IMPALER™

{
Wallachia: 1460
Horrific monstrosities lay waste to the countryside, slaughtering any that cross their path. Faced with no other options, one of history's most notorious madmen commits an unspeakable act in order to fight back.
}

{
New York City: The Present
A derelict freighter is discovered adrift in the waters south of Manhattan, the crew butchered and stacked in the hold like cordwood. An ancient evil has been reawakened. And it's hungry.
}

{
Armageddon: Today
Within two nights, New York City is destroyed, its populace turned into an undead army. An army that thirsts for human blood, an army that will not rest until humanity is completely and utterly destroyed.
}

IMPALER

IMPALER CREATED AND WRITTEN BY WILLIAM HARMS

FOR CINDY

For Top Cow Productions, Inc.:
Marc Silvestri - CEO
Matt Hawkins - President and COO
Filip Sablik - Publisher
Rob Levin - VP - Editorial
Mel Caylo - VP - Marketing & Sales
Chaz Riggs - Graphic Design
Phil Smith - Managing Editor
Joshua Cozine - Assistant Editor
Alyssa Phung - Controller
Adrian Nicita - Webmaster
Scott Newman - Production Lead
Jennifer Chow - Production Assistant

Want more info? Check out:
www.topcow.com and *www.topcowstore.com*
for news and exclusive Top Cow merchandise!

FOR
image
COMICS
Eric Stephenson
image ®
publisher

For this edition
Book Design and Layout by:
Scott Newman

Special Thanks to:
Phil Smith & Chaz Riggs

For this edition
Cover art by:
John Paul Leon

Special Thanks to
Li Kuo, Rob Osborne, Corey Cohen, Sean Cleveland and **Ken F. Levin**

To members of certain religions, particularly among those in the Judeo-Christian-Islamic axis, evil has a name. Be it Satan, Lucifer, the Devil, or the Serpent, evil is a force in the world, existing independent of humanity as it corrupts human action.

To secularists, on the other hand, evil is born in the human heart and exists solely as the result of human action.

But no matter where you've unpacked your bags along the believer-skeptic spectrum, everyone agrees that merely causing harm is not enough. Evil must involve intent.

The Ebola virus can cause untold harm, wiping out entire villages in days. But is it evil? It's simply doing what comes naturally. And what comes naturally for a virus—which, as a mere strand of RNA wrapped in a protein coat, does not meet the criteria for being alive—is pretty much the same for every other organism: Continue its existence and make more of its kind. But a virus can't divide or spawn. It must hijack the cells of another organism and retrofit the nuclear machinery to replicate itself. In the process, the cells are destroyed, but that's no more evil than a lion killing and devouring a wildebeest.

Of course, a virus can be used for evil—imagine someone contaminating a water supply with Ebola—and that brings us back to intent.

Which in turn brings us to the vampire.

The vampire exists on the borderland. It's an intrusion of the supernatural into the real world. In Christian mythology, Satan's purpose is not to do evil, but rather to cause humans to commit evil acts, thus jeopardizing their souls. Not so the vampire. The vampire causes death, but worse, in so doing it creates others like itself.

But are vampires evil?

In many ways they aren't that much different from a virus. Like Ebola, vampires aren't living creatures, can't spawn, and need a host to increase their population. When they sink their teeth into a pulsing carotid and drain the lifeblood, aren't they simply doing what vampires do?

Certainly they do harm, but their intent, at least in the traditional sense, is survival of themselves and their species.

Is that evil? I'll let you decide.

The vampires you'll meet in the following pages are not quite traditional. And their purpose appears to be more than simple preservation of their species. *Impaler* teases us with hints that they are being directed by a malign intelligence—the beast—with perhaps a larger purpose. An evil purpose. We're also left wondering about the man from the past—"the price you paid". . . "you condemned yourself for nothing"—and his methods. Can the evil the city faces be countered only by more evil?

I'm intrigued. I want more. So will you.

~F. Paul Wilson

F. Paul Wilson is the award winning author of **The Keep** and **Repairman Jack** novel series.

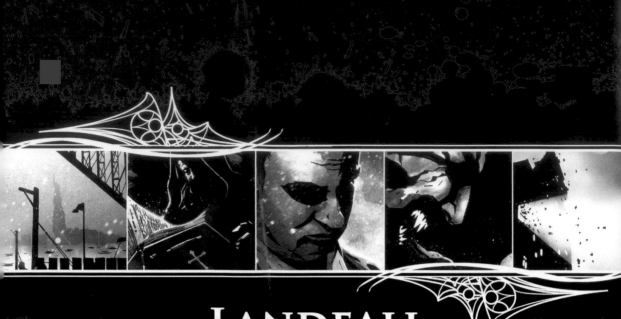

LANDFALL
{Issue #1}

WRITTEN BY:
WILLIAM HARMS

PENCILS & ADDITIONAL INKS BY:
NICK POSTIC

INKS & COLORS BY:
NICK MARINKOVICH

LETTERING BY:
ED DUKESHIRE

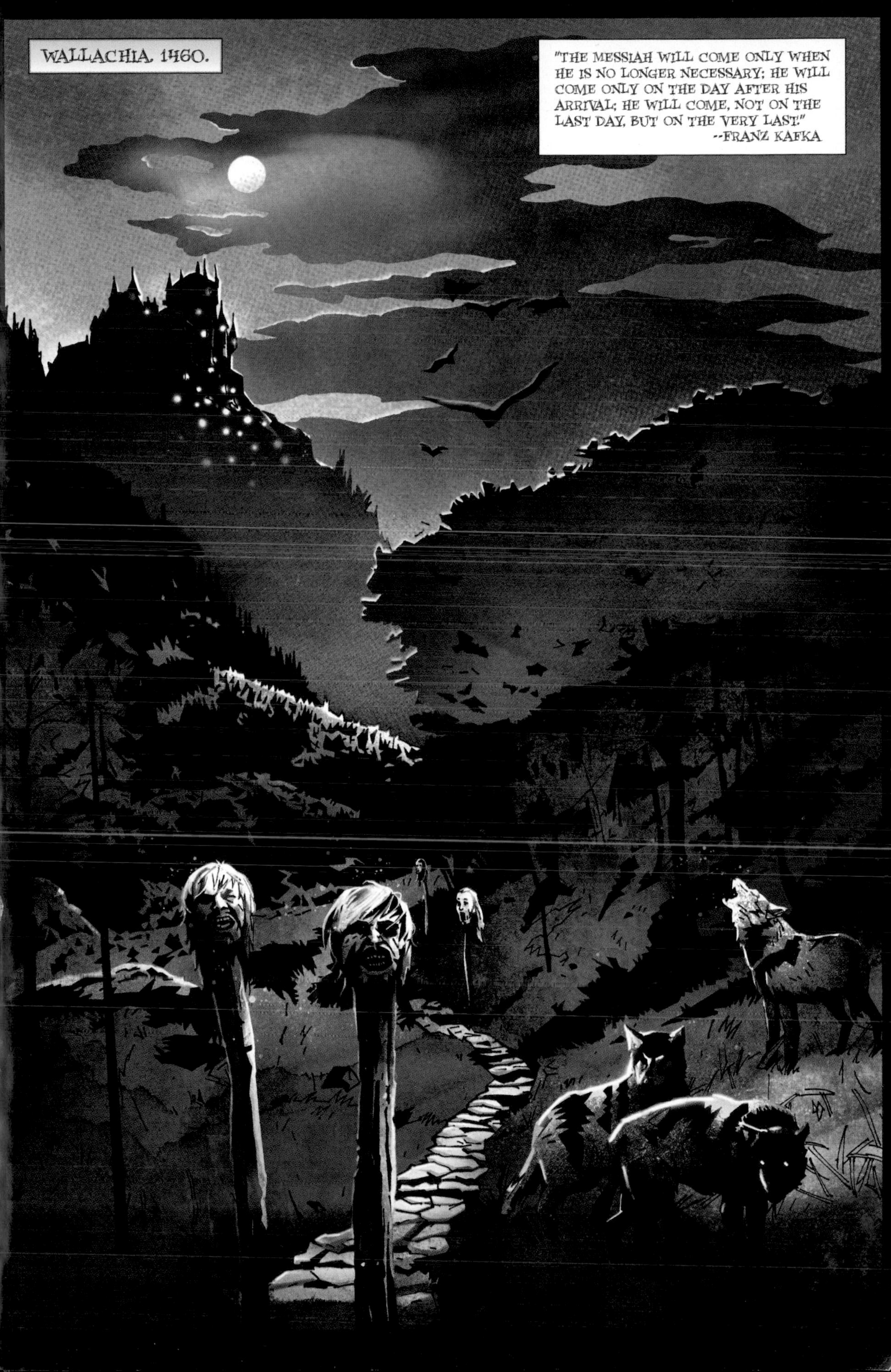
WALLACHIA. 1460.
"THE MESSIAH WILL COME ONLY WHEN HE IS NO LONGER NECESSARY; HE WILL COME ONLY ON THE DAY AFTER HIS ARRIVAL; HE WILL COME, NOT ON THE LAST DAY, BUT ON THE VERY LAST."
--FRANZ KAFKA

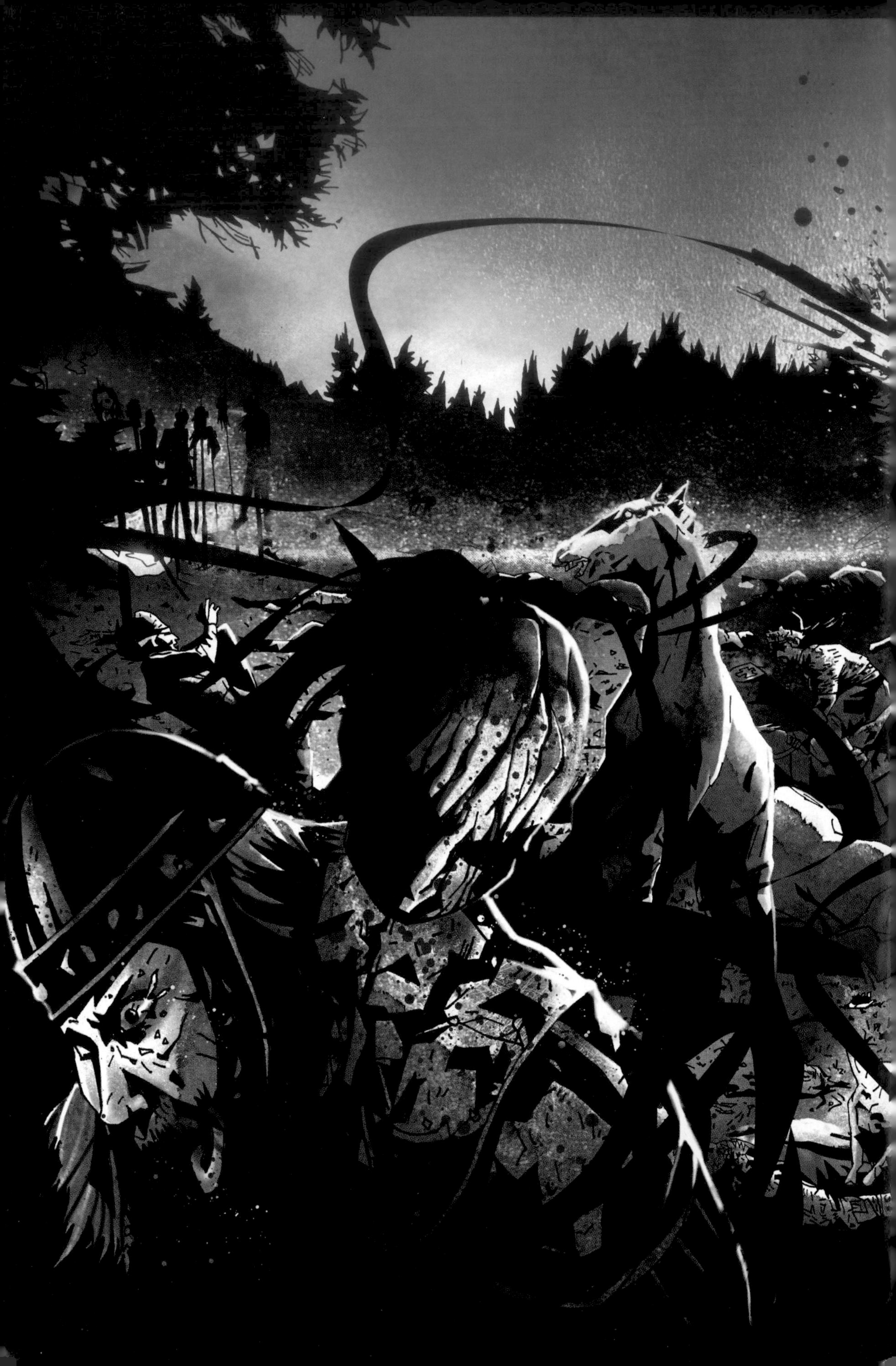

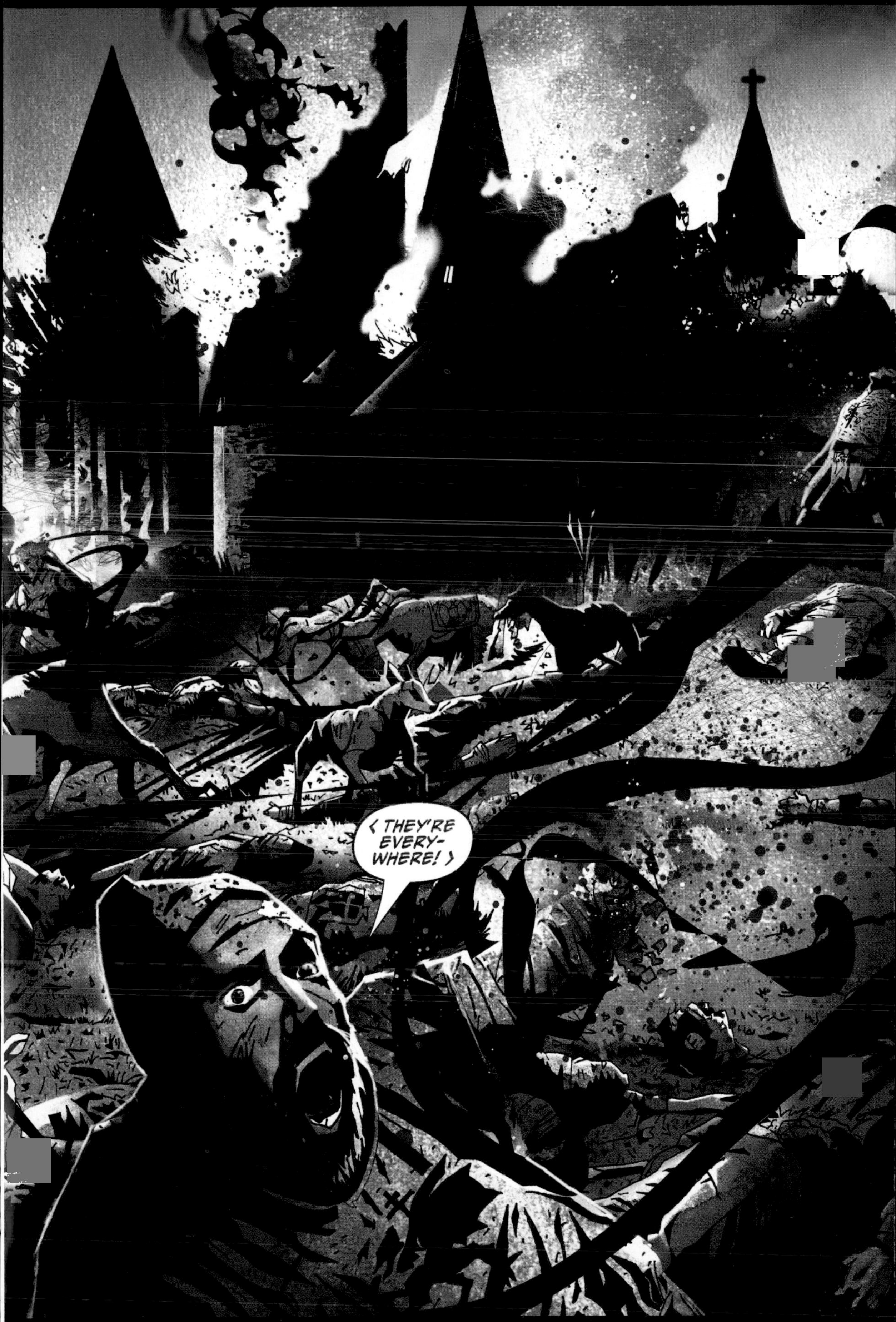
< THEY'RE EVERY-WHERE! >

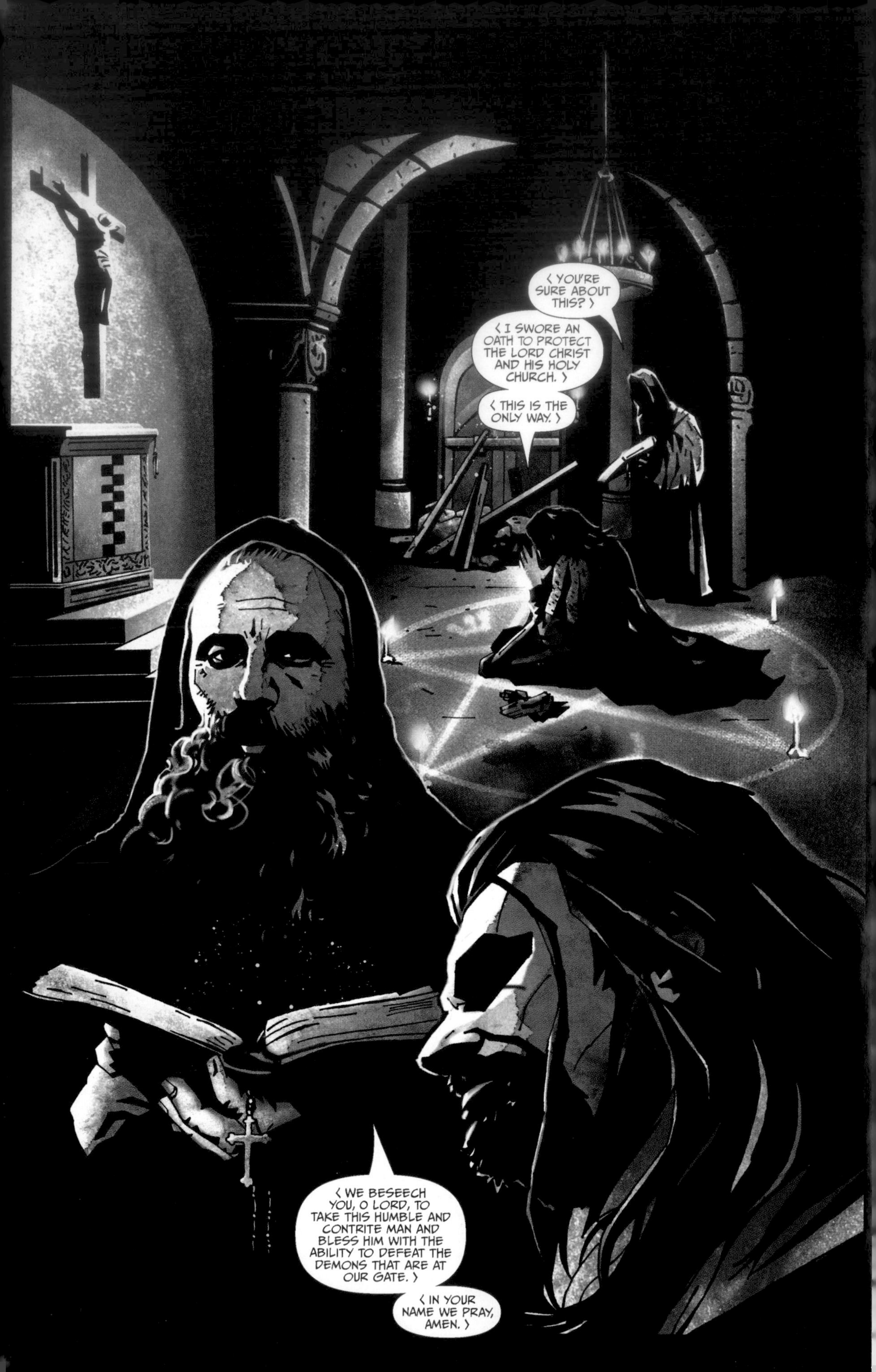

⟨ YOU'RE SURE ABOUT THIS? ⟩
⟨ I SWORE AN OATH TO PROTECT THE LORD CHRIST AND HIS HOLY CHURCH. ⟩
⟨ THIS IS THE ONLY WAY. ⟩
⟨ WE BESEECH YOU, O LORD, TO TAKE THIS HUMBLE AND CONTRITE MAN AND BLESS HIM WITH THE ABILITY TO DEFEAT THE DEMONS THAT ARE AT OUR GATE. ⟩
⟨ IN YOUR NAME WE PRAY, AMEN. ⟩

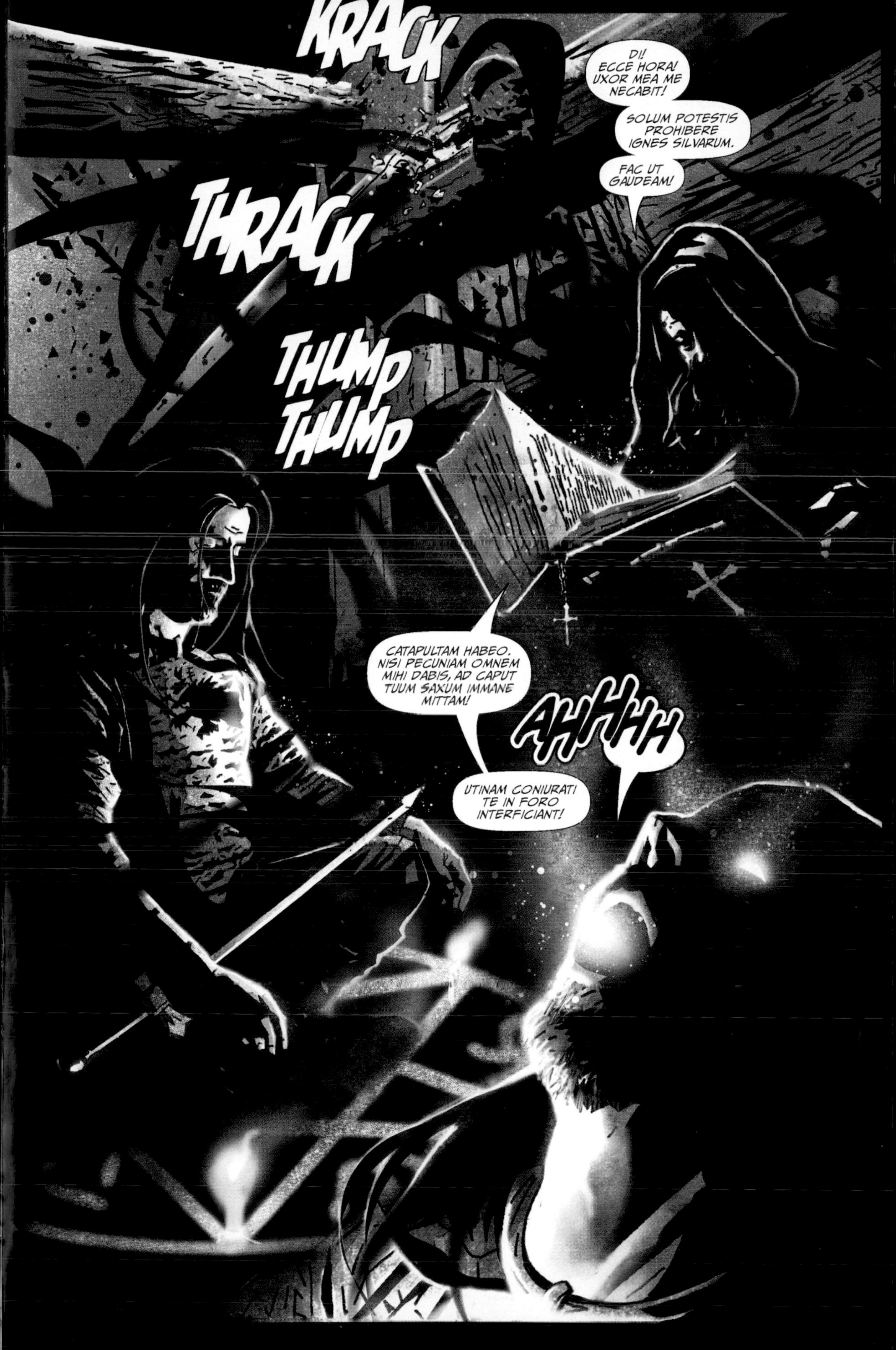
KRACK
THRACK
THUMP THUMP
DI! ECCE HORA! UXOR MEA ME NECABIT!
SOLUM POTESTIS PROHIBERE IGNES SILVARUM.
FAC UT GAUDEAM!
CATAPULTAM HABEO. NISI PECUNIAM OMNEM MIHI DABIS, AD CAPUT TUUM SAXUM IMMANE MITTAM!
AHHHH
UTINAM CONIURATI TE IN FORO INTERFICIANT!

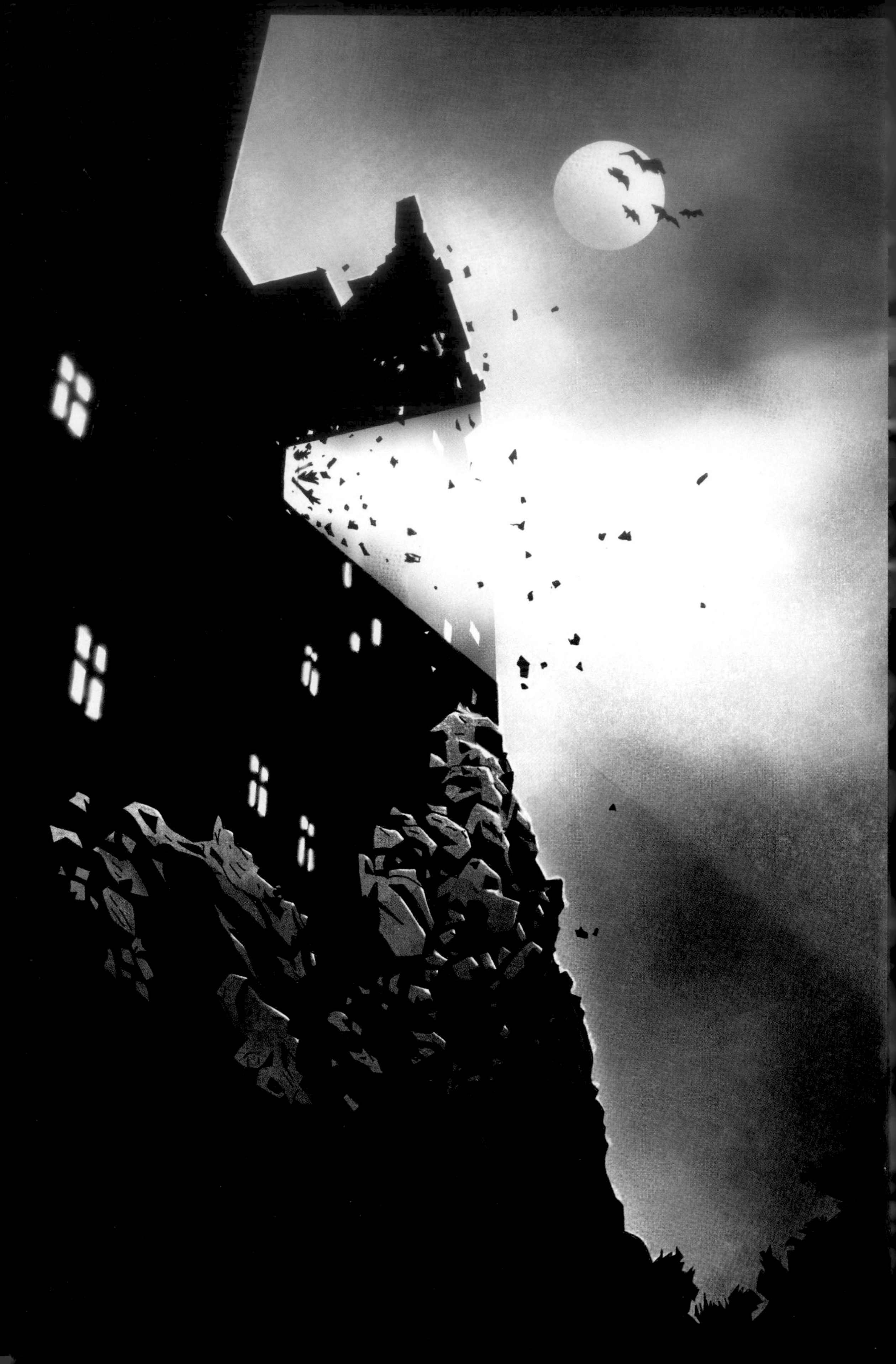

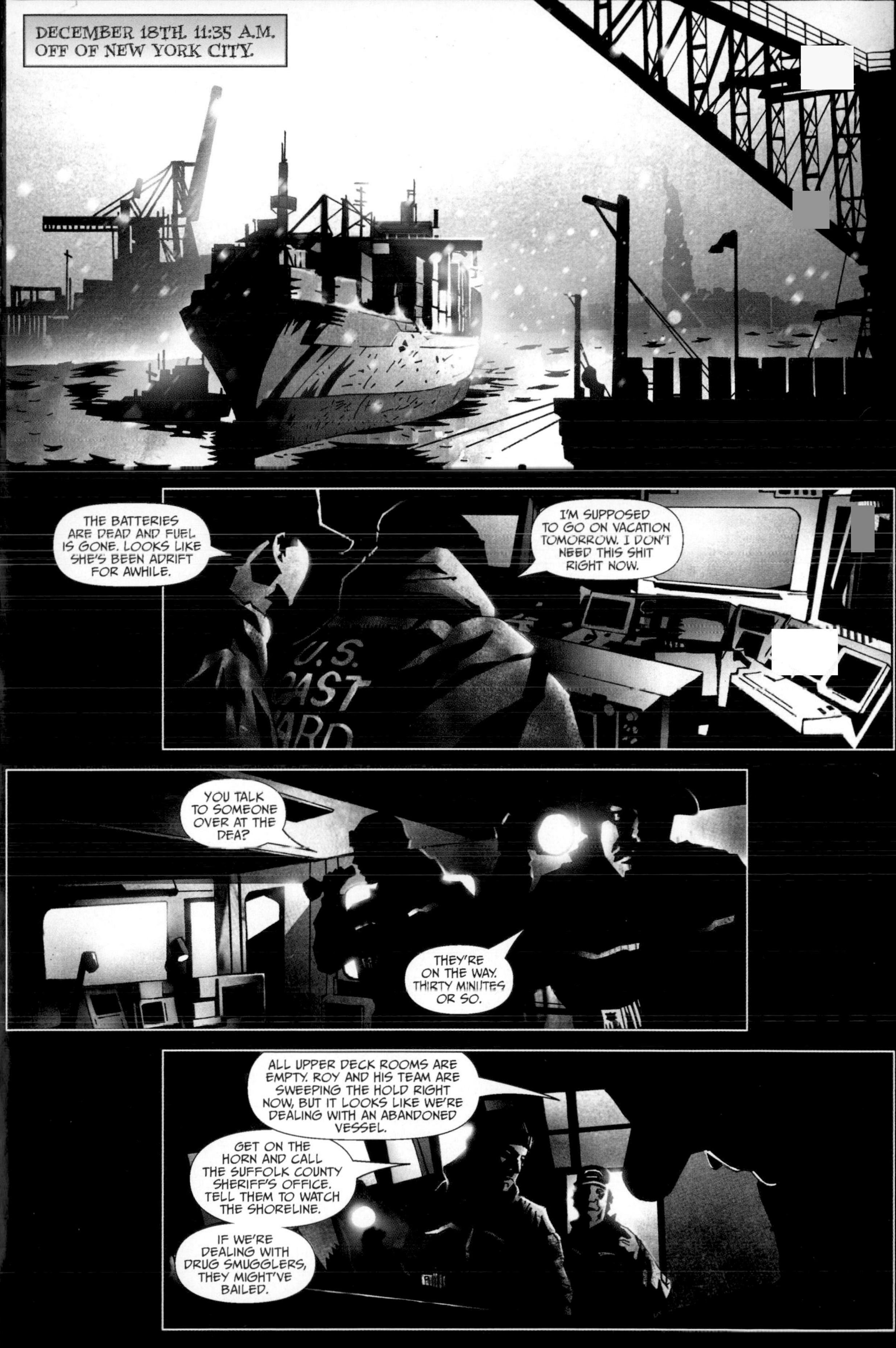
DECEMBER 18TH. 11:35 A.M. OFF OF NEW YORK CITY.
THE BATTERIES ARE DEAD AND FUEL IS GONE. LOOKS LIKE SHE'S BEEN ADRIFT FOR AWHILE.
I'M SUPPOSED TO GO ON VACATION TOMORROW. I DON'T NEED THIS SHIT RIGHT NOW.
YOU TALK TO SOMEONE OVER AT THE DEA?
THEY'RE ON THE WAY. THIRTY MINUTES OR SO.
ALL UPPER DECK ROOMS ARE EMPTY. ROY AND HIS TEAM ARE SWEEPING THE HOLD RIGHT NOW, BUT IT LOOKS LIKE WE'RE DEALING WITH AN ABANDONED VESSEL.
GET ON THE HORN AND CALL THE SUFFOLK COUNTY SHERIFF'S OFFICE. TELL THEM TO WATCH THE SHORELINE.
IF WE'RE DEALING WITH DRUG SMUGGLERS, THEY MIGHT'VE BAILED.

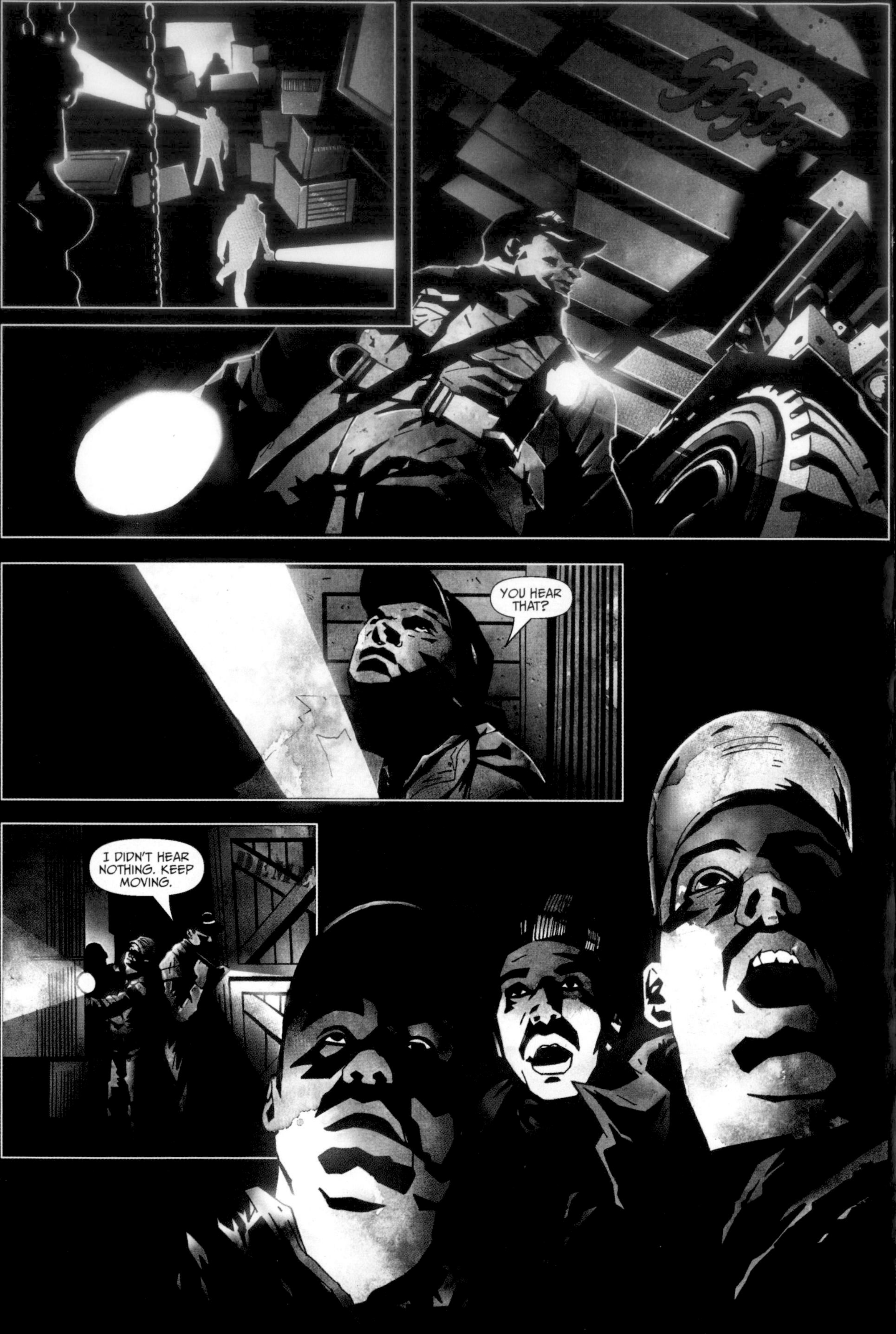
YOU HEAR THAT?
I DIDN'T HEAR NOTHING. KEEP MOVING.

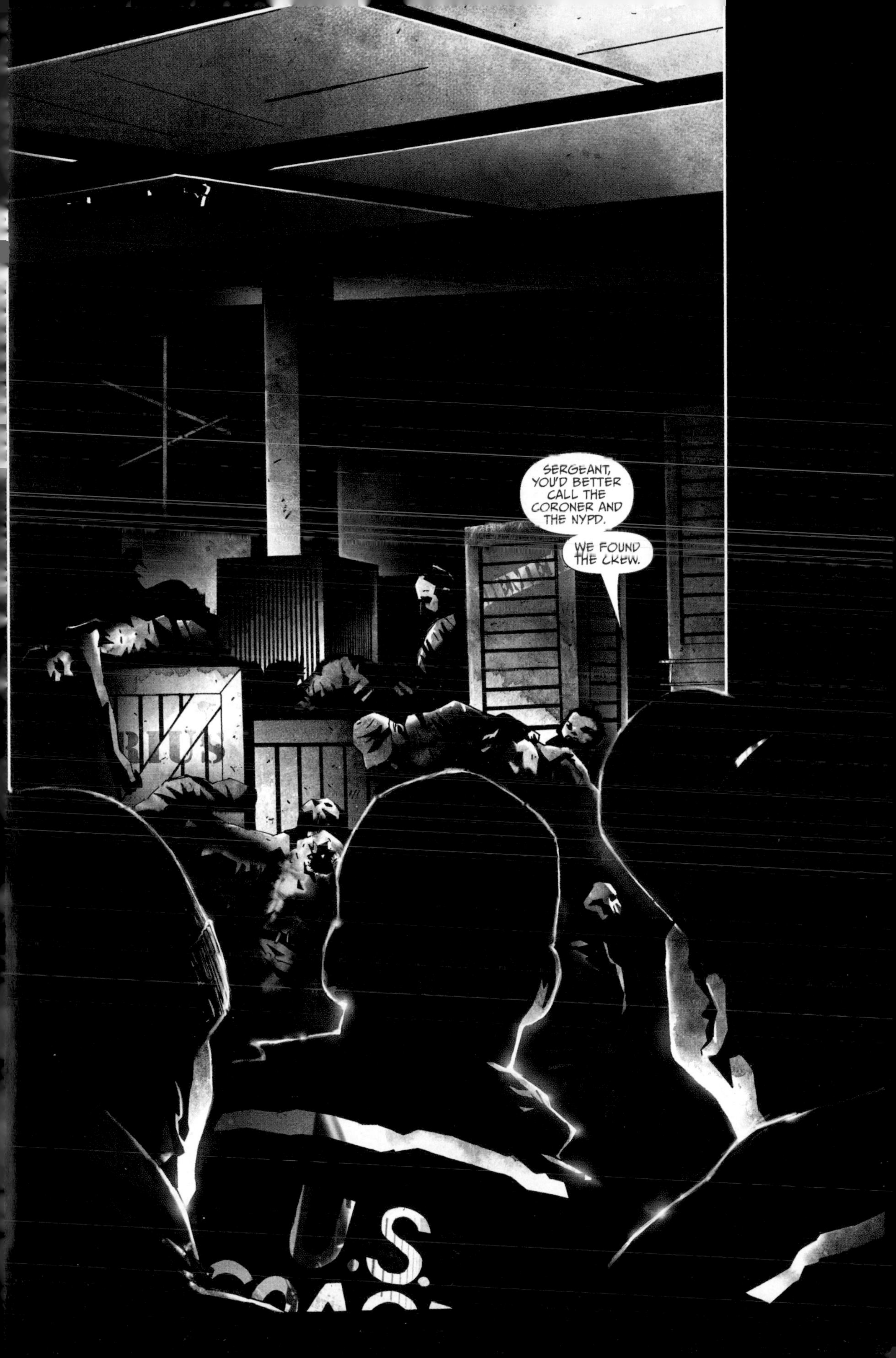
SERGEANT, YOU'D BETTER CALL THE CORONER AND THE NYPD.
WE FOUND THE CREW.
U.S.

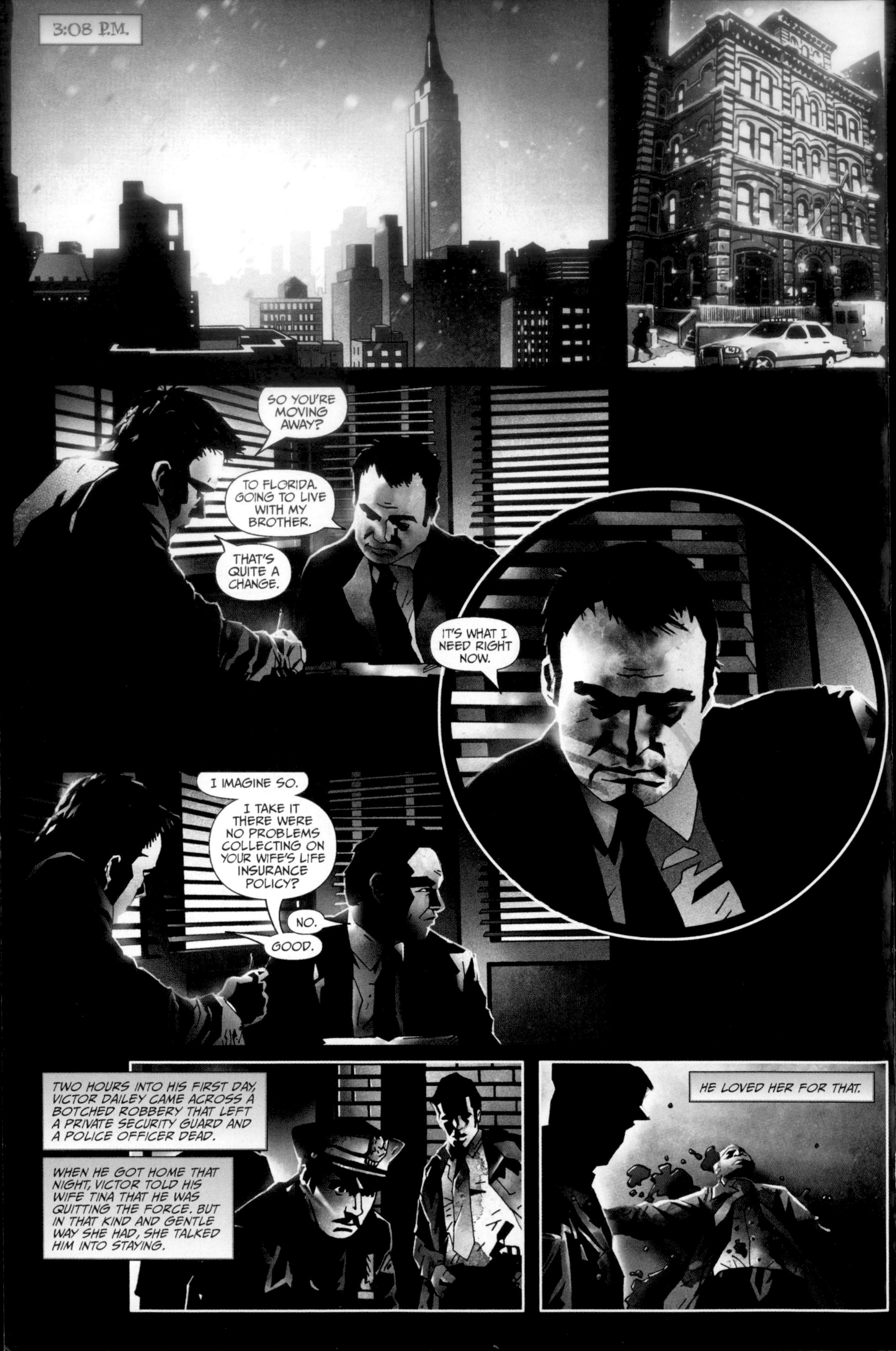
3:08 P.M.
SO YOU'RE MOVING AWAY?
TO FLORIDA. GOING TO LIVE WITH MY BROTHER.
THAT'S QUITE A CHANGE.
IT'S WHAT I NEED RIGHT NOW.
I IMAGINE SO.
I TAKE IT THERE WERE NO PROBLEMS COLLECTING ON YOUR WIFE'S LIFE INSURANCE POLICY?
NO.
GOOD.
TWO HOURS INTO HIS FIRST DAY, VICTOR DAILEY CAME ACROSS A BOTCHED ROBBERY THAT LEFT A PRIVATE SECURITY GUARD AND A POLICE OFFICER DEAD.
WHEN HE GOT HOME THAT NIGHT, VICTOR TOLD HIS WIFE TINA THAT HE WAS QUITTING THE FORCE. BUT IN THAT KIND AND GENTLE WAY SHE HAD, SHE TALKED HIM INTO STAYING.
HE LOVED HER FOR THAT.

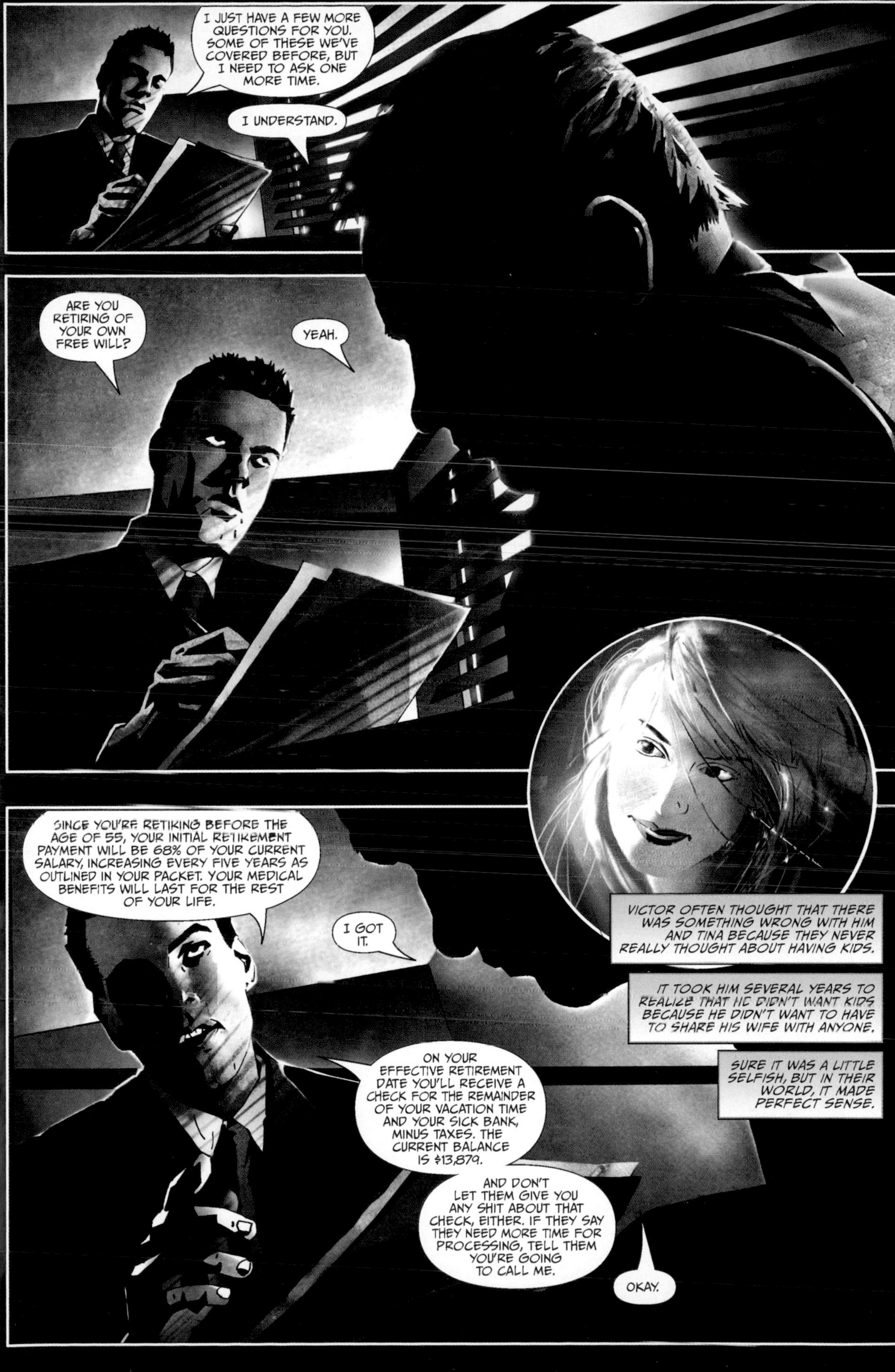
I JUST HAVE A FEW MORE QUESTIONS FOR YOU. SOME OF THESE WE'VE COVERED BEFORE, BUT I NEED TO ASK ONE MORE TIME.
I UNDERSTAND.
ARE YOU RETIRING OF YOUR OWN FREE WILL?
YEAH.
SINCE YOU'RE RETIRING BEFORE THE AGE OF 55, YOUR INITIAL RETIREMENT PAYMENT WILL BE 68% OF YOUR CURRENT SALARY, INCREASING EVERY FIVE YEARS AS OUTLINED IN YOUR PACKET. YOUR MEDICAL BENEFITS WILL LAST FOR THE REST OF YOUR LIFE.
I GOT IT.
VICTOR OFTEN THOUGHT THAT THERE WAS SOMETHING WRONG WITH HIM AND TINA BECAUSE THEY NEVER REALLY THOUGHT ABOUT HAVING KIDS.
IT TOOK HIM SEVERAL YEARS TO REALIZE THAT HE DIDN'T WANT KIDS BECAUSE HE DIDN'T WANT TO HAVE TO SHARE HIS WIFE WITH ANYONE.
SURE IT WAS A LITTLE SELFISH, BUT IN THEIR WORLD, IT MADE PERFECT SENSE.
ON YOUR EFFECTIVE RETIREMENT DATE YOU'LL RECEIVE A CHECK FOR THE REMAINDER OF YOUR VACATION TIME AND YOUR SICK BANK, MINUS TAXES. THE CURRENT BALANCE IS $13,879.
AND DON'T LET THEM GIVE YOU ANY SHIT ABOUT THAT CHECK, EITHER. IF THEY SAY THEY NEED MORE TIME FOR PROCESSING, TELL THEM YOU'RE GOING TO CALL ME.
OKAY.

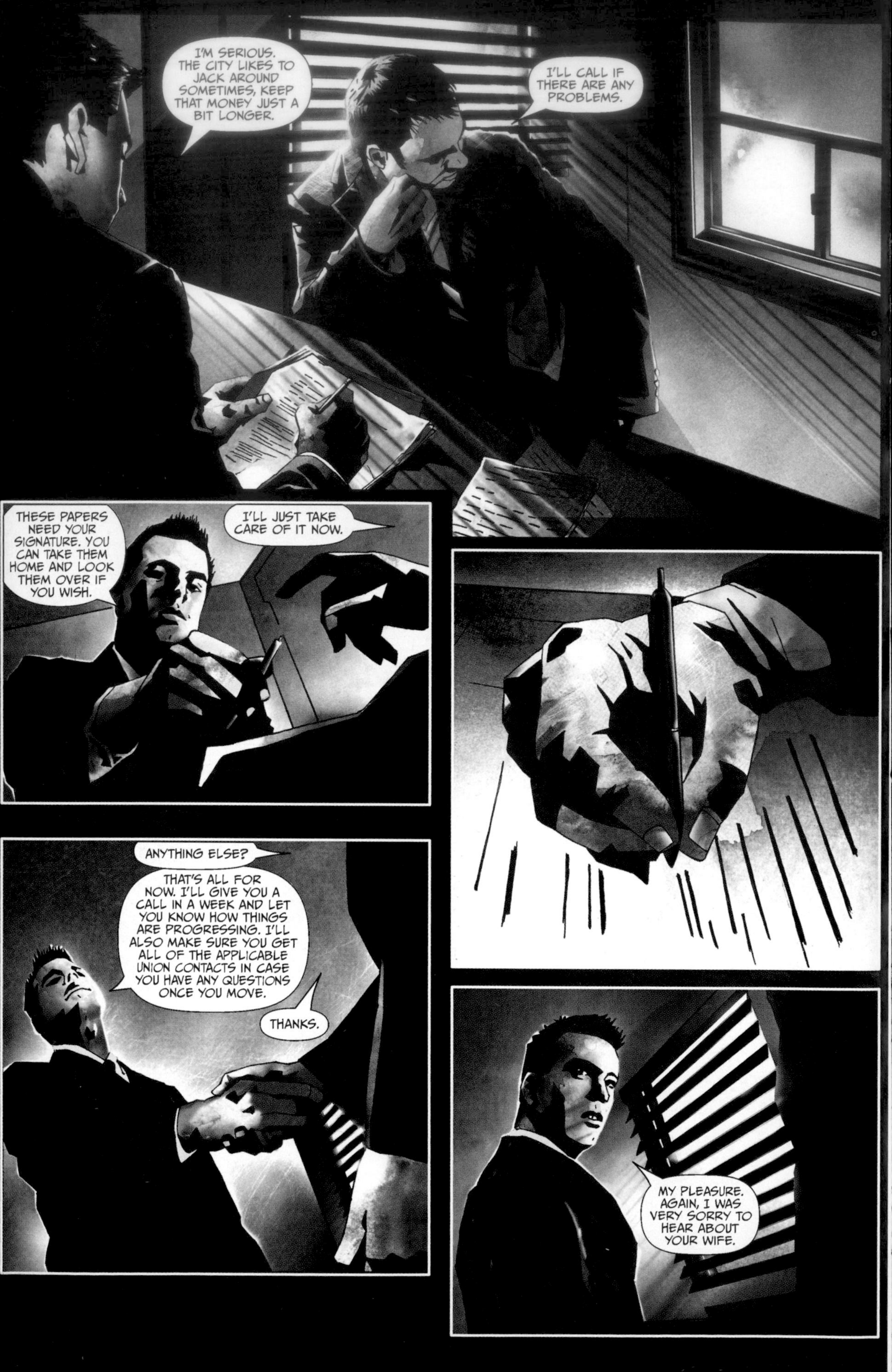
I'M SERIOUS. THE CITY LIKES TO JACK AROUND SOMETIMES, KEEP THAT MONEY JUST A BIT LONGER.
I'LL CALL IF THERE ARE ANY PROBLEMS.
THESE PAPERS NEED YOUR SIGNATURE. YOU CAN TAKE THEM HOME AND LOOK THEM OVER IF YOU WISH.
I'LL JUST TAKE CARE OF IT NOW.
ANYTHING ELSE?
THAT'S ALL FOR NOW. I'LL GIVE YOU A CALL IN A WEEK AND LET YOU KNOW HOW THINGS ARE PROGRESSING. I'LL ALSO MAKE SURE YOU GET ALL OF THE APPLICABLE UNION CONTACTS IN CASE YOU HAVE ANY QUESTIONS ONCE YOU MOVE.
THANKS.
MY PLEASURE. AGAIN, I WAS VERY SORRY TO HEAR ABOUT YOUR WIFE.

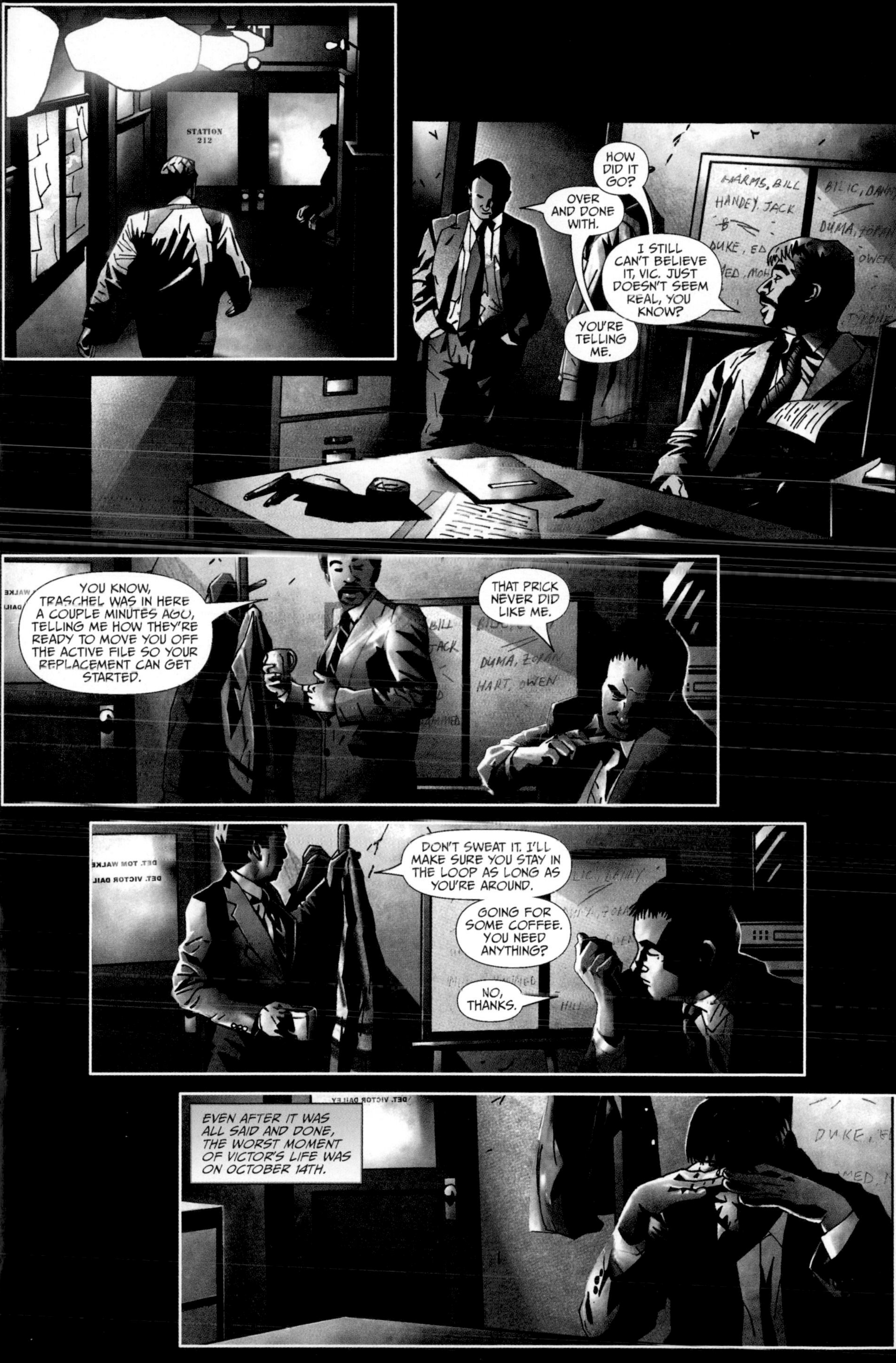

STATION 212
HOW DID IT GO?
OVER AND DONE WITH.
I STILL CAN'T BELIEVE IT, VIC. JUST DOESN'T SEEM REAL, YOU KNOW?
YOU'RE TELLING ME.
YOU KNOW, TRASCHEL WAS IN HERE A COUPLE MINUTES AGO, TELLING ME HOW THEY'RE READY TO MOVE YOU OFF THE ACTIVE FILE SO YOUR REPLACEMENT CAN GET STARTED.
THAT PRICK NEVER DID LIKE ME.
DON'T SWEAT IT. I'LL MAKE SURE YOU STAY IN THE LOOP AS LONG AS YOU'RE AROUND.
GOING FOR SOME COFFEE. YOU NEED ANYTHING?
NO, THANKS.
EVEN AFTER IT WAS ALL SAID AND DONE, THE WORST MOMENT OF VICTOR'S LIFE WAS ON OCTOBER 14TH.

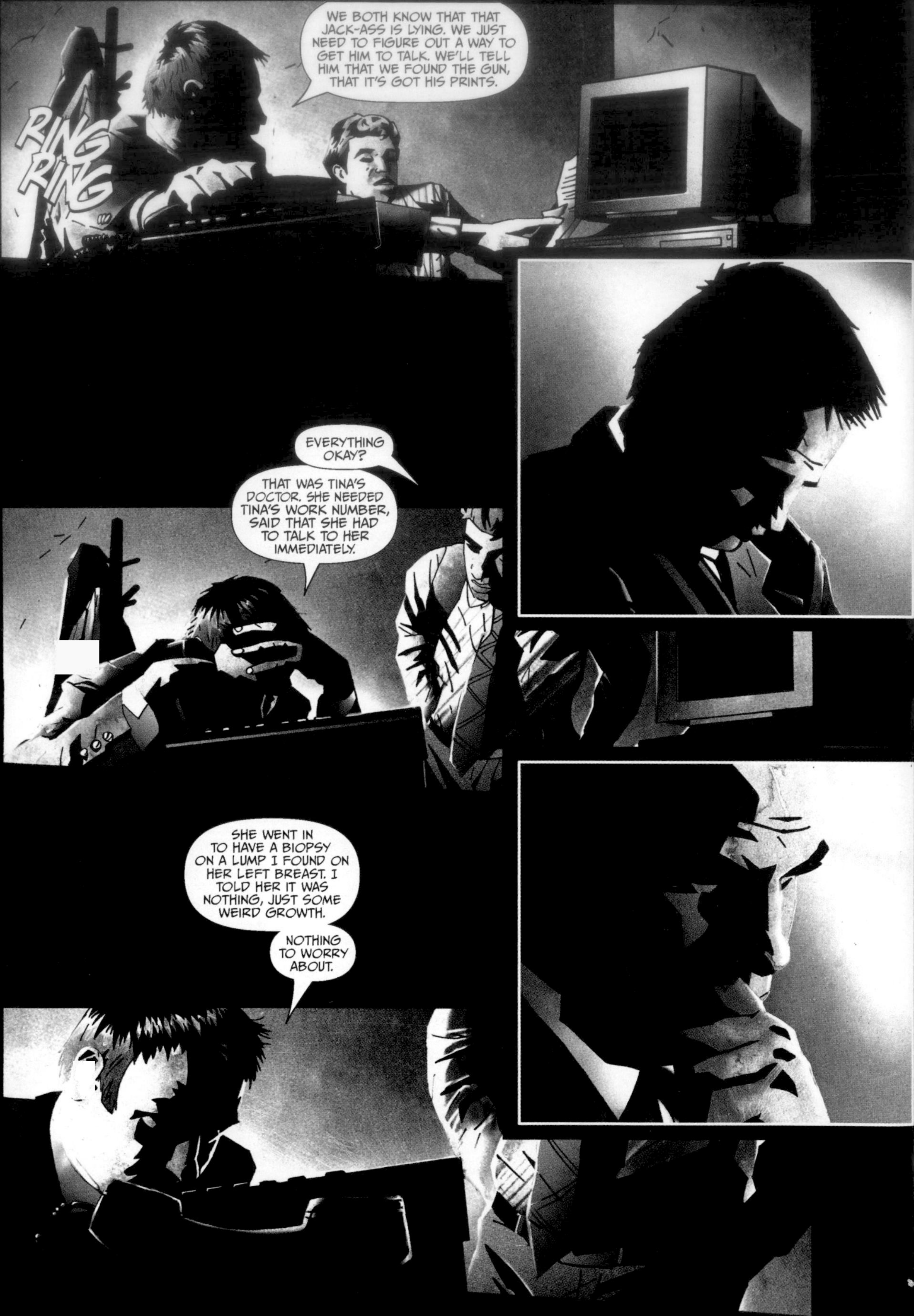
WE BOTH KNOW THAT THAT JACK-ASS IS LYING. WE JUST NEED TO FIGURE OUT A WAY TO GET HIM TO TALK. WE'LL TELL HIM THAT WE FOUND THE GUN, THAT IT'S GOT HIS PRINTS.
RING RING
EVERYTHING OKAY?
THAT WAS TINA'S DOCTOR. SHE NEEDED TINA'S WORK NUMBER, SAID THAT SHE HAD TO TALK TO HER IMMEDIATELY.
SHE WENT IN TO HAVE A BIOPSY ON A LUMP I FOUND ON HER LEFT BREAST. I TOLD HER IT WAS NOTHING, JUST SOME WEIRD GROWTH.
NOTHING TO WORRY ABOUT.

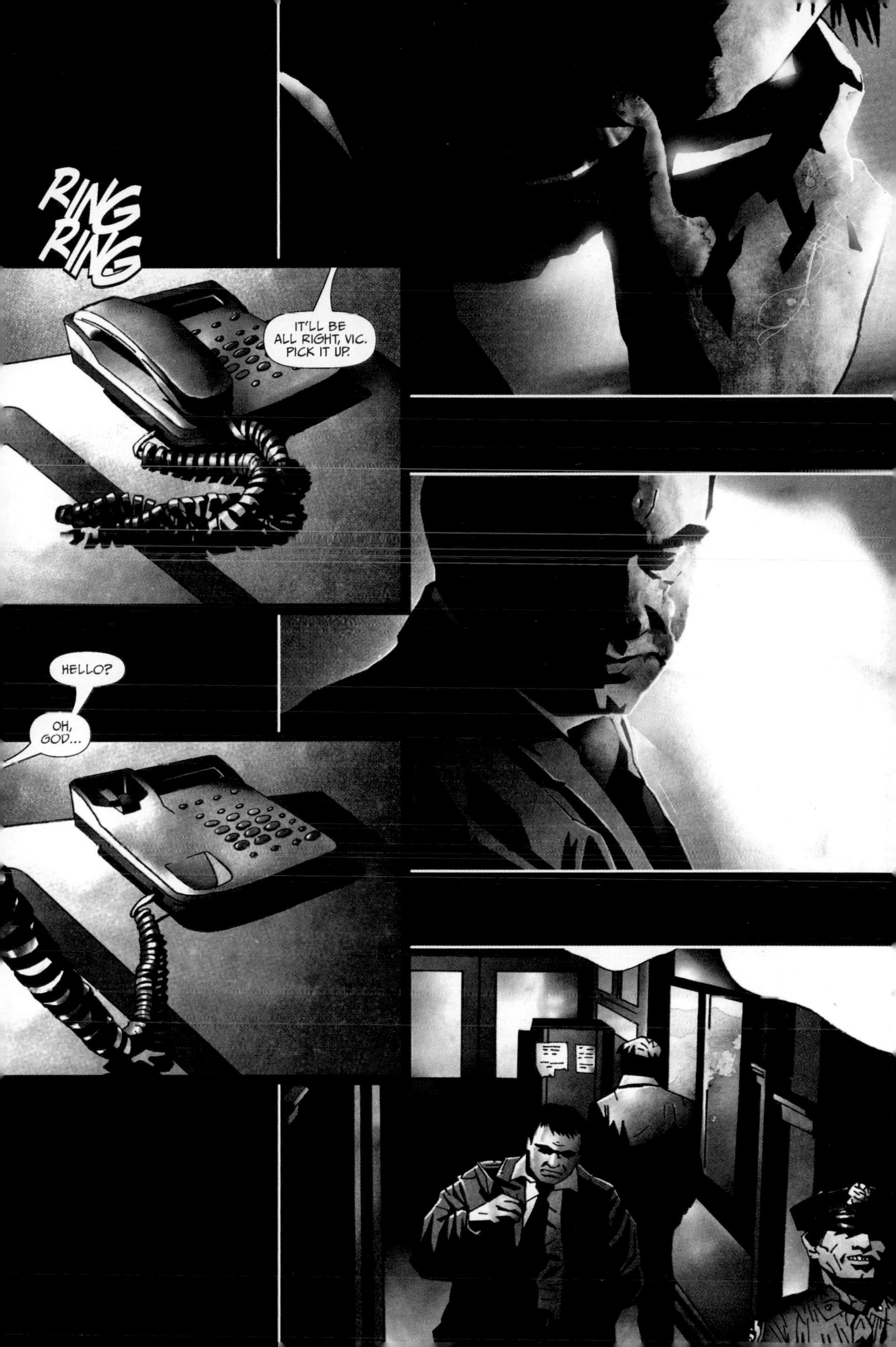
RING RING
IT'LL BE ALL RIGHT, VIC. PICK IT UP.
HELLO?
OH, GOD...

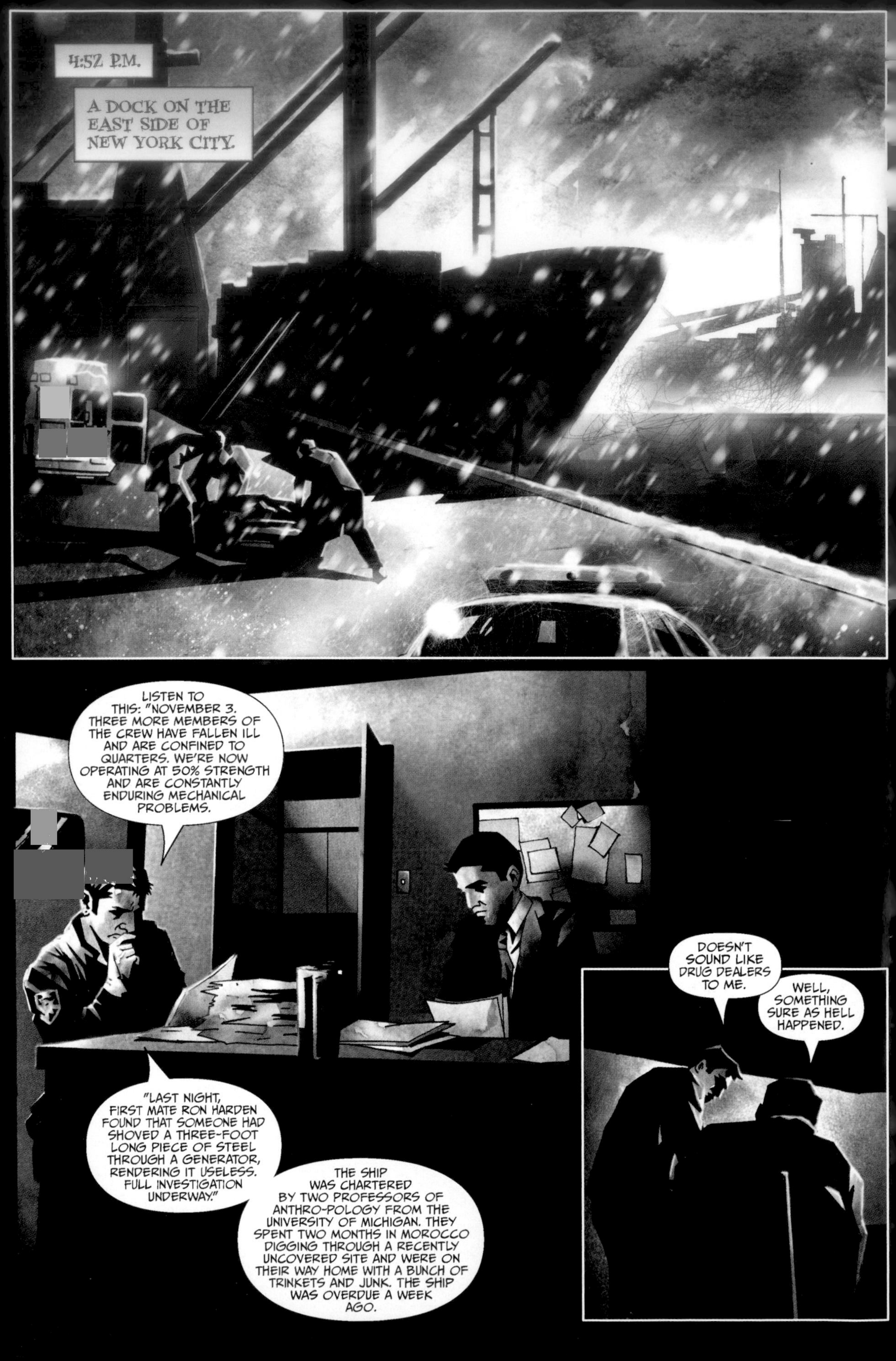
4:52 P.M.
A DOCK ON THE EAST SIDE OF NEW YORK CITY.
LISTEN TO THIS: "NOVEMBER 3. THREE MORE MEMBERS OF THE CREW HAVE FALLEN ILL AND ARE CONFINED TO QUARTERS. WE'RE NOW OPERATING AT 50% STRENGTH AND ARE CONSTANTLY ENDURING MECHANICAL PROBLEMS.
"LAST NIGHT, FIRST MATE RON HARDEN FOUND THAT SOMEONE HAD SHOVED A THREE-FOOT LONG PIECE OF STEEL THROUGH A GENERATOR, RENDERING IT USELESS. FULL INVESTIGATION UNDERWAY."
THE SHIP WAS CHARTERED BY TWO PROFESSORS OF ANTHRO-POLOGY FROM THE UNIVERSITY OF MICHIGAN. THEY SPENT TWO MONTHS IN MOROCCO DIGGING THROUGH A RECENTLY UNCOVERED SITE AND WERE ON THEIR WAY HOME WITH A BUNCH OF TRINKETS AND JUNK. THE SHIP WAS OVERDUE A WEEK AGO.
DOESN'T SOUND LIKE DRUG DEALERS TO ME.
WELL, SOMETHING SURE AS HELL HAPPENED.

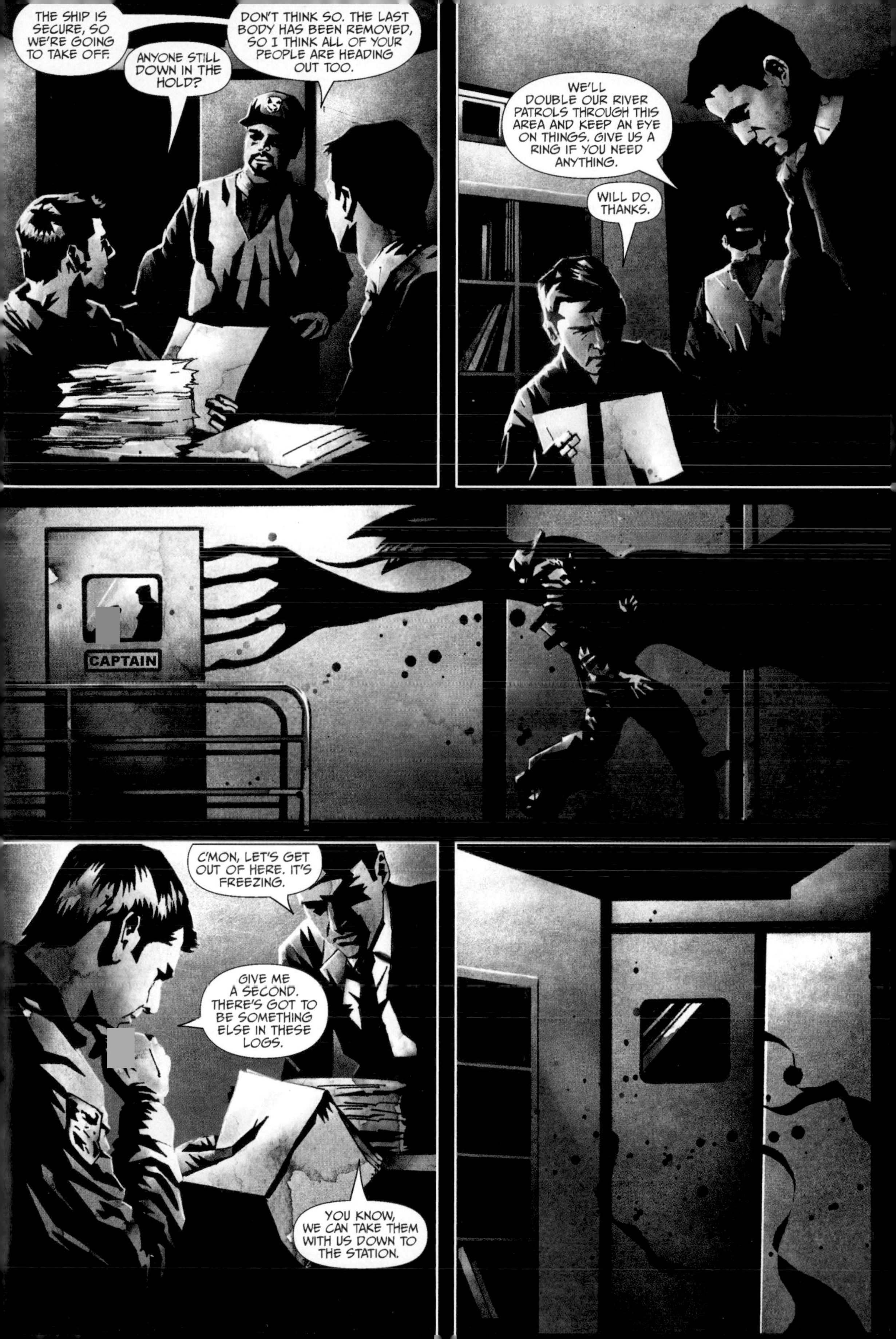
THE SHIP IS SECURE, SO WE'RE GOING TO TAKE OFF.
ANYONE STILL DOWN IN THE HOLD?
DON'T THINK SO. THE LAST BODY HAS BEEN REMOVED, SO I THINK ALL OF YOUR PEOPLE ARE HEADING OUT TOO.
WE'LL DOUBLE OUR RIVER PATROLS THROUGH THIS AREA AND KEEP AN EYE ON THINGS. GIVE US A RING IF YOU NEED ANYTHING.
WILL DO. THANKS.
CAPTAIN
C'MON, LET'S GET OUT OF HERE. IT'S FREEZING.
GIVE ME A SECOND. THERE'S GOT TO BE SOMETHING ELSE IN THESE LOGS.
YOU KNOW, WE CAN TAKE THEM WITH US DOWN TO THE STATION.

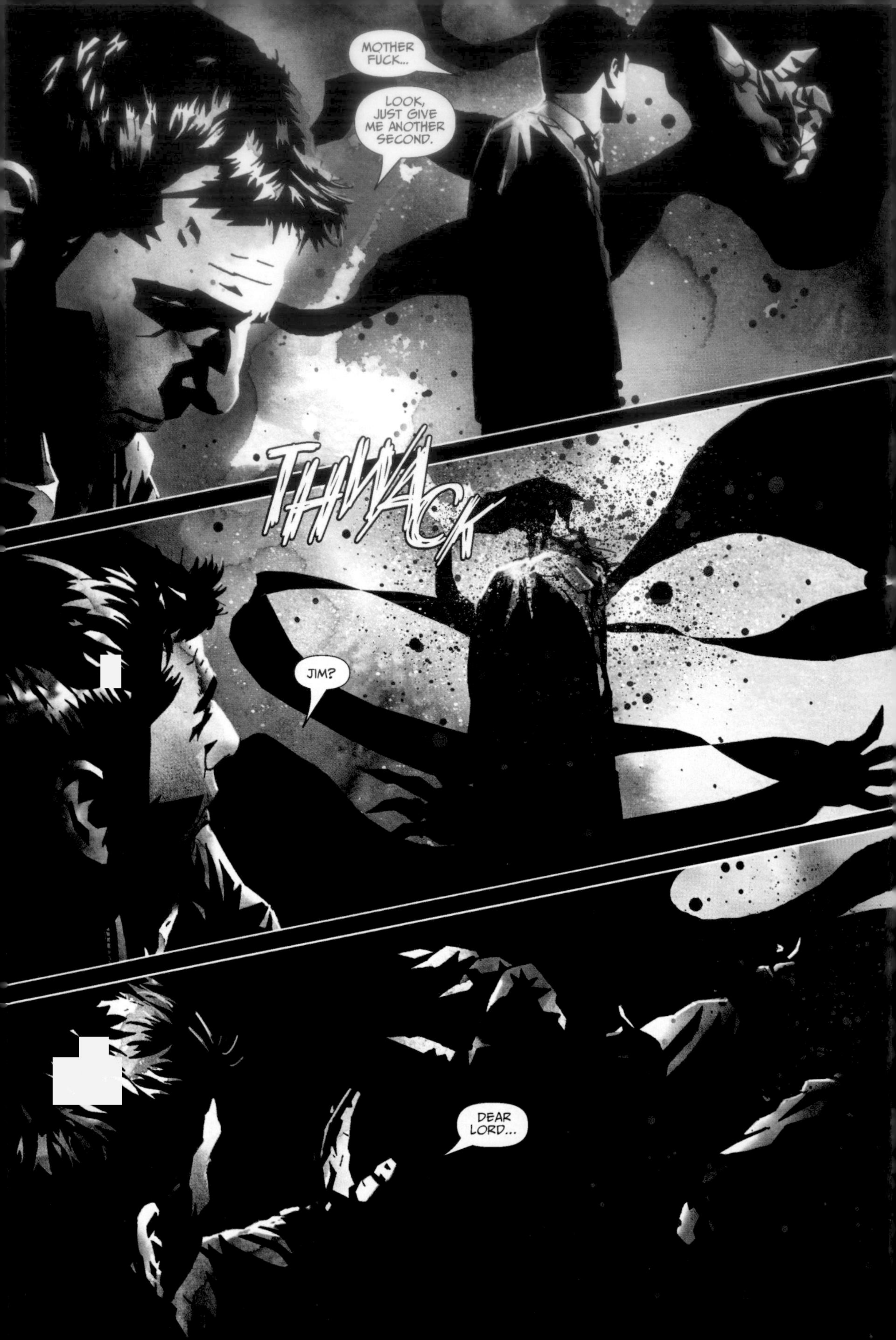
MOTHER FUCK...
LOOK, JUST GIVE ME ANOTHER SECOND.
THWACK
JIM?
DEAR LORD...

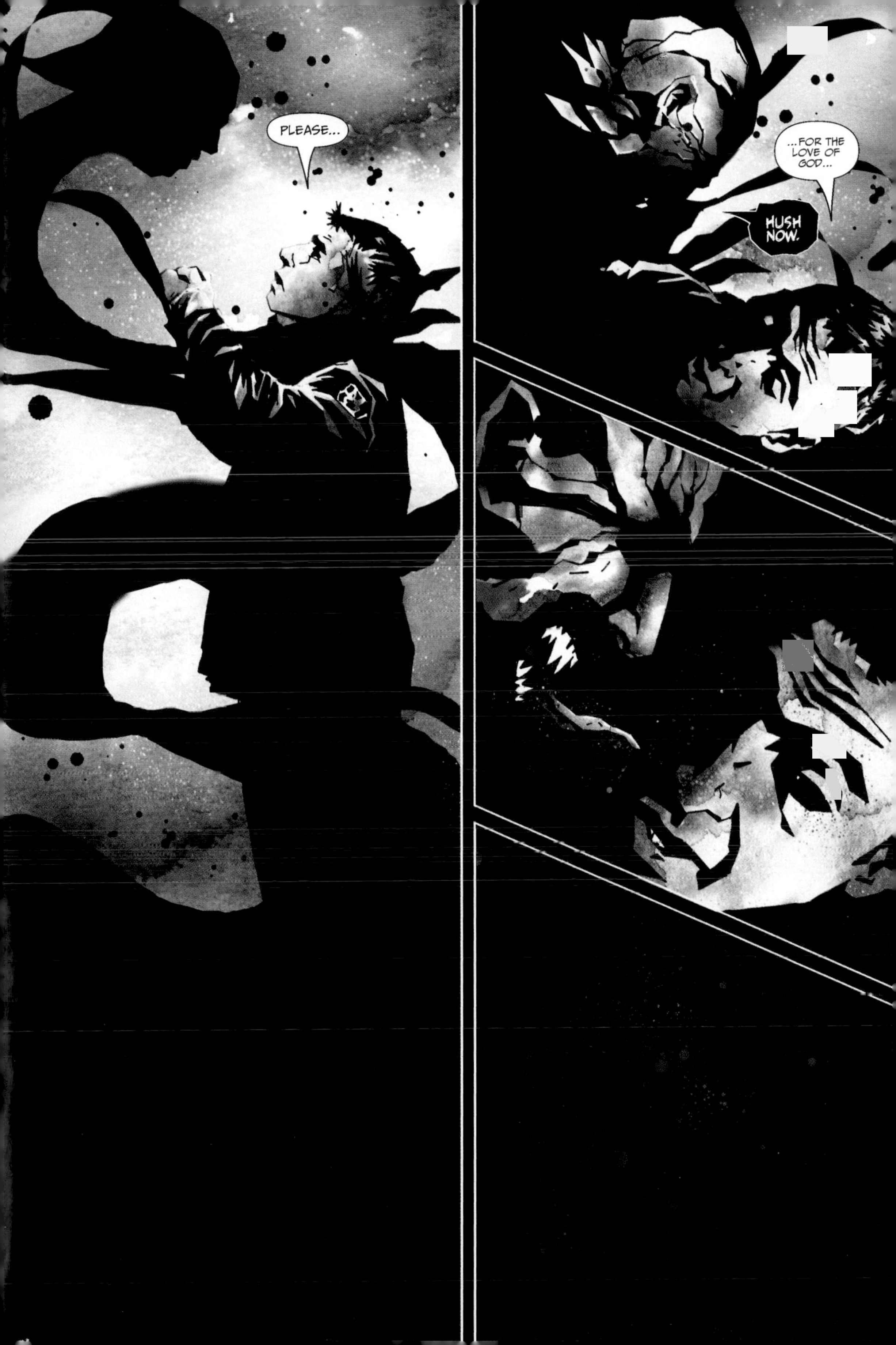
PLEASE...
...FOR THE LOVE OF GOD...
HUSH NOW.

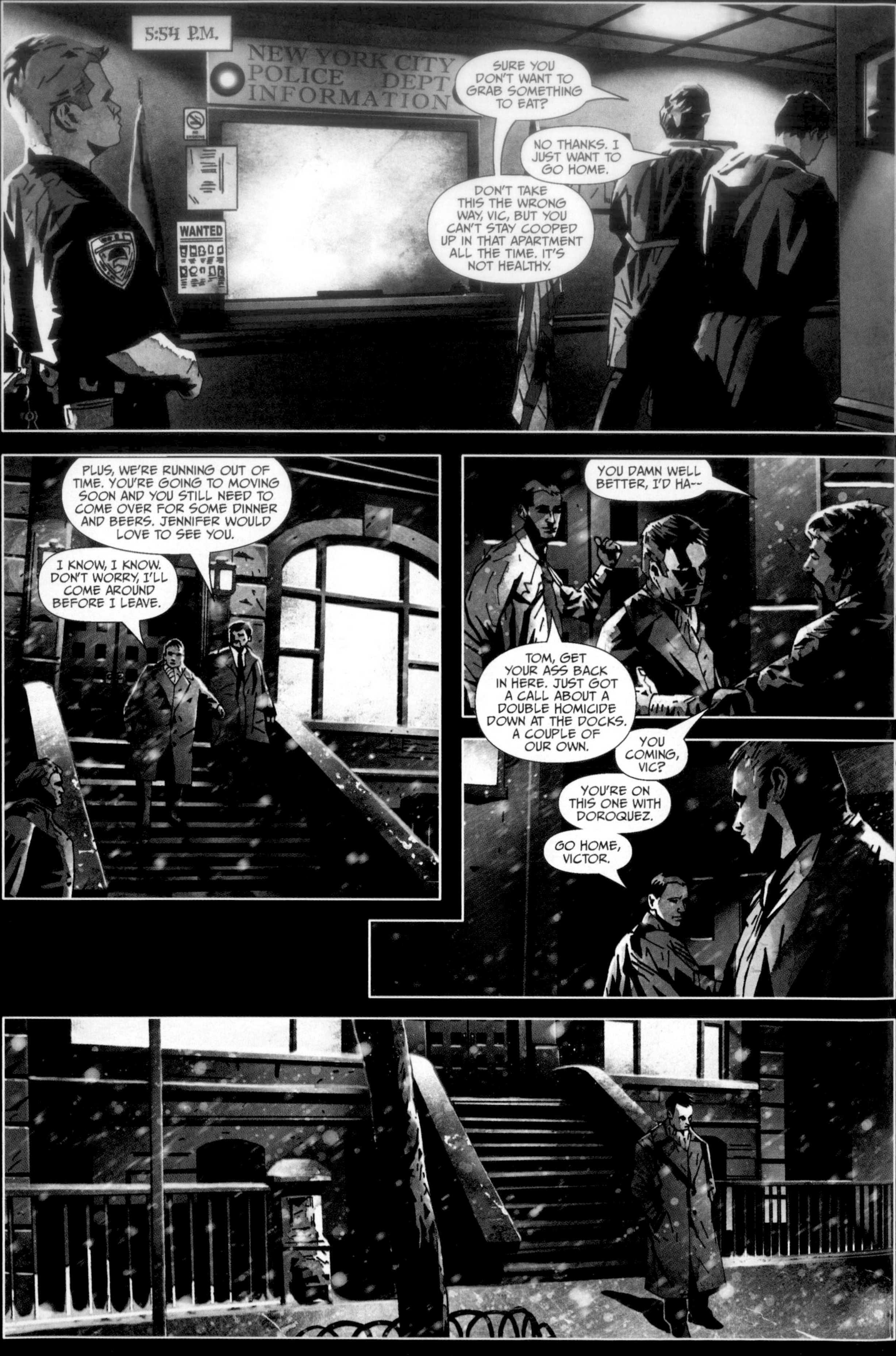
5:54 P.M.
NEW YORK CITY POLICE DEPT INFORMATION
WANTED
SURE YOU DON'T WANT TO GRAB SOMETHING TO EAT?
NO THANKS. I JUST WANT TO GO HOME.
DON'T TAKE THIS THE WRONG WAY, VIC, BUT YOU CAN'T STAY COOPED UP IN THAT APARTMENT ALL THE TIME. IT'S NOT HEALTHY.
PLUS, WE'RE RUNNING OUT OF TIME. YOU'RE GOING TO MOVING SOON AND YOU STILL NEED TO COME OVER FOR SOME DINNER AND BEERS. JENNIFER WOULD LOVE TO SEE YOU.
I KNOW, I KNOW. DON'T WORRY, I'LL COME AROUND BEFORE I LEAVE.
YOU DAMN WELL BETTER, I'D HA--
TOM, GET YOUR ASS BACK IN HERE. JUST GOT A CALL ABOUT A DOUBLE HOMICIDE DOWN AT THE DOCKS. A COUPLE OF OUR OWN.
YOU COMING, VIC?
YOU'RE ON THIS ONE WITH DOROQUEZ.
GO HOME, VICTOR.

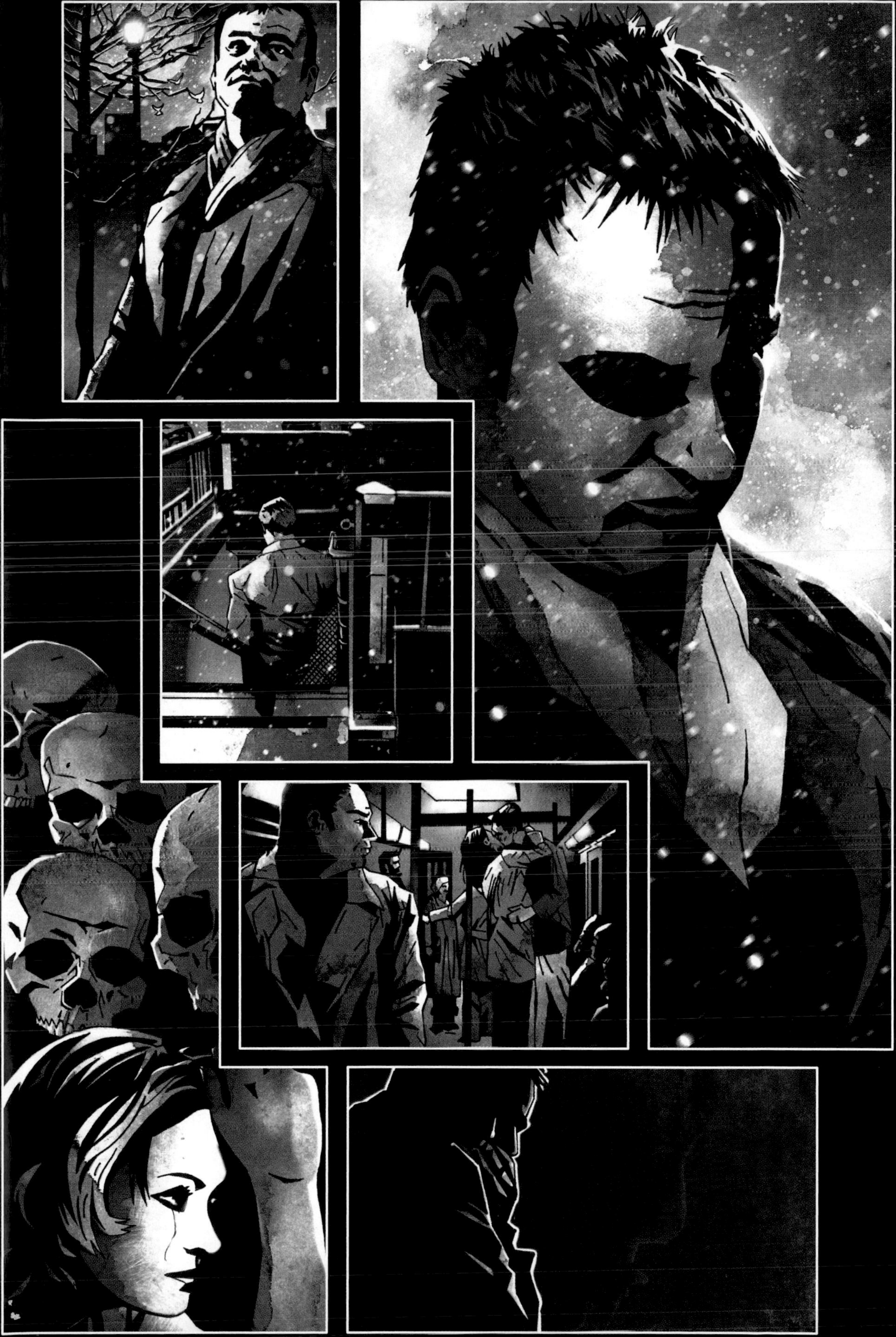

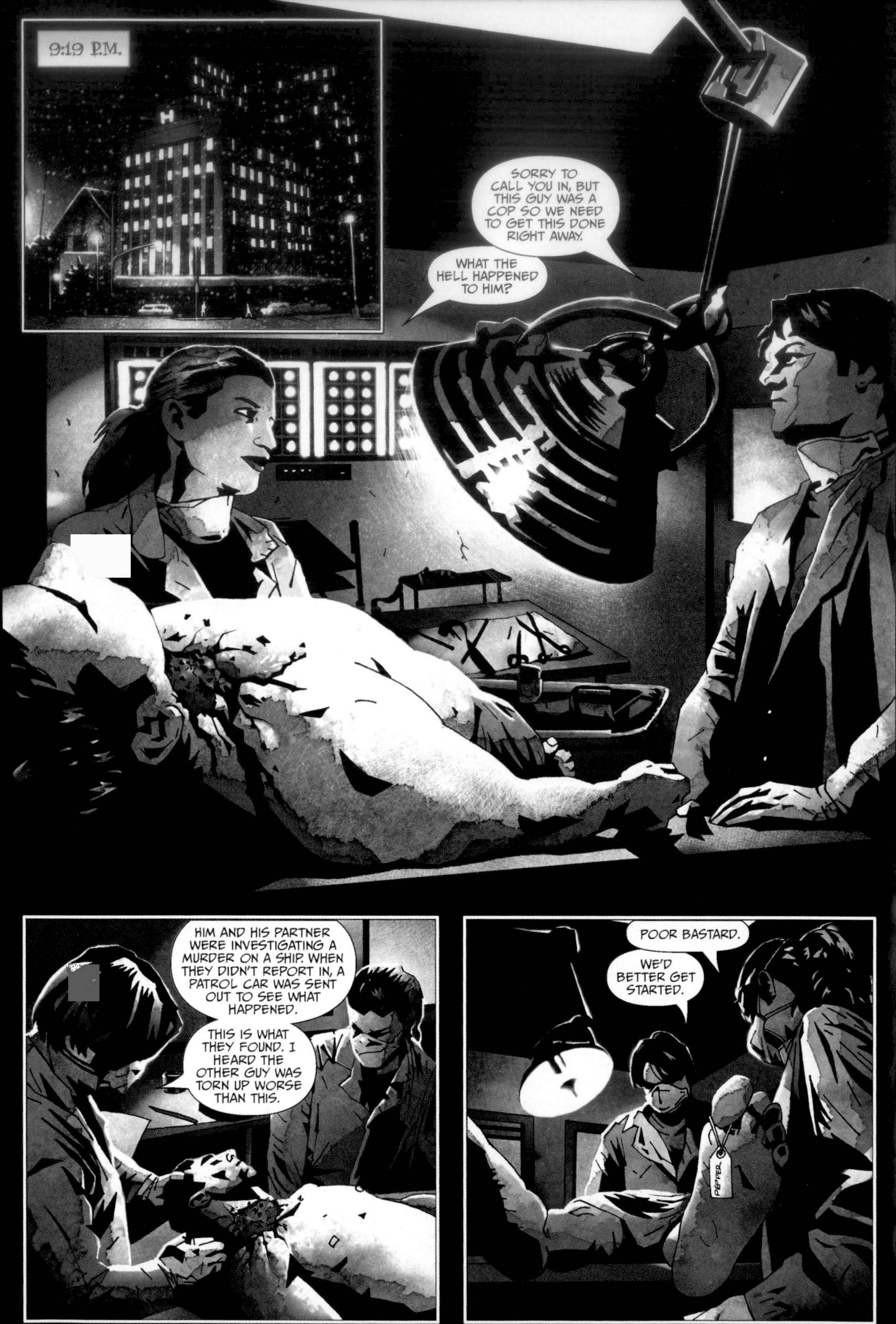
9:19 P.M.
SORRY TO CALL YOU IN, BUT THIS GUY WAS A COP SO WE NEED TO GET THIS DONE RIGHT AWAY.
WHAT THE HELL HAPPENED TO HIM?
HIM AND HIS PARTNER WERE INVESTIGATING A MURDER ON A SHIP. WHEN THEY DIDN'T REPORT IN, A PATROL CAR WAS SENT OUT TO SEE WHAT HAPPENED.
THIS IS WHAT THEY FOUND. I HEARD THE OTHER GUY WAS TORN UP WORSE THAN THIS.
POOR BASTARD.
WE'D BETTER GET STARTED.
PEPPER

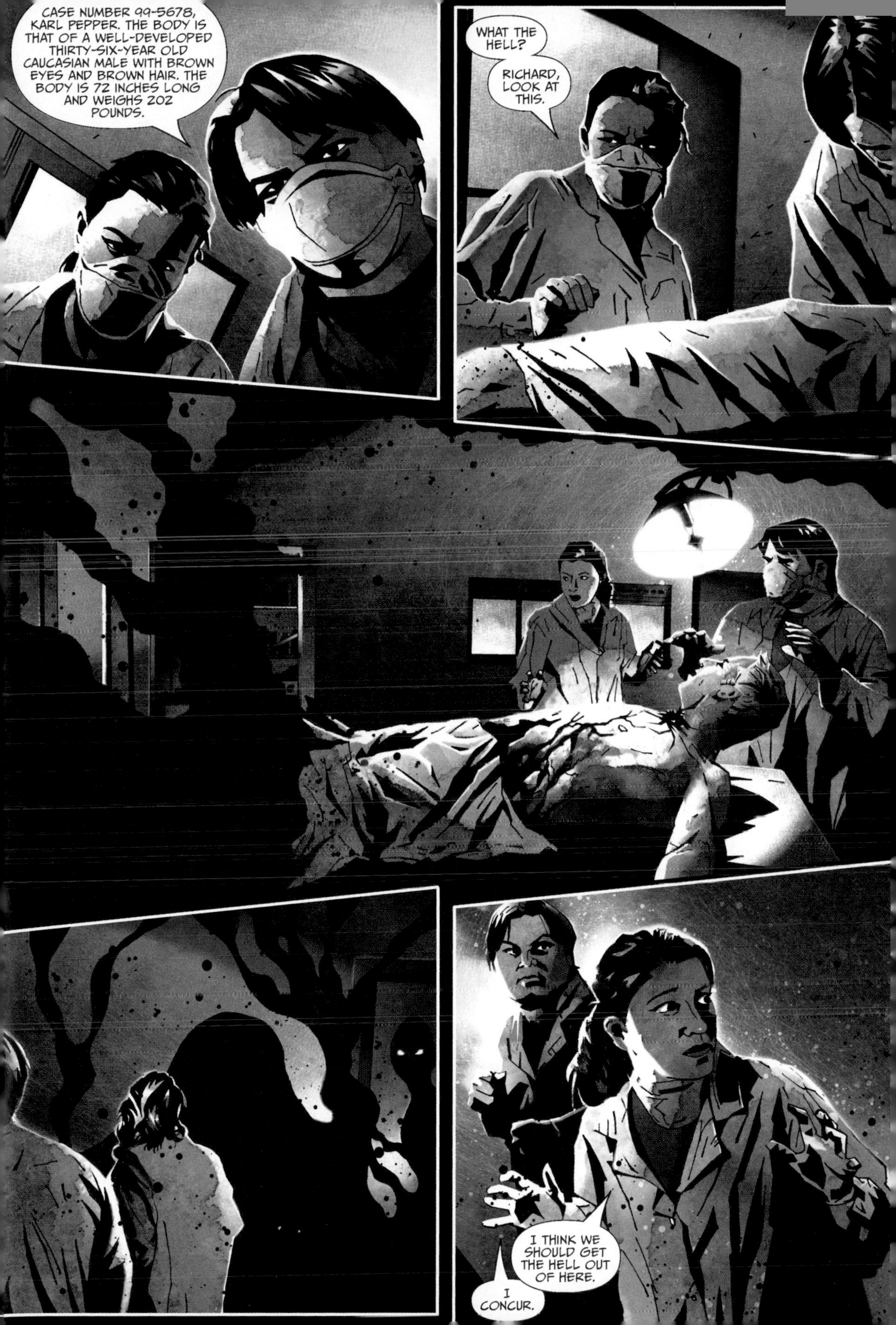
CASE NUMBER 99-5678, KARL PEPPER. THE BODY IS THAT OF A WELL-DEVELOPED THIRTY-SIX-YEAR OLD CAUCASIAN MALE WITH BROWN EYES AND BROWN HAIR. THE BODY IS 72 INCHES LONG AND WEIGHS 202 POUNDS.
WHAT THE HELL?
RICHARD, LOOK AT THIS.
I THINK WE SHOULD GET THE HELL OUT OF HERE.
I CONCUR.

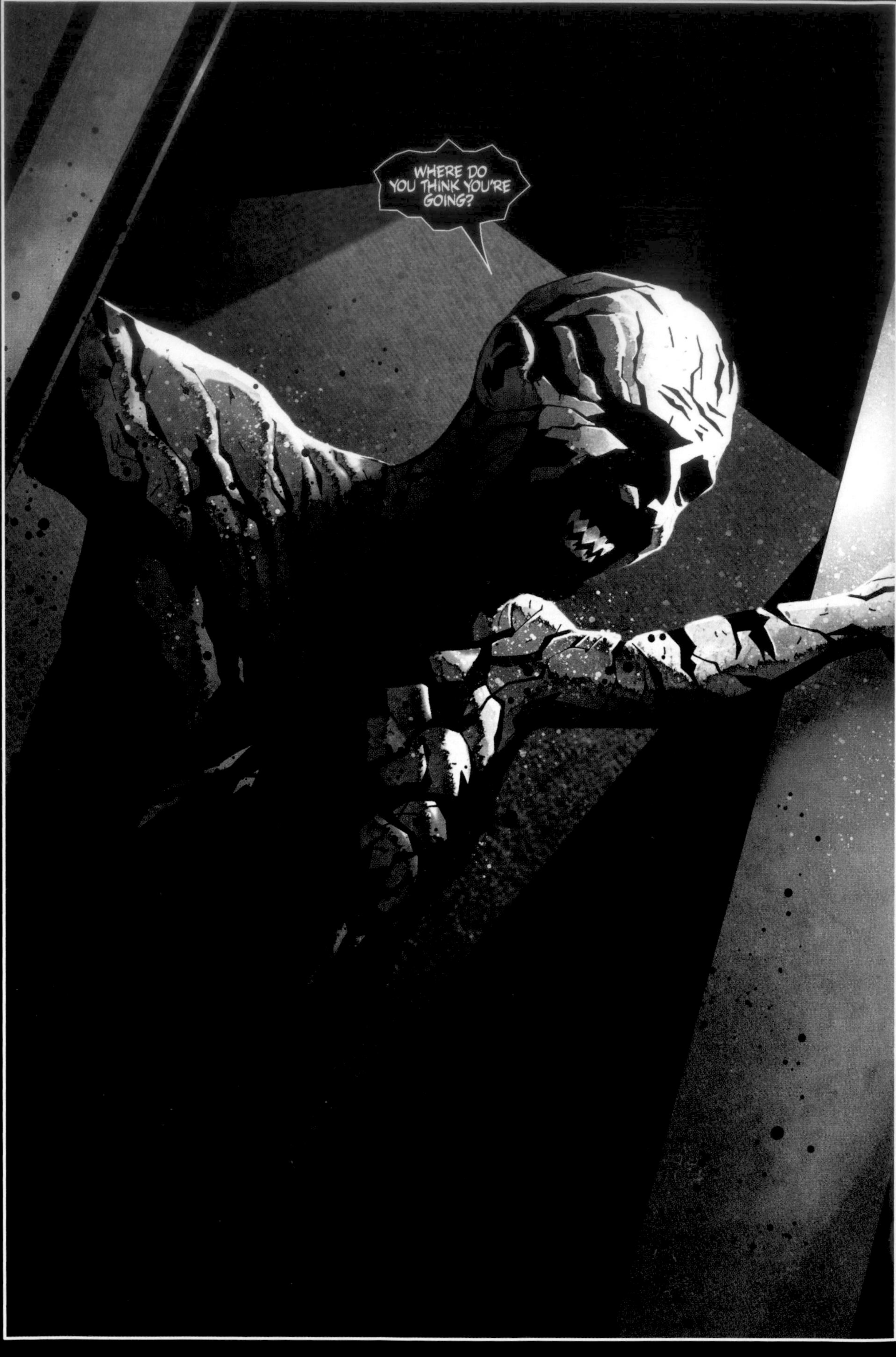
WHERE DO YOU THINK YOU'RE GOING?

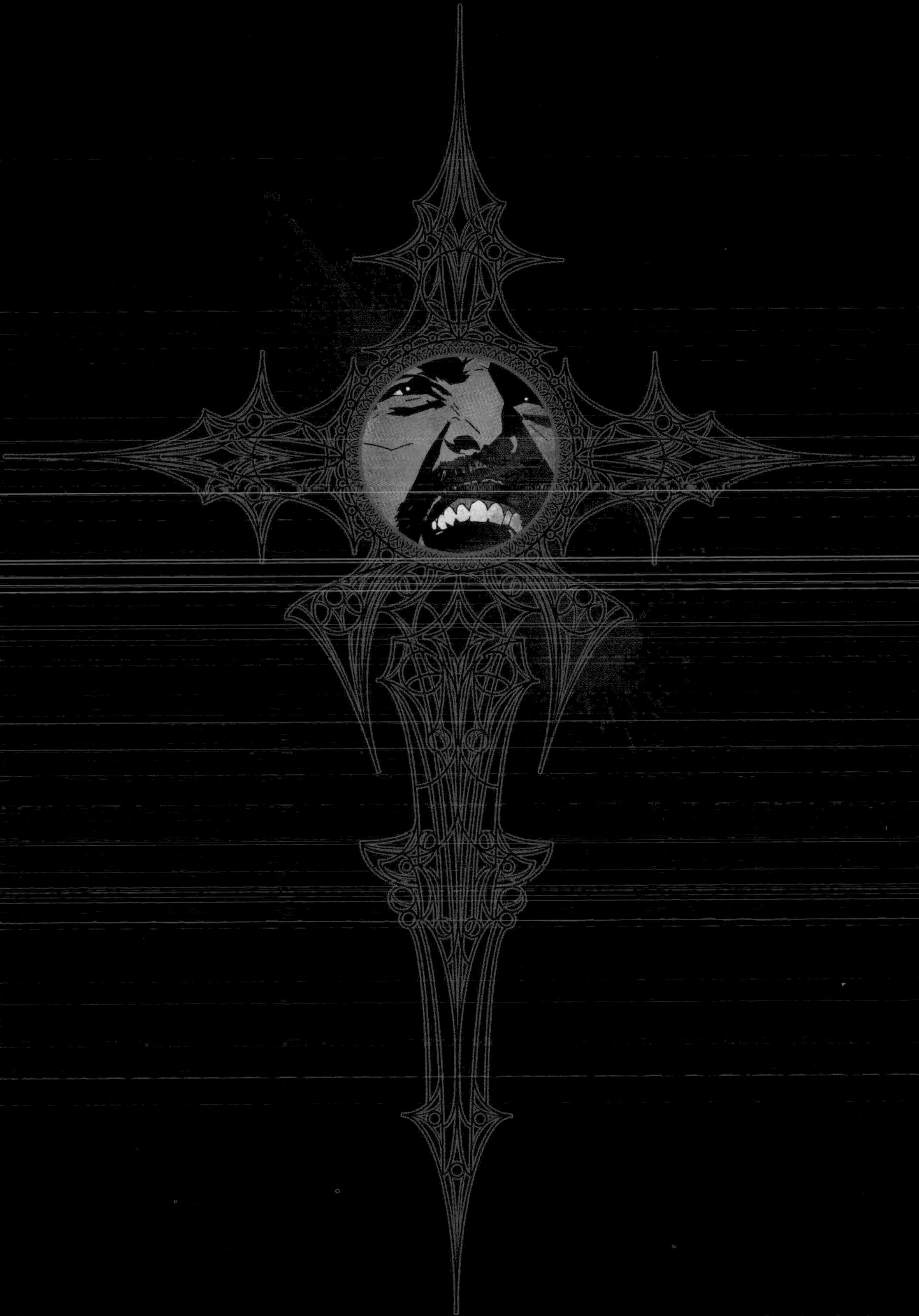

CHAOS
{Issue #2}

WRITTEN BY:
WILLIAM HARMS

PENCILS & ADDITIONAL INKS BY:
NICK POSTIC

INKS & COLORS BY:
NICK MARINKOVICH

LETTERING BY:
ED DUKESHIRE

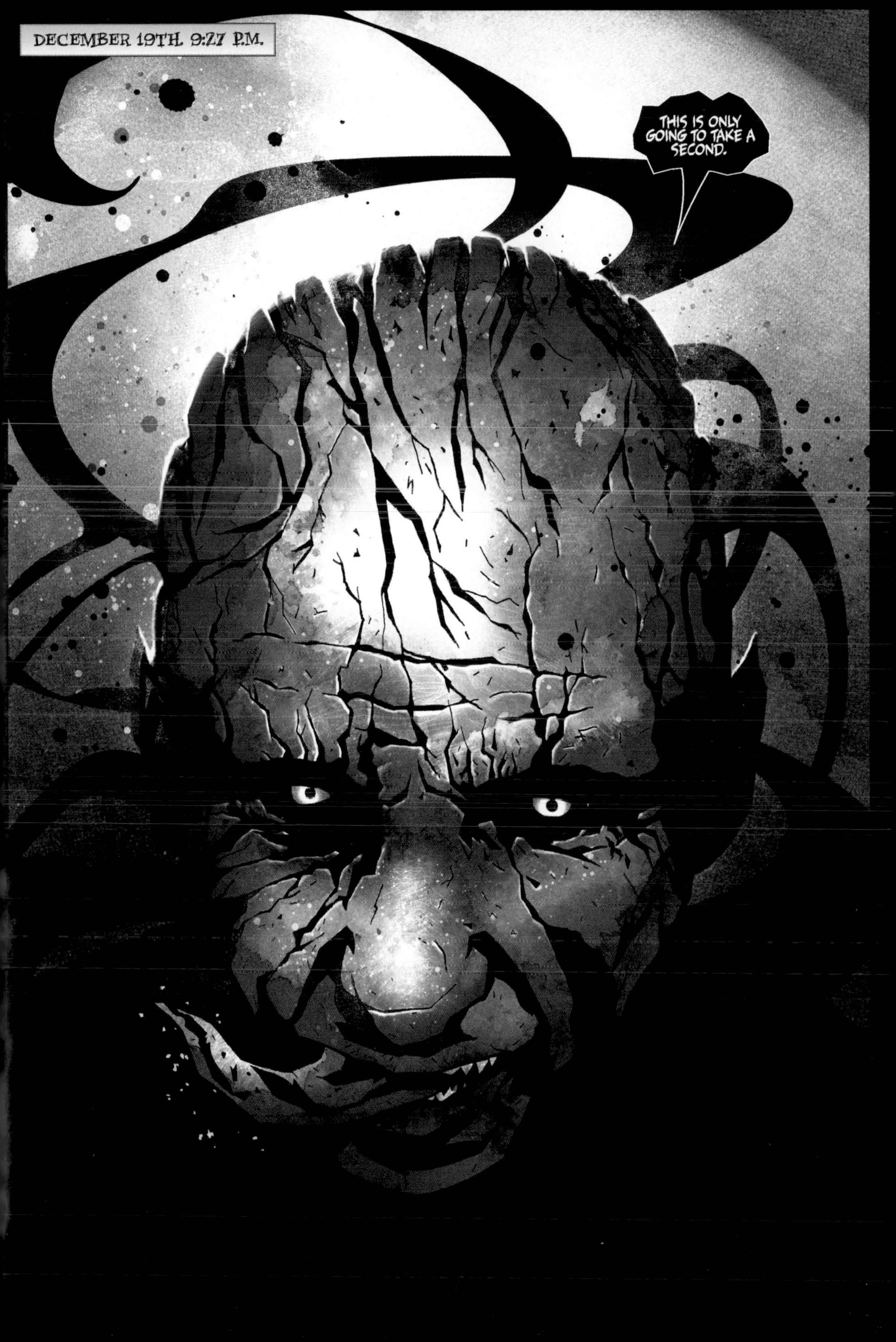
DECEMBER 19TH. 9:27 P.M.
THIS IS ONLY GOING TO TAKE A SECOND.

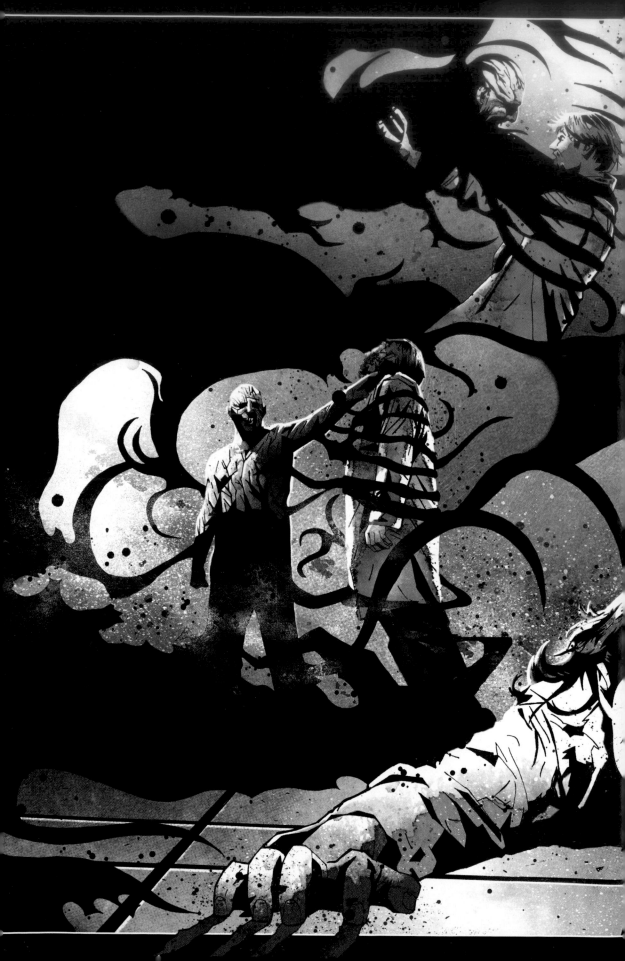

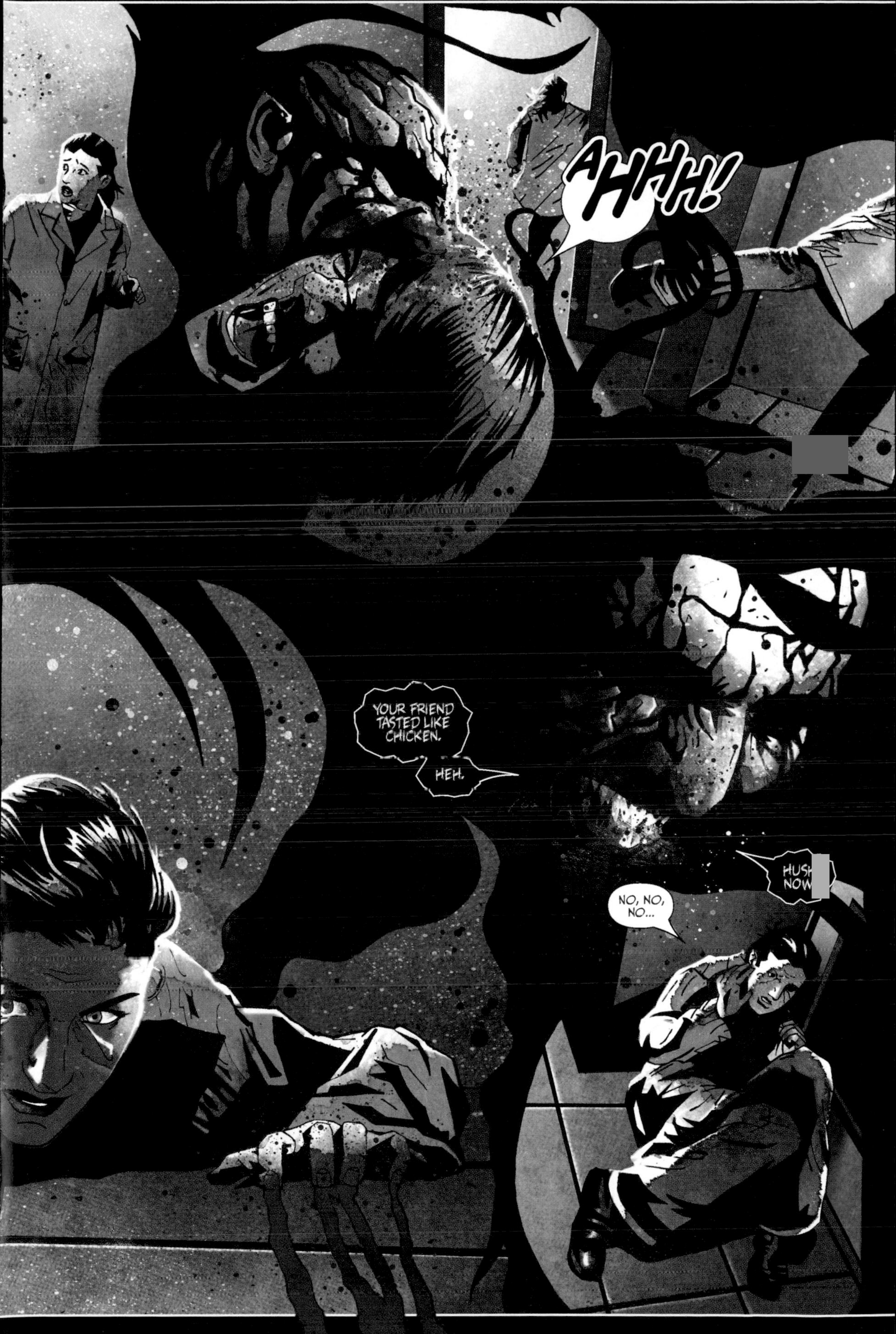
AHHH!
YOUR FRIEND TASTED LIKE CHICKEN.
HEH.
HUSH NOW
NO, NO, NO...

DECEMBER 20TH 12:13 A.M.

...LIBERALS WILL STOP AT NOTHING. THEY WANT NOTHING MORE THAN THE COMPLETE AND UTTER DESTRUCTION OF THIS COUNTRY.

DAMN STRAIGHT.

WHAT THE...

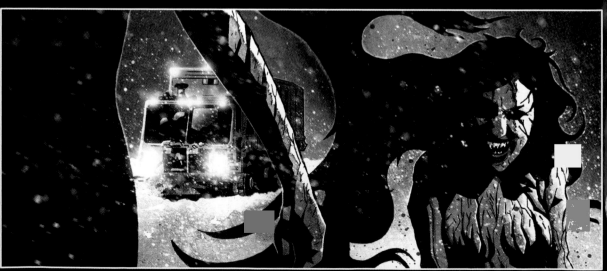

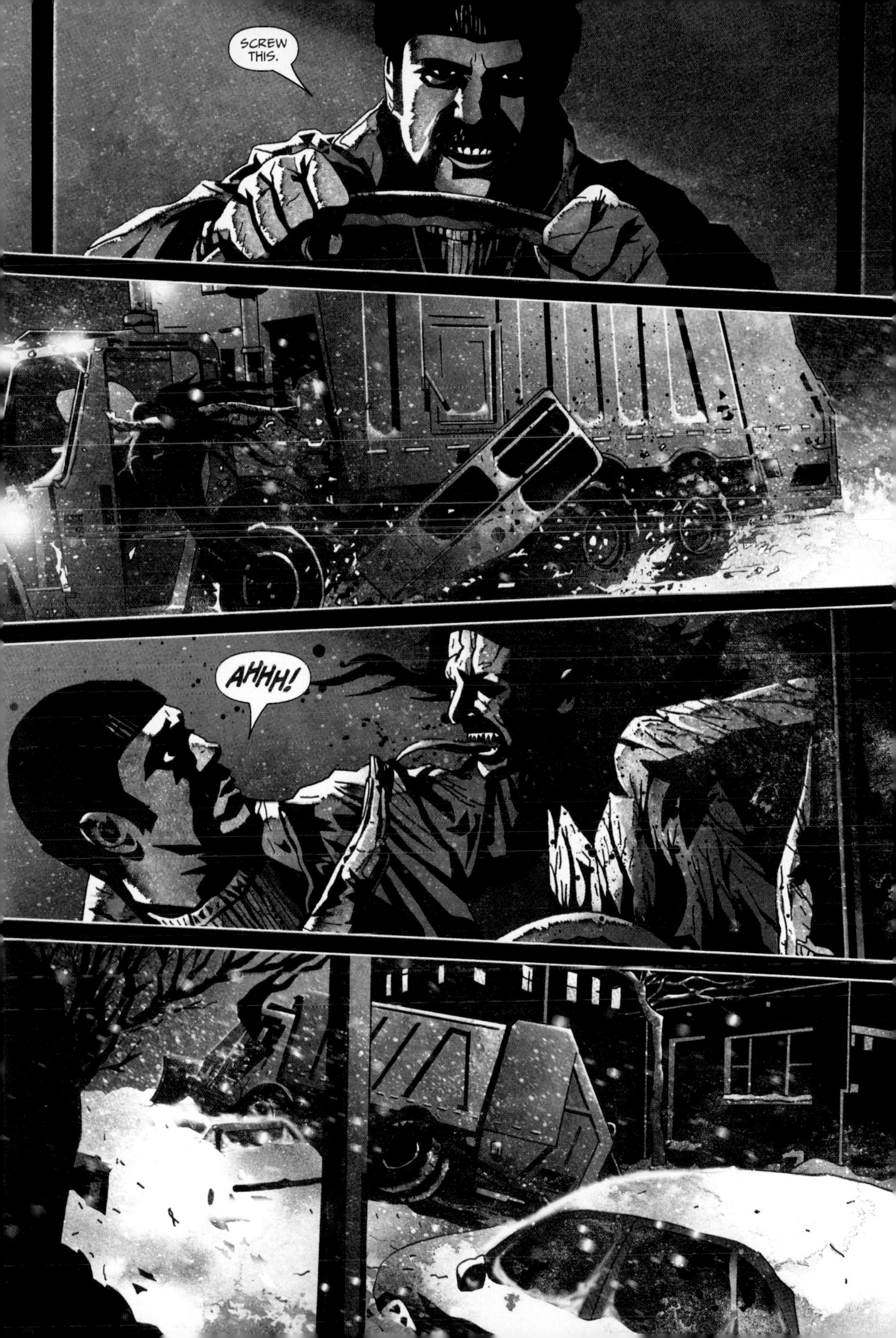
SCREW THIS.
AHHH!

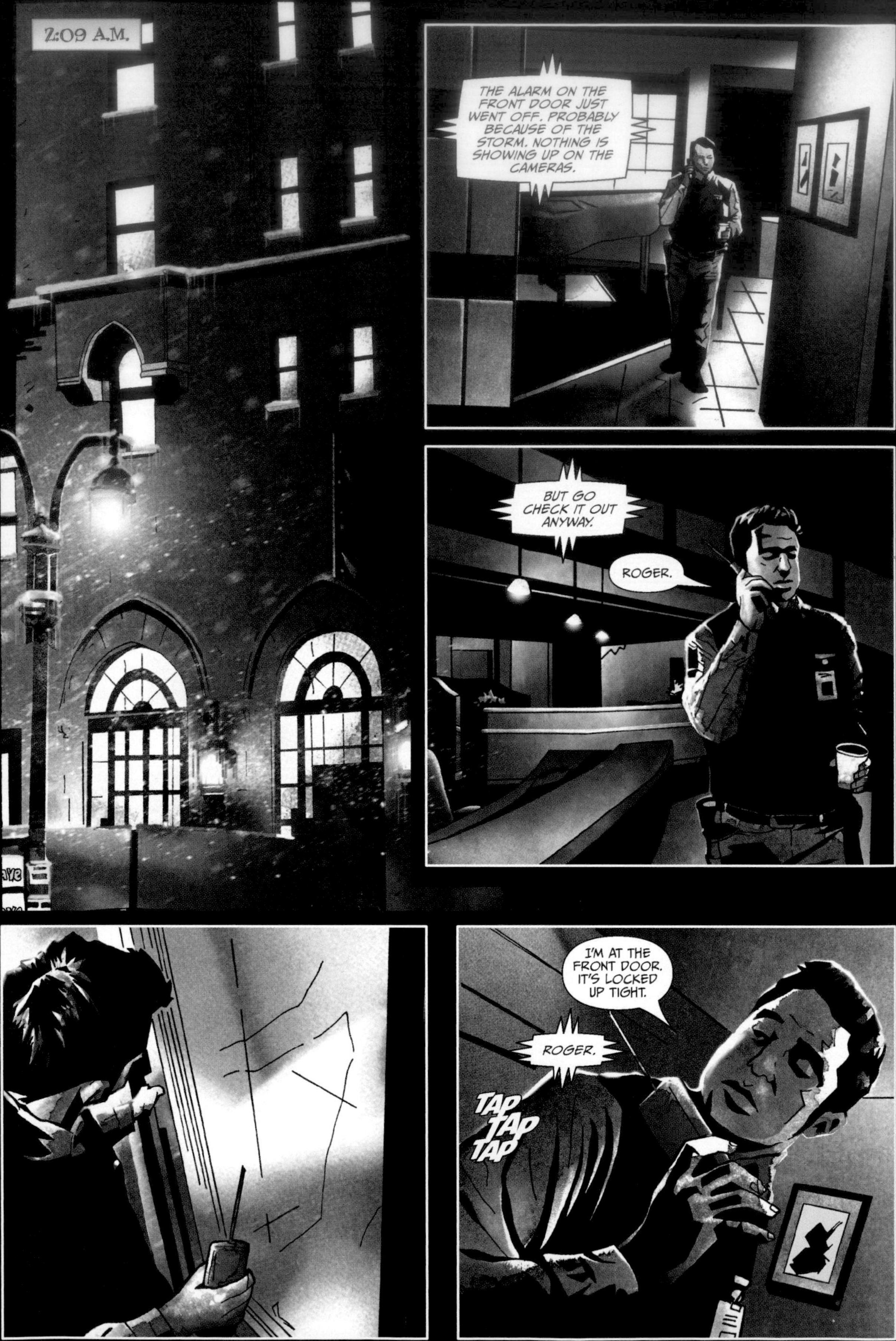
2:09 A.M.
THE ALARM ON THE FRONT DOOR JUST WENT OFF. PROBABLY BECAUSE OF THE STORM. NOTHING IS SHOWING UP ON THE CAMERAS.
BUT GO CHECK IT OUT ANYWAY.
ROGER.
I'M AT THE FRONT DOOR. IT'S LOCKED UP TIGHT.
ROGER.
TAP TAP TAP

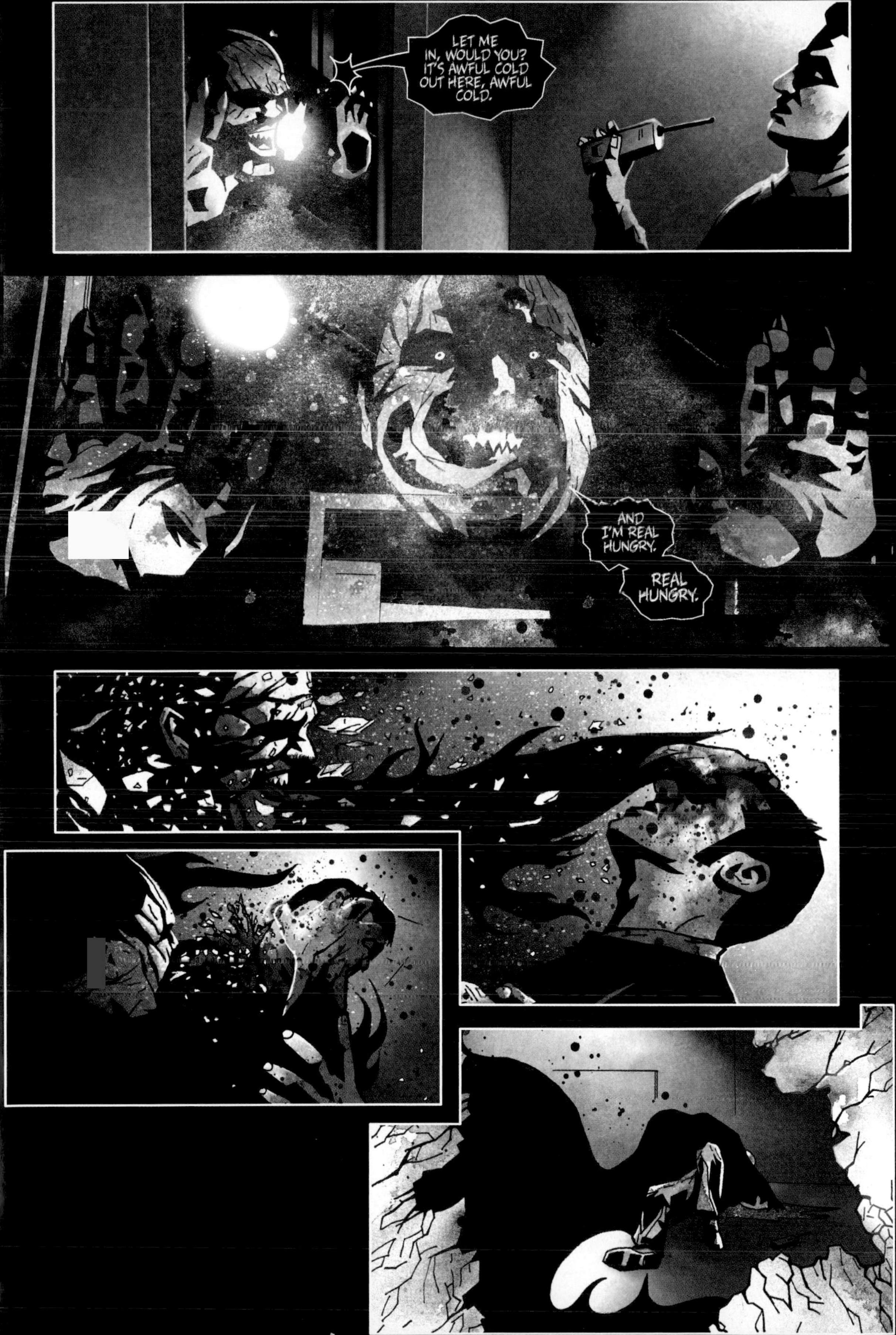
LET ME IN, WOULD YOU? IT'S AWFUL COLD OUT HERE, AWFUL COLD.
AND I'M REAL HUNGRY.
REAL HUNGRY.

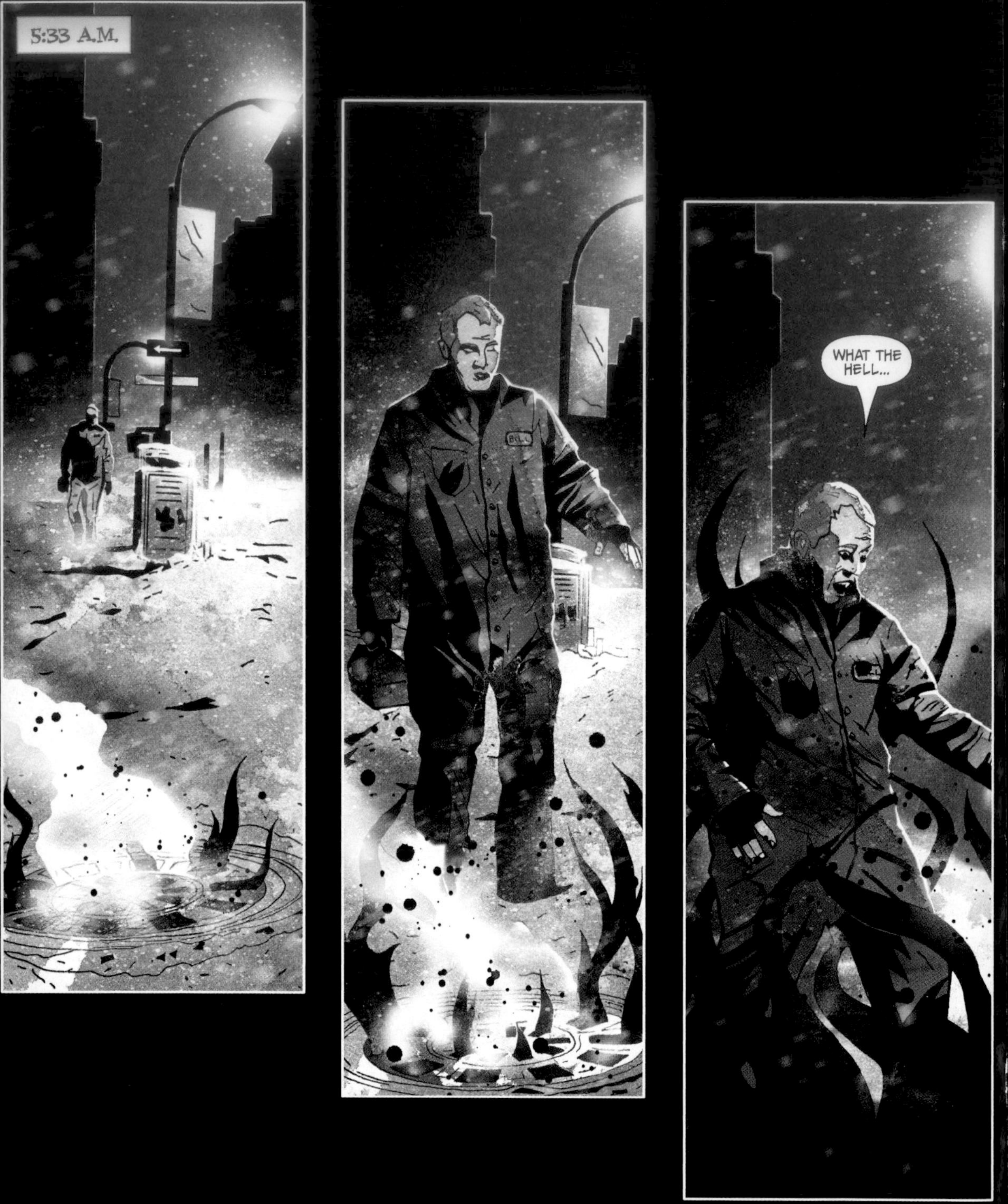
5:33 A.M.
WHAT THE HELL...

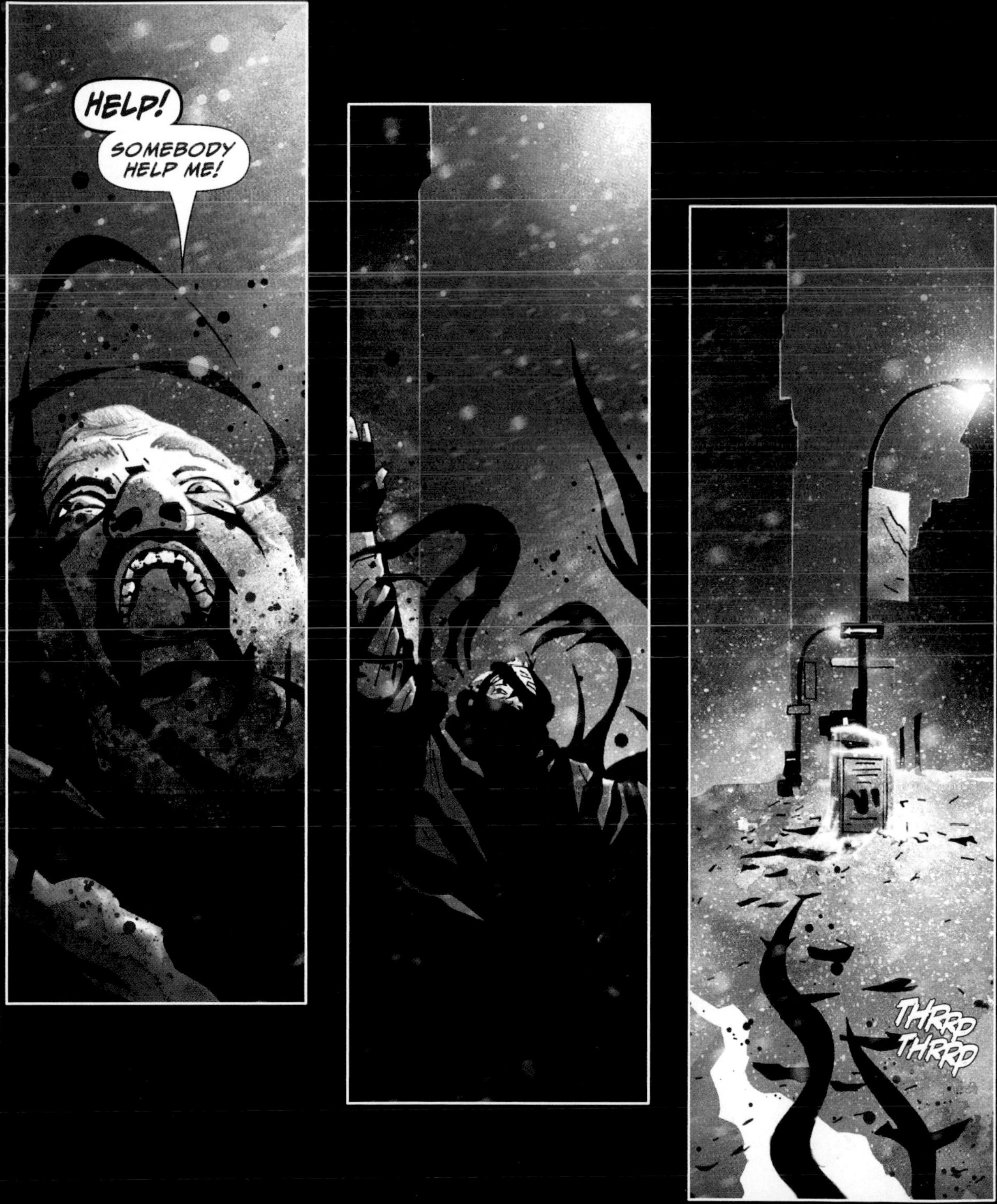
HELP!
SOMEBODY HELP ME!
THRRP THRRP

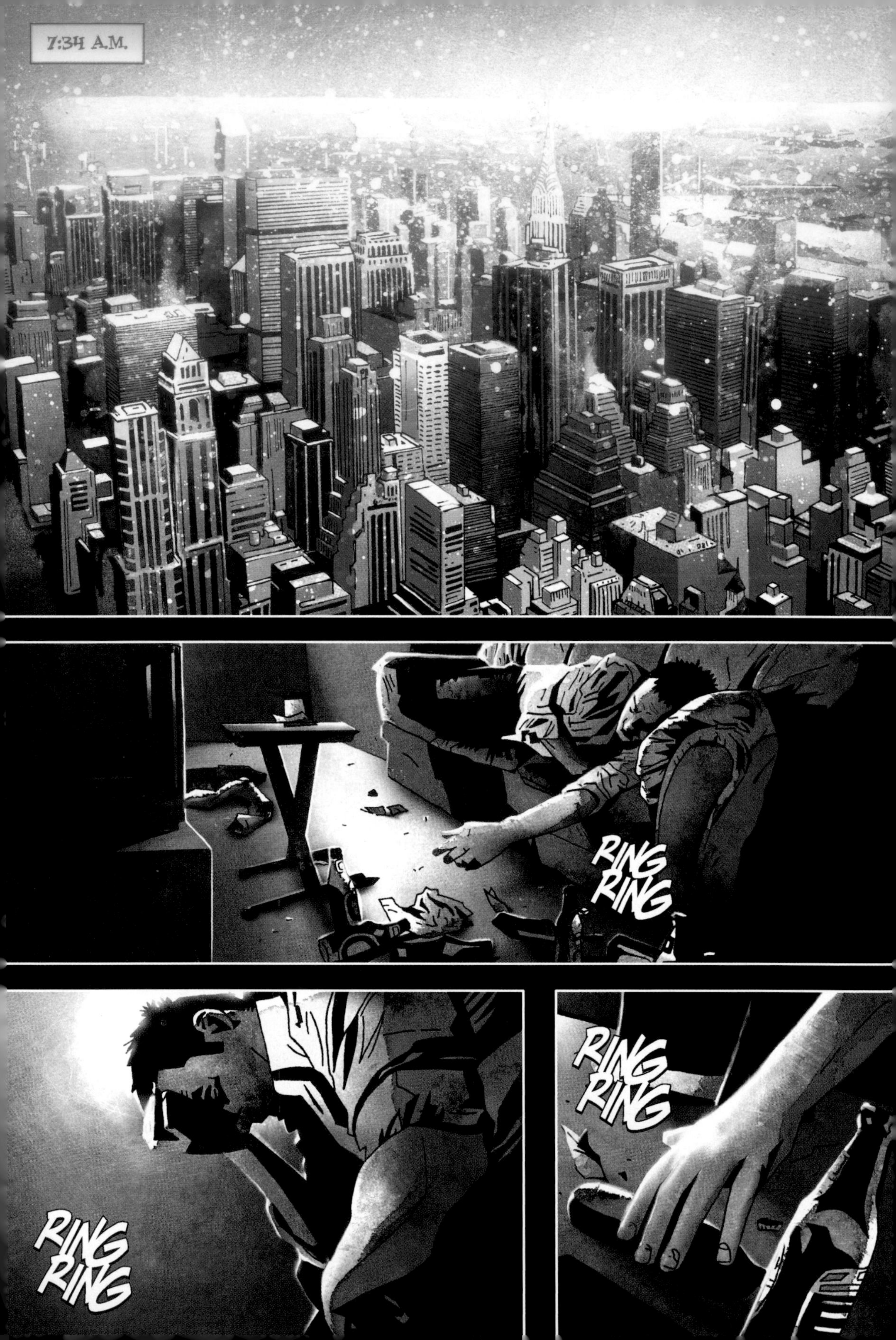
7:34 A.M.
RING RING
RING RING
RING RING

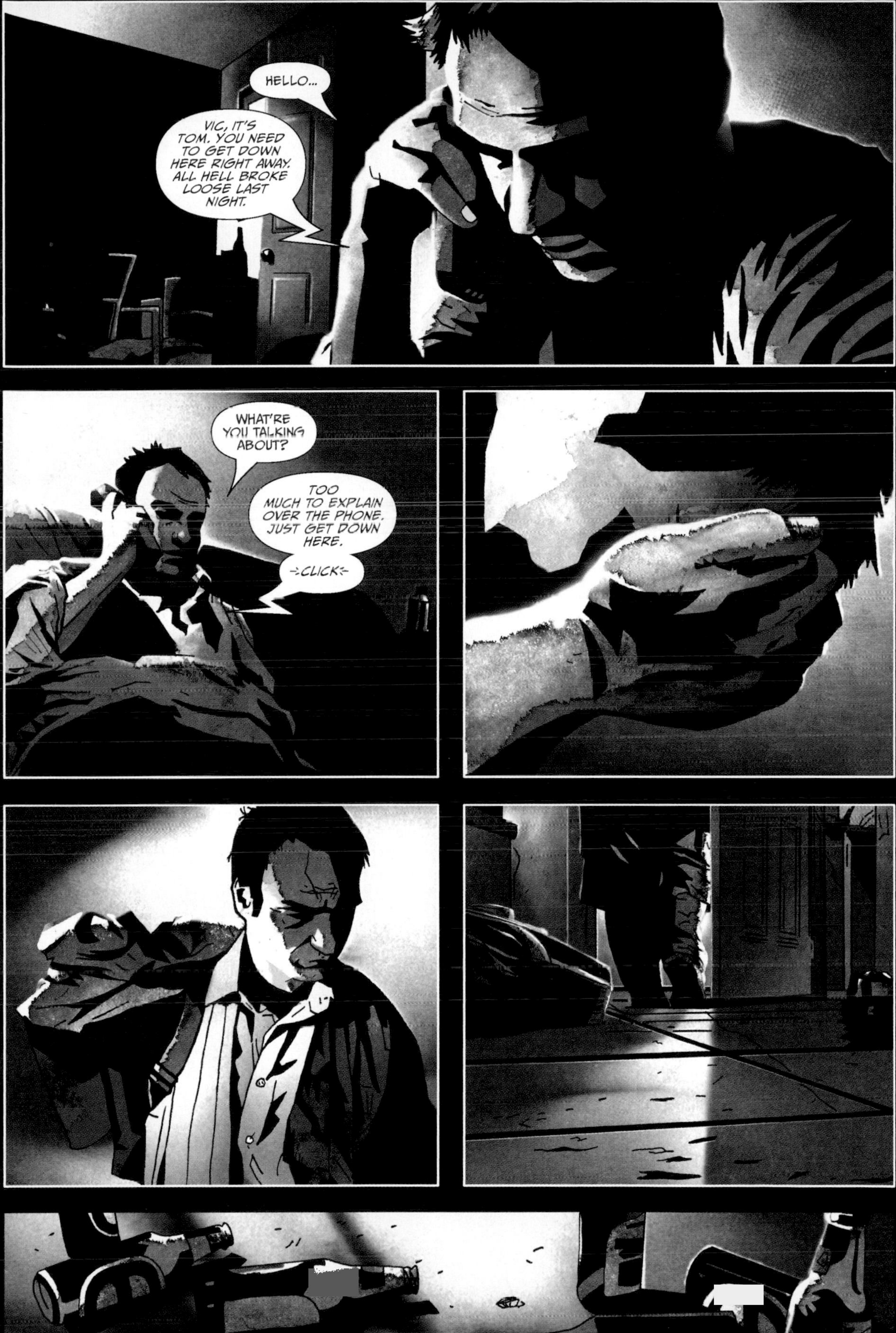
HELLO...
VIC, IT'S TOM. YOU NEED TO GET DOWN HERE RIGHT AWAY. ALL HELL BROKE LOOSE LAST NIGHT.
WHAT'RE YOU TALKING ABOUT?
TOO MUCH TO EXPLAIN OVER THE PHONE. JUST GET DOWN HERE.
CLICK

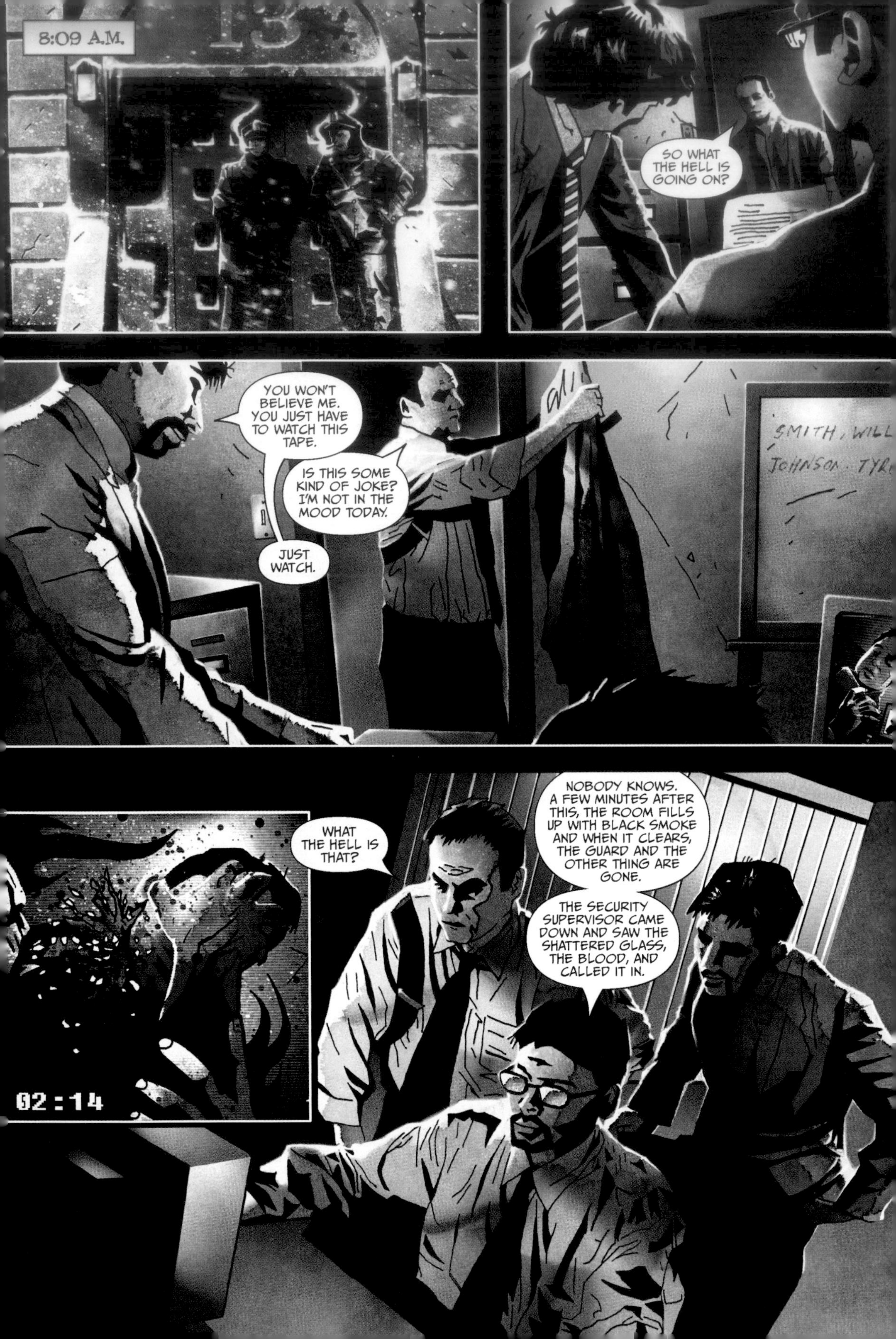
8:09 A.M.
SO WHAT THE HELL IS GOING ON?
YOU WON'T BELIEVE ME. YOU JUST HAVE TO WATCH THIS TAPE.
IS THIS SOME KIND OF JOKE? I'M NOT IN THE MOOD TODAY.
JUST WATCH.
WHAT THE HELL IS THAT?
NOBODY KNOWS. A FEW MINUTES AFTER THIS, THE ROOM FILLS UP WITH BLACK SMOKE AND WHEN IT CLEARS, THE GUARD AND THE OTHER THING ARE GONE.
THE SECURITY SUPERVISOR CAME DOWN AND SAW THE SHATTERED GLASS, THE BLOOD, AND CALLED IT IN.
02:14

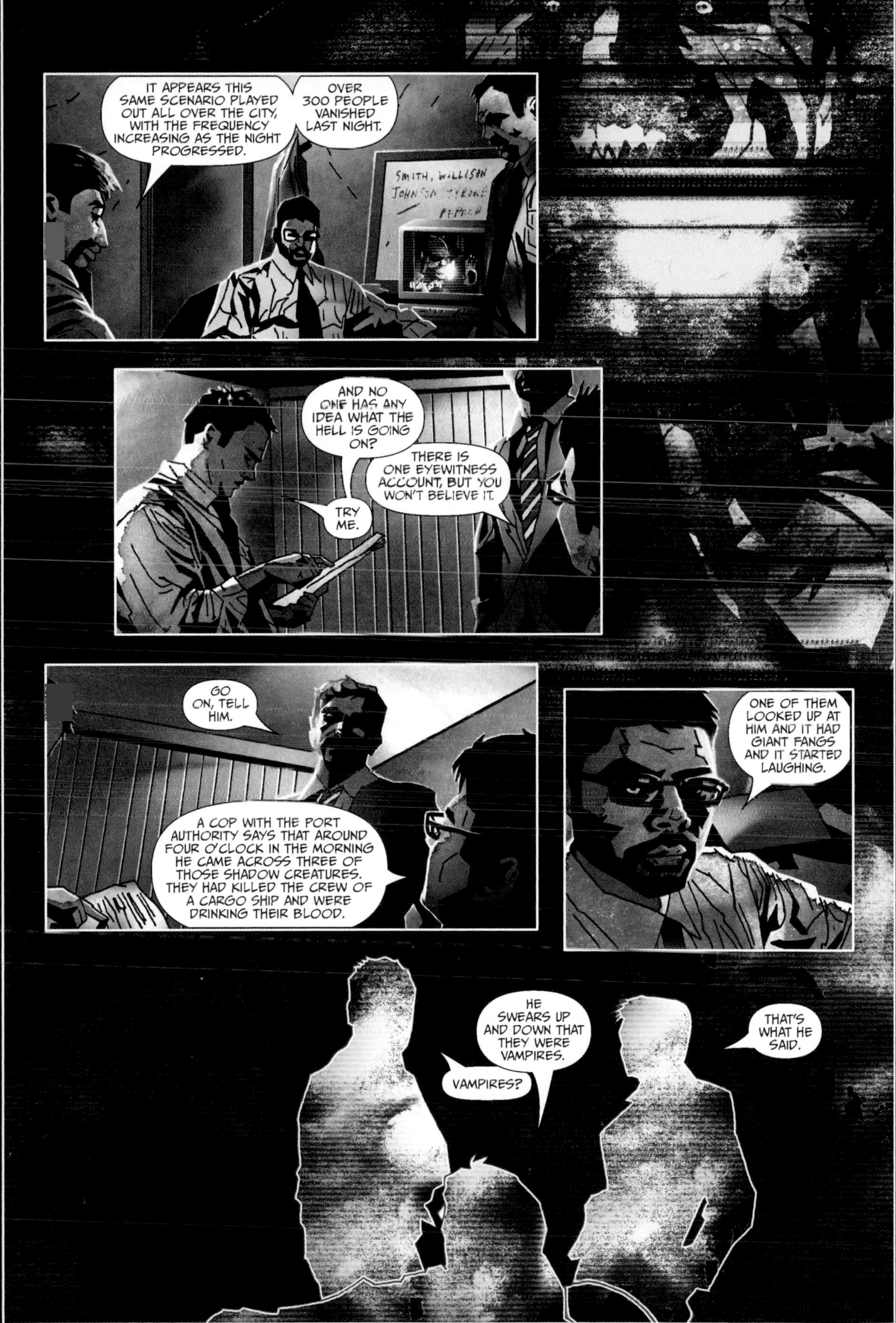
IT APPEARS THIS SAME SCENARIO PLAYED OUT ALL OVER THE CITY, WITH THE FREQUENCY INCREASING AS THE NIGHT PROGRESSED.
OVER 300 PEOPLE VANISHED LAST NIGHT.
AND NO ONE HAS ANY IDEA WHAT THE HELL IS GOING ON?
THERE IS ONE EYEWITNESS ACCOUNT, BUT YOU WON'T BELIEVE IT.
TRY ME.
GO ON, TELL HIM.
A COP WITH THE PORT AUTHORITY SAYS THAT AROUND FOUR O'CLOCK IN THE MORNING HE CAME ACROSS THREE OF THOSE SHADOW CREATURES. THEY HAD KILLED THE CREW OF A CARGO SHIP AND WERE DRINKING THEIR BLOOD.
ONE OF THEM LOOKED UP AT HIM AND IT HAD GIANT FANGS AND IT STARTED LAUGHING.
HE SWEARS UP AND DOWN THAT THEY WERE VAMPIRES.
VAMPIRES?
THAT'S WHAT HE SAID.

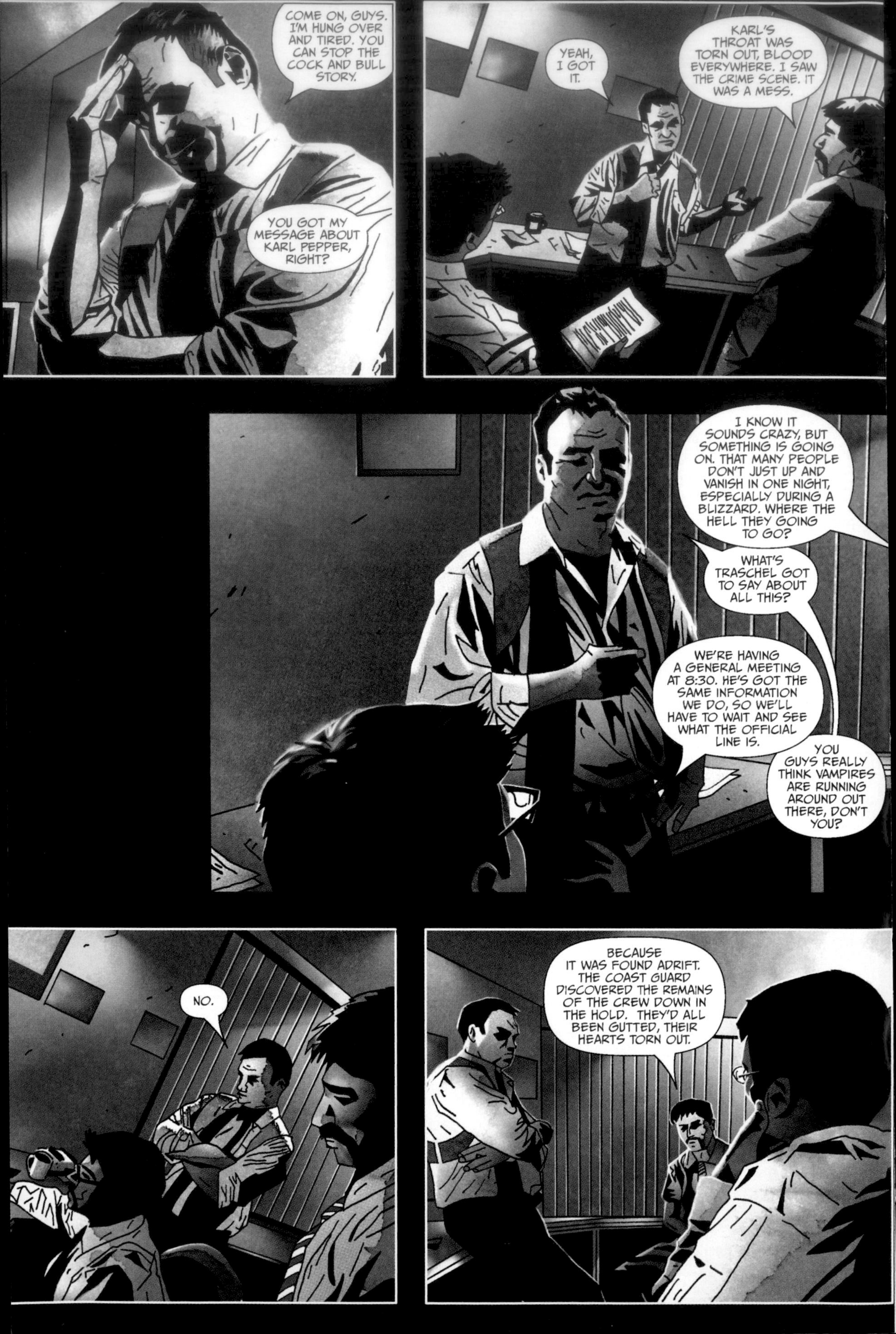
COME ON, GUYS. I'M HUNG OVER AND TIRED. YOU CAN STOP THE COCK AND BULL STORY.
YOU GOT MY MESSAGE ABOUT KARL PEPPER, RIGHT?
YEAH, I GOT IT.
KARL'S THROAT WAS TORN OUT, BLOOD EVERYWHERE. I SAW THE CRIME SCENE. IT WAS A MESS.
I KNOW IT SOUNDS CRAZY, BUT SOMETHING IS GOING ON. THAT MANY PEOPLE DON'T JUST UP AND VANISH IN ONE NIGHT, ESPECIALLY DURING A BLIZZARD. WHERE THE HELL THEY GOING TO GO?
WHAT'S TRASCHEL GOT TO SAY ABOUT ALL THIS?
WE'RE HAVING A GENERAL MEETING AT 8:30. HE'S GOT THE SAME INFORMATION WE DO, SO WE'LL HAVE TO WAIT AND SEE WHAT THE OFFICIAL LINE IS.
YOU GUYS REALLY THINK VAMPIRES ARE RUNNING AROUND OUT THERE, DON'T YOU?
NO.
BECAUSE IT WAS FOUND ADRIFT. THE COAST GUARD DISCOVERED THE REMAINS OF THE CREW DOWN IN THE HOLD. THEY'D ALL BEEN GUTTED, THEIR HEARTS TORN OUT.

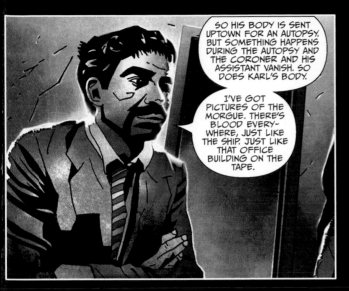

SO HIS BODY IS SENT UPTOWN FOR AN AUTOPSY. BUT SOMETHING HAPPENS DURING THE AUTOPSY AND THE CORONER AND HIS ASSISTANT VANISH. SO DOES KARL'S BODY.

I'VE GOT PICTURES OF THE MORGUE. THERE'S BLOOD EVERY-WHERE, JUST LIKE THE SHIP. JUST LIKE THAT OFFICE BUILDING ON THE TAPE.

SO WHAT ARE YOU SAYING, THAT PEPPER WAS TURNED INTO A VAMPIRE AND HE KILLED THE CORONER?

LISTEN, I DON'T KNOW IF THEY'RE VAMPIRES. BUT I DO THINK THAT THEY'RE SOMETHING SUPERNATURAL. YOU KNOW WHY PEPPER WAS ON THAT SHIP?

THE ENTIRE SHIP IS SEARCHED, TOP TO BOTTOM, AND THEN SEALED OFF, WITH PEPPER LEADING THE INVESTIGATION. AN HOUR LATER, PEPPER AND HIS PARTNER ARE FOUND DEAD.

WHATEVER KILLED THEM WAS WHAT KILLED THE CREW. AND IT WAS STILL ON THAT SHIP.

YOU'RE SERIOUS ABOUT THIS, AREN'T YOU?

LATER THIS AFTERNOON, WE'RE GOING TO GO DOWN AND CHECK OUT THAT SHIP, SEE IF WE CAN FIND ANYTHING.

WE NEED YOU TO COVER FOR US, CASE SOMEONE COMES AROUND WONDERING WHERE WE'RE AT.

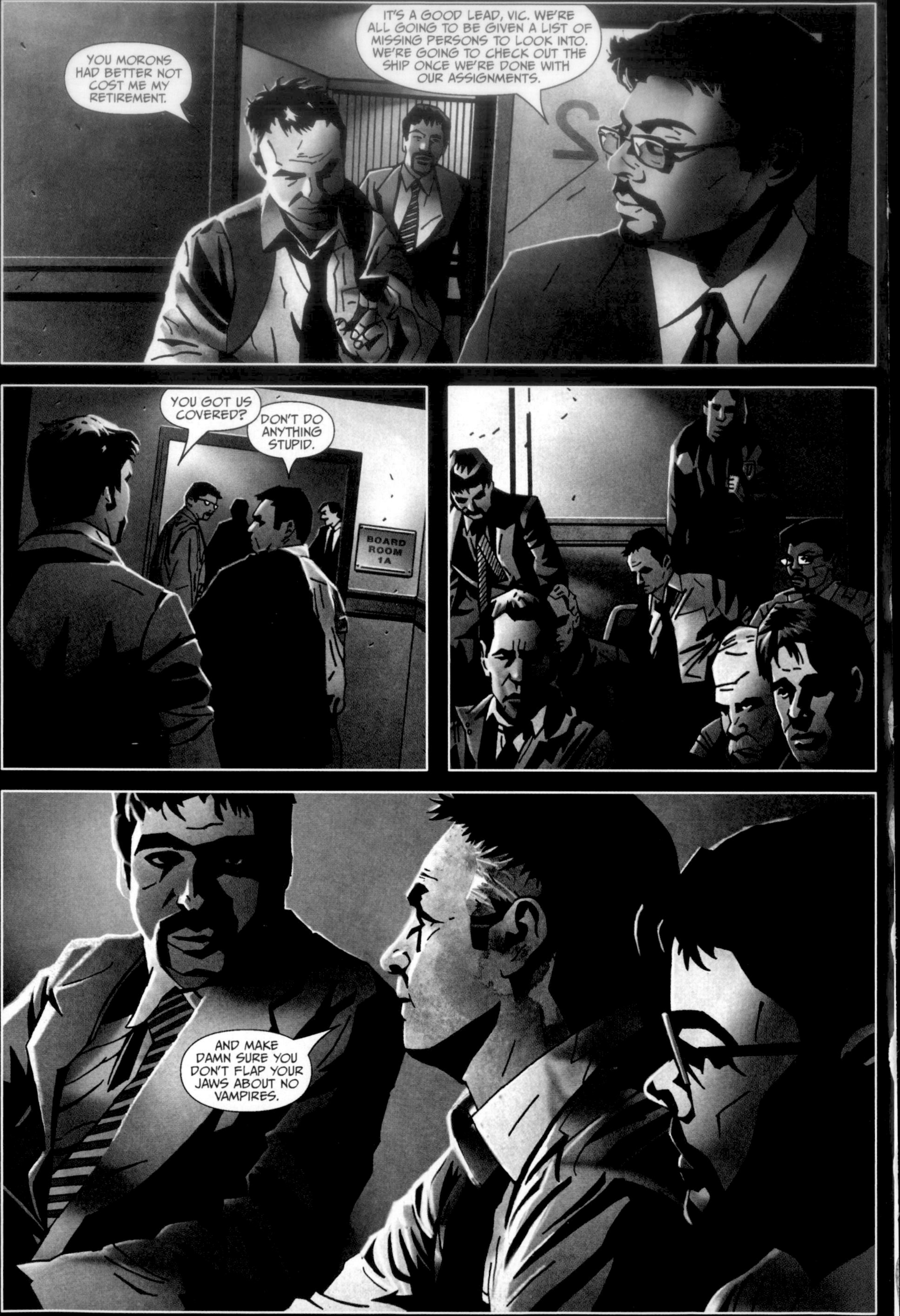
YOU MORONS HAD BETTER NOT COST ME MY RETIREMENT.
IT'S A GOOD LEAD, VIC. WE'RE ALL GOING TO BE GIVEN A LIST OF MISSING PERSONS TO LOOK INTO. WE'RE GOING TO CHECK OUT THE SHIP ONCE WE'RE DONE WITH OUR ASSIGNMENTS.
YOU GOT US COVERED?
DON'T DO ANYTHING STUPID.
BOARD ROOM 1A
AND MAKE DAMN SURE YOU DON'T FLAP YOUR JAWS ABOUT NO VAMPIRES.

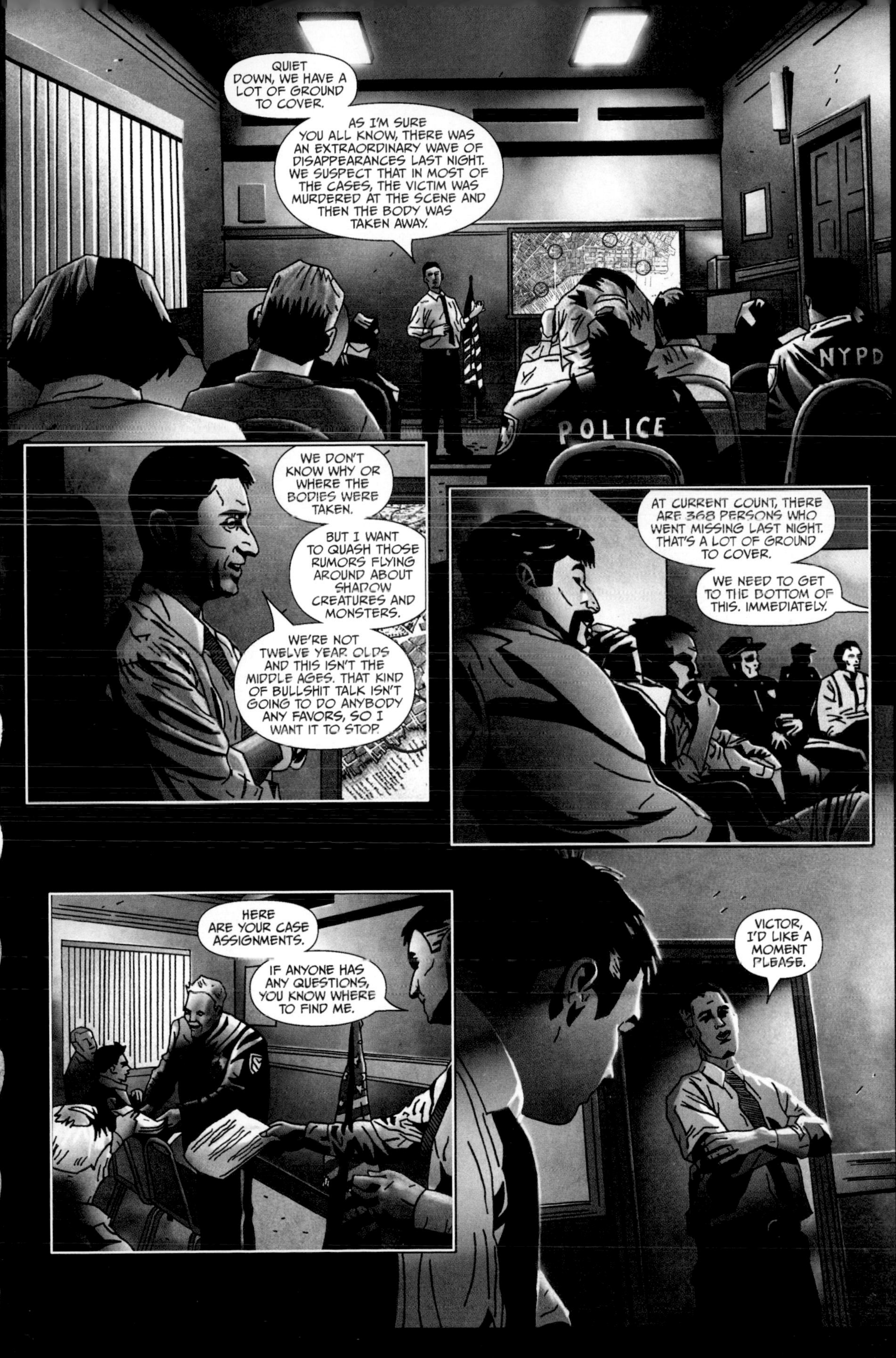
QUIET DOWN, WE HAVE A LOT OF GROUND TO COVER.
AS I'M SURE YOU ALL KNOW, THERE WAS AN EXTRAORDINARY WAVE OF DISAPPEARANCES LAST NIGHT. WE SUSPECT THAT IN MOST OF THE CASES, THE VICTIM WAS MURDERED AT THE SCENE AND THEN THE BODY WAS TAKEN AWAY.
NYPD
POLICE
WE DON'T KNOW WHY OR WHERE THE BODIES WERE TAKEN.
BUT I WANT TO QUASH THOSE RUMORS FLYING AROUND ABOUT SHADOW CREATURES AND MONSTERS.
WE'RE NOT TWELVE YEAR OLDS AND THIS ISN'T THE MIDDLE AGES. THAT KIND OF BULLSHIT TALK ISN'T GOING TO DO ANYBODY ANY FAVORS, SO I WANT IT TO STOP.
AT CURRENT COUNT, THERE ARE 368 PERSONS WHO WENT MISSING LAST NIGHT. THAT'S A LOT OF GROUND TO COVER.
WE NEED TO GET TO THE BOTTOM OF THIS. IMMEDIATELY.
HERE ARE YOUR CASE ASSIGNMENTS.
IF ANYONE HAS ANY QUESTIONS, YOU KNOW WHERE TO FIND ME.
VICTOR, I'D LIKE A MOMENT PLEASE.

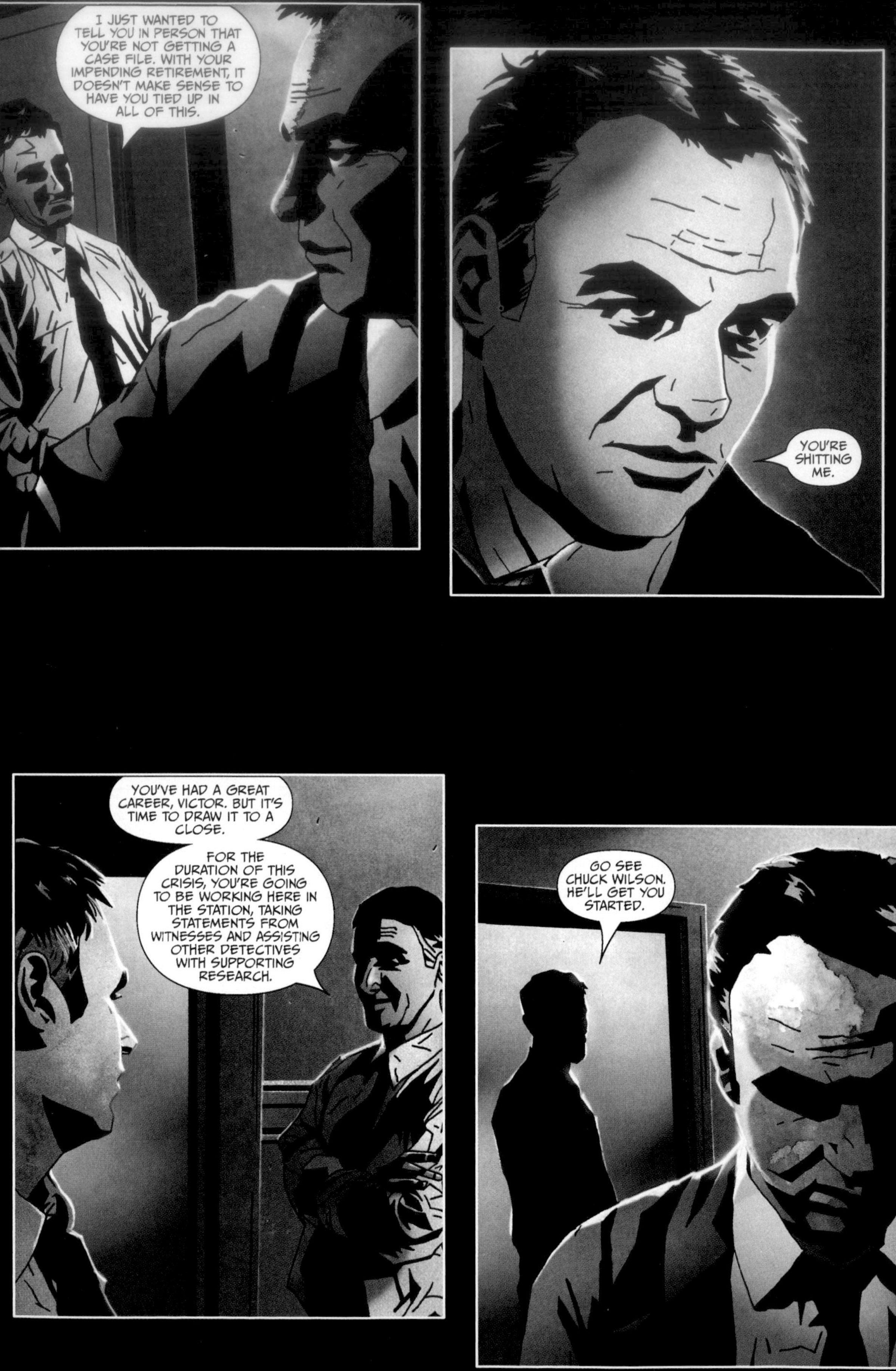
I JUST WANTED TO TELL YOU IN PERSON THAT YOU'RE NOT GETTING A CASE FILE. WITH YOUR IMPENDING RETIREMENT, IT DOESN'T MAKE SENSE TO HAVE YOU TIED UP IN ALL OF THIS.
YOU'RE SHITTING ME.
YOU'VE HAD A GREAT CAREER, VICTOR. BUT IT'S TIME TO DRAW IT TO A CLOSE.
FOR THE DURATION OF THIS CRISIS, YOU'RE GOING TO BE WORKING HERE IN THE STATION, TAKING STATEMENTS FROM WITNESSES AND ASSISTING OTHER DETECTIVES WITH SUPPORTING RESEARCH.
GO SEE CHUCK WILSON. HE'LL GET YOU STARTED.

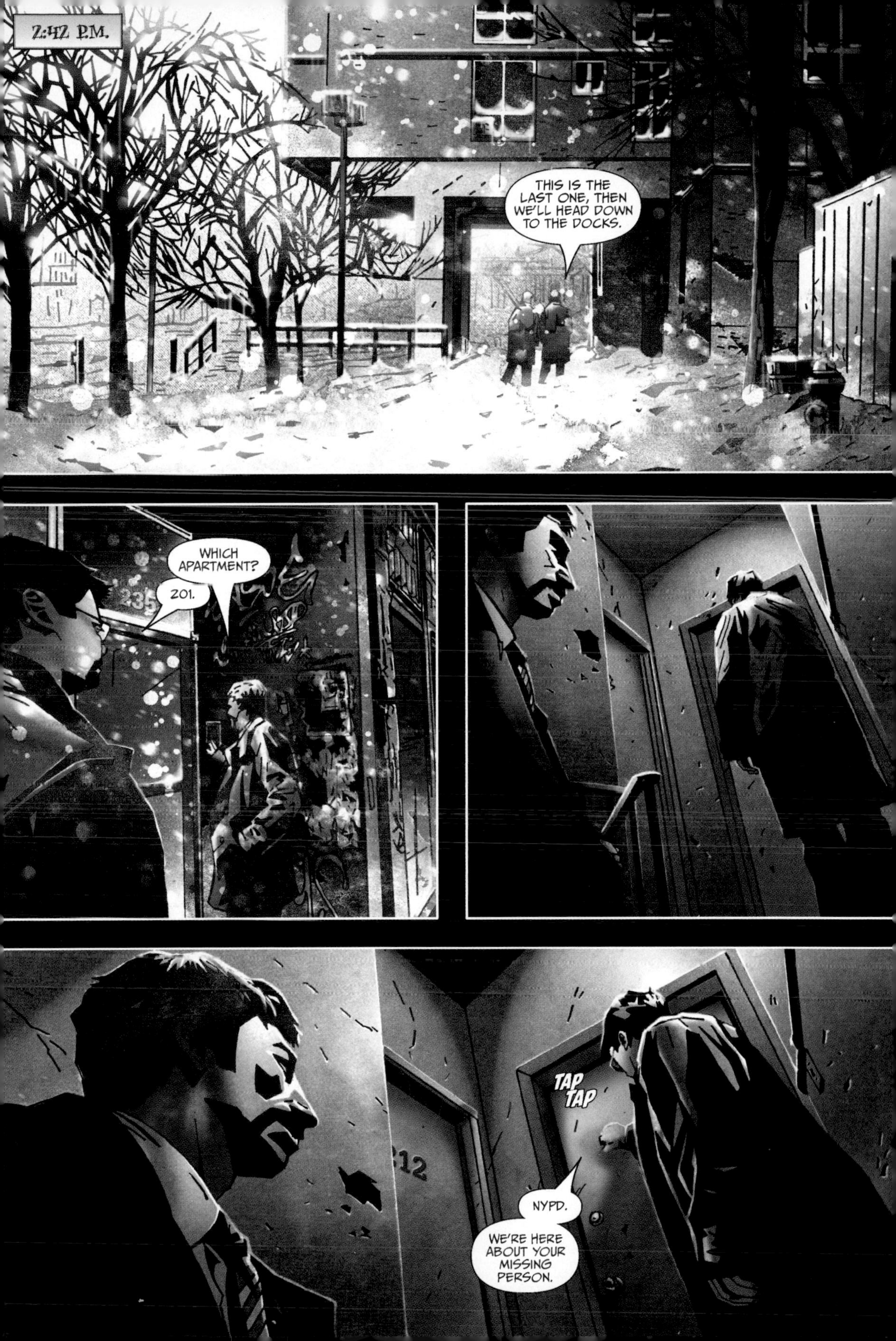
2:42 P.M.
THIS IS THE LAST ONE, THEN WE'LL HEAD DOWN TO THE DOCKS.
WHICH APARTMENT?
201.
TAP TAP
NYPD.
WE'RE HERE ABOUT YOUR MISSING PERSON.

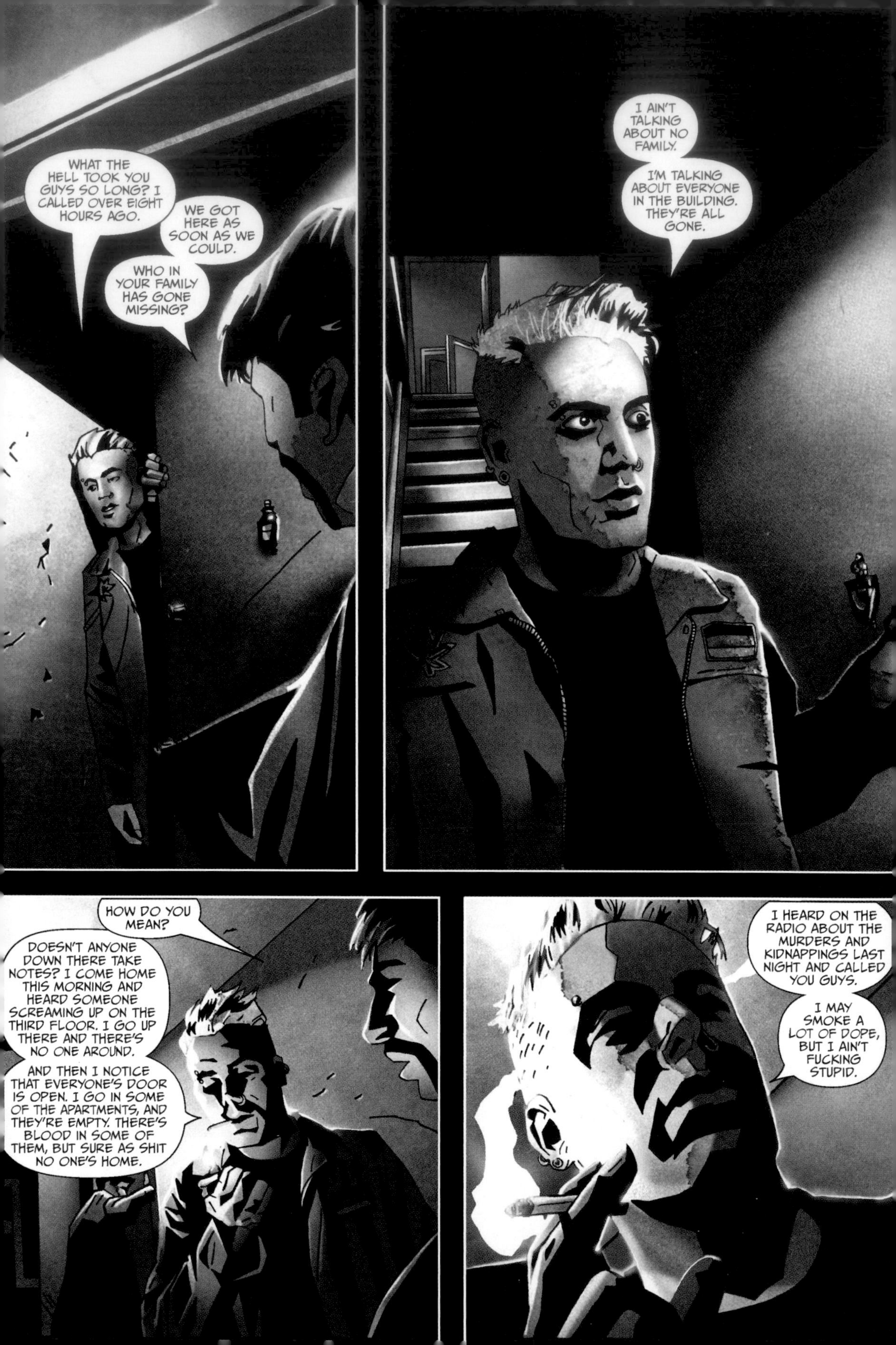
WHAT THE HELL TOOK YOU GUYS SO LONG? I CALLED OVER EIGHT HOURS AGO.
WE GOT HERE AS SOON AS WE COULD.
WHO IN YOUR FAMILY HAS GONE MISSING?
I AIN'T TALKING ABOUT NO FAMILY.
I'M TALKING ABOUT EVERYONE IN THE BUILDING. THEY'RE ALL GONE.
HOW DO YOU MEAN?
DOESN'T ANYONE DOWN THERE TAKE NOTES? I COME HOME THIS MORNING AND HEARD SOMEONE SCREAMING UP ON THE THIRD FLOOR. I GO UP THERE AND THERE'S NO ONE AROUND.
AND THEN I NOTICE THAT EVERYONE'S DOOR IS OPEN. I GO IN SOME OF THE APARTMENTS, AND THEY'RE EMPTY. THERE'S BLOOD IN SOME OF THEM, BUT SURE AS SHIT NO ONE'S HOME.
I HEARD ON THE RADIO ABOUT THE MURDERS AND KIDNAPPINGS LAST NIGHT AND CALLED YOU GUYS.
I MAY SMOKE A LOT OF DOPE, BUT I AIN'T FUCKING STUPID.

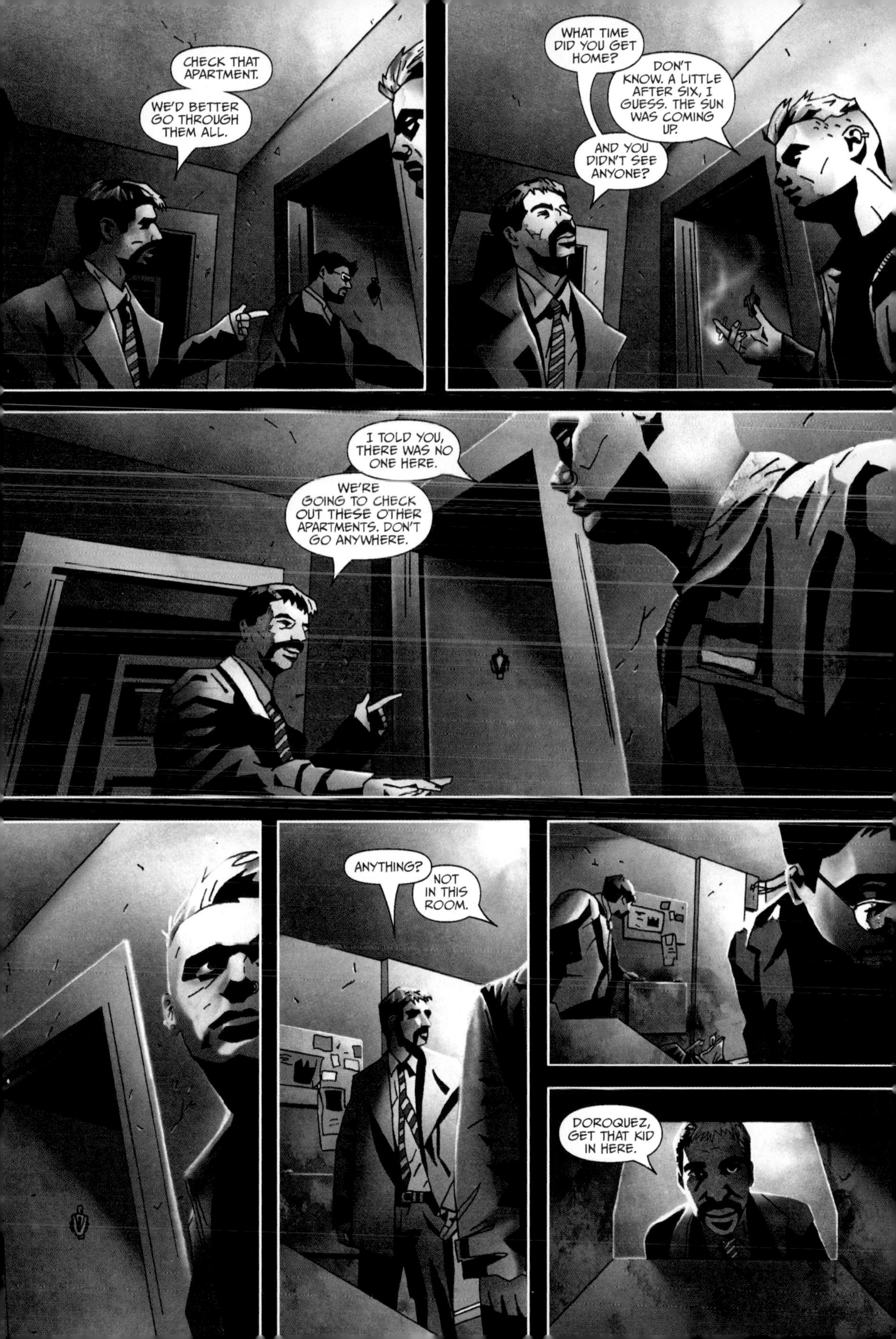
CHECK THAT APARTMENT.
WE'D BETTER GO THROUGH THEM ALL.
WHAT TIME DID YOU GET HOME?
DON'T KNOW. A LITTLE AFTER SIX, I GUESS. THE SUN WAS COMING UP.
AND YOU DIDN'T SEE ANYONE?
I TOLD YOU, THERE WAS NO ONE HERE.
WE'RE GOING TO CHECK OUT THESE OTHER APARTMENTS. DON'T GO ANYWHERE.
ANYTHING?
NOT IN THIS ROOM.
DOROQUEZ, GET THAT KID IN HERE.

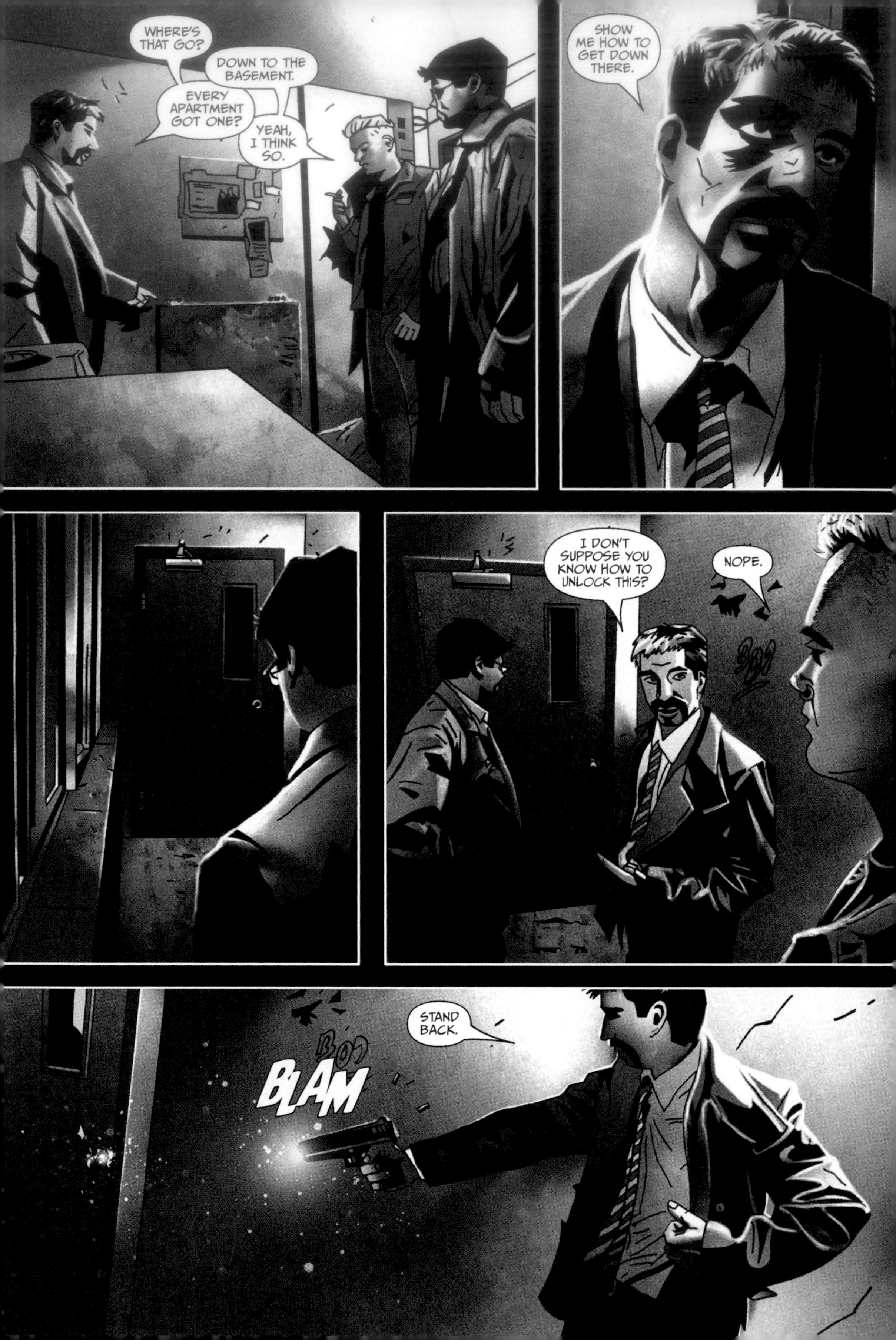
WHERE'S THAT GO?
DOWN TO THE BASEMENT.
EVERY APARTMENT GOT ONE?
YEAH, I THINK SO.
SHOW ME HOW TO GET DOWN THERE.
I DON'T SUPPOSE YOU KNOW HOW TO UNLOCK THIS?
NOPE.
STAND BACK.
BLAM

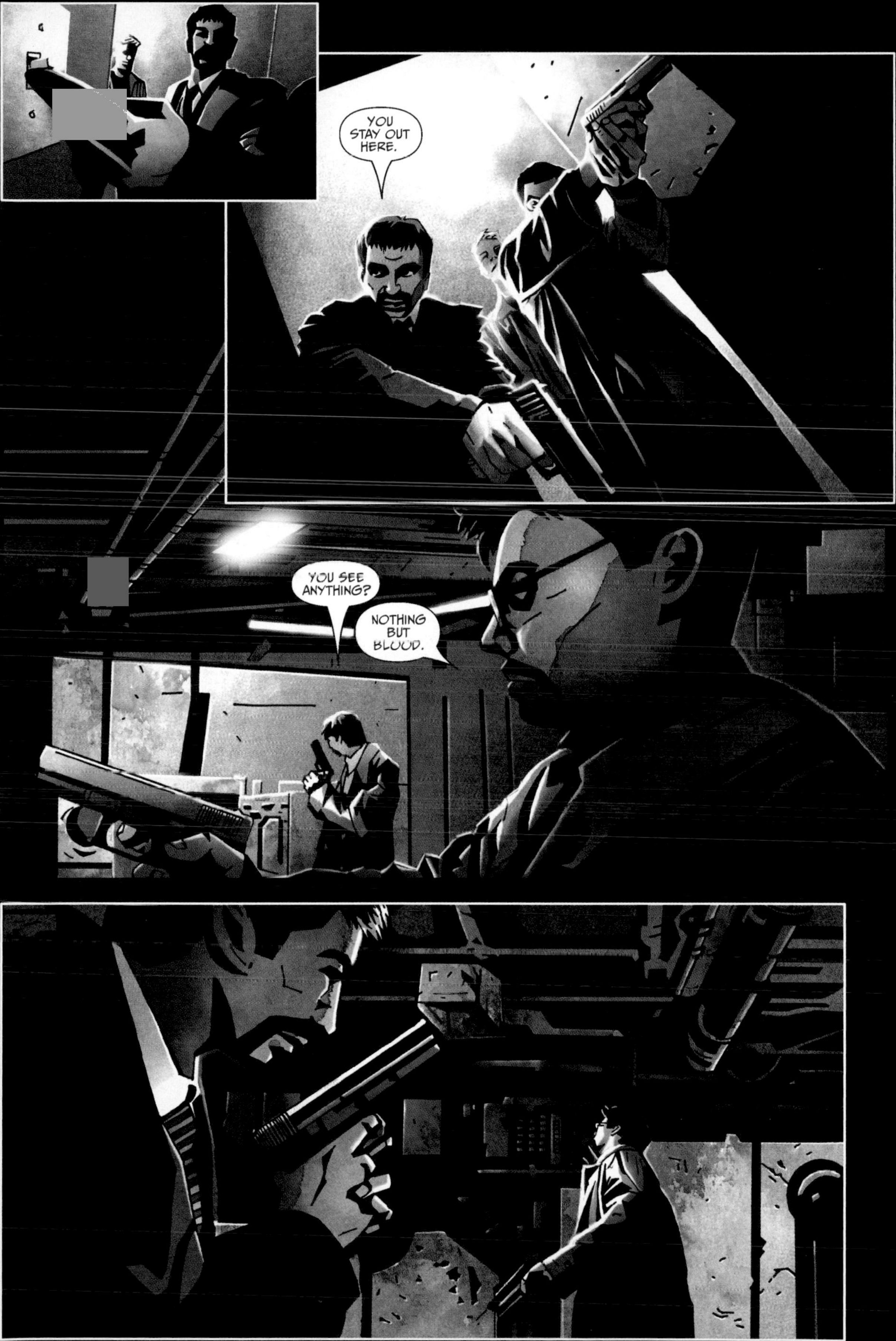
YOU STAY OUT HERE.
YOU SEE ANYTHING?
NOTHING BUT BLOOD.

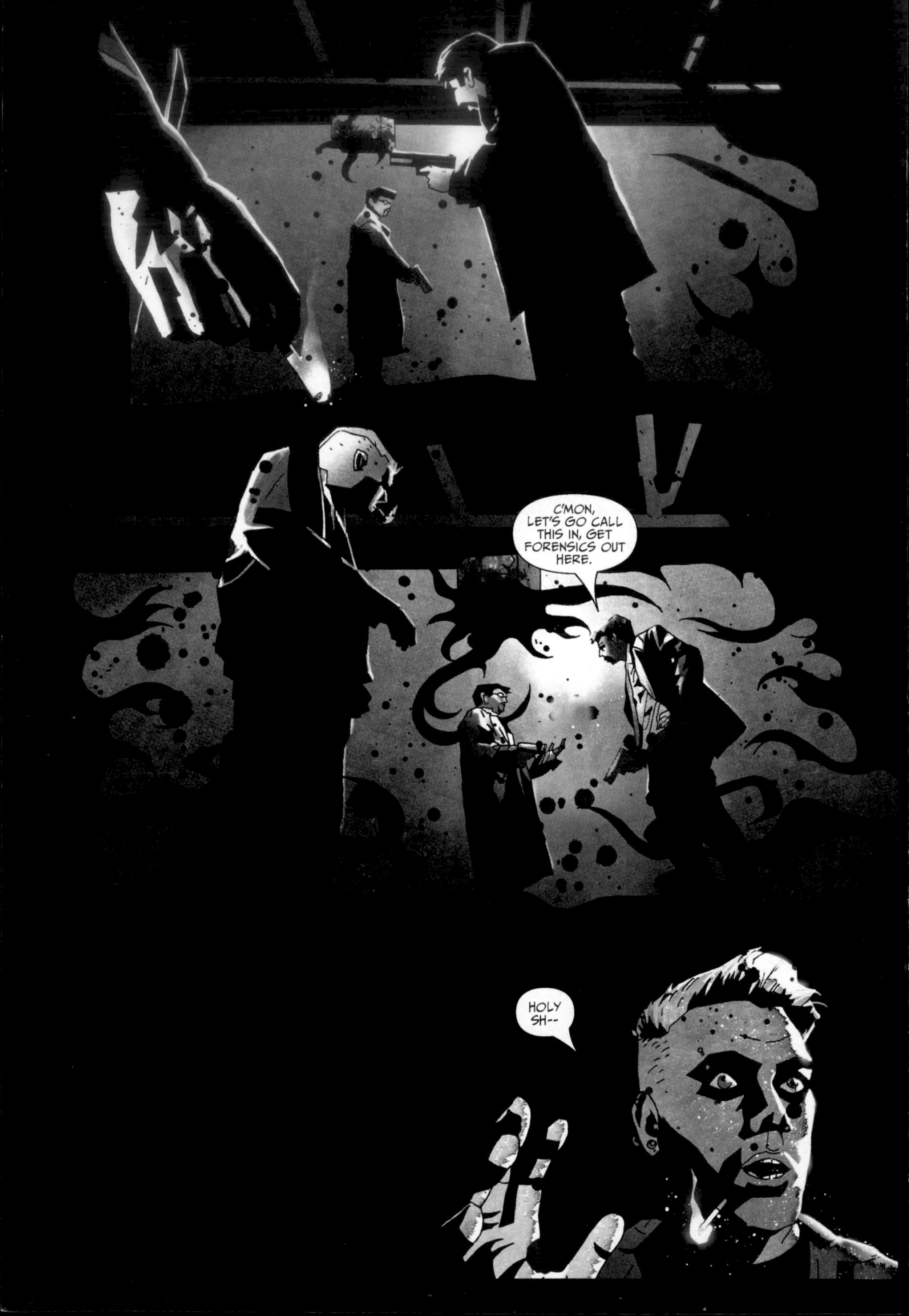
C'MON, LET'S GO CALL THIS IN, GET FORENSICS OUT HERE.
HOLY SH--

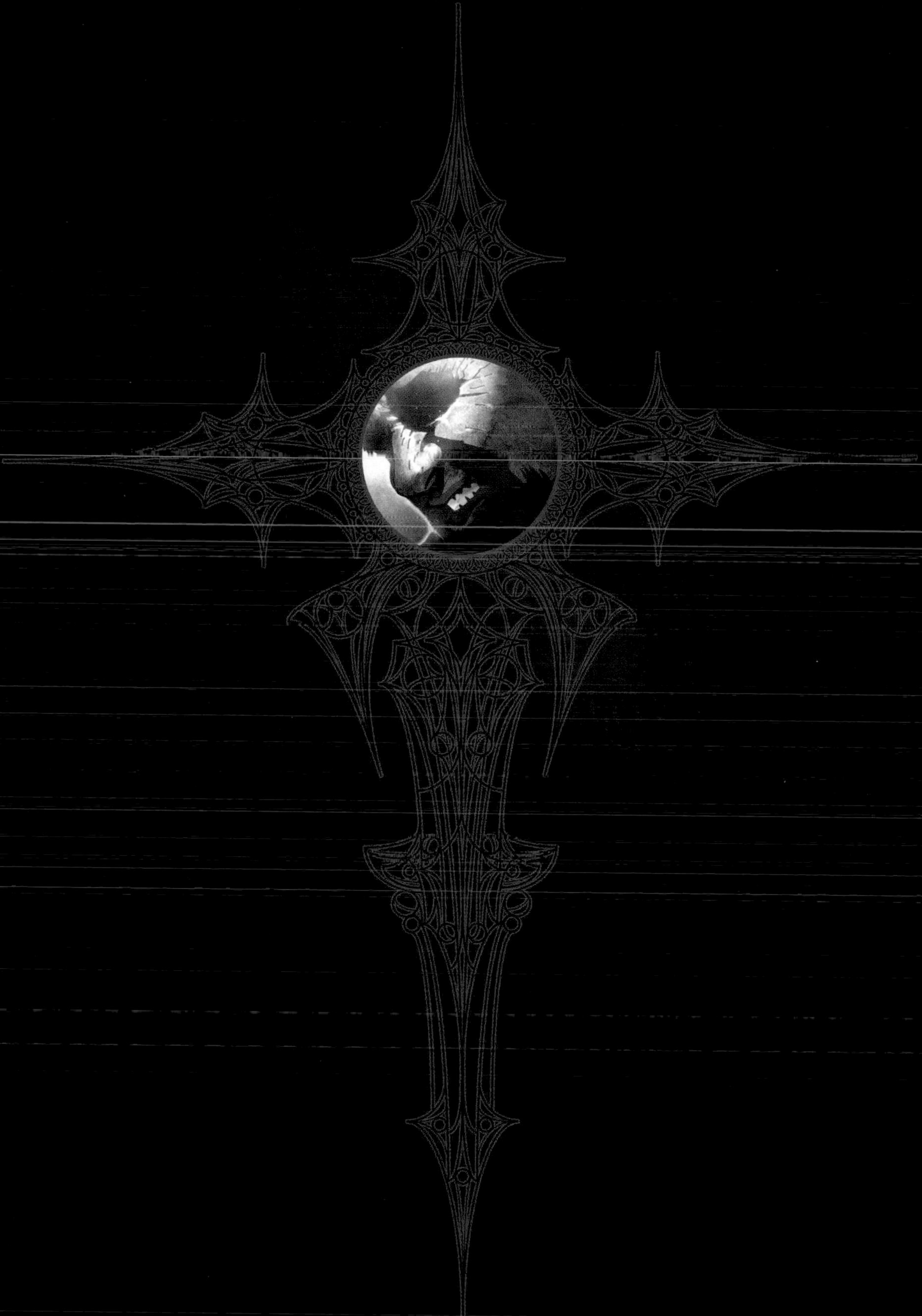

Rebirth
{Issue #3}

WRITTEN BY:
WILLIAM HARMS

PENCILS & INKS BY:
NICK POSTIC

COLORS & ADDITIONAL INKS BY:
NICK MARINKOVICH

LETTERING BY:
ED DUKESHIRE

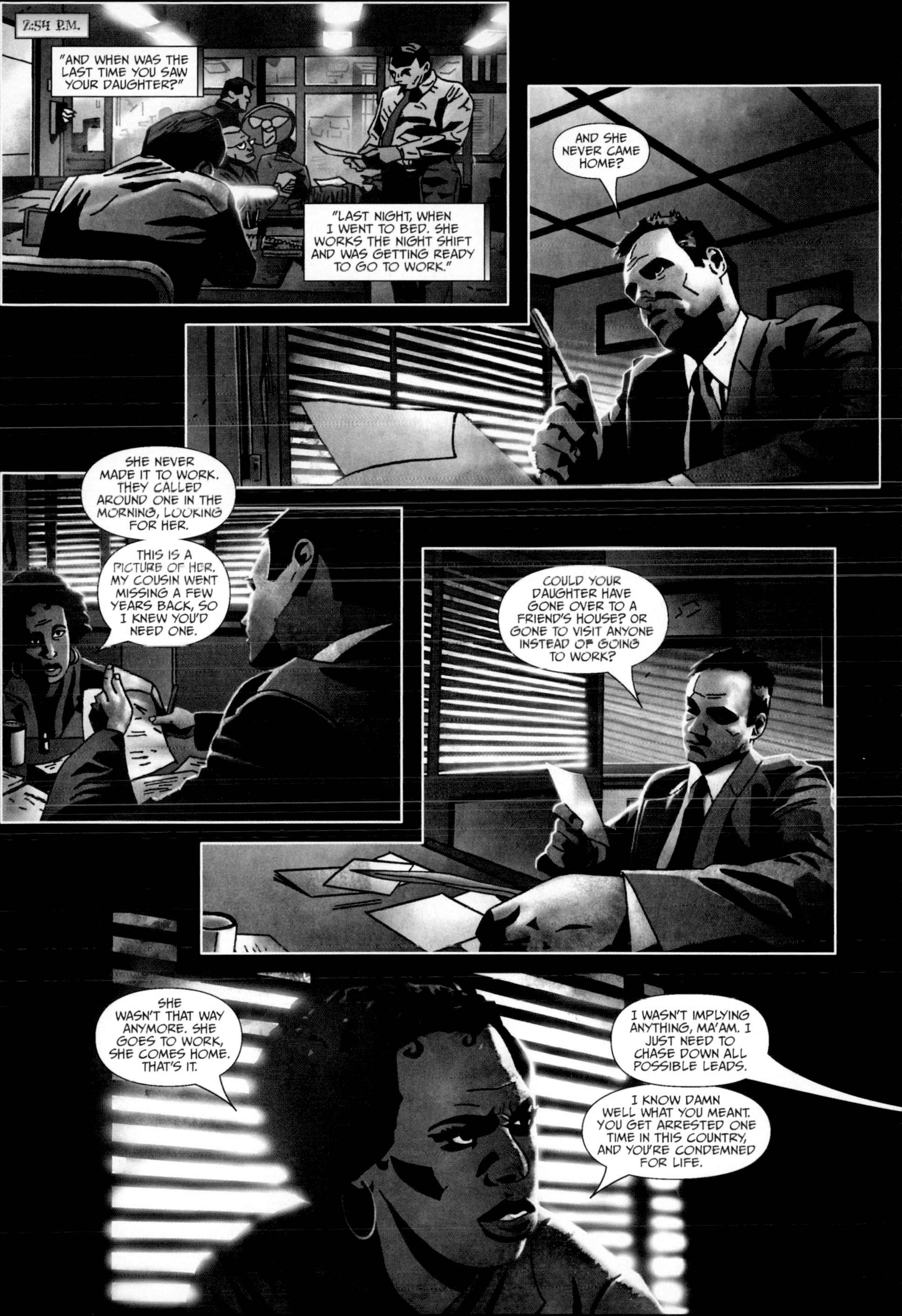
2:54 P.M.
"AND WHEN WAS THE LAST TIME YOU SAW YOUR DAUGHTER?"
"LAST NIGHT, WHEN I WENT TO BED. SHE WORKS THE NIGHT SHIFT AND WAS GETTING READY TO GO TO WORK."
AND SHE NEVER CAME HOME?
SHE NEVER MADE IT TO WORK. THEY CALLED AROUND ONE IN THE MORNING, LOOKING FOR HER.
THIS IS A PICTURE OF HER. MY COUSIN WENT MISSING A FEW YEARS BACK, SO I KNEW YOU'D NEED ONE.
COULD YOUR DAUGHTER HAVE GONE OVER TO A FRIEND'S HOUSE? OR GONE TO VISIT ANYONE INSTEAD OF GOING TO WORK?
SHE WASN'T THAT WAY ANYMORE. SHE GOES TO WORK, SHE COMES HOME. THAT'S IT.
I WASN'T IMPLYING ANYTHING, MA'AM. I JUST NEED TO CHASE DOWN ALL POSSIBLE LEADS.
I KNOW DAMN WELL WHAT YOU MEANT. YOU GET ARRESTED ONE TIME IN THIS COUNTRY, AND YOU'RE CONDEMNED FOR LIFE.

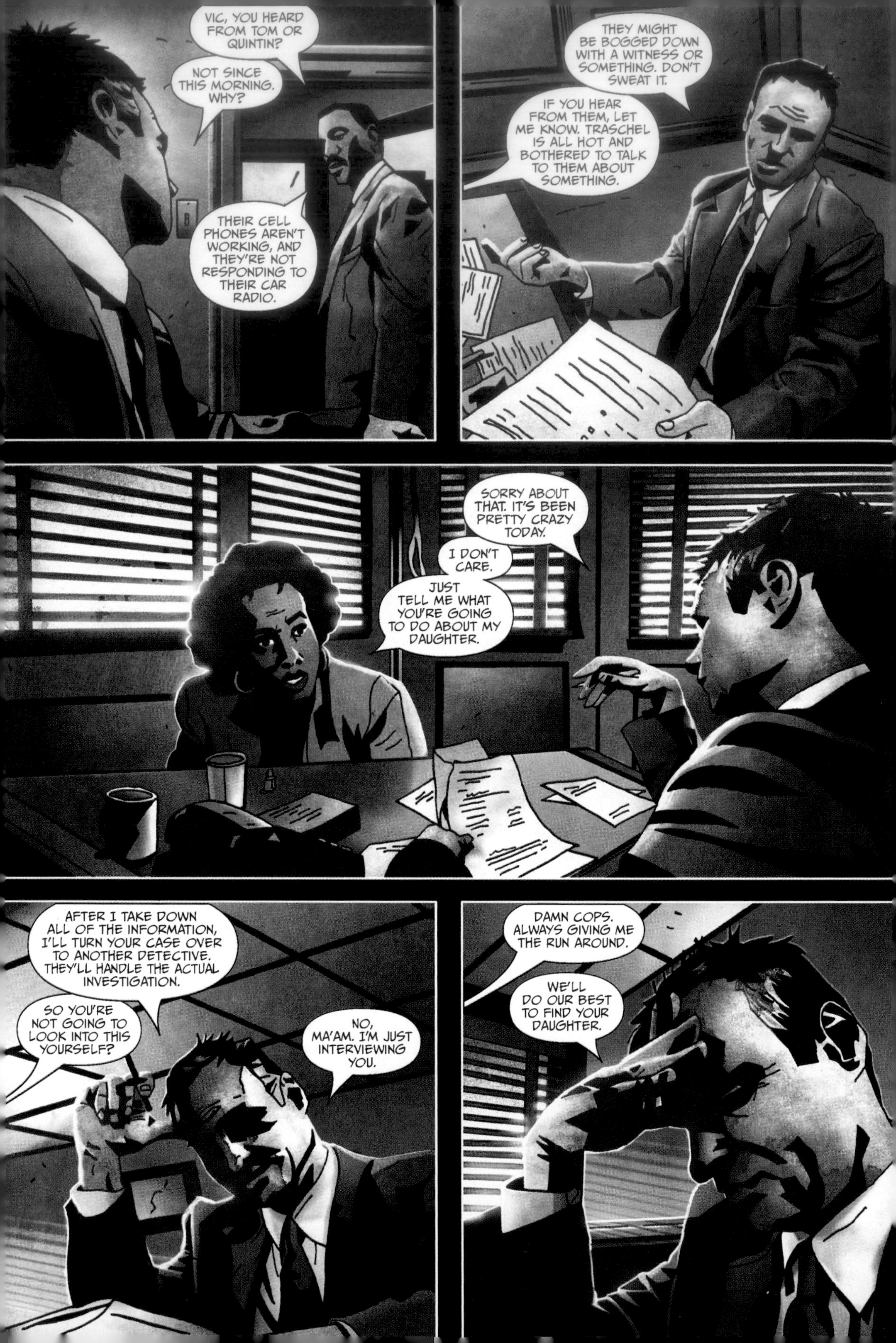
VIC, YOU HEARD FROM TOM OR QUINTIN?
NOT SINCE THIS MORNING. WHY?
THEIR CELL PHONES AREN'T WORKING, AND THEY'RE NOT RESPONDING TO THEIR CAR RADIO.
THEY MIGHT BE BOGGED DOWN WITH A WITNESS OR SOMETHING. DON'T SWEAT IT.
IF YOU HEAR FROM THEM, LET ME KNOW. TRASCHEL IS ALL HOT AND BOTHERED TO TALK TO THEM ABOUT SOMETHING.
SORRY ABOUT THAT. IT'S BEEN PRETTY CRAZY TODAY.
I DON'T CARE.
JUST TELL ME WHAT YOU'RE GOING TO DO ABOUT MY DAUGHTER.
AFTER I TAKE DOWN ALL OF THE INFORMATION, I'LL TURN YOUR CASE OVER TO ANOTHER DETECTIVE. THEY'LL HANDLE THE ACTUAL INVESTIGATION.
SO YOU'RE NOT GOING TO LOOK INTO THIS YOURSELF?
NO, MA'AM. I'M JUST INTERVIEWING YOU.
DAMN COPS. ALWAYS GIVING ME THE RUN AROUND.
WE'LL DO OUR BEST TO FIND YOUR DAUGHTER.

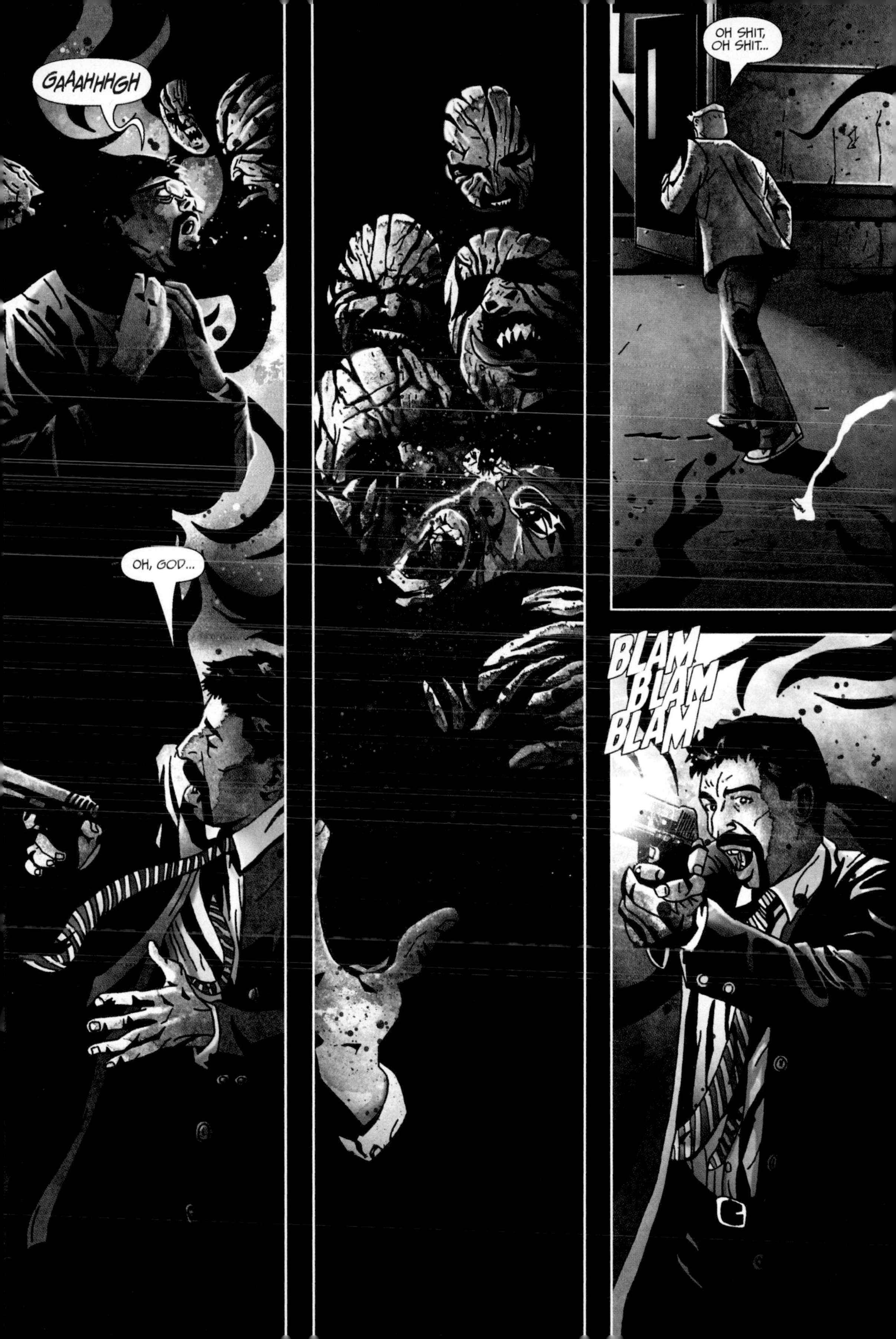
GAAAHHHGH
OH, GOD...
OH SHIT,
OH SHIT...
BLAM
BLAM
BLAM

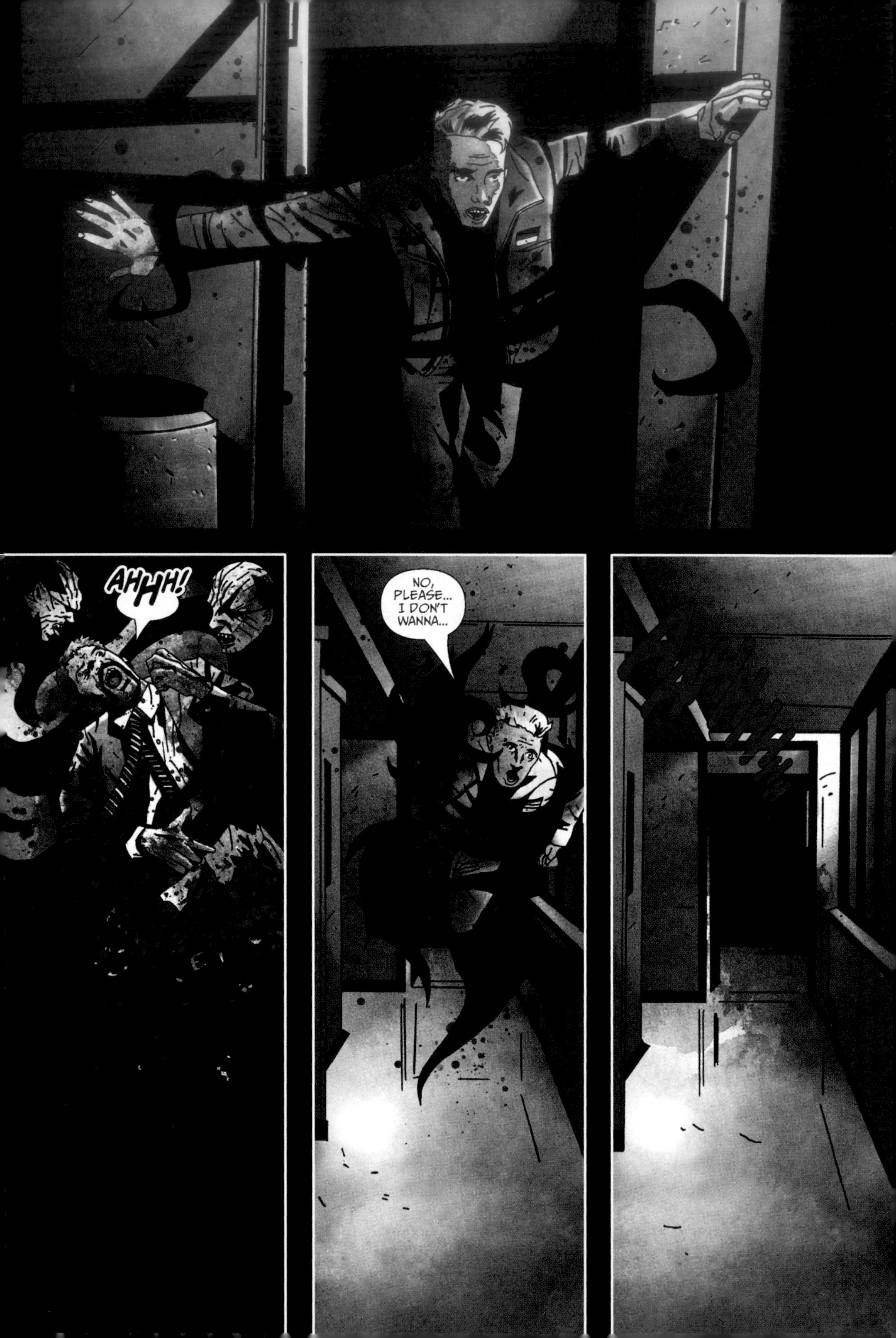
AHHH!
NO, PLEASE... I DON'T WANNA...

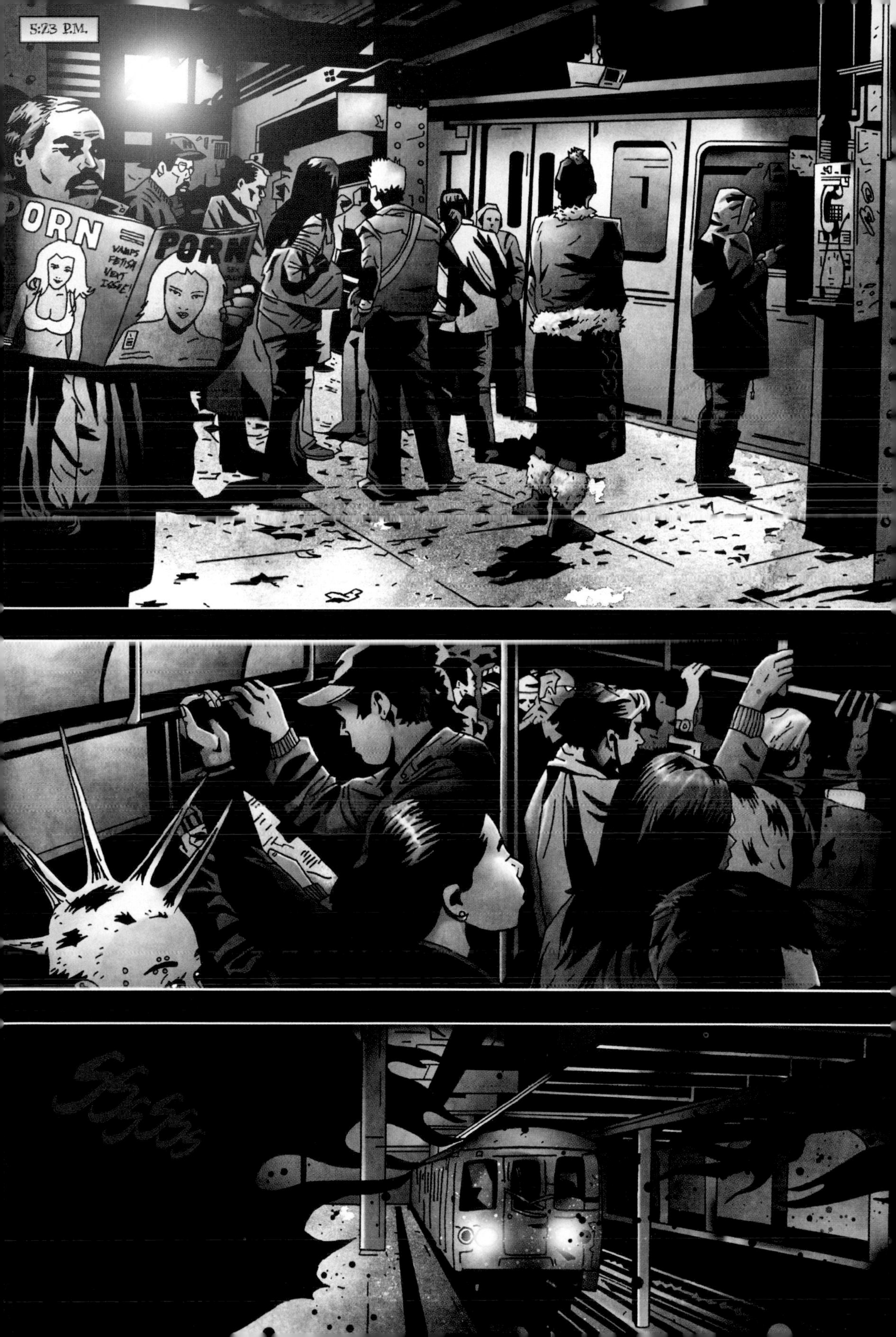
5:23 P.M.
PORN
PORN
VAMPS FETISH NEXT ISSUE!

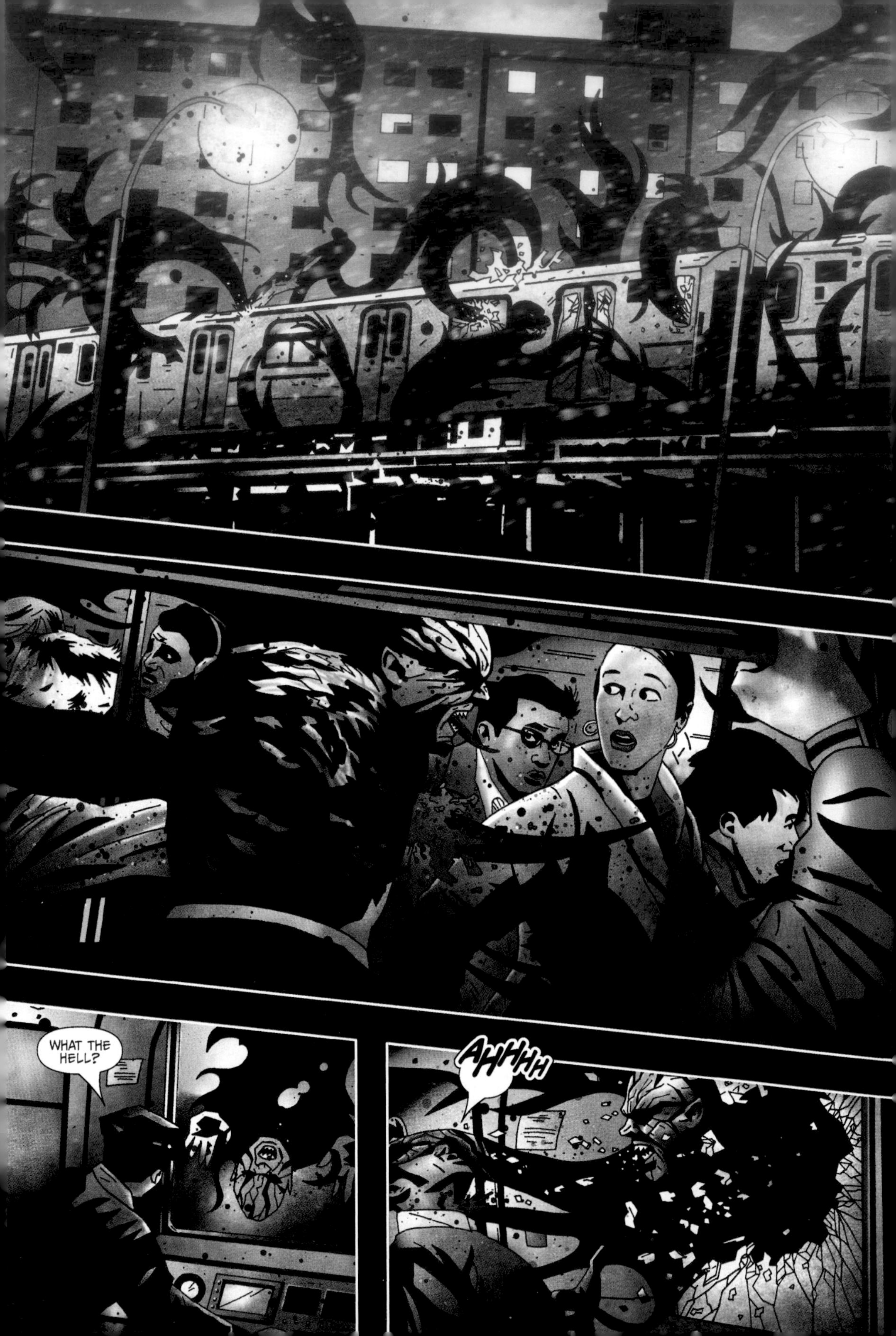
WHAT THE HELL?
AHHHH

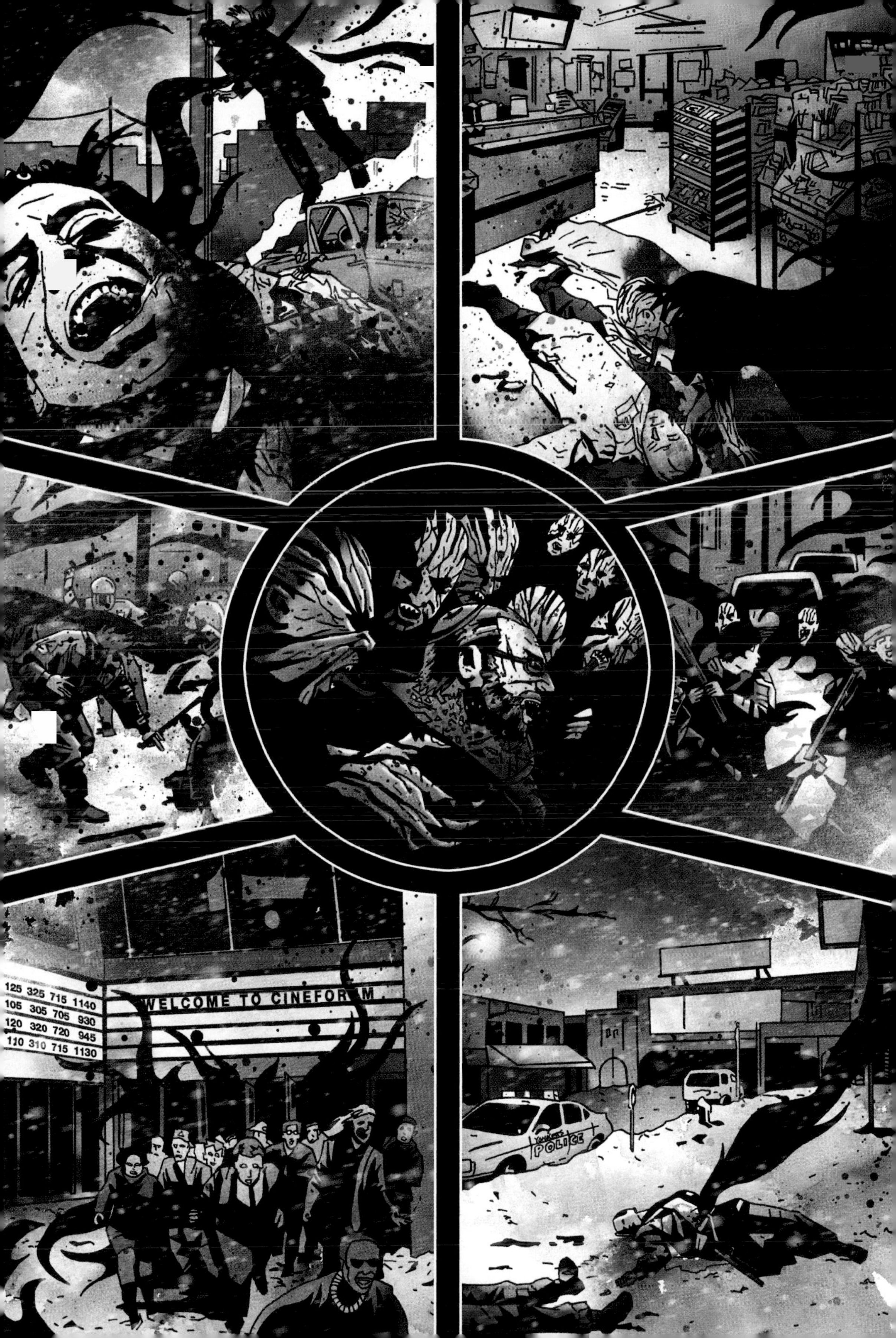
125 325 715 1140
105 305 705 930
120 320 720 945
110 310 715 1130
WELCOME TO CINEFORUM
POLICE

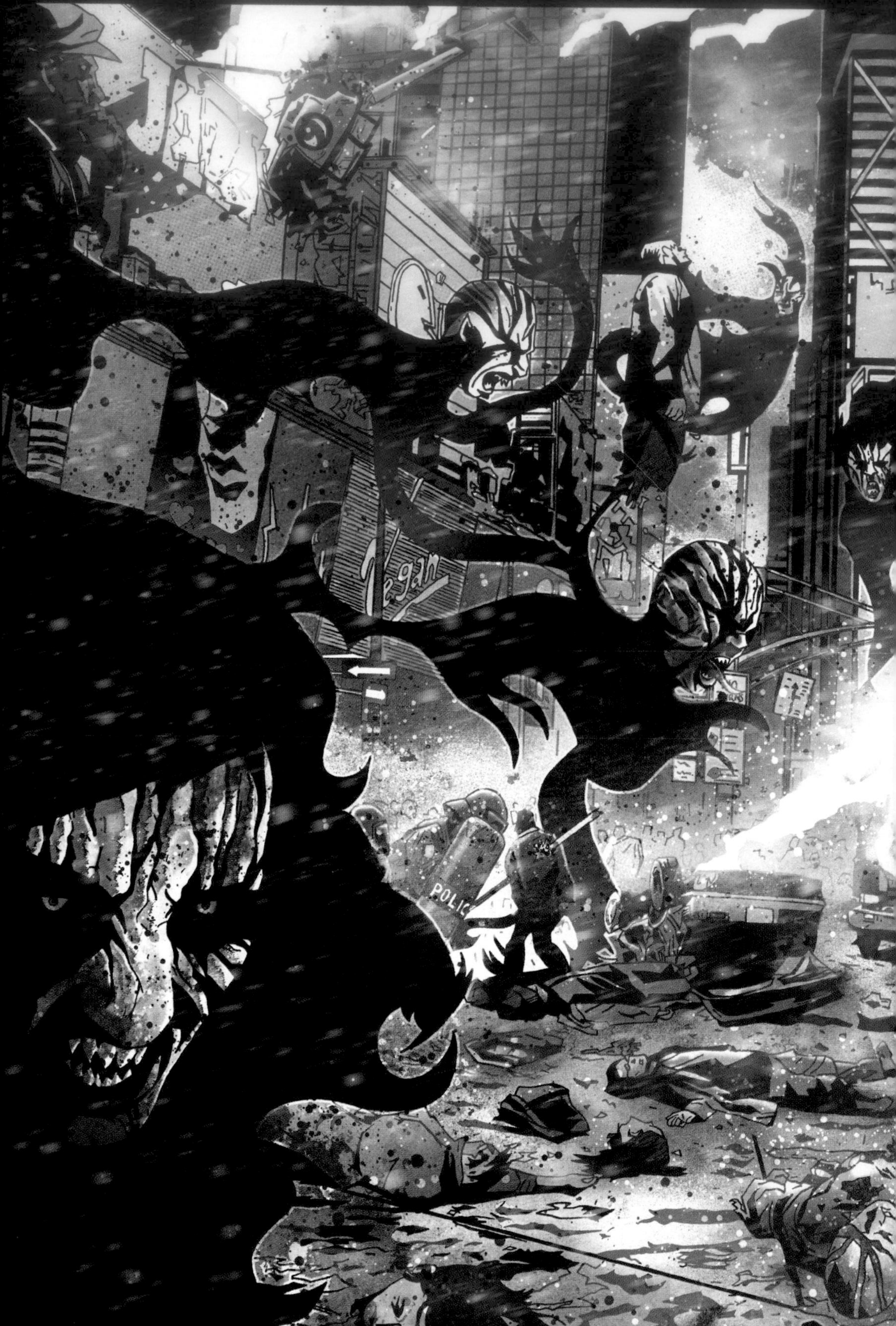
Vegan
POLIC

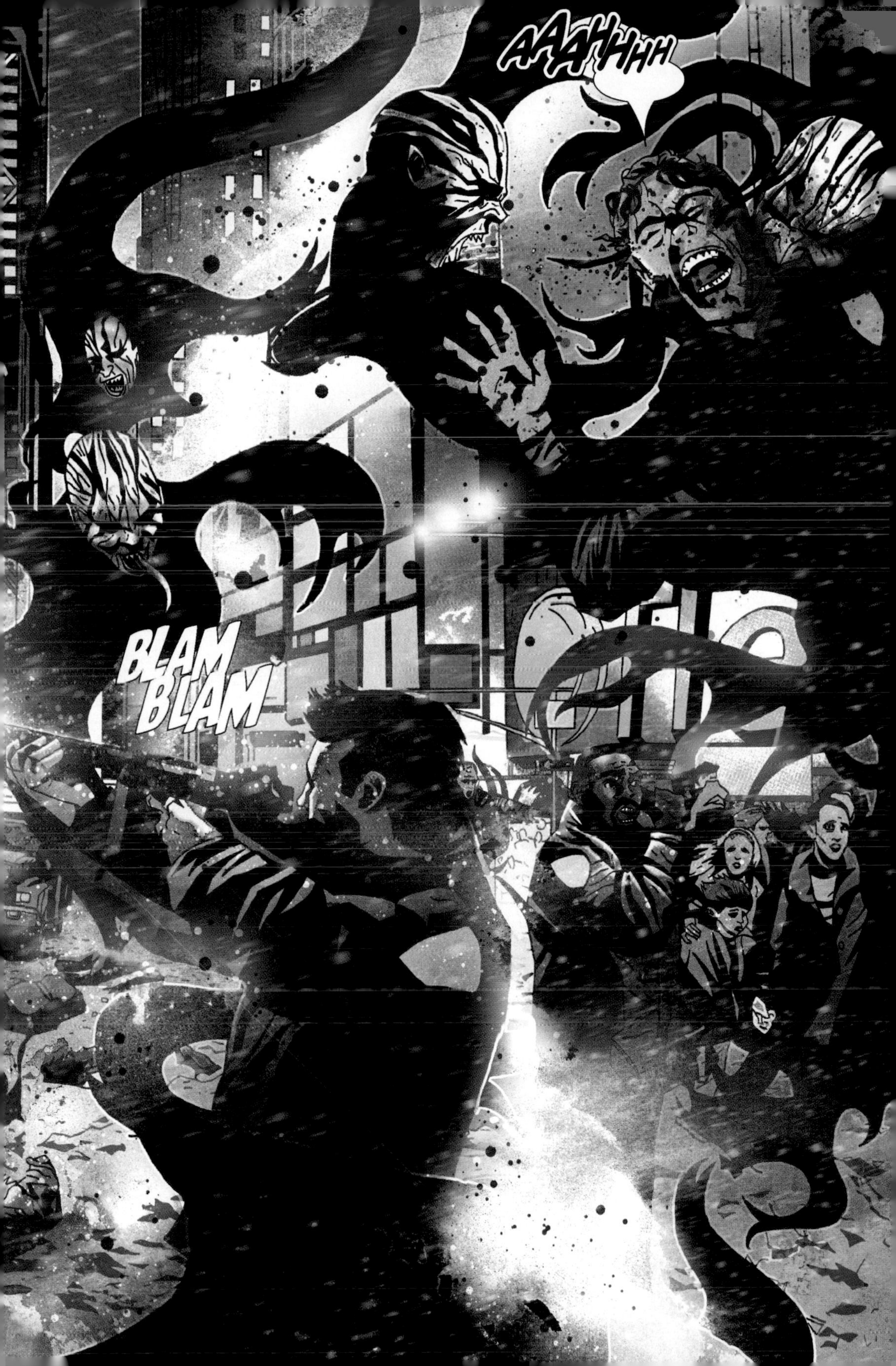
AAAHHHH
BLAM
BLAM

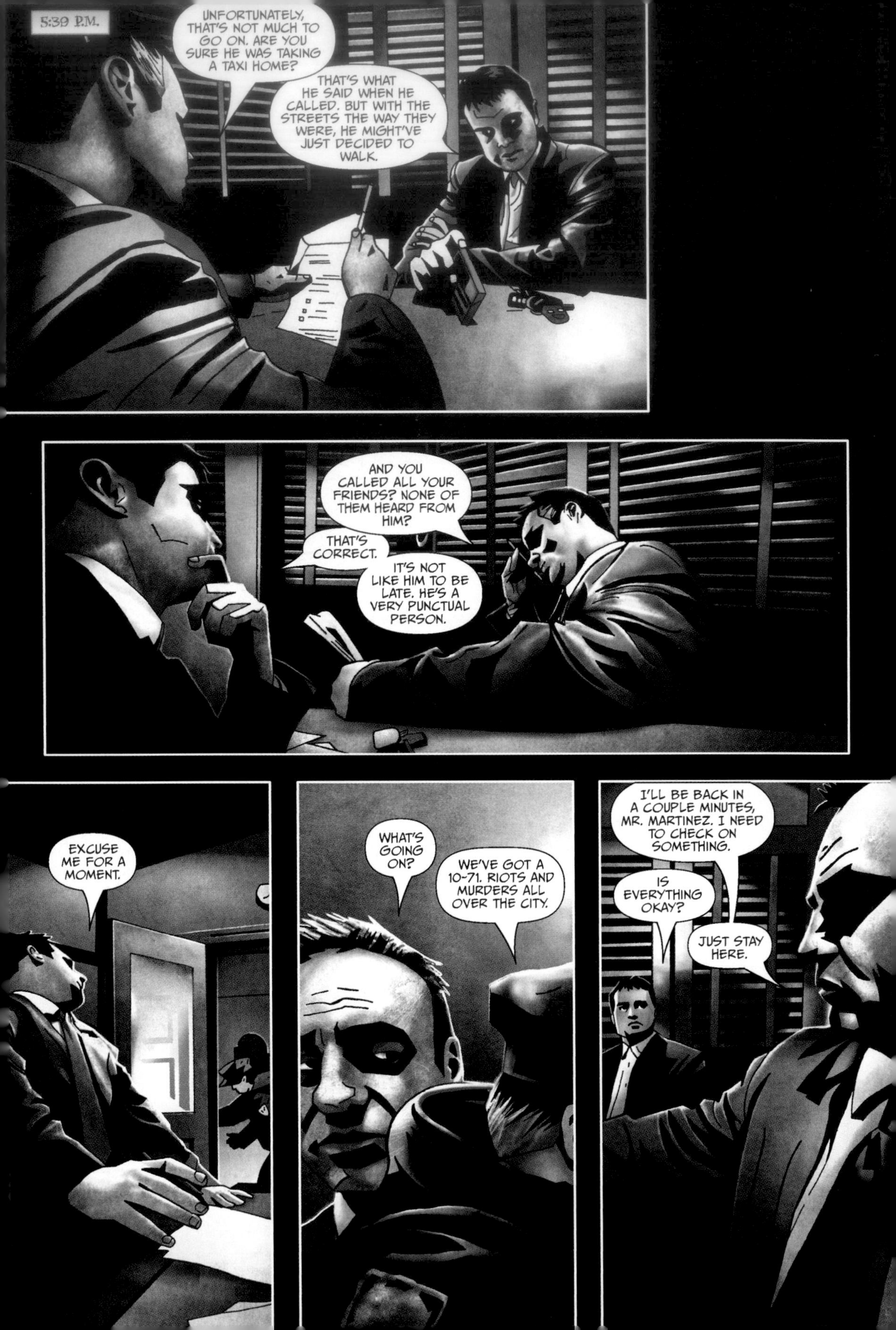
5:39 P.M.
UNFORTUNATELY, THAT'S NOT MUCH TO GO ON. ARE YOU SURE HE WAS TAKING A TAXI HOME?
THAT'S WHAT HE SAID WHEN HE CALLED. BUT WITH THE STREETS THE WAY THEY WERE, HE MIGHT'VE JUST DECIDED TO WALK.
AND YOU CALLED ALL YOUR FRIENDS? NONE OF THEM HEARD FROM HIM?
THAT'S CORRECT.
IT'S NOT LIKE HIM TO BE LATE. HE'S A VERY PUNCTUAL PERSON.
EXCUSE ME FOR A MOMENT.
WHAT'S GOING ON?
WE'VE GOT A 10-71. RIOTS AND MURDERS ALL OVER THE CITY.
I'LL BE BACK IN A COUPLE MINUTES, MR. MARTINEZ. I NEED TO CHECK ON SOMETHING.
IS EVERYTHING OKAY?
JUST STAY HERE.

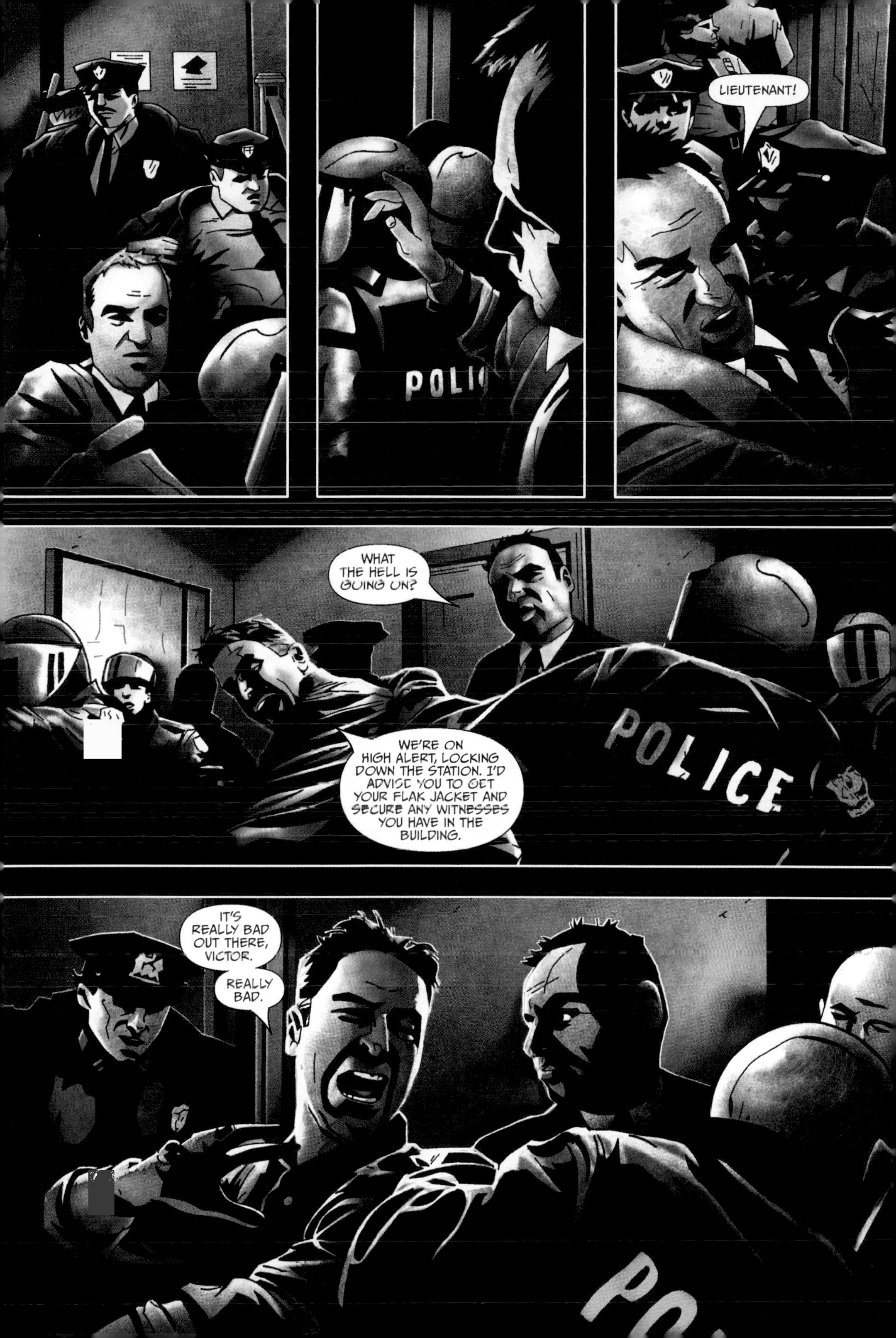
LIEUTENANT!
POLIC
WHAT THE HELL IS GOING ON?
WE'RE ON HIGH ALERT, LOCKING DOWN THE STATION. I'D ADVISE YOU TO GET YOUR FLAK JACKET AND SECURE ANY WITNESSES YOU HAVE IN THE BUILDING.
POLICE
IT'S REALLY BAD OUT THERE, VICTOR.
REALLY BAD.

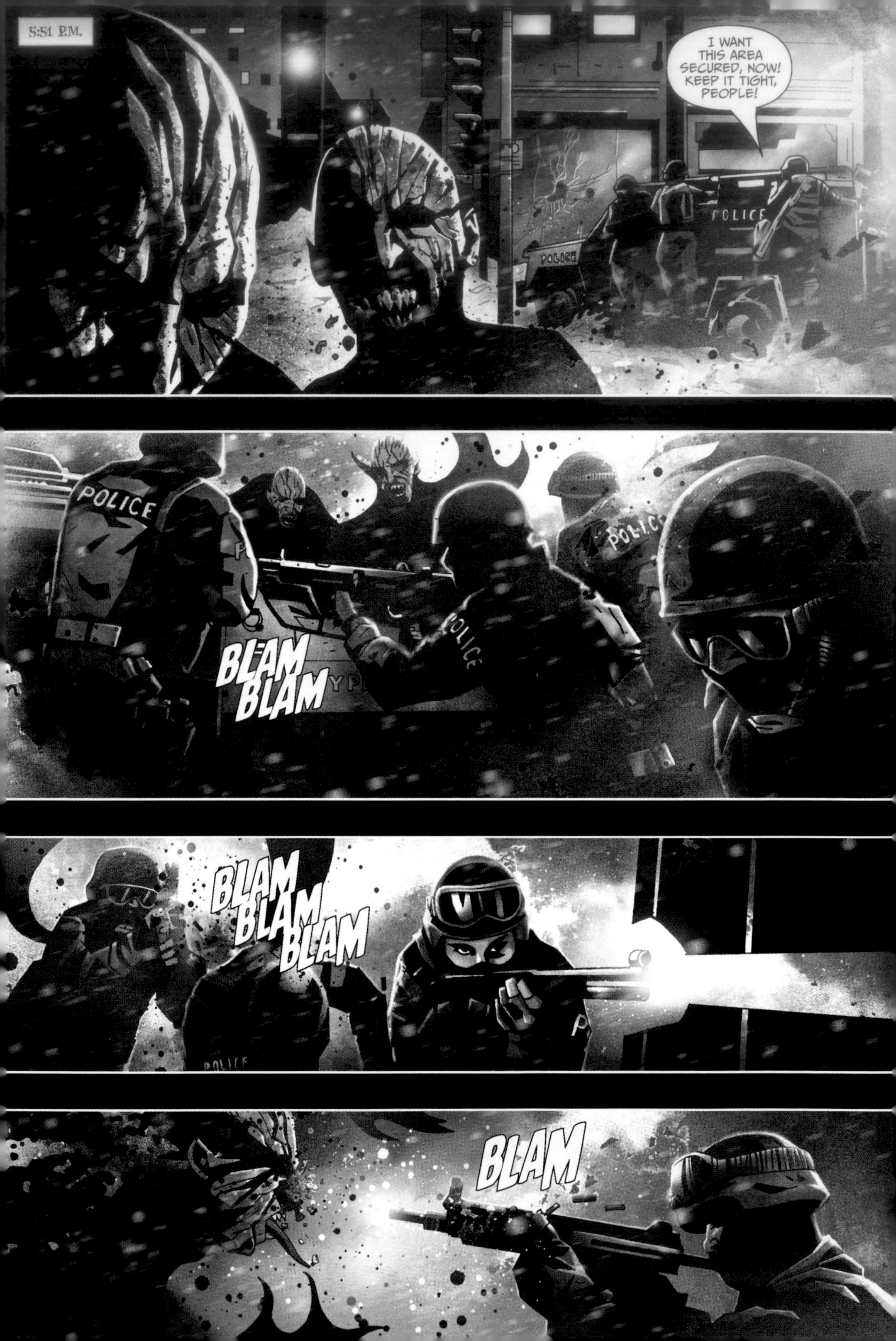
5:51 P.M.
I WANT THIS AREA SECURED, NOW! KEEP IT TIGHT, PEOPLE!
POLICE
BLAM BLAM
BLAM BLAM BLAM
BLAM

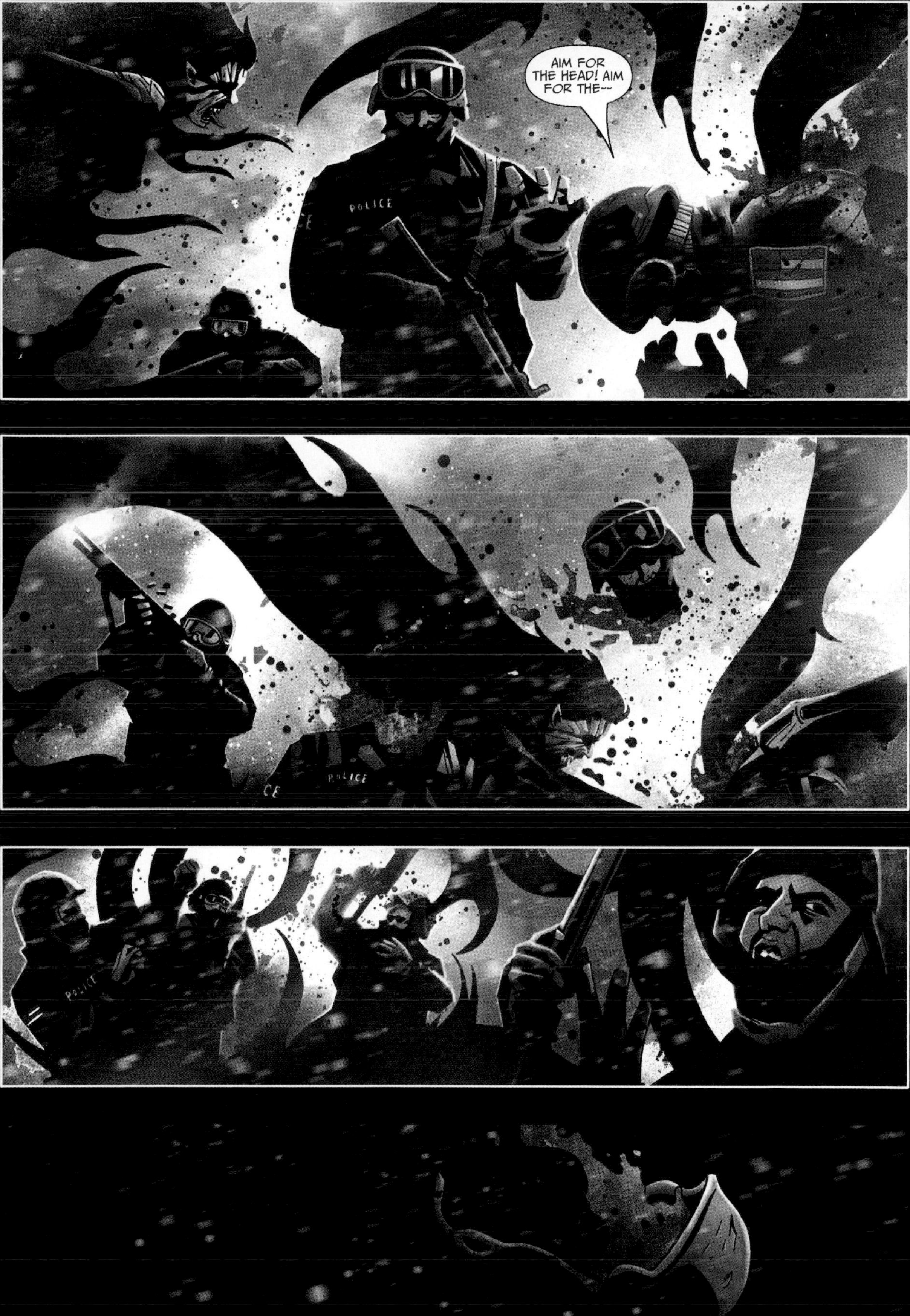
AIM FOR THE HEAD! AIM FOR THE--
POLICE
POLICE
POLICE

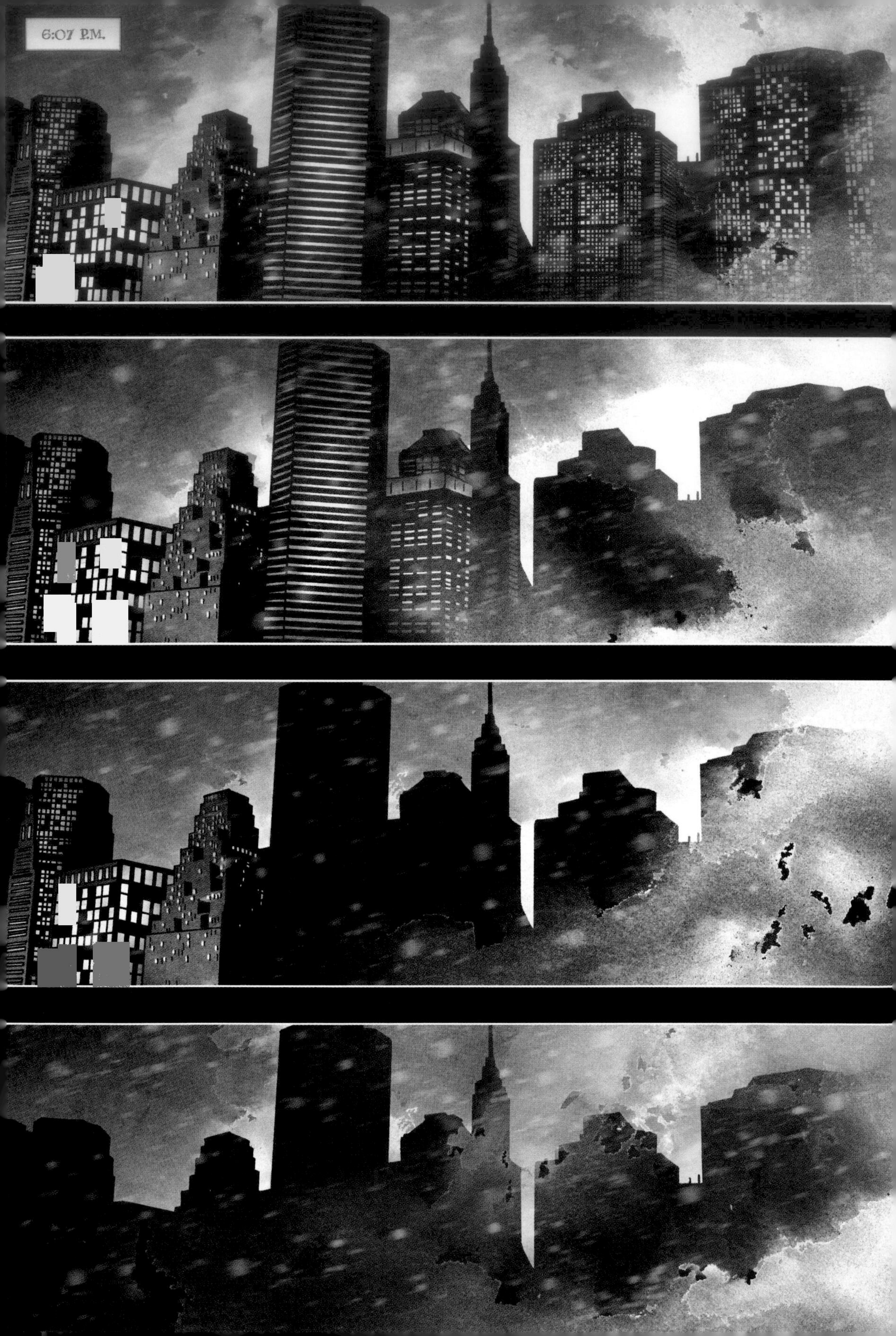
6:07 P.M.

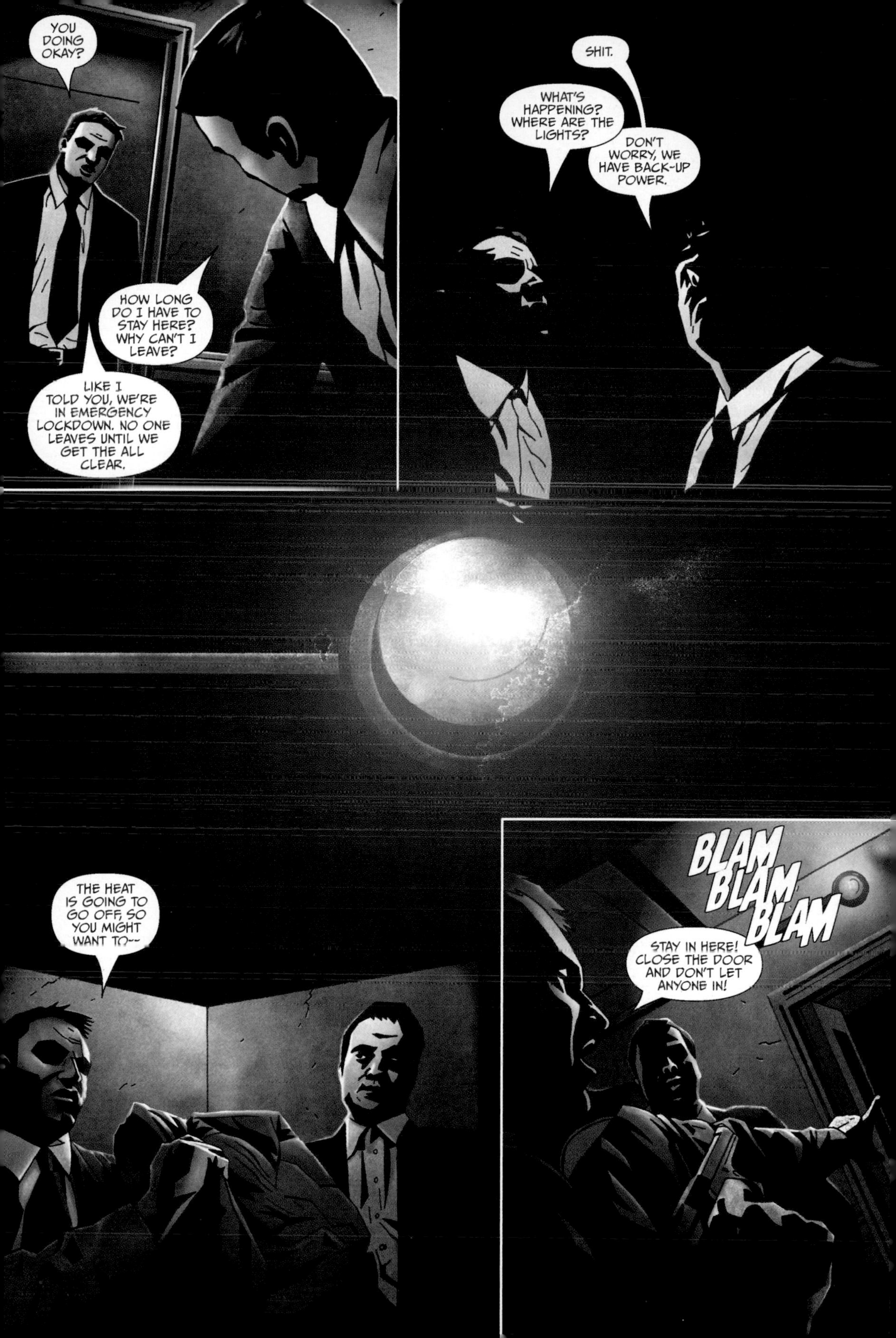
YOU DOING OKAY?
HOW LONG DO I HAVE TO STAY HERE? WHY CAN'T I LEAVE?
LIKE I TOLD YOU, WE'RE IN EMERGENCY LOCKDOWN. NO ONE LEAVES UNTIL WE GET THE ALL CLEAR.
SHIT.
WHAT'S HAPPENING? WHERE ARE THE LIGHTS?
DON'T WORRY, WE HAVE BACK-UP POWER.
THE HEAT IS GOING TO GO OFF, SO YOU MIGHT WANT TO--
BLAM BLAM BLAM
STAY IN HERE! CLOSE THE DOOR AND DON'T LET ANYONE IN!

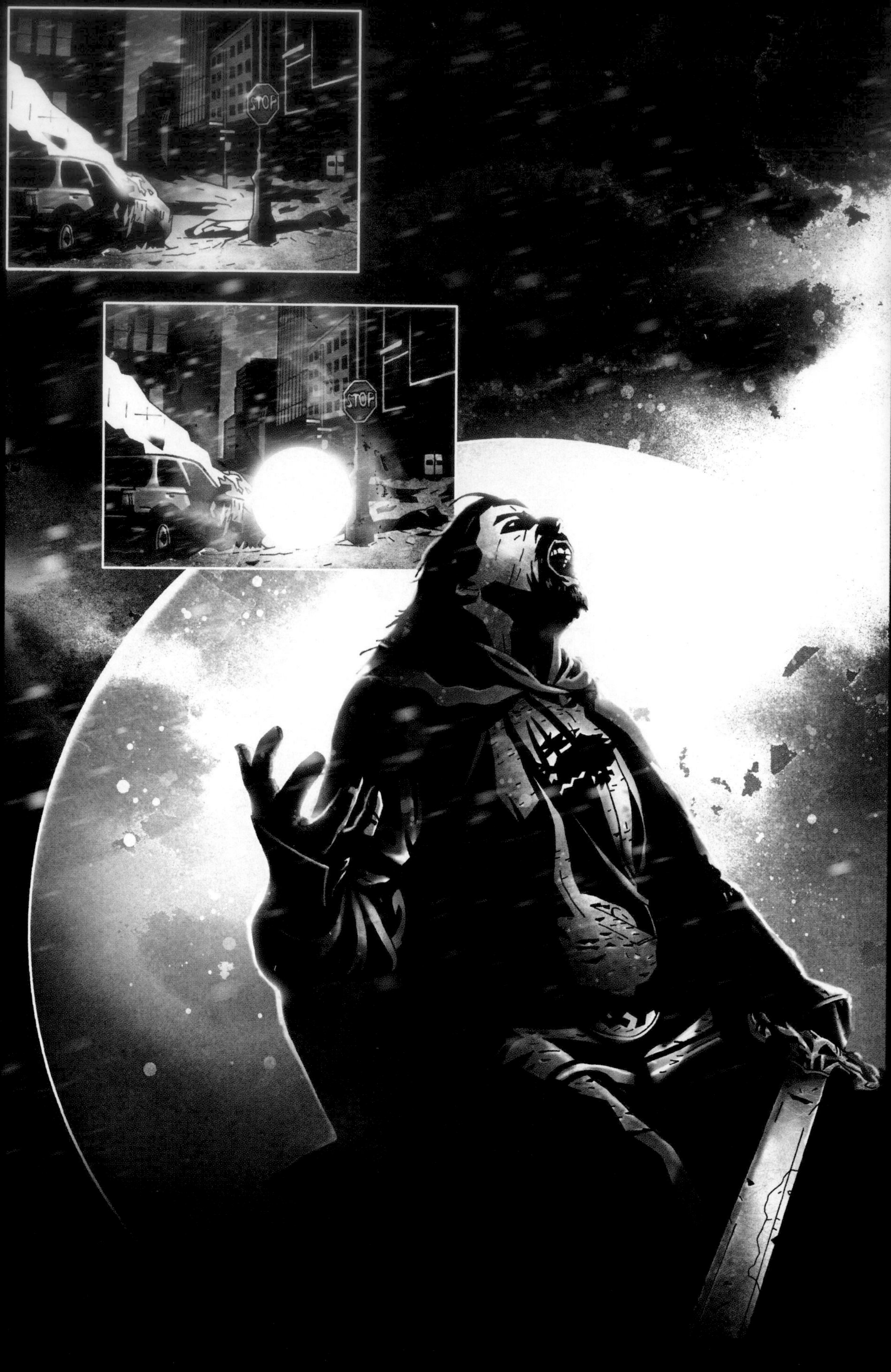
STOP
STOP

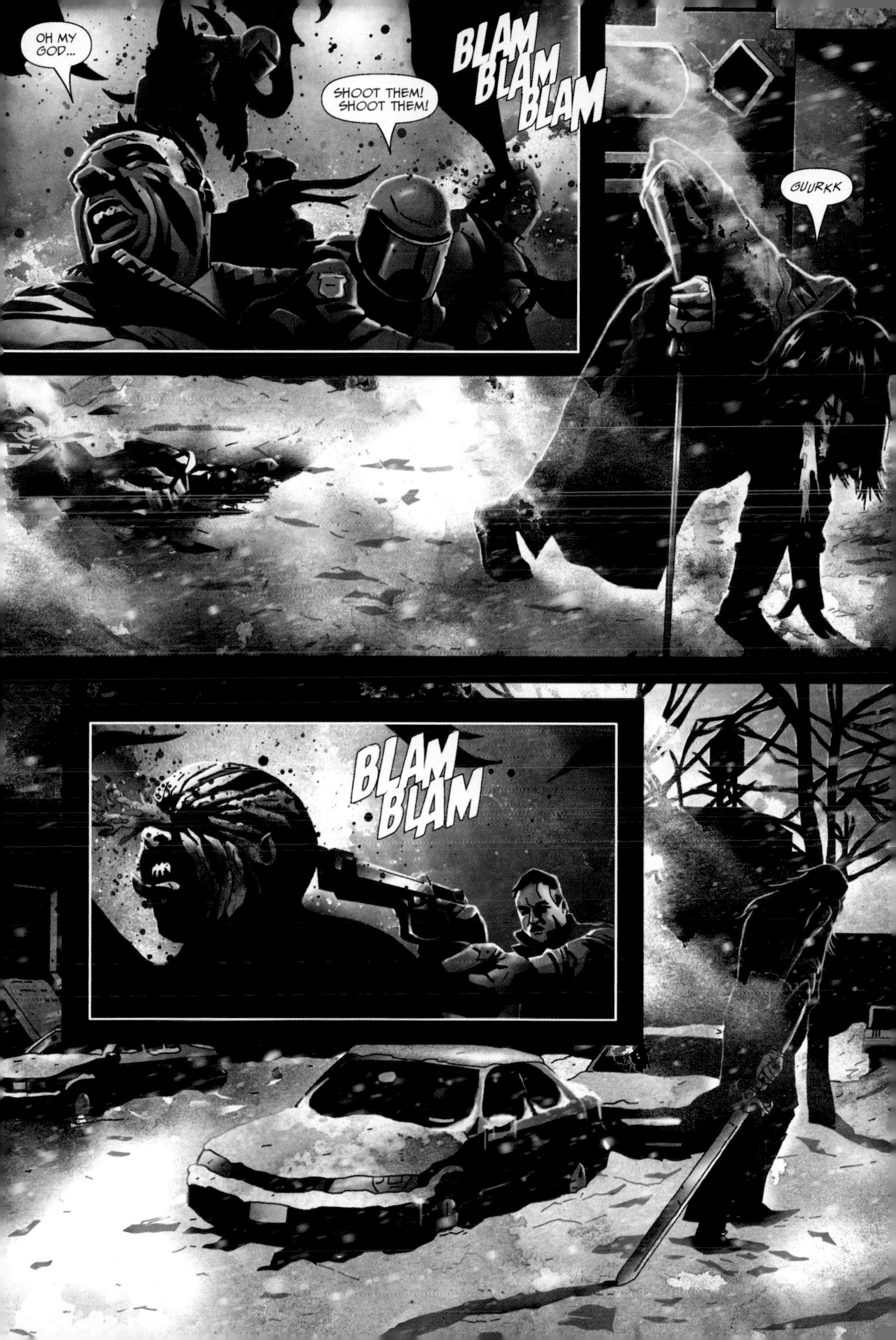
OH MY GOD...
SHOOT THEM! SHOOT THEM!
BLAM BLAM BLAM
GUURKK
BLAM BLAM

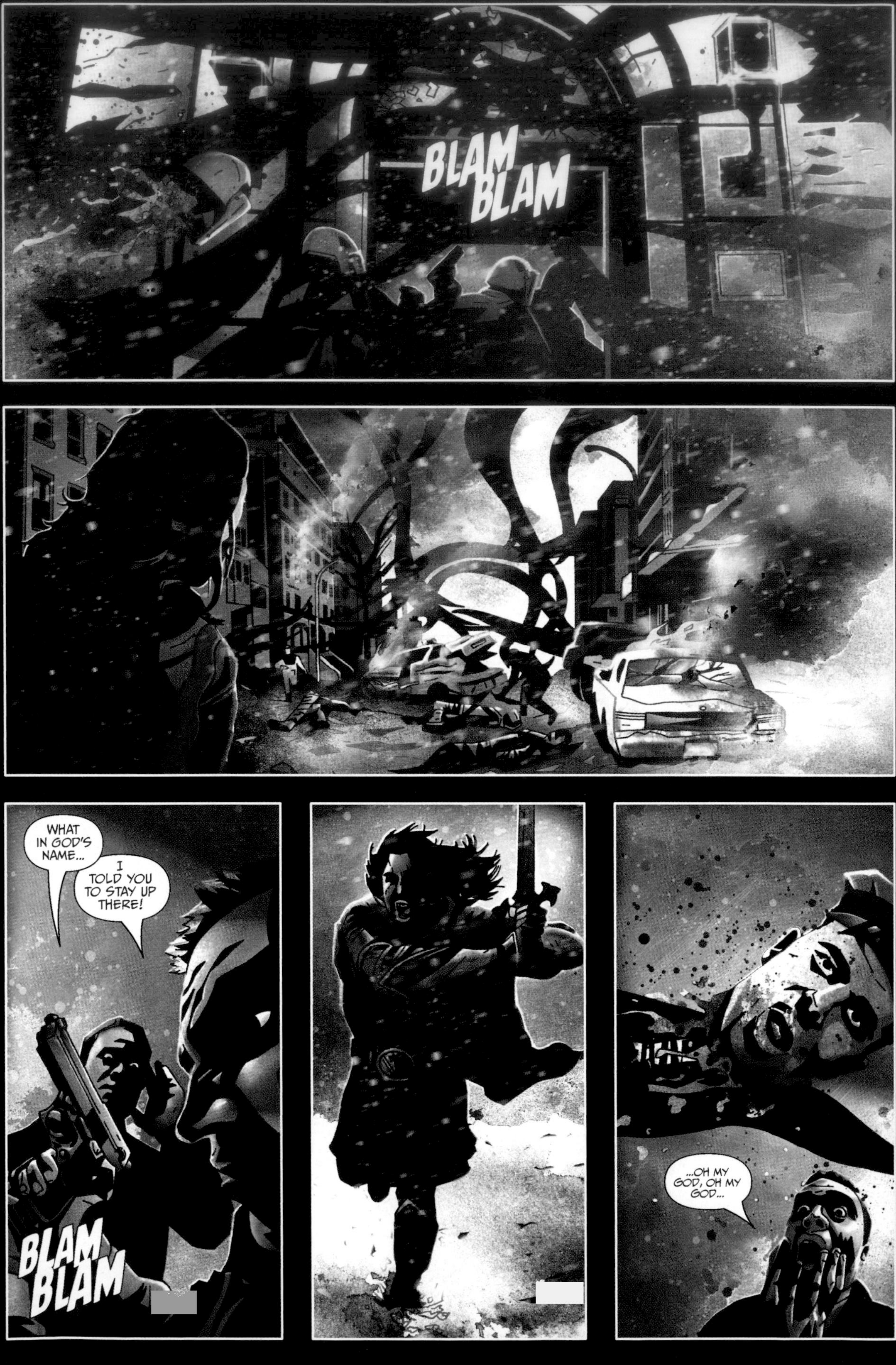
BLAM BLAM
WHAT IN GOD'S NAME...
I TOLD YOU TO STAY UP THERE!
BLAM BLAM
...OH MY GOD, OH MY GOD...

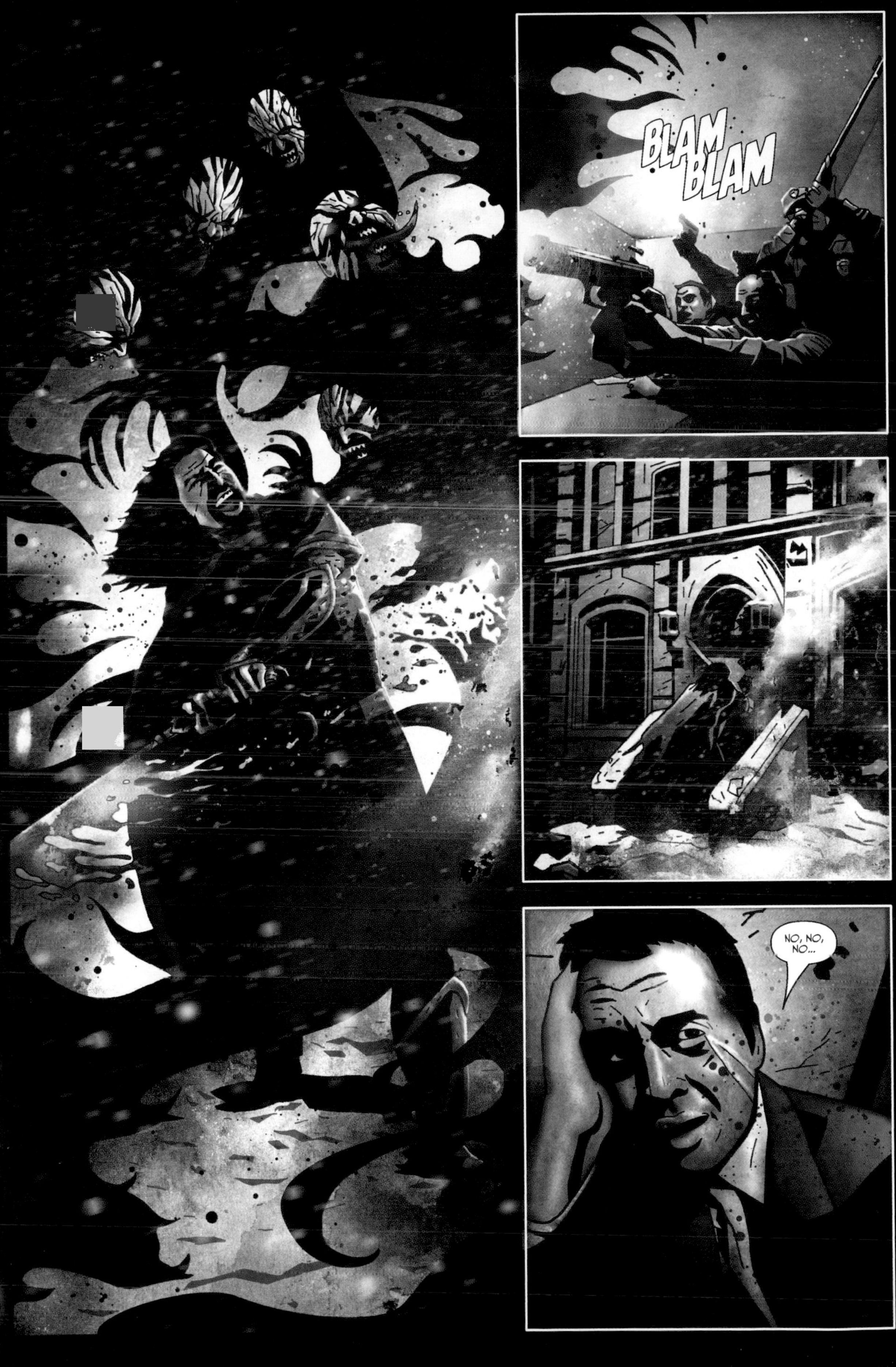
BLAM BLAM
NO, NO, NO...

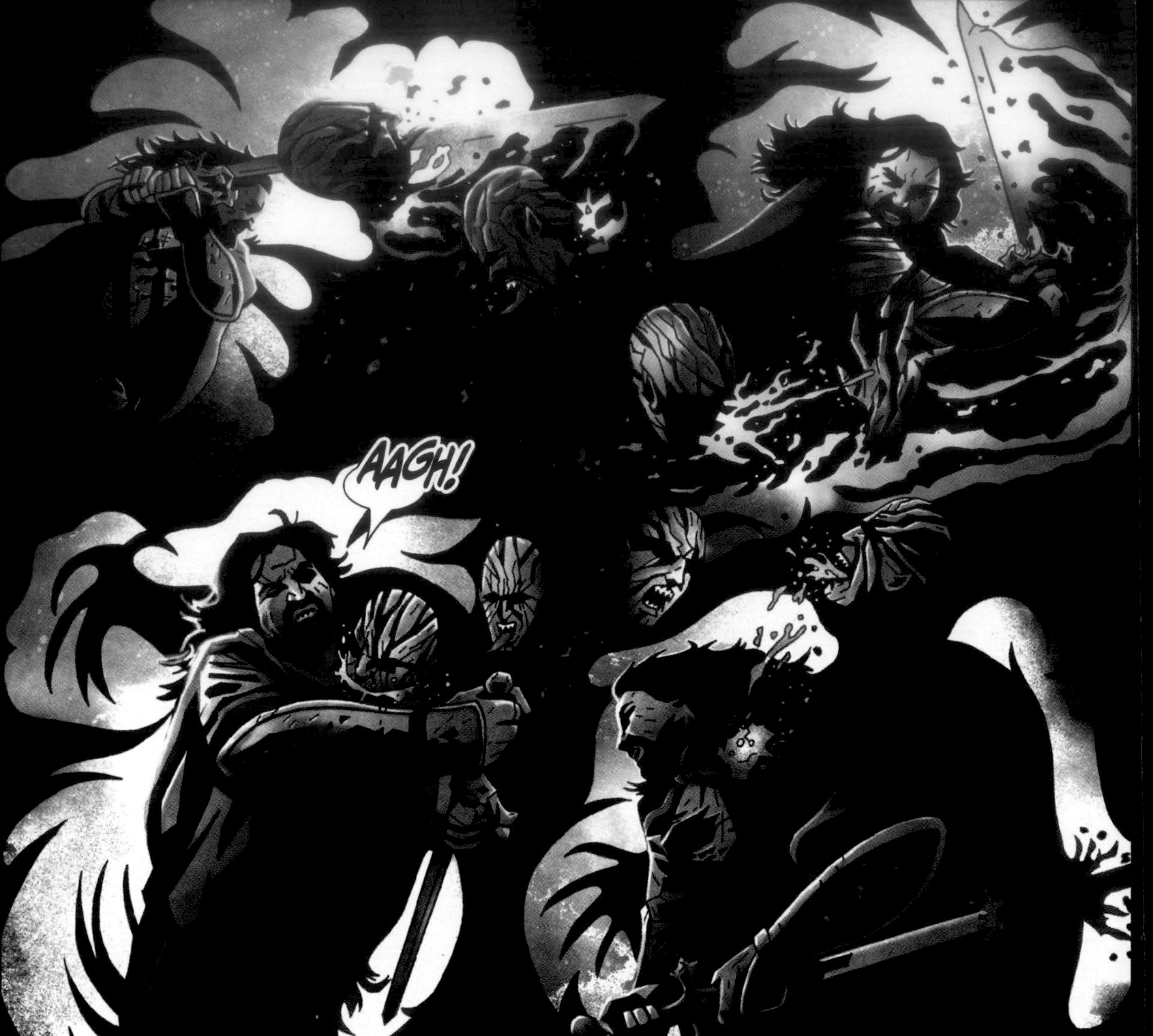
AAGH!

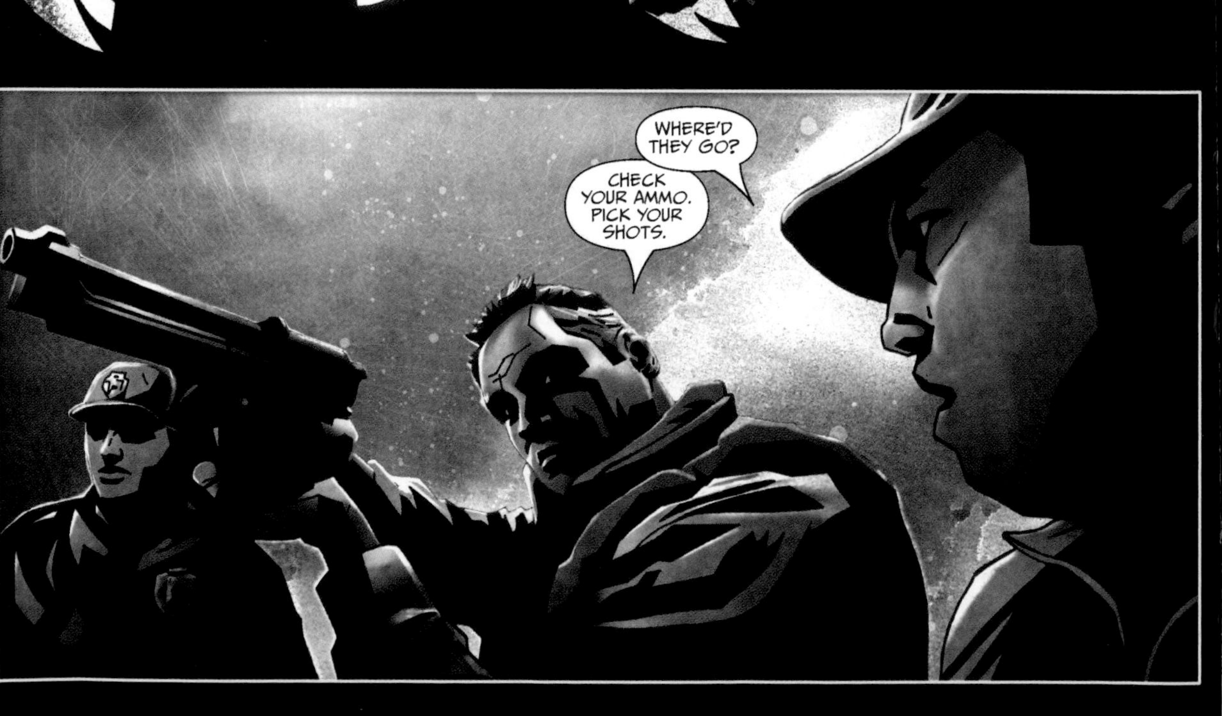
WHERE'D THEY GO?
CHECK YOUR AMMO. PICK YOUR SHOTS.

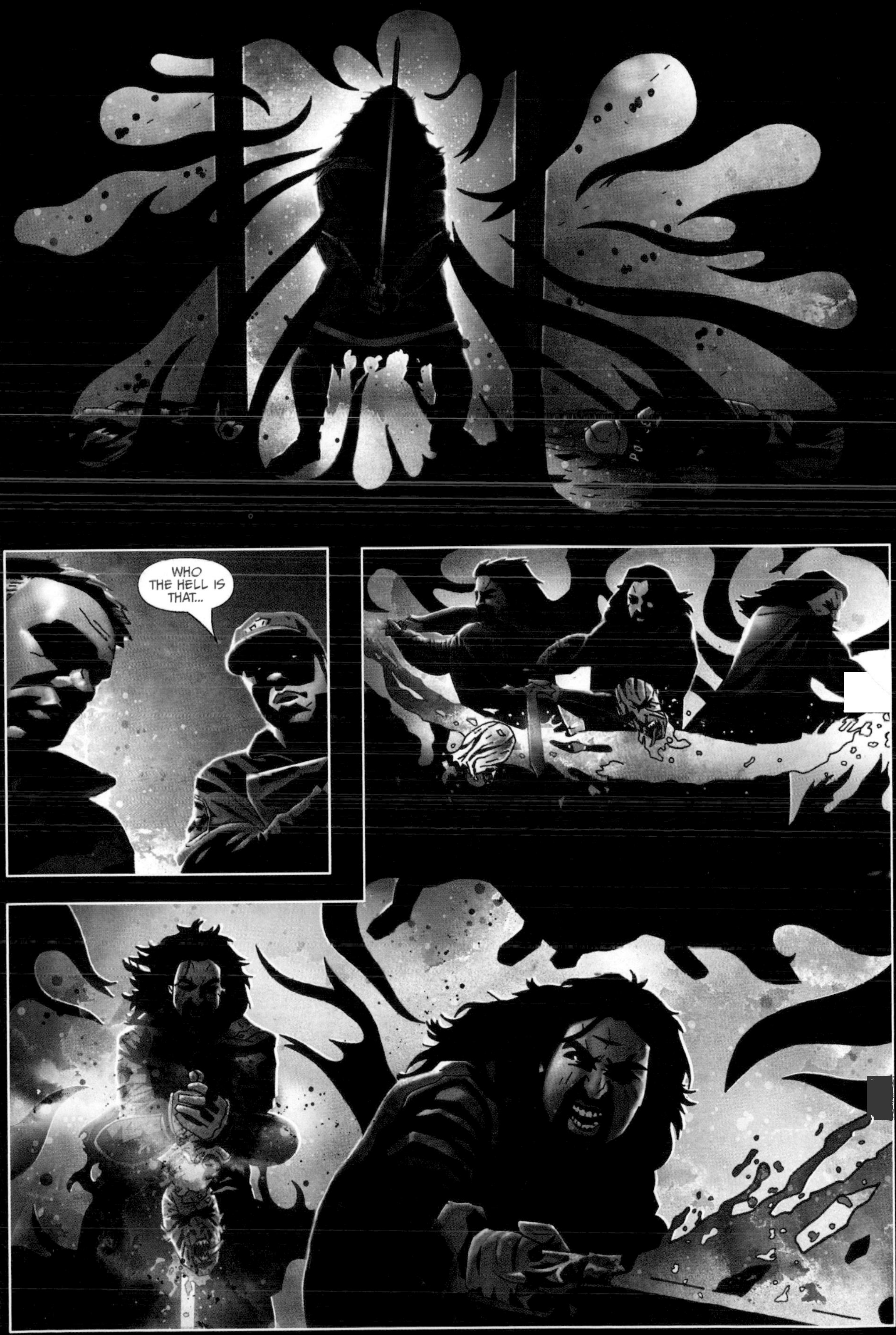
WHO THE HELL IS THAT...

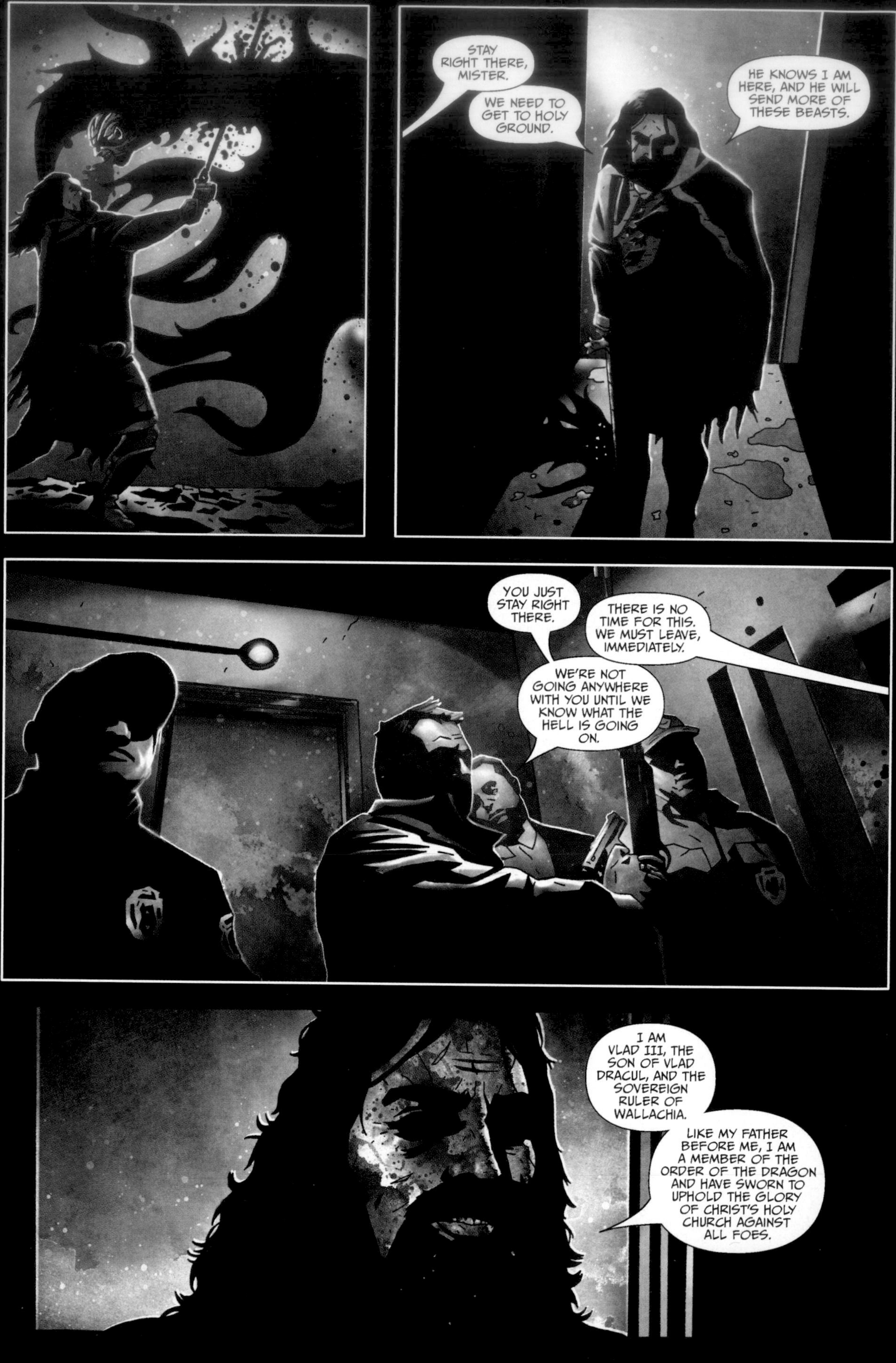
STAY RIGHT THERE, MISTER.
WE NEED TO GET TO HOLY GROUND.
HE KNOWS I AM HERE, AND HE WILL SEND MORE OF THESE BEASTS.
YOU JUST STAY RIGHT THERE.
THERE IS NO TIME FOR THIS. WE MUST LEAVE, IMMEDIATELY.
WE'RE NOT GOING ANYWHERE WITH YOU UNTIL WE KNOW WHAT THE HELL IS GOING ON.
I AM VLAD III, THE SON OF VLAD DRACUL, AND THE SOVEREIGN RULER OF WALLACHIA.
LIKE MY FATHER BEFORE ME, I AM A MEMBER OF THE ORDER OF THE DRAGON AND HAVE SWORN TO UPHOLD THE GLORY OF CHRIST'S HOLY CHURCH AGAINST ALL FOES.

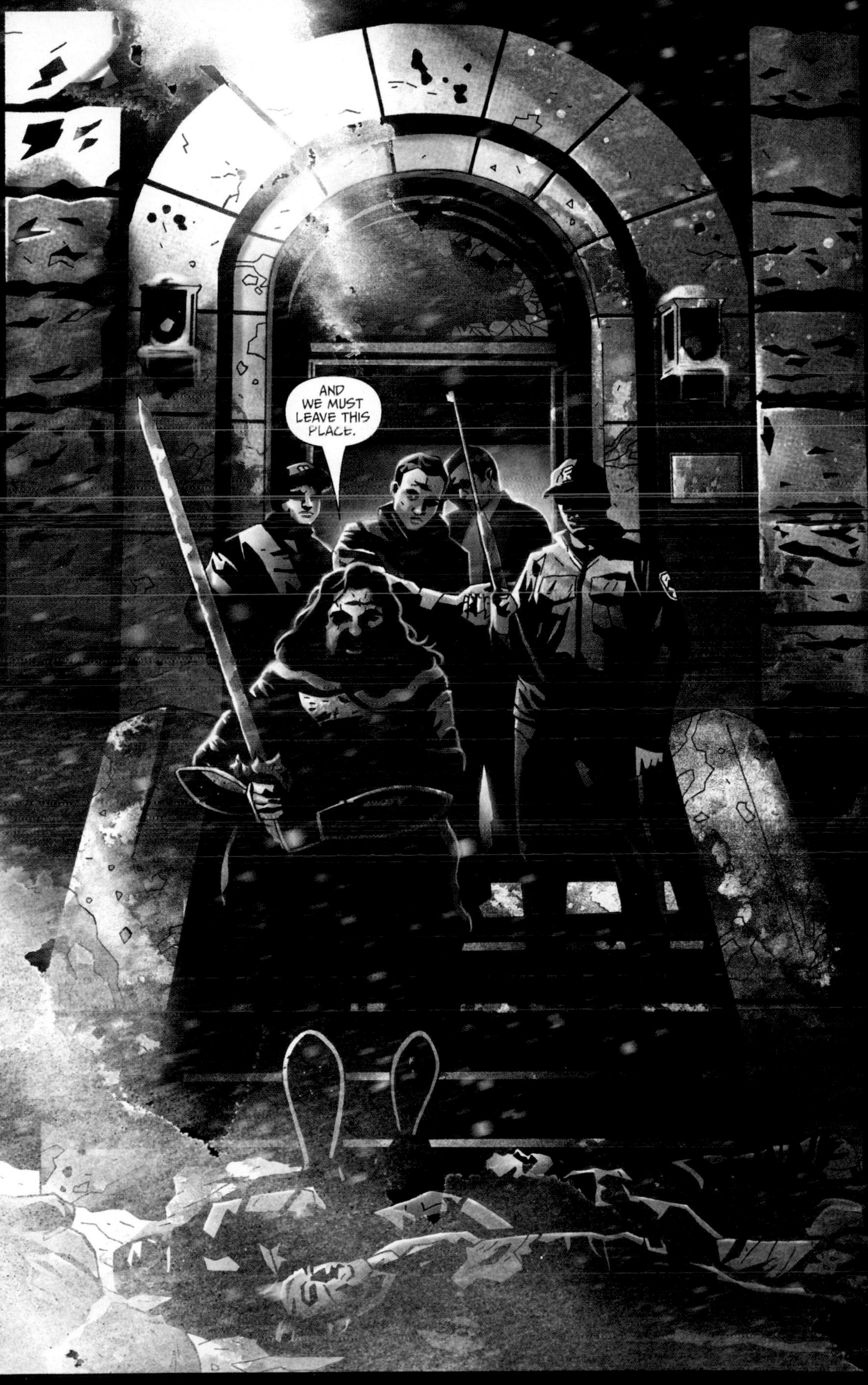
AND WE MUST LEAVE THIS PLACE.

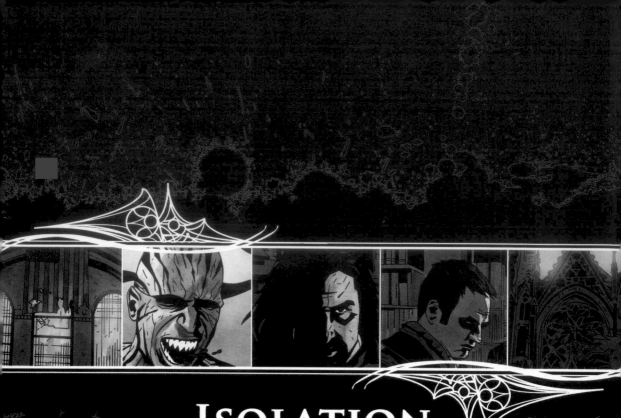

ISOLATION
{Issue #4}

WRITTEN BY:
WILLIAM HARMS

PENCILS & INKS BY:
NICK POSTIC

COLORS BY:
FRANCIS TSAI

LETTERING BY:
TROY PETERI

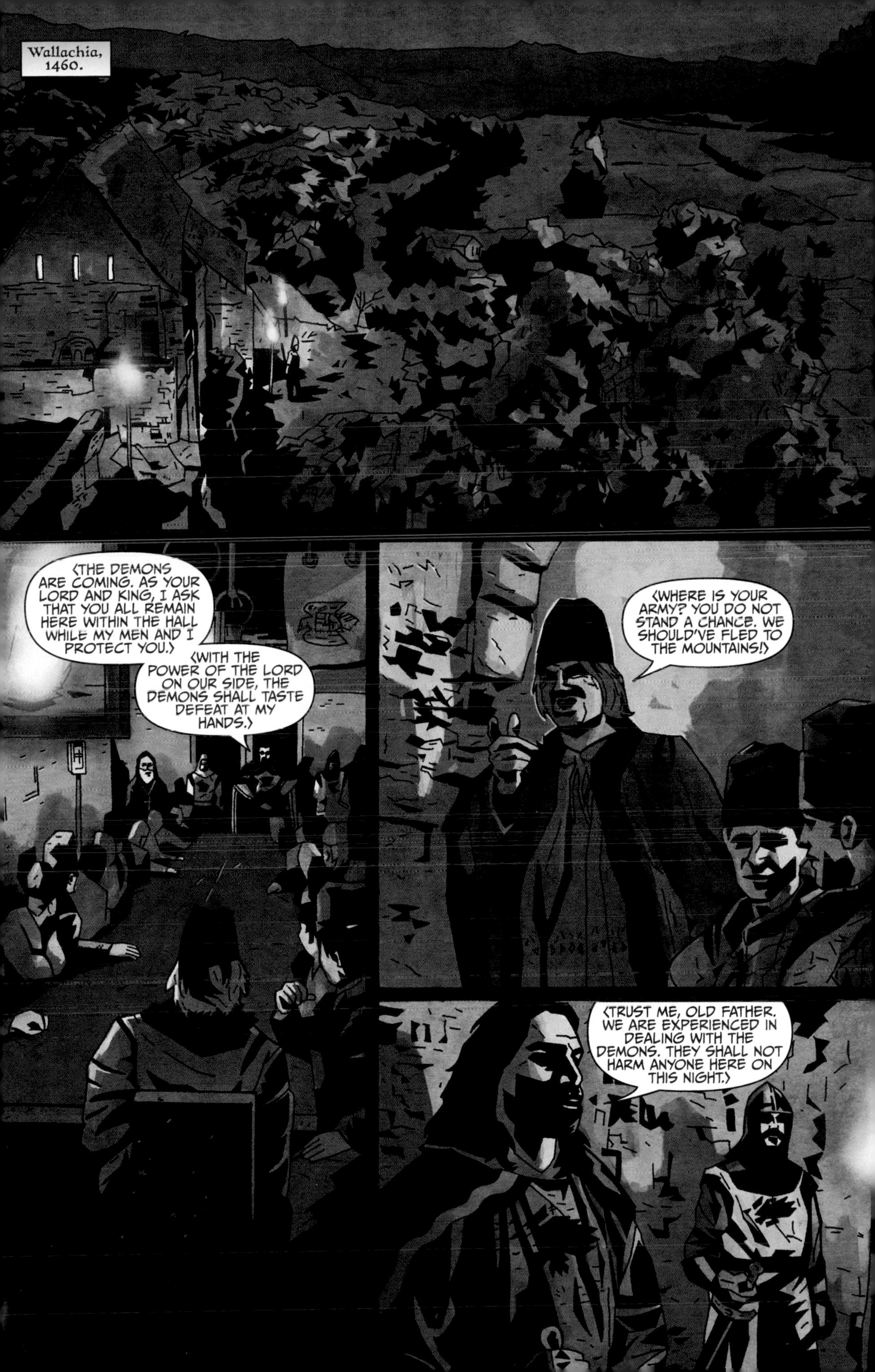

Wallachia, 1460.
‹THE DEMONS ARE COMING. AS YOUR LORD AND KING, I ASK THAT YOU ALL REMAIN HERE WITHIN THE HALL WHILE MY MEN AND I PROTECT YOU.›
‹WITH THE POWER OF THE LORD ON OUR SIDE, THE DEMONS SHALL TASTE DEFEAT AT MY HANDS.›
‹WHERE IS YOUR ARMY? YOU DO NOT STAND A CHANCE. WE SHOULD'VE FLED TO THE MOUNTAINS!›
‹TRUST ME, OLD FATHER. WE ARE EXPERIENCED IN DEALING WITH THE DEMONS. THEY SHALL NOT HARM ANYONE HERE ON THIS NIGHT.›

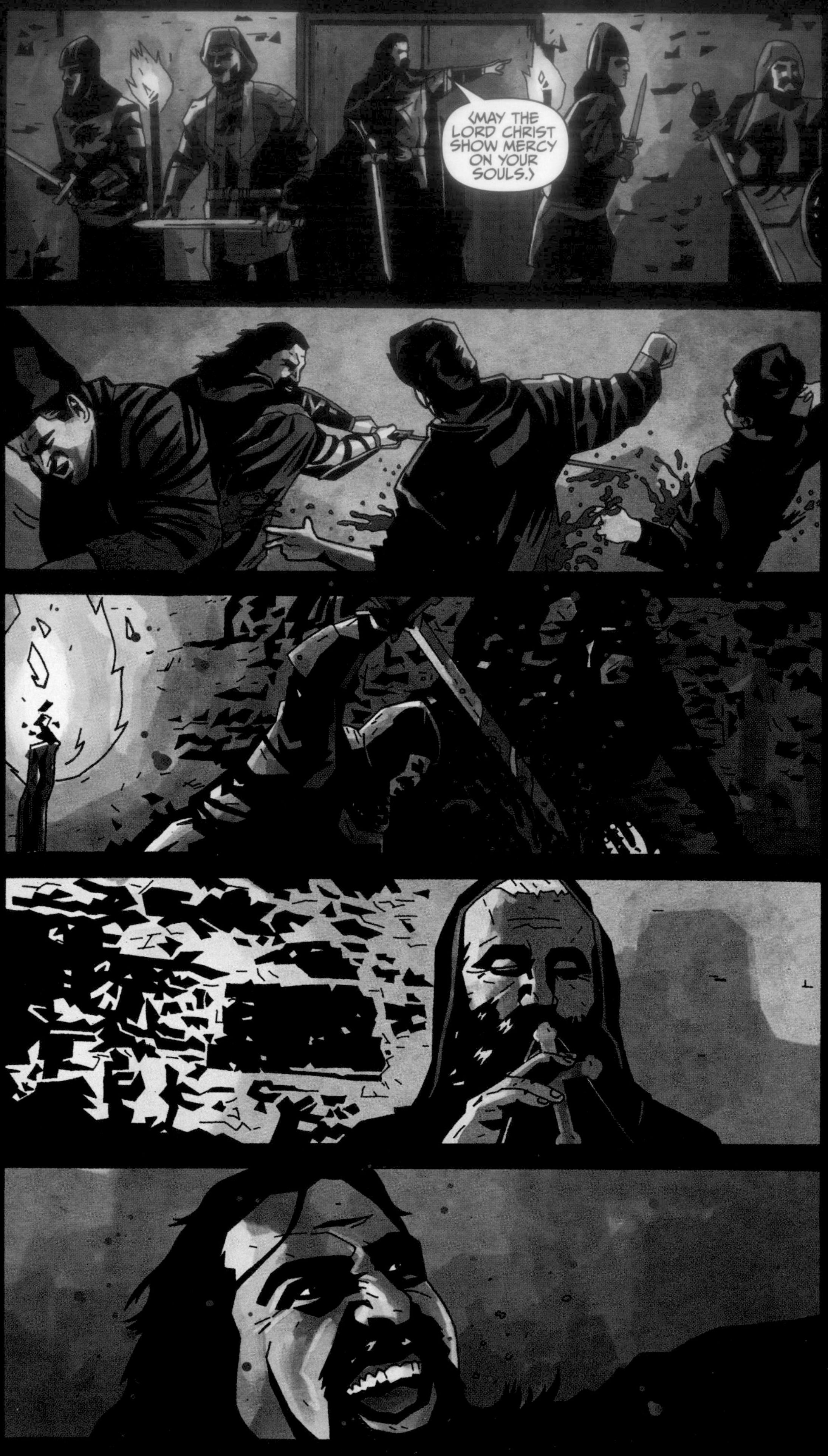

⟨MAY THE LORD CHRIST SHOW MERCY ON YOUR SOULS.⟩

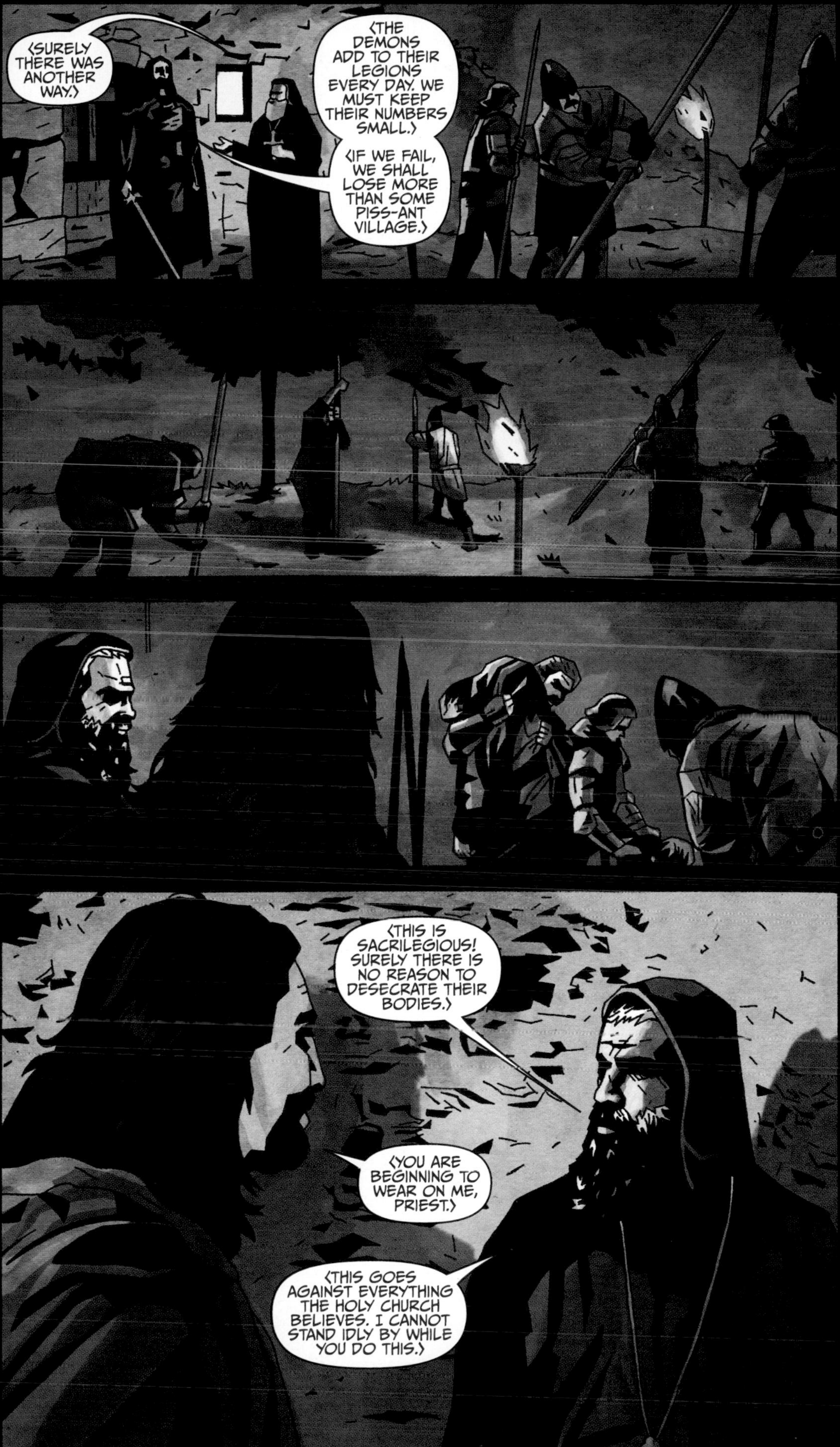
⟨SURELY THERE WAS ANOTHER WAY.⟩
⟨THE DEMONS ADD TO THEIR LEGIONS EVERY DAY. WE MUST KEEP THEIR NUMBERS SMALL.⟩
⟨IF WE FAIL, WE SHALL LOSE MORE THAN SOME PISS-ANT VILLAGE.⟩
⟨THIS IS SACRILEGIOUS! SURELY THERE IS NO REASON TO DESECRATE THEIR BODIES.⟩
⟨YOU ARE BEGINNING TO WEAR ON ME, PRIEST.⟩
⟨THIS GOES AGAINST EVERYTHING THE HOLY CHURCH BELIEVES. I CANNOT STAND IDLY BY WHILE YOU DO THIS.⟩

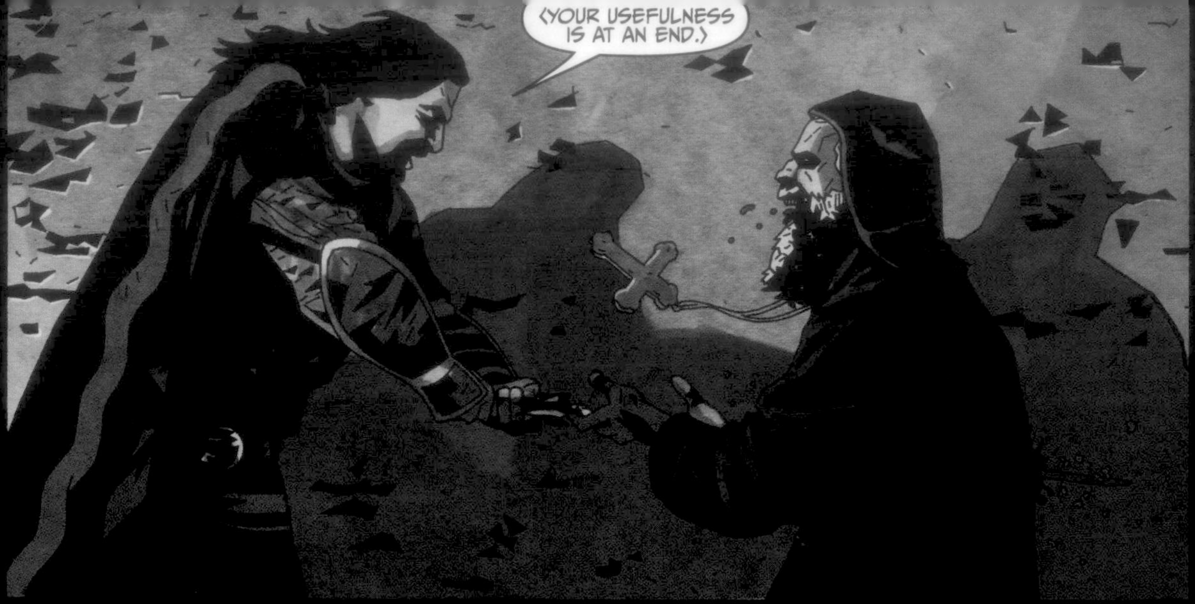
‹YOUR USEFULNESS IS AT AN END.›

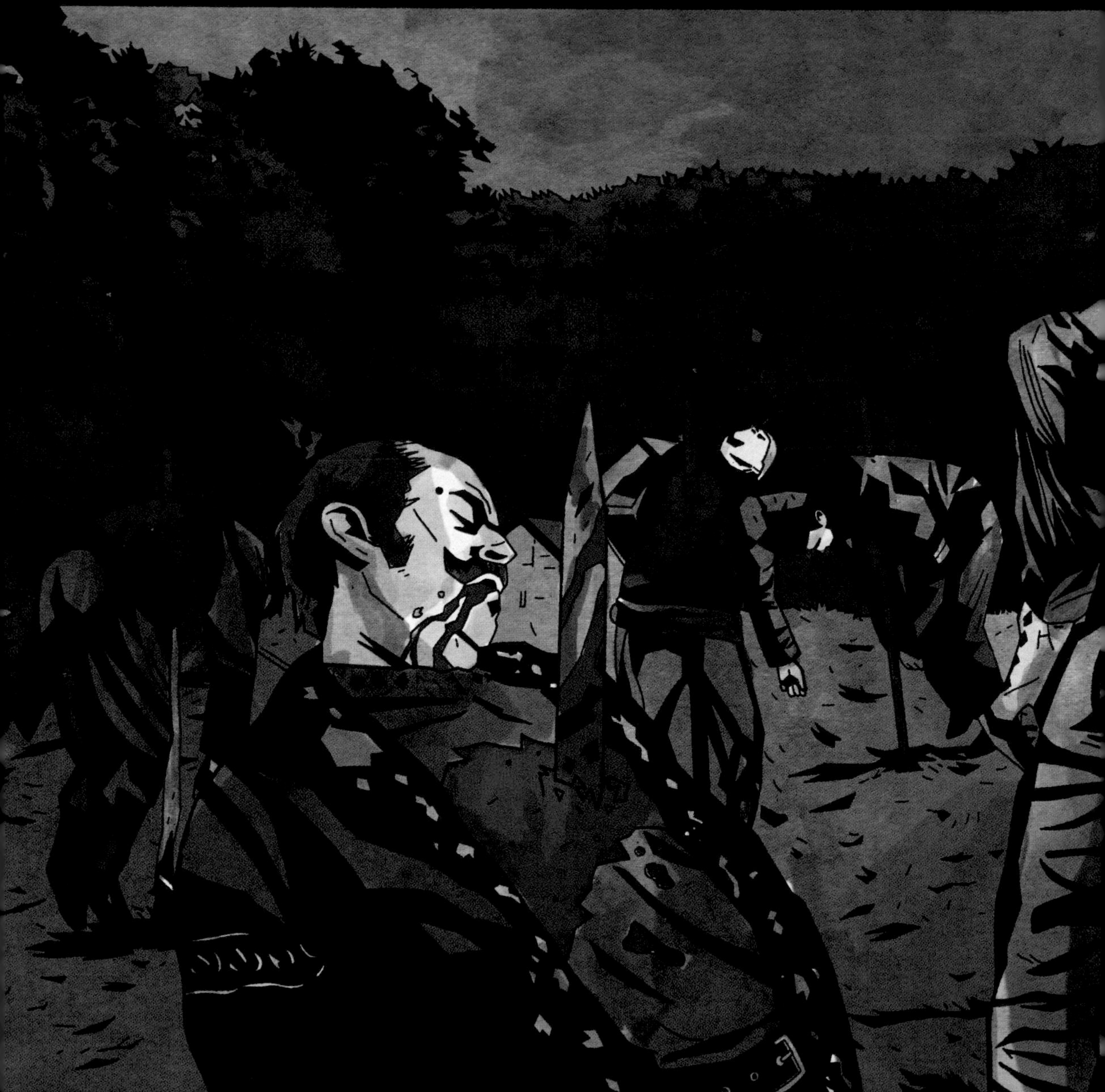

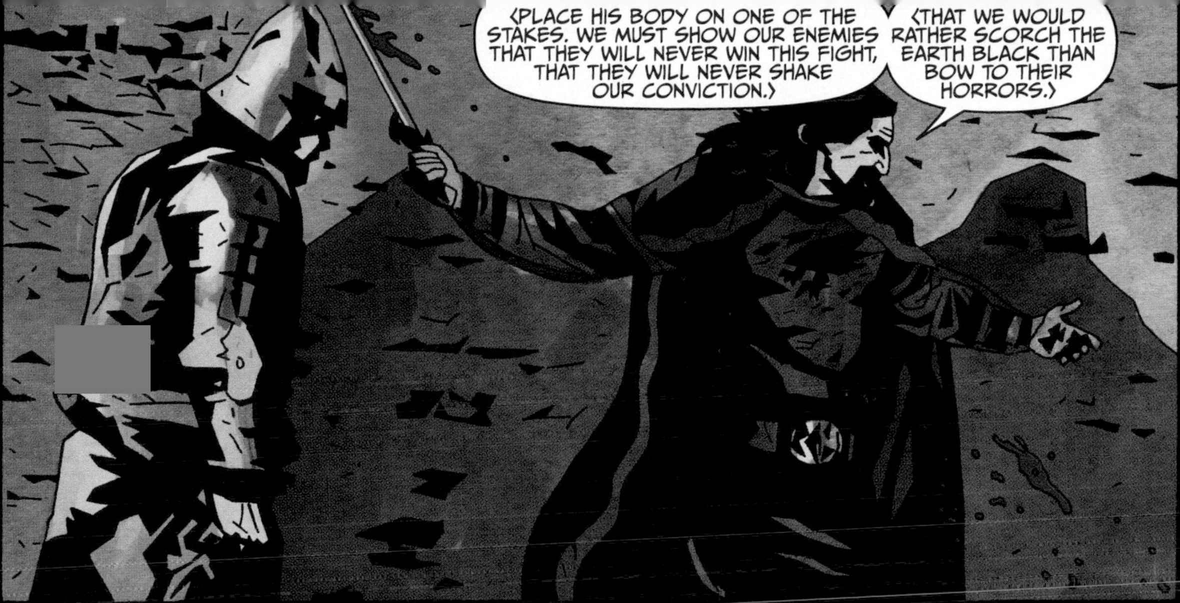
<PLACE HIS BODY ON ONE OF THE STAKES. WE MUST SHOW OUR ENEMIES THAT THEY WILL NEVER WIN THIS FIGHT, THAT THEY WILL NEVER SHAKE OUR CONVICTION.>
<THAT WE WOULD RATHER SCORCH THE EARTH BLACK THAN BOW TO THEIR HORRORS.>

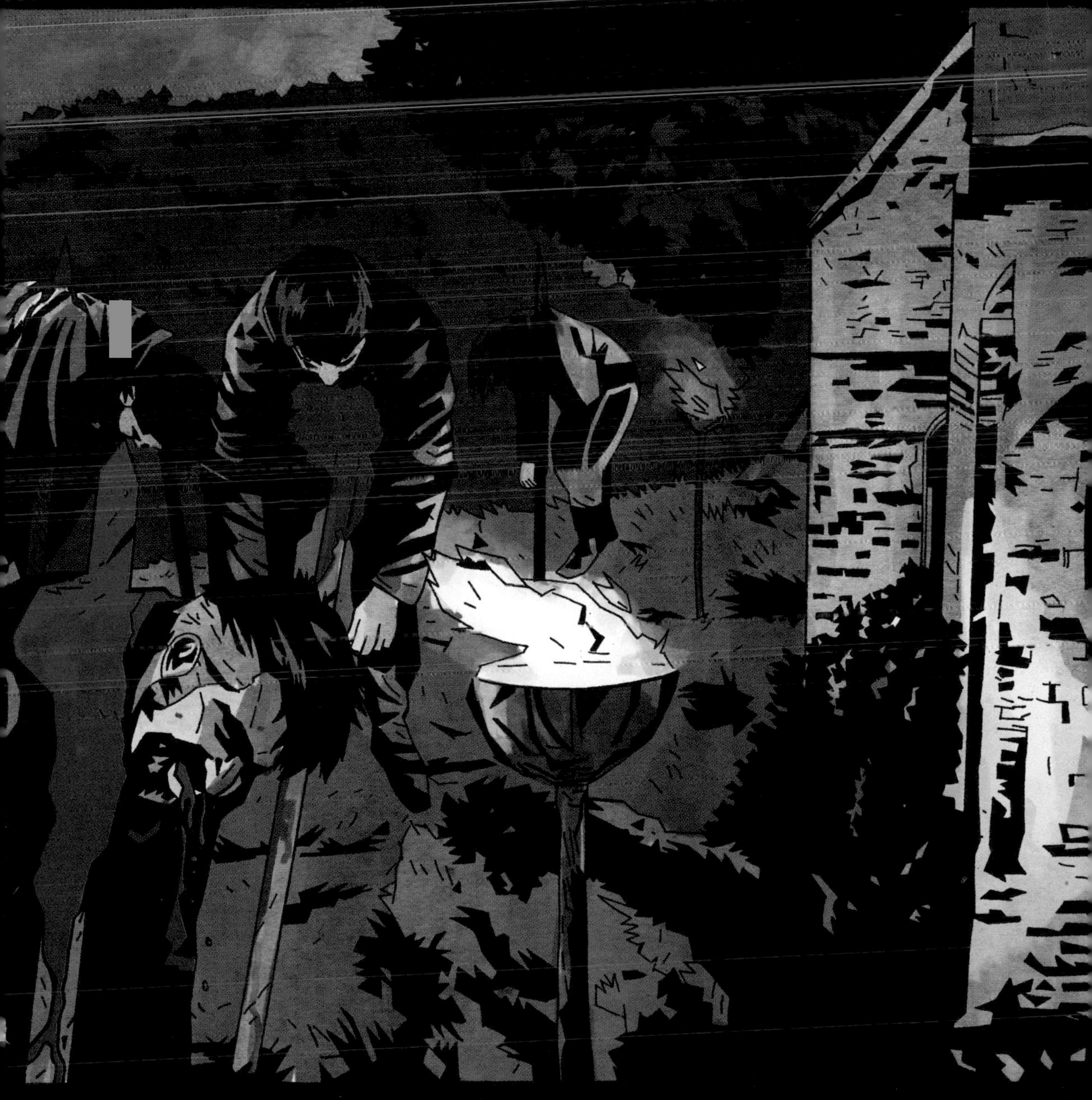

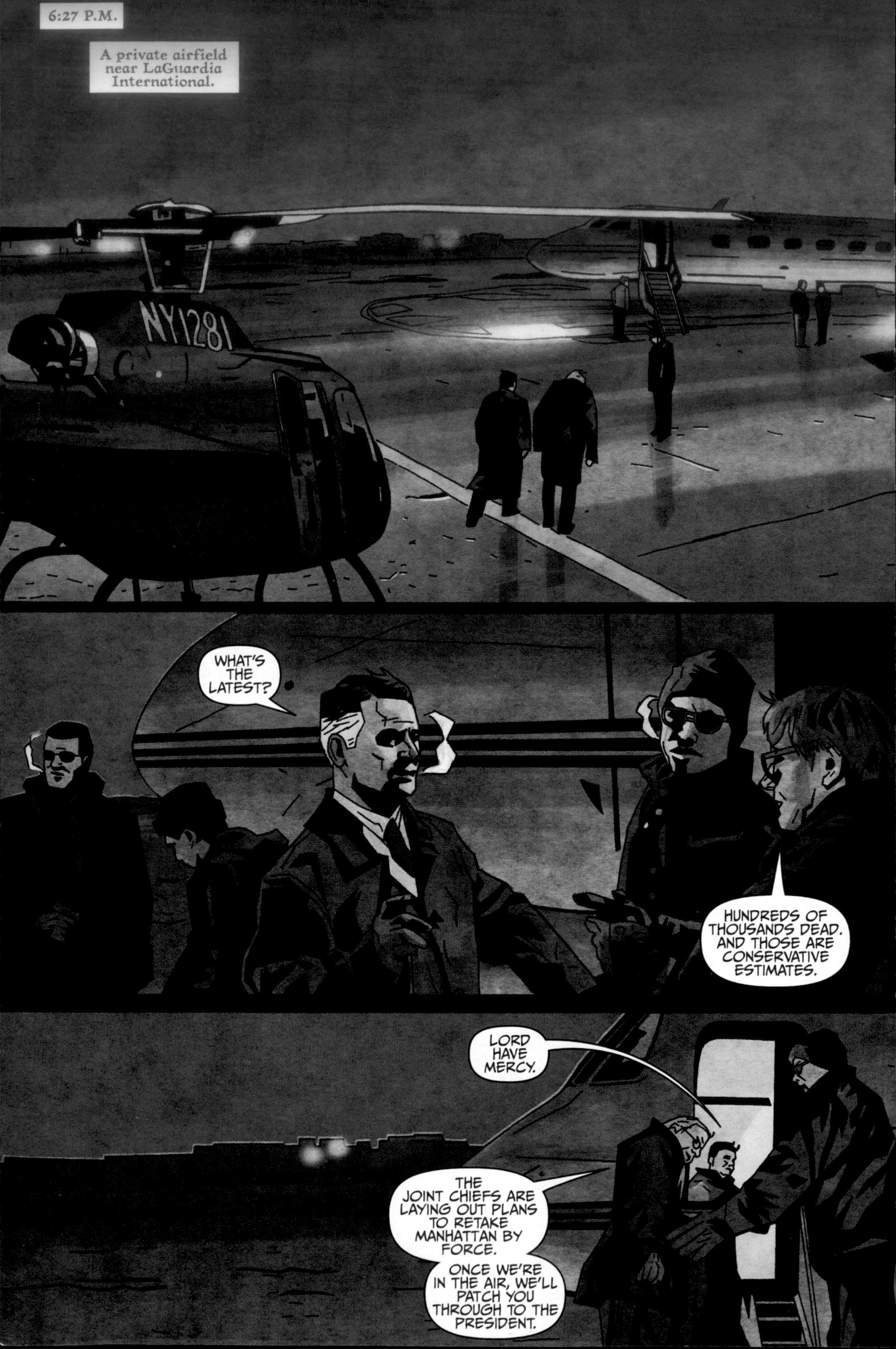
6:27 P.M.
A private airfield near LaGuardia International.
NY1281
WHAT'S THE LATEST?
HUNDREDS OF THOUSANDS DEAD. AND THOSE ARE CONSERVATIVE ESTIMATES.
LORD HAVE MERCY.
THE JOINT CHIEFS ARE LAYING OUT PLANS TO RETAKE MANHATTAN BY FORCE.
ONCE WE'RE IN THE AIR, WE'LL PATCH YOU THROUGH TO THE PRESIDENT.

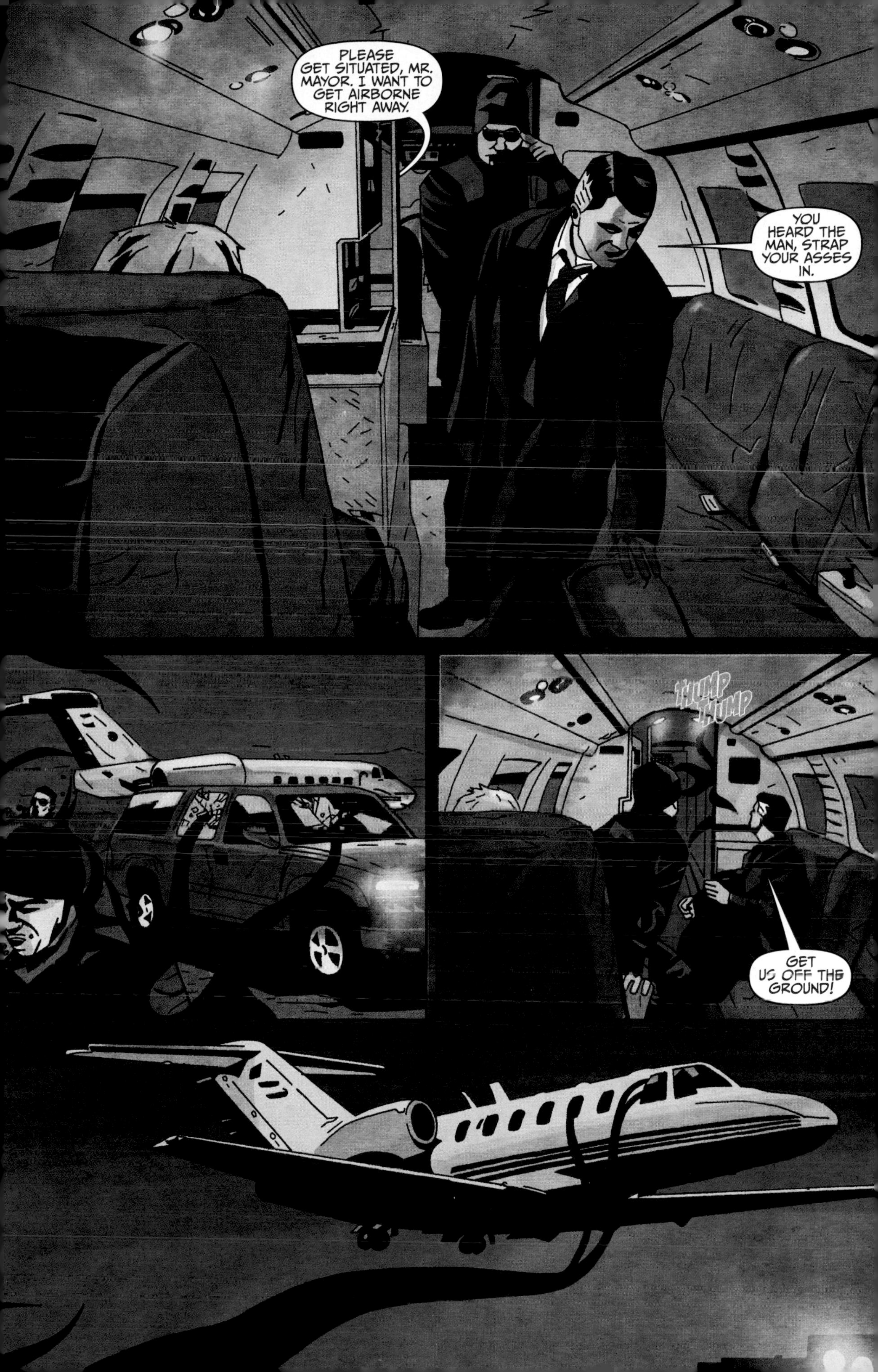
PLEASE GET SITUATED, MR. MAYOR. I WANT TO GET AIRBORNE RIGHT AWAY.
YOU HEARD THE MAN, STRAP YOUR ASSES IN.
THUMP THUMP
GET US OFF THE GROUND!

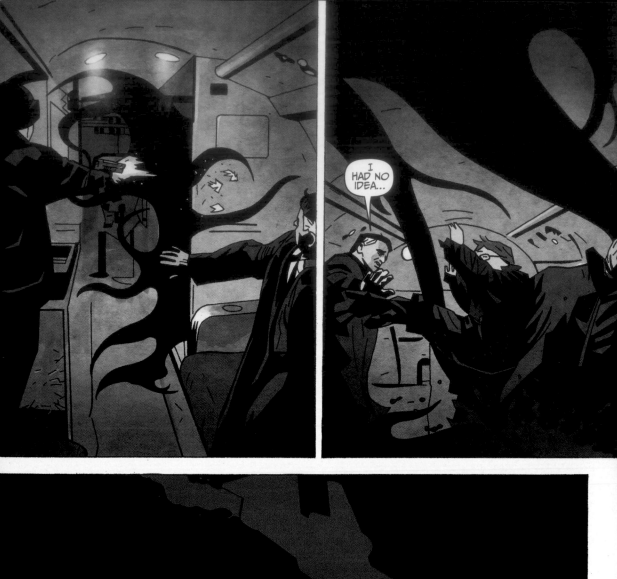

I HAD NO IDEA...

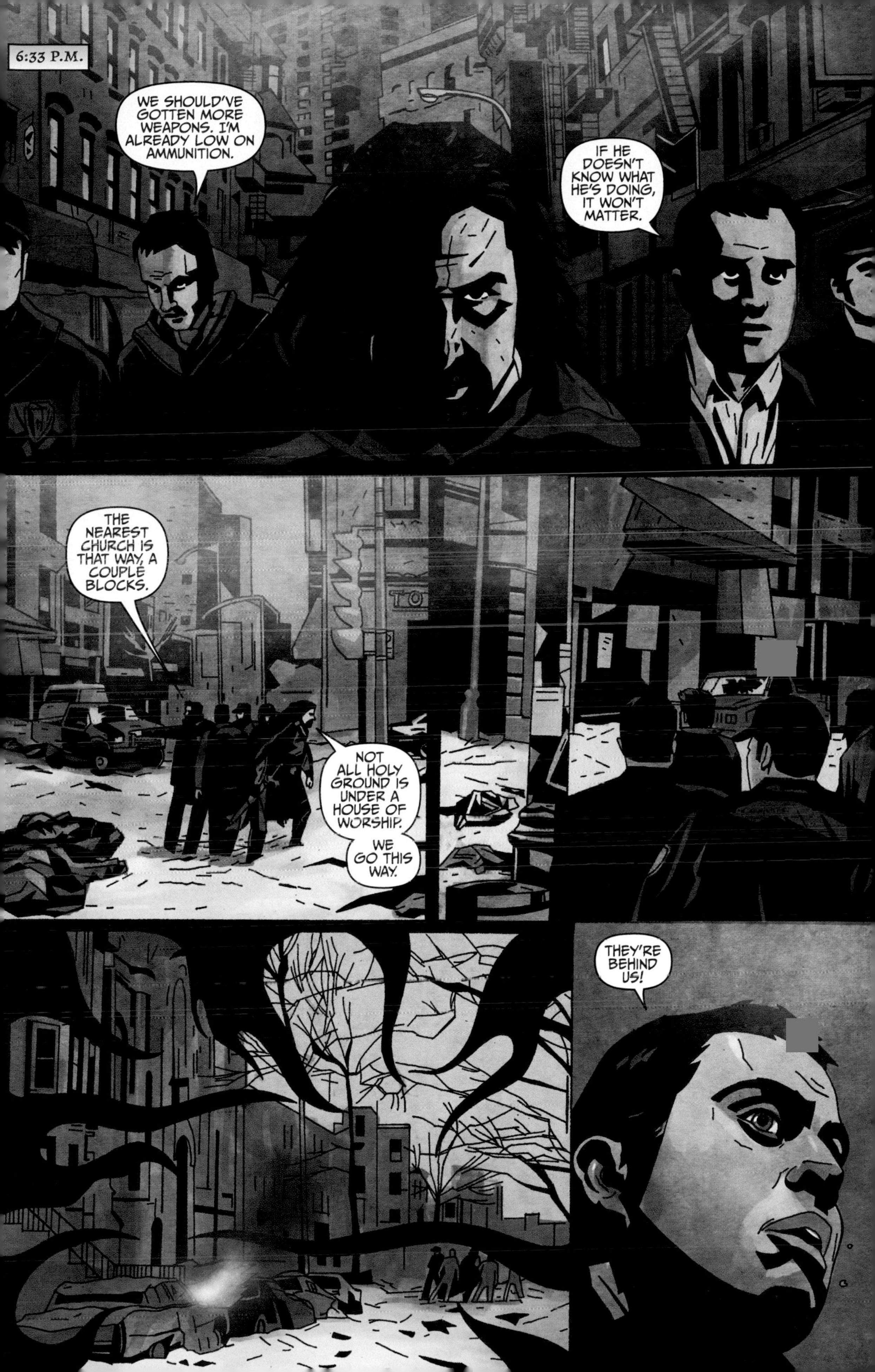
6:33 P.M.
WE SHOULD'VE GOTTEN MORE WEAPONS. I'M ALREADY LOW ON AMMUNITION.
IF HE DOESN'T KNOW WHAT HE'S DOING, IT WON'T MATTER.
THE NEAREST CHURCH IS THAT WAY, A COUPLE BLOCKS.
NOT ALL HOLY GROUND IS UNDER A HOUSE OF WORSHIP.
WE GO THIS WAY.
THEY'RE BEHIND US!

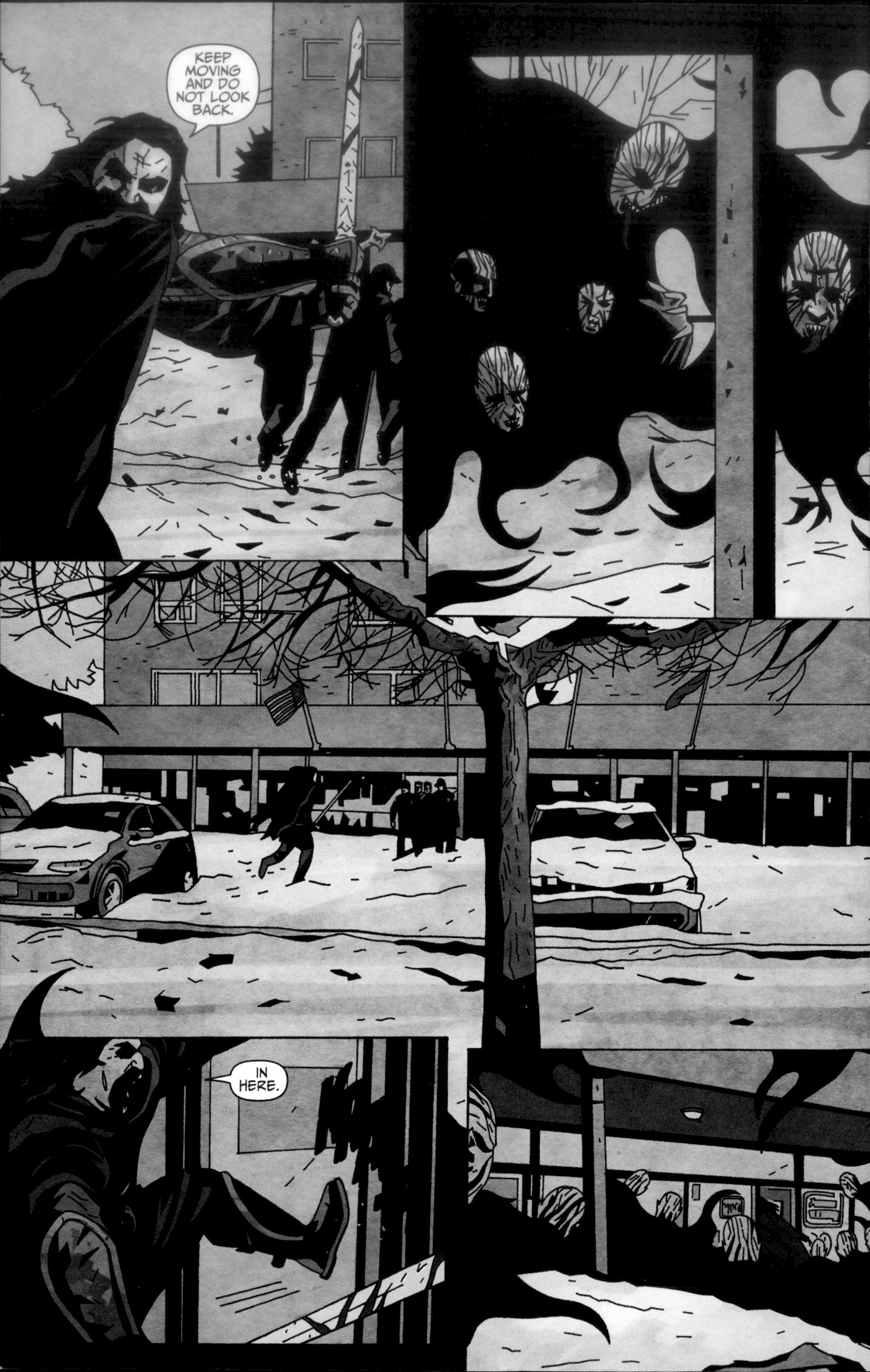
KEEP MOVING AND DO NOT LOOK BACK.
IN HERE.

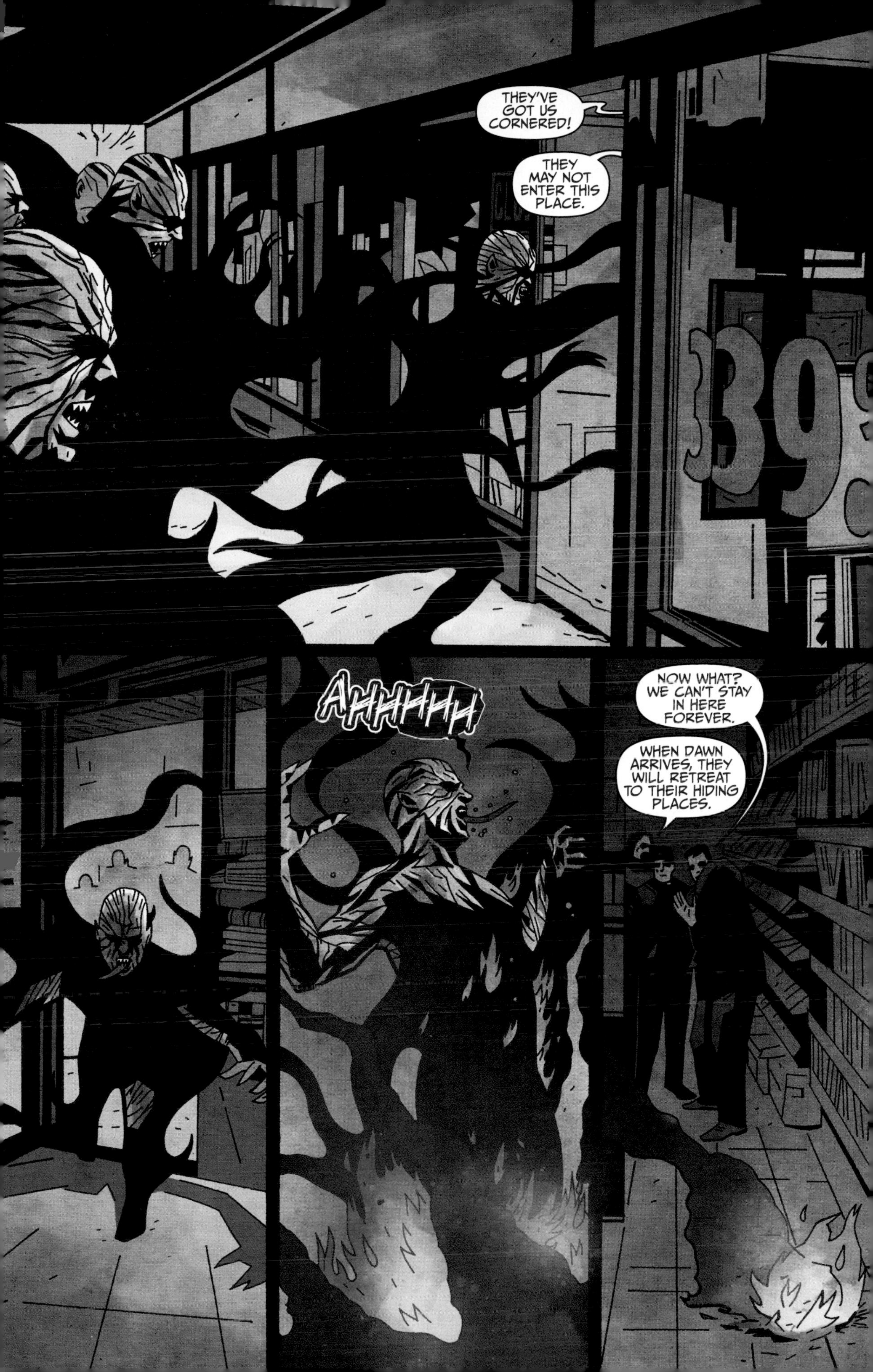
THEY'VE GOT US CORNERED!
THEY MAY NOT ENTER THIS PLACE.
AHHHHHH
NOW WHAT? WE CAN'T STAY IN HERE FOREVER.
WHEN DAWN ARRIVES, THEY WILL RETREAT TO THEIR HIDING PLACES.

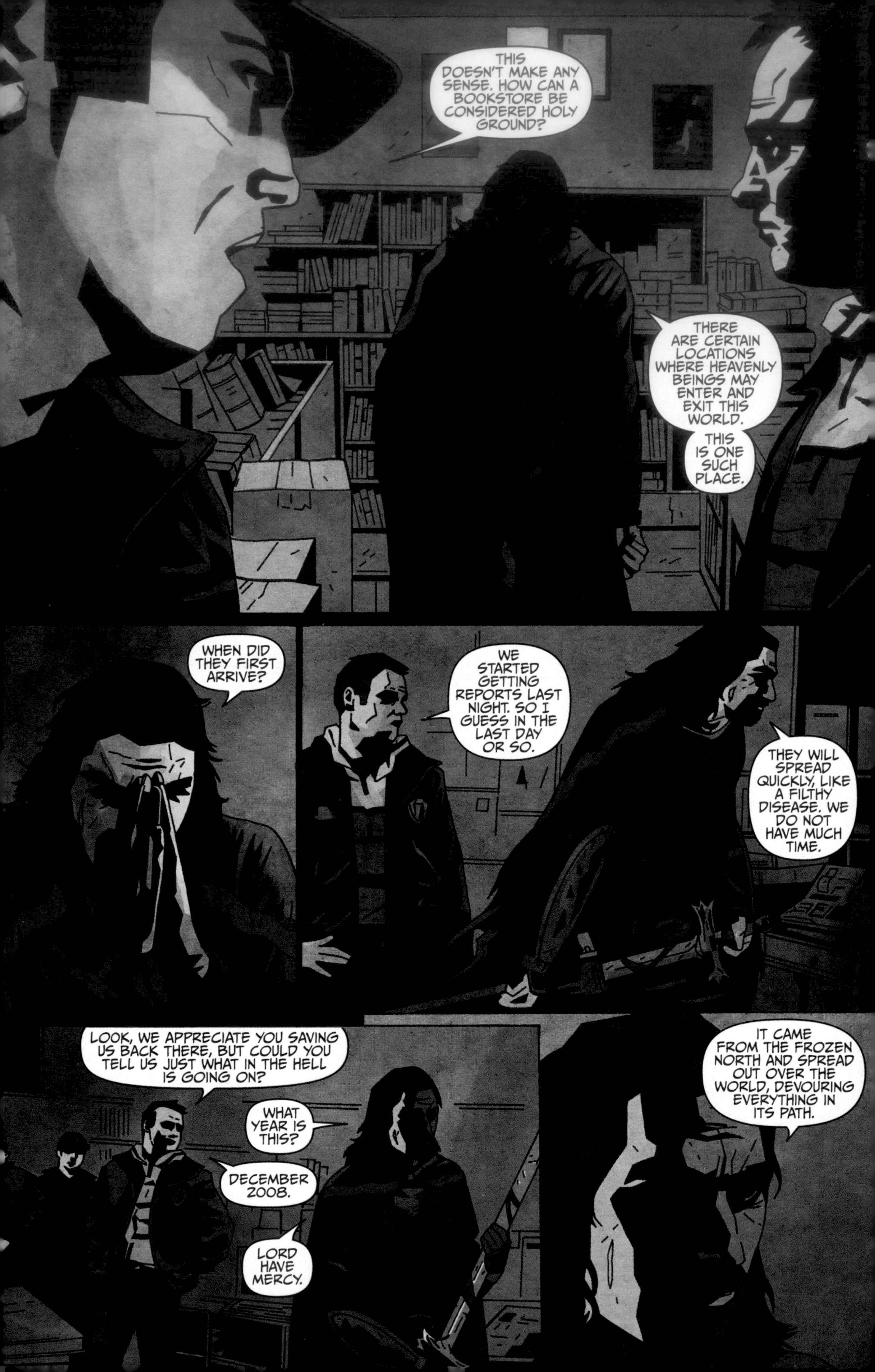

THIS DOESN'T MAKE ANY SENSE. HOW CAN A BOOKSTORE BE CONSIDERED HOLY GROUND?
THERE ARE CERTAIN LOCATIONS WHERE HEAVENLY BEINGS MAY ENTER AND EXIT THIS WORLD.
THIS IS ONE SUCH PLACE.
WHEN DID THEY FIRST ARRIVE?
WE STARTED GETTING REPORTS LAST NIGHT. SO I GUESS IN THE LAST DAY OR SO.
THEY WILL SPREAD QUICKLY, LIKE A FILTHY DISEASE. WE DO NOT HAVE MUCH TIME.
LOOK, WE APPRECIATE YOU SAVING US BACK THERE, BUT COULD YOU TELL US JUST WHAT IN THE HELL IS GOING ON?
WHAT YEAR IS THIS?
DECEMBER 2008.
LORD HAVE MERCY.
IT CAME FROM THE FROZEN NORTH AND SPREAD OUT OVER THE WORLD, DEVOURING EVERYTHING IN ITS PATH.

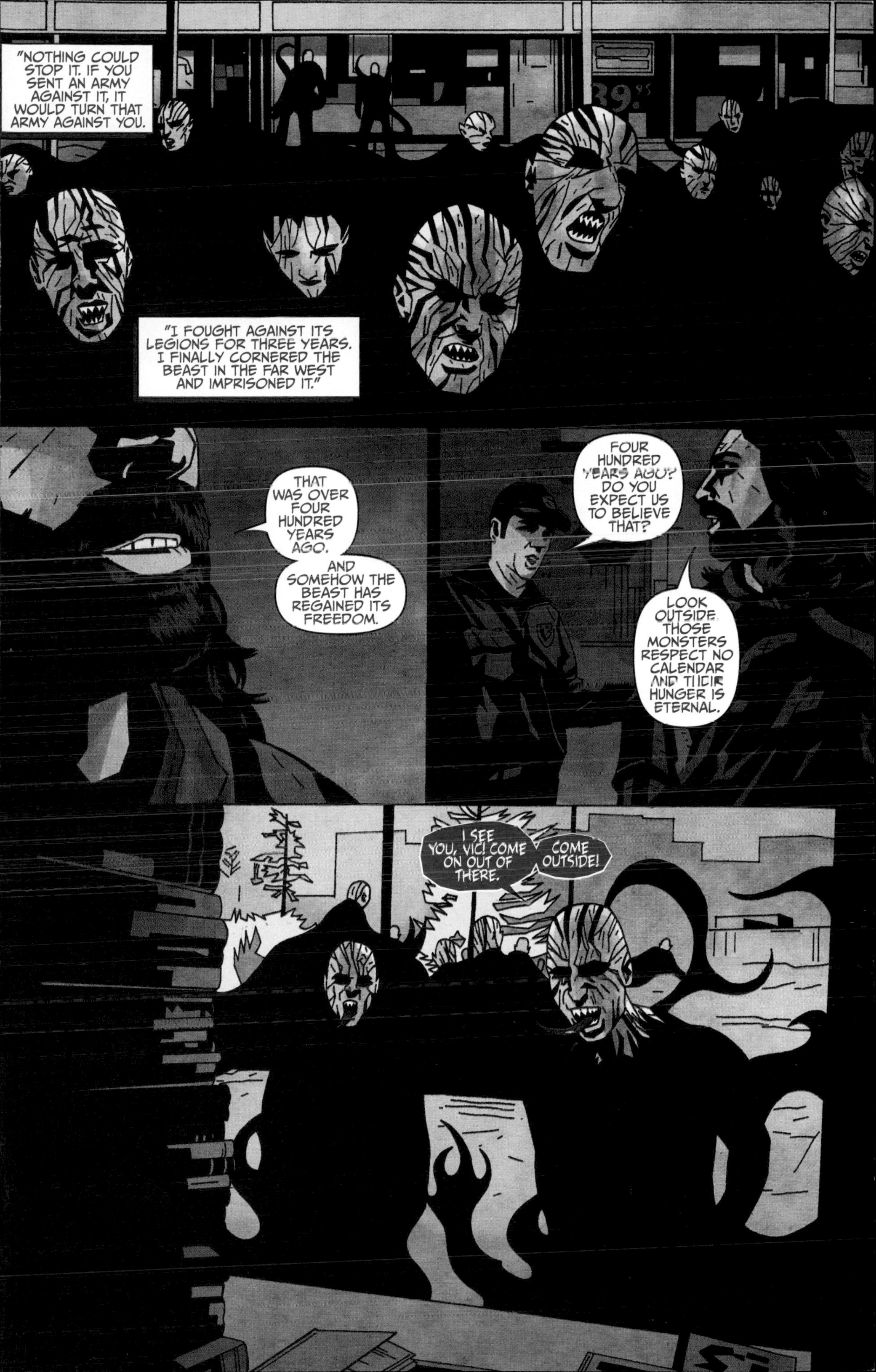
"NOTHING COULD STOP IT. IF YOU SENT AN ARMY AGAINST IT, IT WOULD TURN THAT ARMY AGAINST YOU.
"I FOUGHT AGAINST ITS LEGIONS FOR THREE YEARS. I FINALLY CORNERED THE BEAST IN THE FAR WEST AND IMPRISONED IT."
THAT WAS OVER FOUR HUNDRED YEARS AGO.
AND SOMEHOW THE BEAST HAS REGAINED ITS FREEDOM.
FOUR HUNDRED YEARS AGO? DO YOU EXPECT US TO BELIEVE THAT?
LOOK OUTSIDE. THOSE MONSTERS RESPECT NO CALENDAR AND THEIR HUNGER IS ETERNAL.
I SEE YOU, VIC! COME ON OUT OF THERE.
COME OUTSIDE!

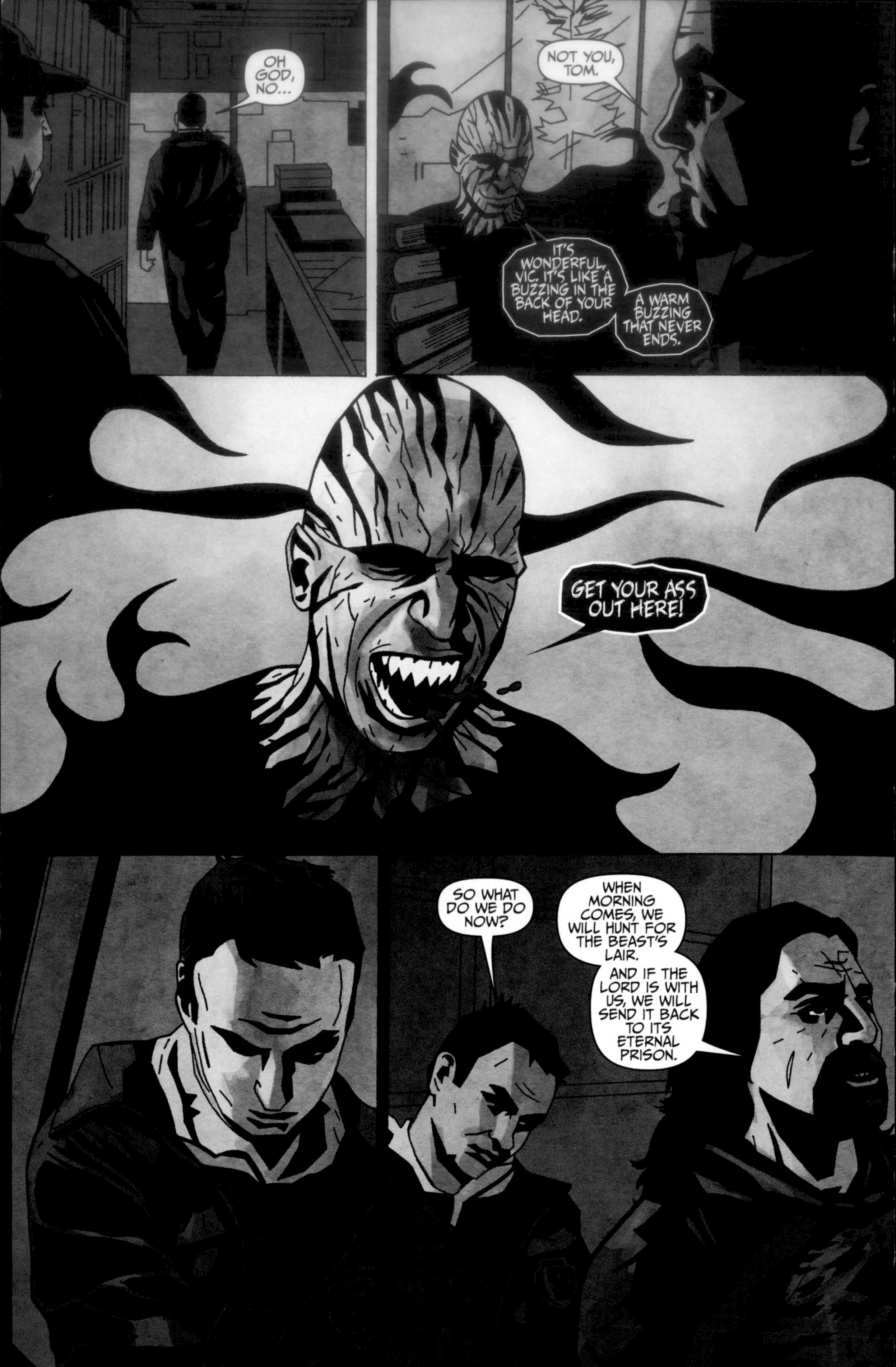
OH GOD, NO...
NOT YOU, TOM.
IT'S WONDERFUL, VIC. IT'S LIKE A BUZZING IN THE BACK OF YOUR HEAD.
A WARM BUZZING THAT NEVER ENDS.
GET YOUR ASS OUT HERE!
SO WHAT DO WE DO NOW?
WHEN MORNING COMES, WE WILL HUNT FOR THE BEAST'S LAIR.
AND IF THE LORD IS WITH US, WE WILL SEND IT BACK TO ITS ETERNAL PRISON.

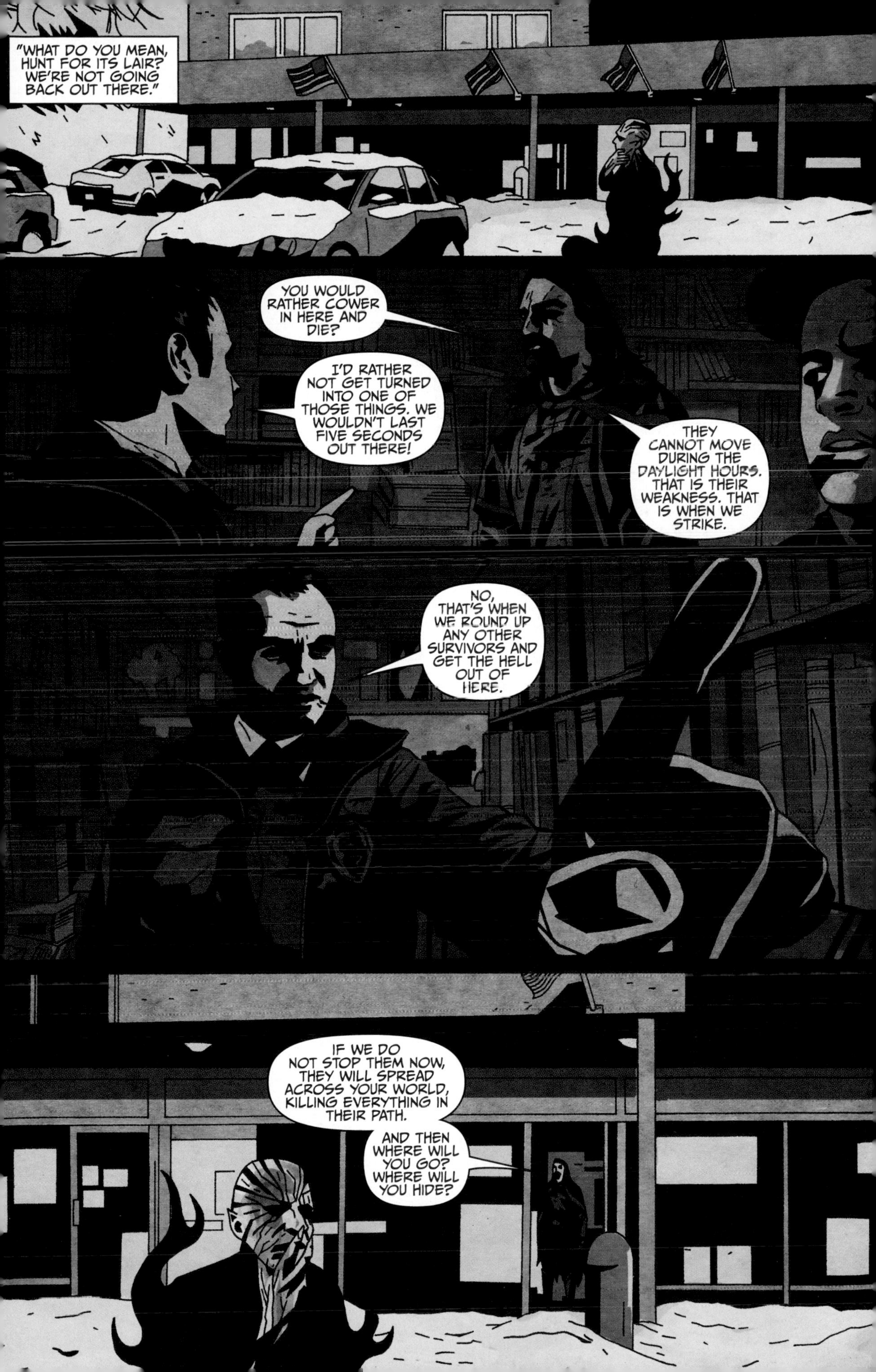
"WHAT DO YOU MEAN, HUNT FOR ITS LAIR? WE'RE NOT GOING BACK OUT THERE."
YOU WOULD RATHER COWER IN HERE AND DIE?
I'D RATHER NOT GET TURNED INTO ONE OF THOSE THINGS. WE WOULDN'T LAST FIVE SECONDS OUT THERE!
THEY CANNOT MOVE DURING THE DAYLIGHT HOURS. THAT IS THEIR WEAKNESS. THAT IS WHEN WE STRIKE.
NO, THAT'S WHEN WE ROUND UP ANY OTHER SURVIVORS AND GET THE HELL OUT OF HERE.
IF WE DO NOT STOP THEM NOW, THEY WILL SPREAD ACROSS YOUR WORLD, KILLING EVERYTHING IN THEIR PATH.
AND THEN WHERE WILL YOU GO? WHERE WILL YOU HIDE?

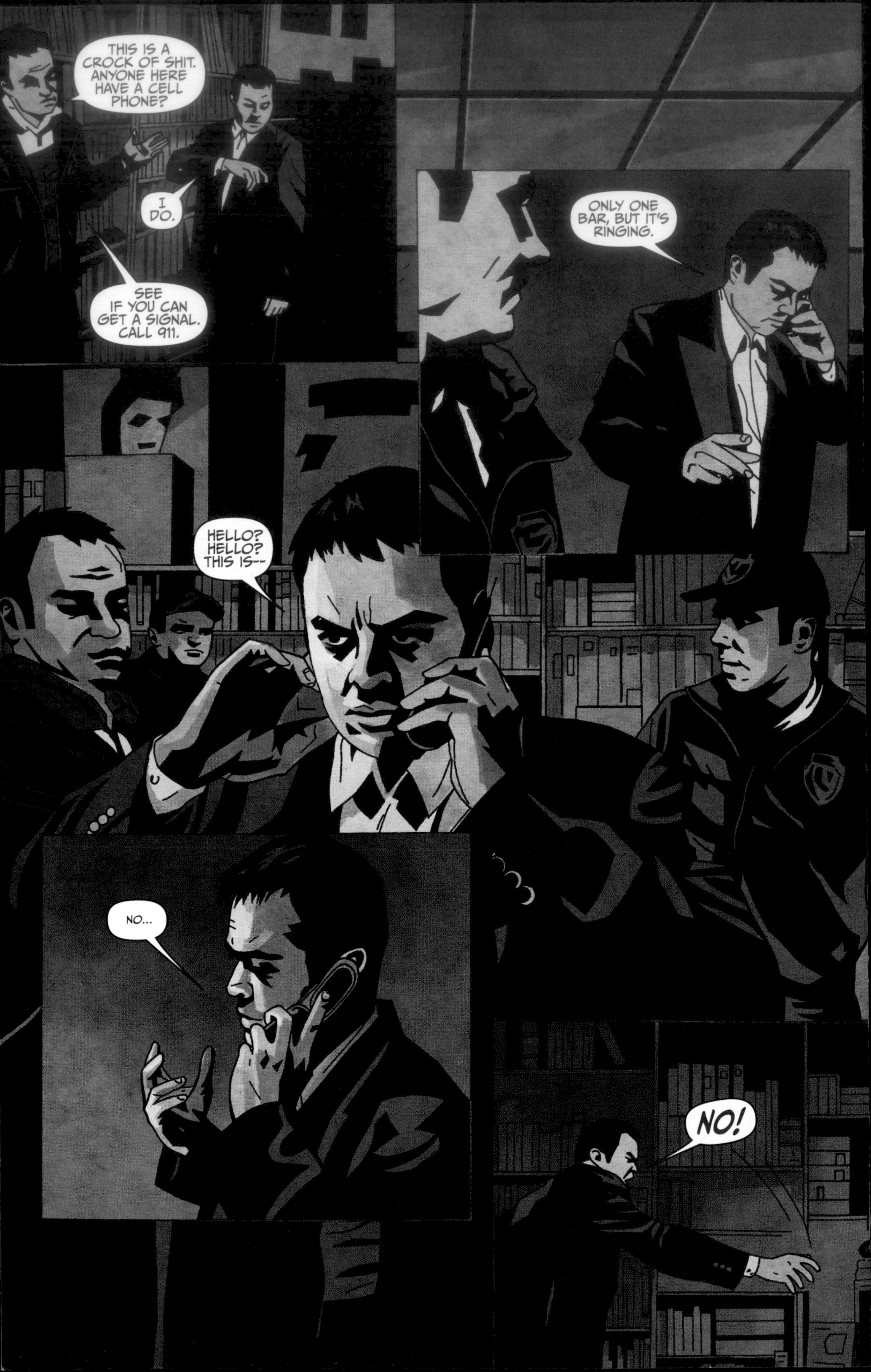
THIS IS A CROCK OF SHIT. ANYONE HERE HAVE A CELL PHONE?
I DO.
SEE IF YOU CAN GET A SIGNAL. CALL 911.
ONLY ONE BAR, BUT IT'S RINGING.
HELLO? HELLO? THIS IS--
NO...
NO!

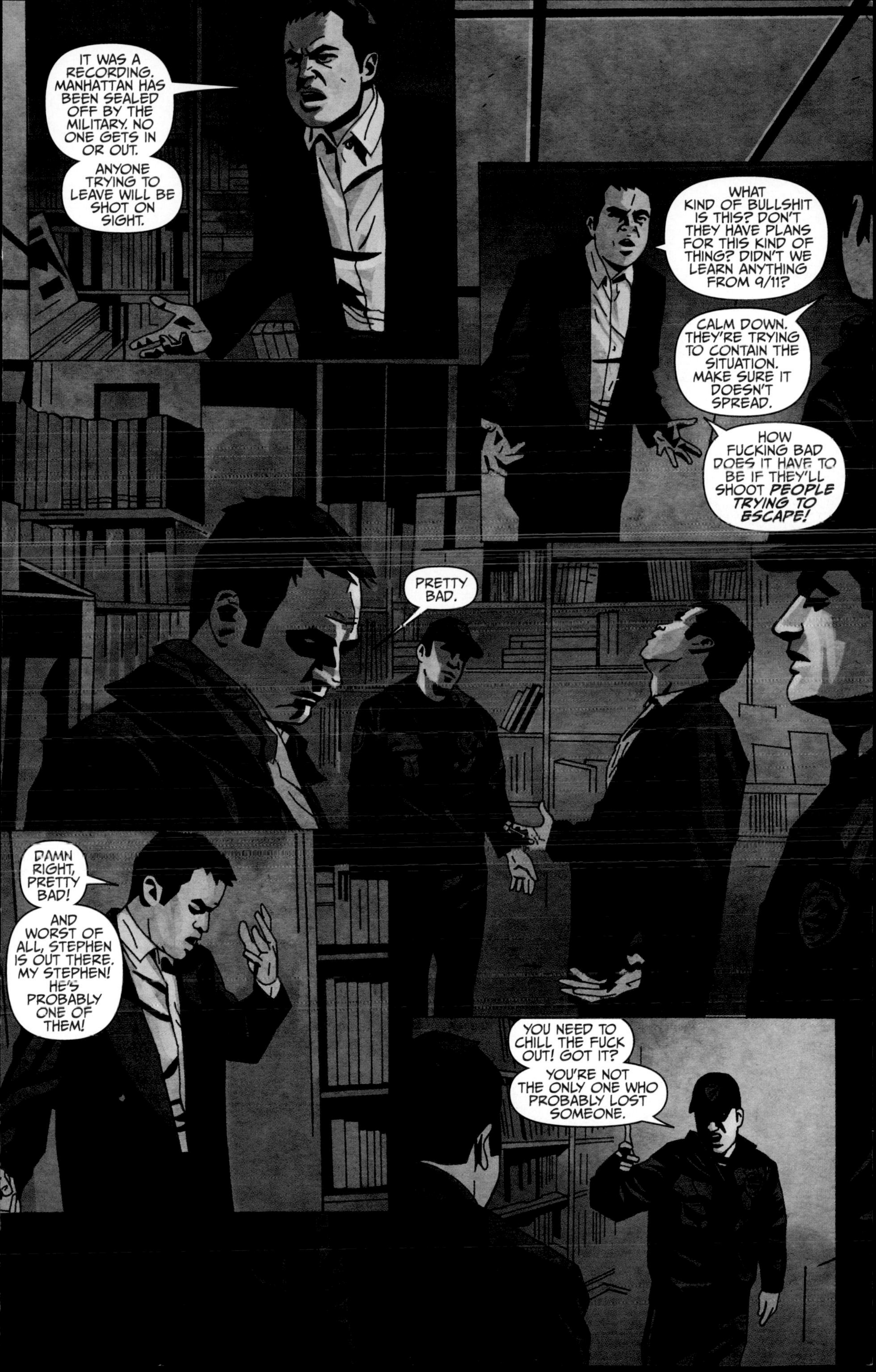
IT WAS A RECORDING. MANHATTAN HAS BEEN SEALED OFF BY THE MILITARY. NO ONE GETS IN OR OUT.
ANYONE TRYING TO LEAVE WILL BE SHOT ON SIGHT.
WHAT KIND OF BULLSHIT IS THIS? DON'T THEY HAVE PLANS FOR THIS KIND OF THING? DIDN'T WE LEARN ANYTHING FROM 9/11?
CALM DOWN. THEY'RE TRYING TO CONTAIN THE SITUATION. MAKE SURE IT DOESN'T SPREAD.
HOW FUCKING BAD DOES IT HAVE TO BE IF THEY'LL SHOOT *PEOPLE TRYING TO ESCAPE!*
PRETTY BAD.
DAMN RIGHT, PRETTY BAD!
AND WORST OF ALL, STEPHEN IS OUT THERE. MY STEPHEN! HE'S PROBABLY ONE OF THEM!
YOU NEED TO CHILL THE FUCK OUT! GOT IT?
YOU'RE NOT THE ONLY ONE WHO PROBABLY LOST SOMEONE.

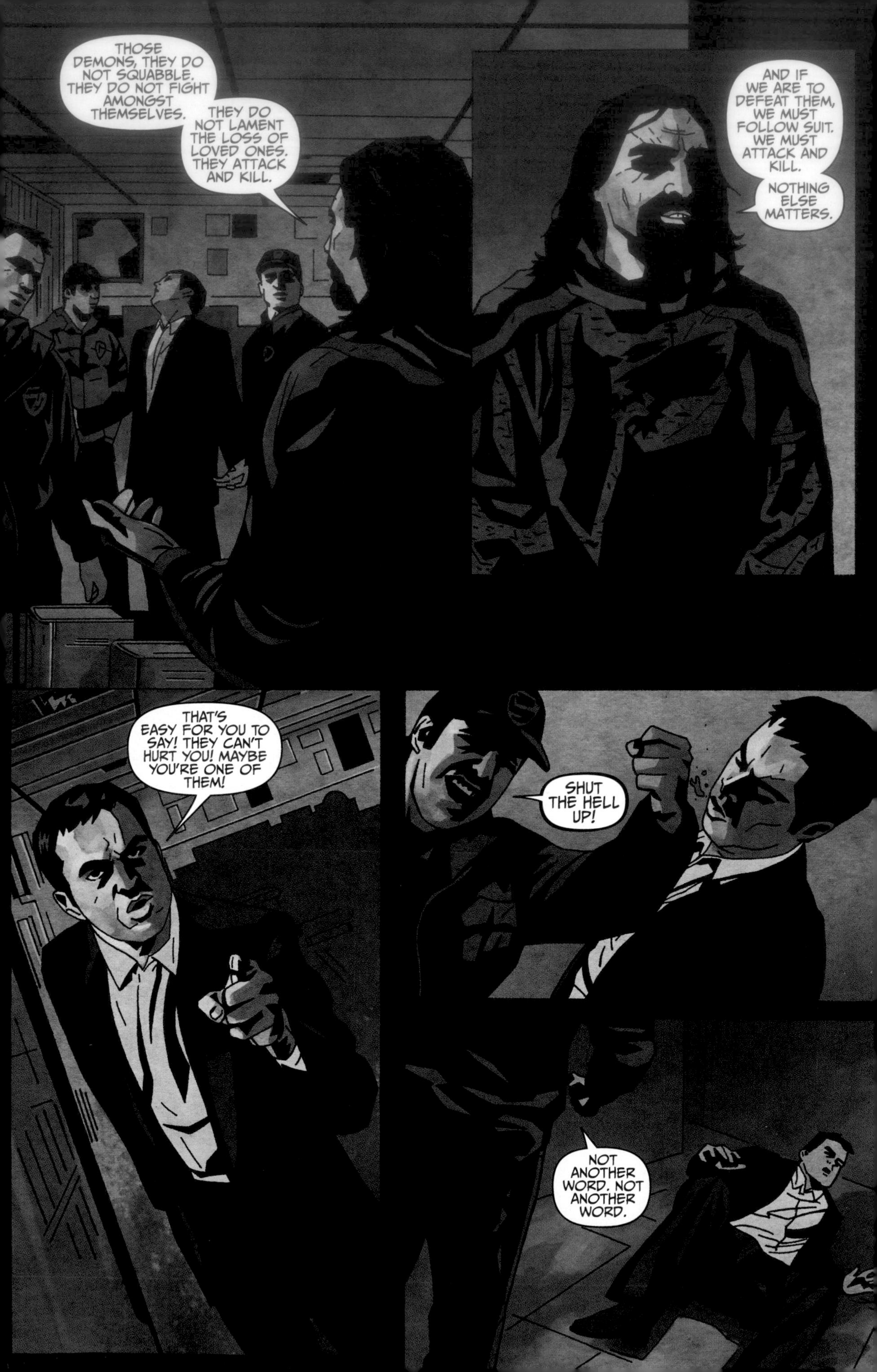
THOSE DEMONS, THEY DO NOT SQUABBLE. THEY DO NOT FIGHT AMONGST THEMSELVES.
THEY DO NOT LAMENT THE LOSS OF LOVED ONES. THEY ATTACK AND KILL.
AND IF WE ARE TO DEFEAT THEM, WE MUST FOLLOW SUIT. WE MUST ATTACK AND KILL.
NOTHING ELSE MATTERS.
THAT'S EASY FOR YOU TO SAY! THEY CAN'T HURT YOU! MAYBE YOU'RE ONE OF THEM!
SHUT THE HELL UP!
NOT ANOTHER WORD. NOT ANOTHER WORD.

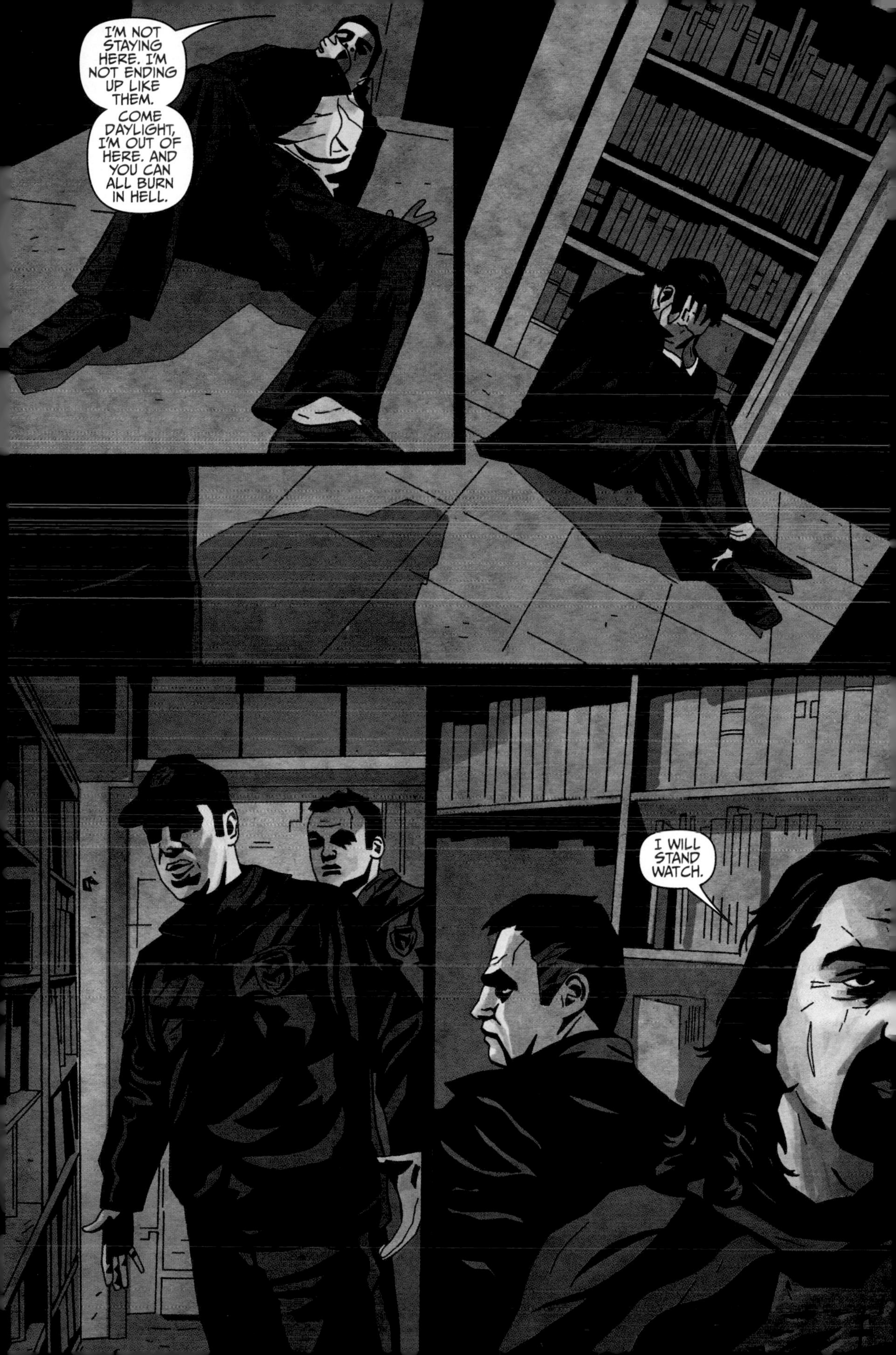
I'M NOT STAYING HERE. I'M NOT ENDING UP LIKE THEM.
COME DAYLIGHT, I'M OUT OF HERE. AND YOU CAN ALL BURN IN HELL.
I WILL STAND WATCH.

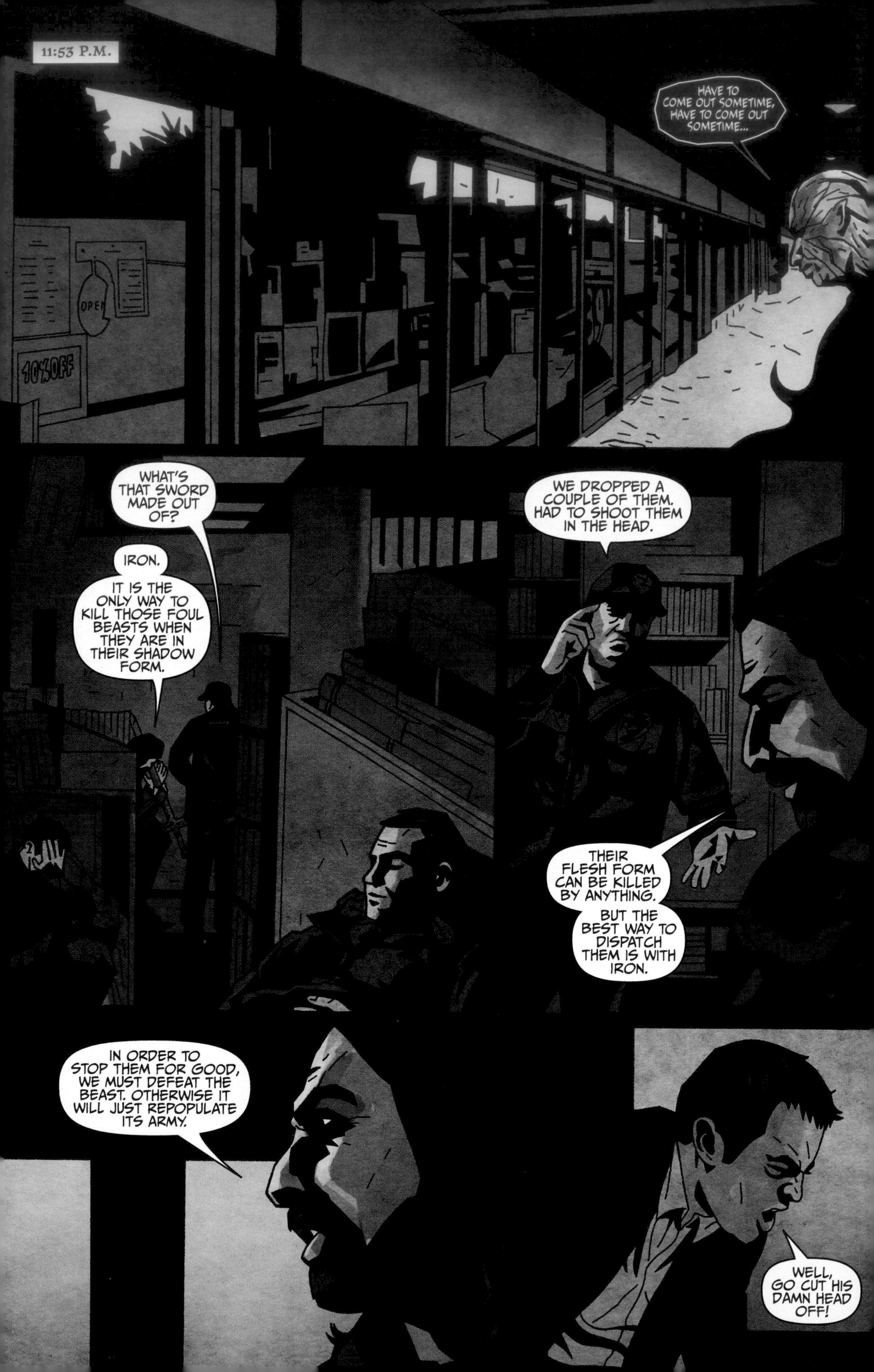
11:53 P.M.
HAVE TO COME OUT SOMETIME, HAVE TO COME OUT SOMETIME...
OPEN
10%OFF
WHAT'S THAT SWORD MADE OUT OF?
IRON.
IT IS THE ONLY WAY TO KILL THOSE FOUL BEASTS WHEN THEY ARE IN THEIR SHADOW FORM.
WE DROPPED A COUPLE OF THEM. HAD TO SHOOT THEM IN THE HEAD.
THEIR FLESH FORM CAN BE KILLED BY ANYTHING.
BUT THE BEST WAY TO DISPATCH THEM IS WITH IRON.
IN ORDER TO STOP THEM FOR GOOD, WE MUST DEFEAT THE BEAST. OTHERWISE IT WILL JUST REPOPULATE ITS ARMY.
WELL, GO CUT HIS DAMN HEAD OFF!

IF IT WERE THAT SIMPLE, I WOULD HAVE DONE THE DEED A LONG TIME AGO.
THERE IS A CEREMONY THAT I MUST PERFORM. ONCE IT IS COMPLETE, THE BEAST SHALL ONCE AGAIN BE IMPRISONED.
I DON'T SUPPOSE YOU CAN DO THAT FROM HERE?
WE MUST JOURNEY INTO ITS LAIR. ALL OF US.
THIS KEEPS GETTING BETTER AND BETTER.

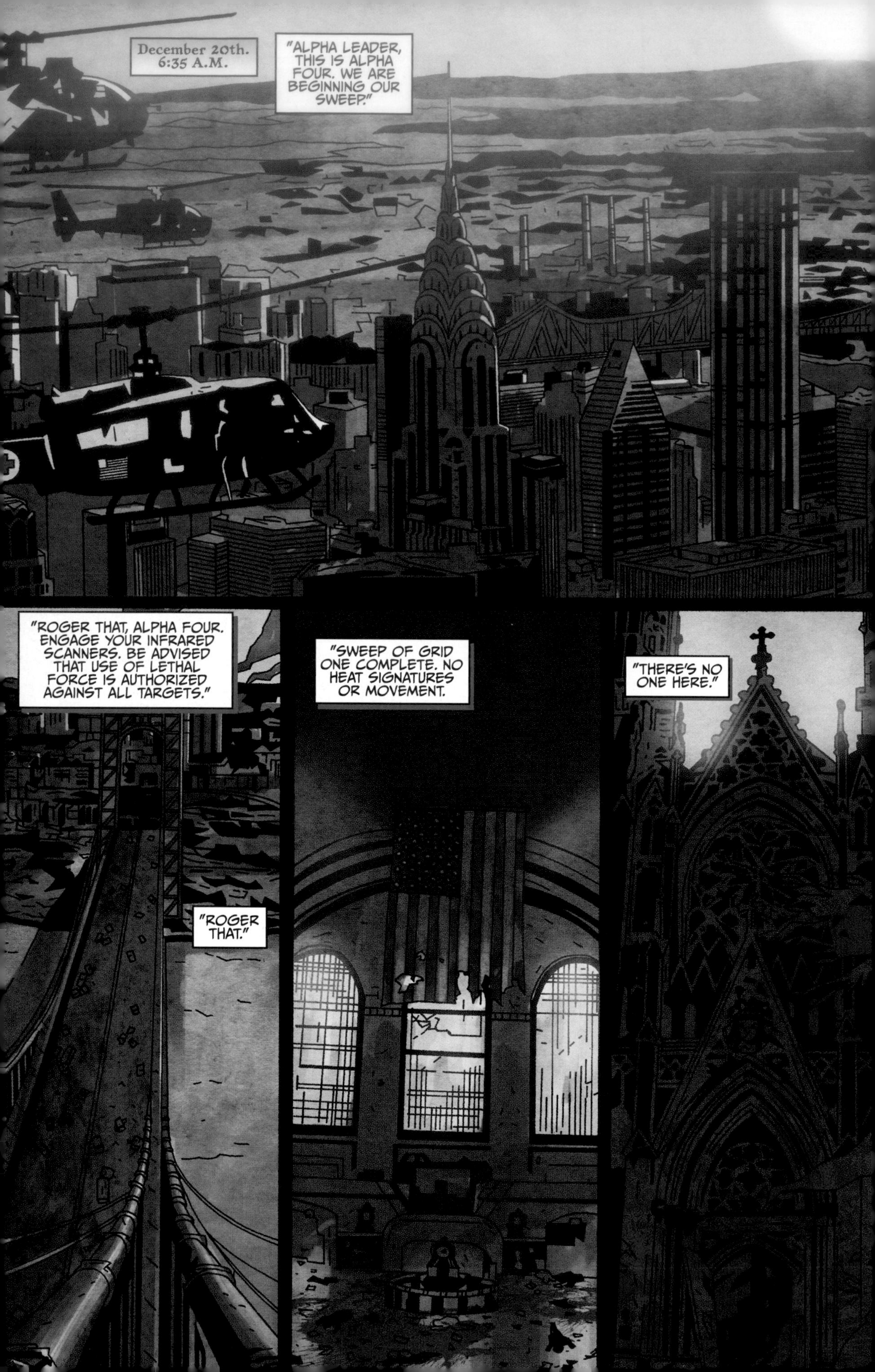
December 20th. 6:35 A.M.
"ALPHA LEADER, THIS IS ALPHA FOUR. WE ARE BEGINNING OUR SWEEP."
"ROGER THAT, ALPHA FOUR. ENGAGE YOUR INFRARED SCANNERS. BE ADVISED THAT USE OF LETHAL FORCE IS AUTHORIZED AGAINST ALL TARGETS."
"ROGER THAT."
"SWEEP OF GRID ONE COMPLETE. NO HEAT SIGNATURES OR MOVEMENT.
"THERE'S NO ONE HERE."

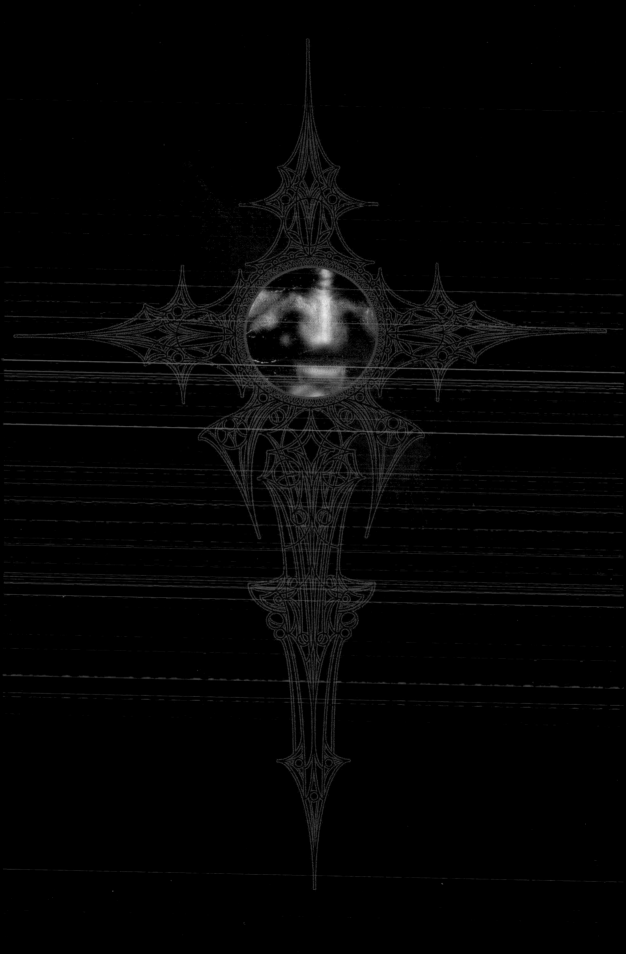

FORSAKEN
{Issue #5}

WRITTEN BY:
WILLIAM HARMS

PENCILS, INKS & COLORS BY:
FRANCIS TSAI

LETTERING BY:
TROY PETERI

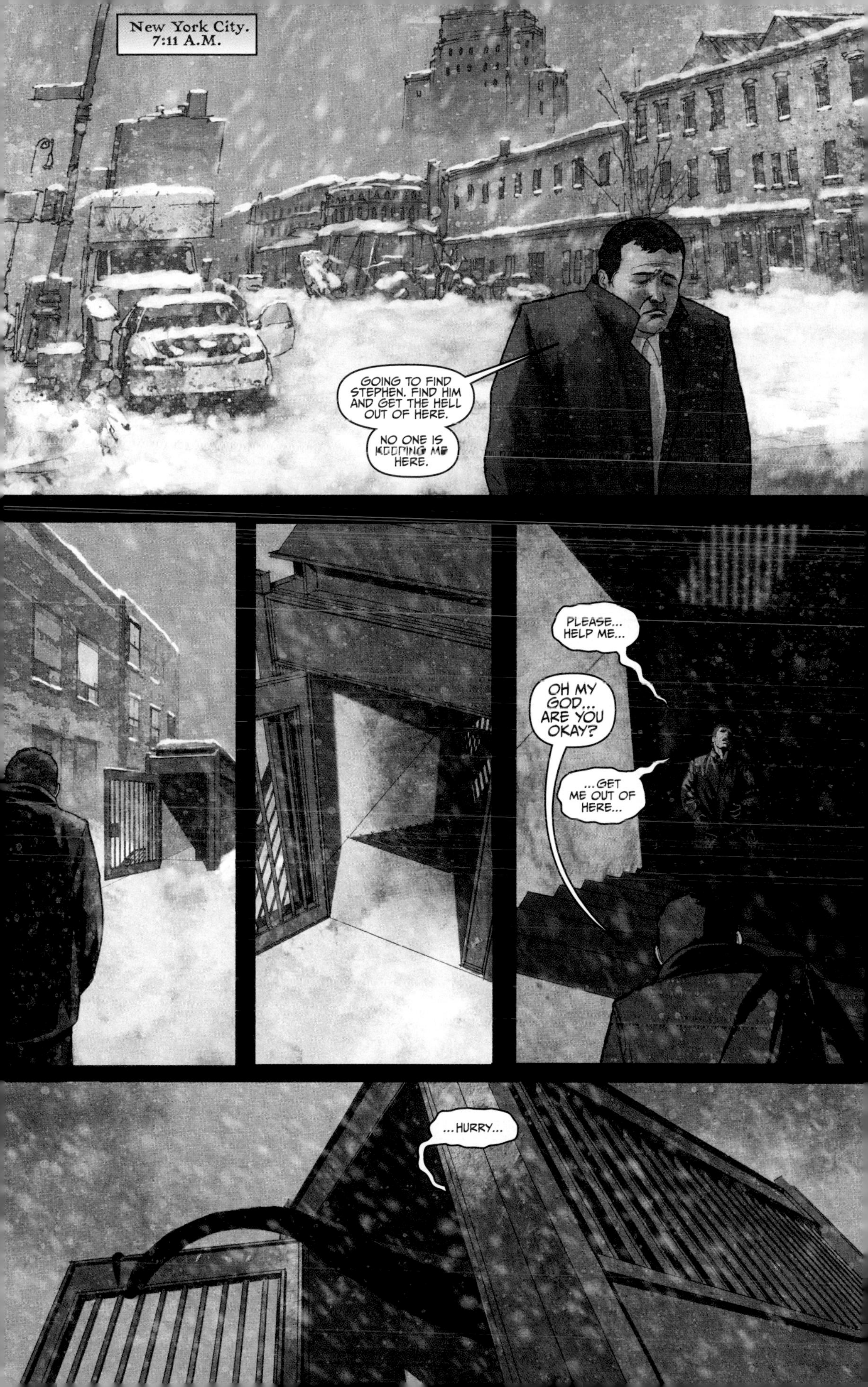
New York City.
7:11 A.M.
GOING TO FIND STEPHEN. FIND HIM AND GET THE HELL OUT OF HERE.
NO ONE IS KEEPING ME HERE.
PLEASE... HELP ME...
OH MY GOD... ARE YOU OKAY?
...GET ME OUT OF HERE...
...HURRY...

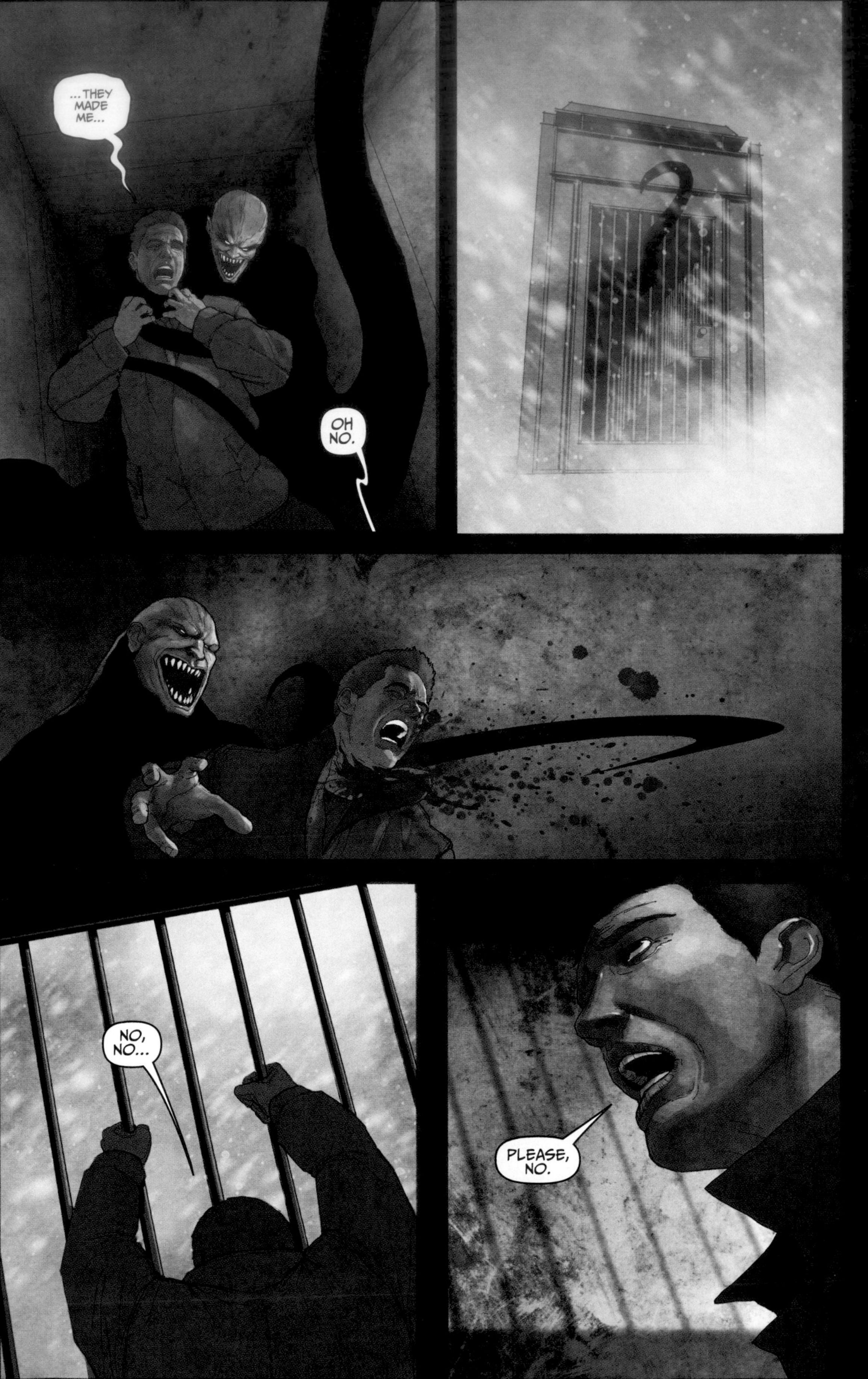
...THEY MADE ME...
OH NO.
NO, NO...
PLEASE, NO.

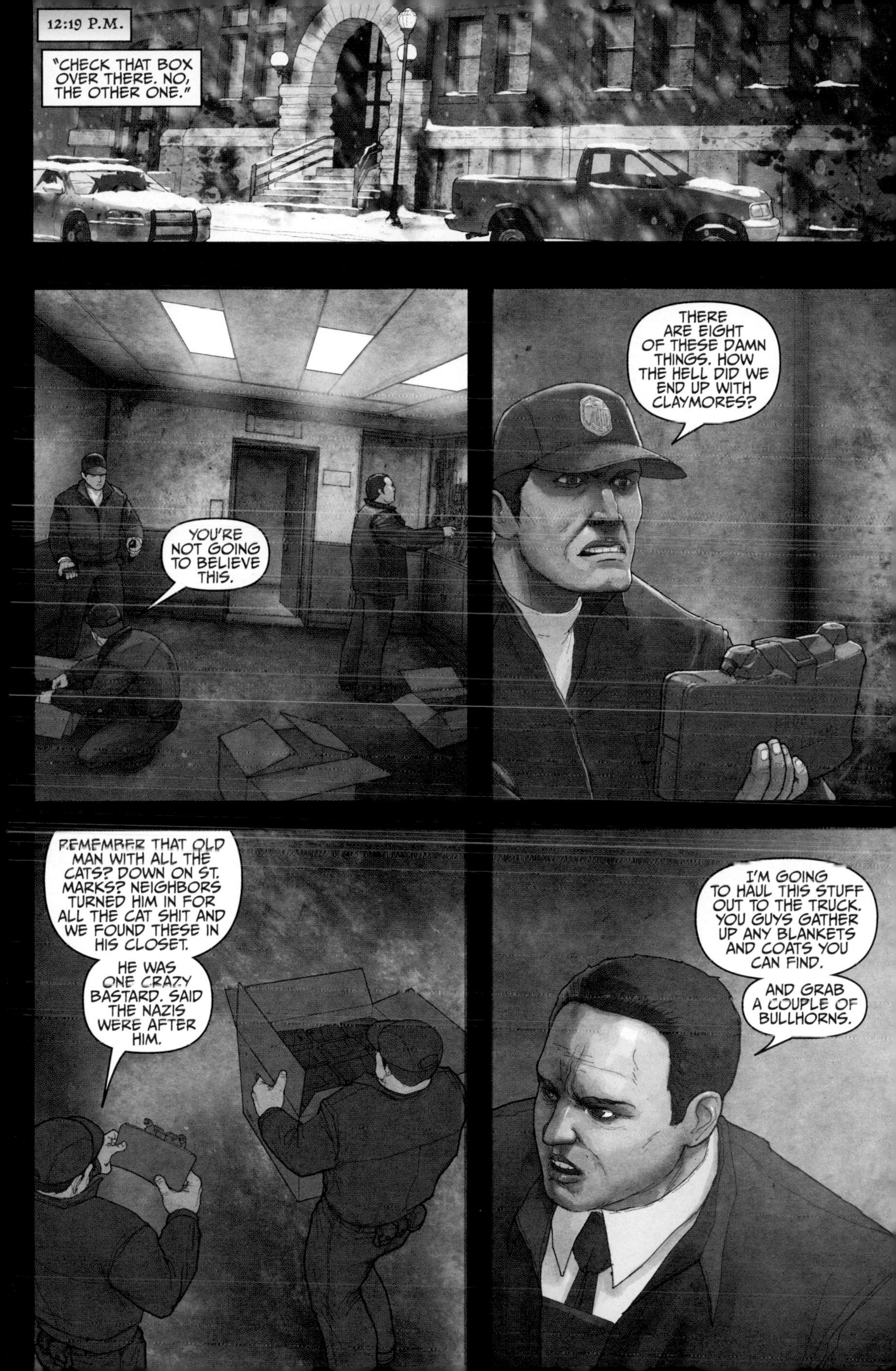
12:19 P.M.
"CHECK THAT BOX OVER THERE. NO, THE OTHER ONE."
YOU'RE NOT GOING TO BELIEVE THIS.
THERE ARE EIGHT OF THESE DAMN THINGS. HOW THE HELL DID WE END UP WITH CLAYMORES?
REMEMBER THAT OLD MAN WITH ALL THE CATS? DOWN ON ST. MARKS? NEIGHBORS TURNED HIM IN FOR ALL THE CAT SHIT AND WE FOUND THESE IN HIS CLOSET.
HE WAS ONE CRAZY BASTARD. SAID THE NAZIS WERE AFTER HIM.
I'M GOING TO HAUL THIS STUFF OUT TO THE TRUCK. YOU GUYS GATHER UP ANY BLANKETS AND COATS YOU CAN FIND.
AND GRAB A COUPLE OF BULLHORNS.

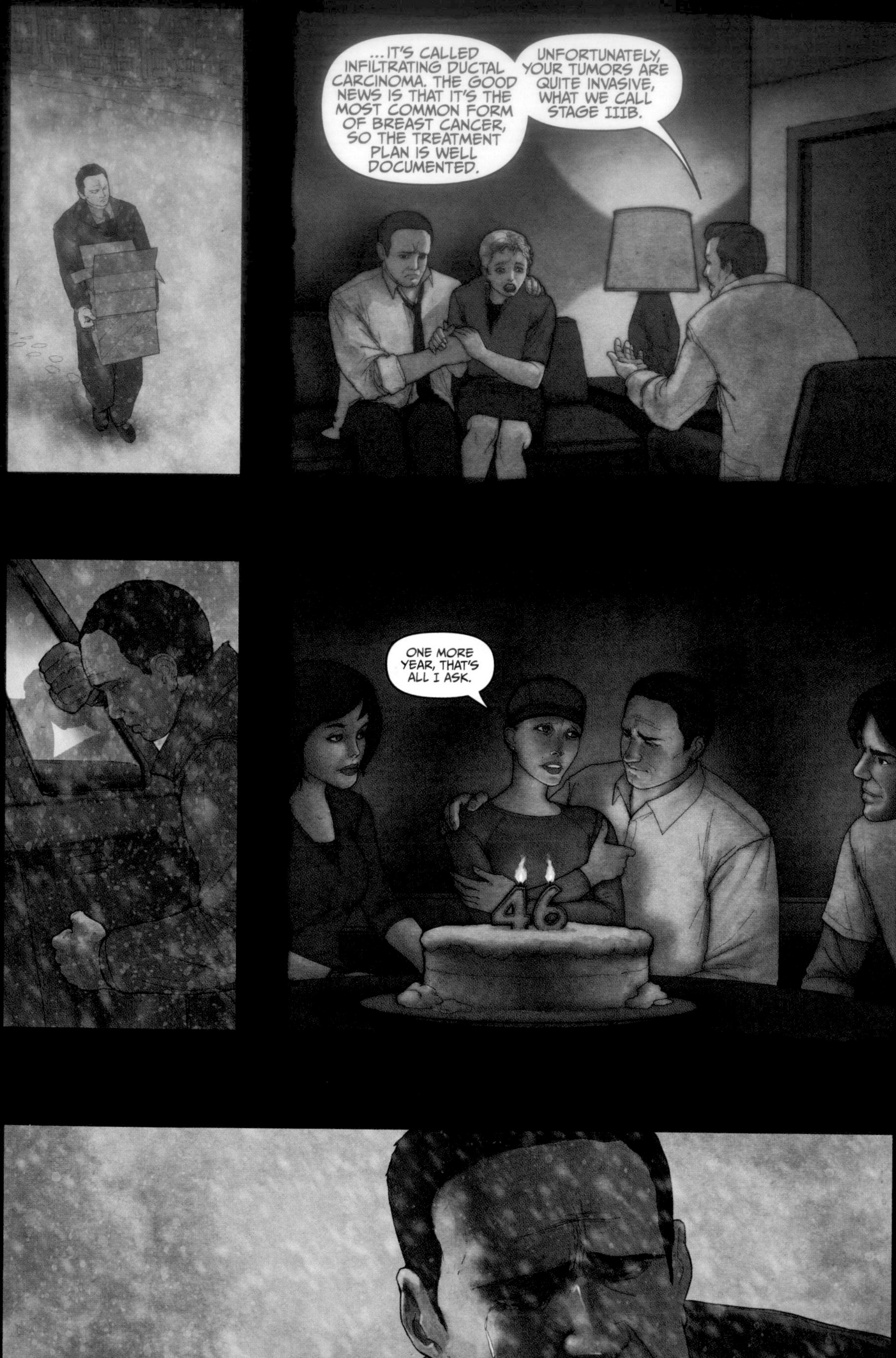
...IT'S CALLED INFILTRATING DUCTAL CARCINOMA. THE GOOD NEWS IS THAT IT'S THE MOST COMMON FORM OF BREAST CANCER, SO THE TREATMENT PLAN IS WELL DOCUMENTED.
UNFORTUNATELY, YOUR TUMORS ARE QUITE INVASIVE, WHAT WE CALL STAGE IIIB.
ONE MORE YEAR, THAT'S ALL I ASK.
46

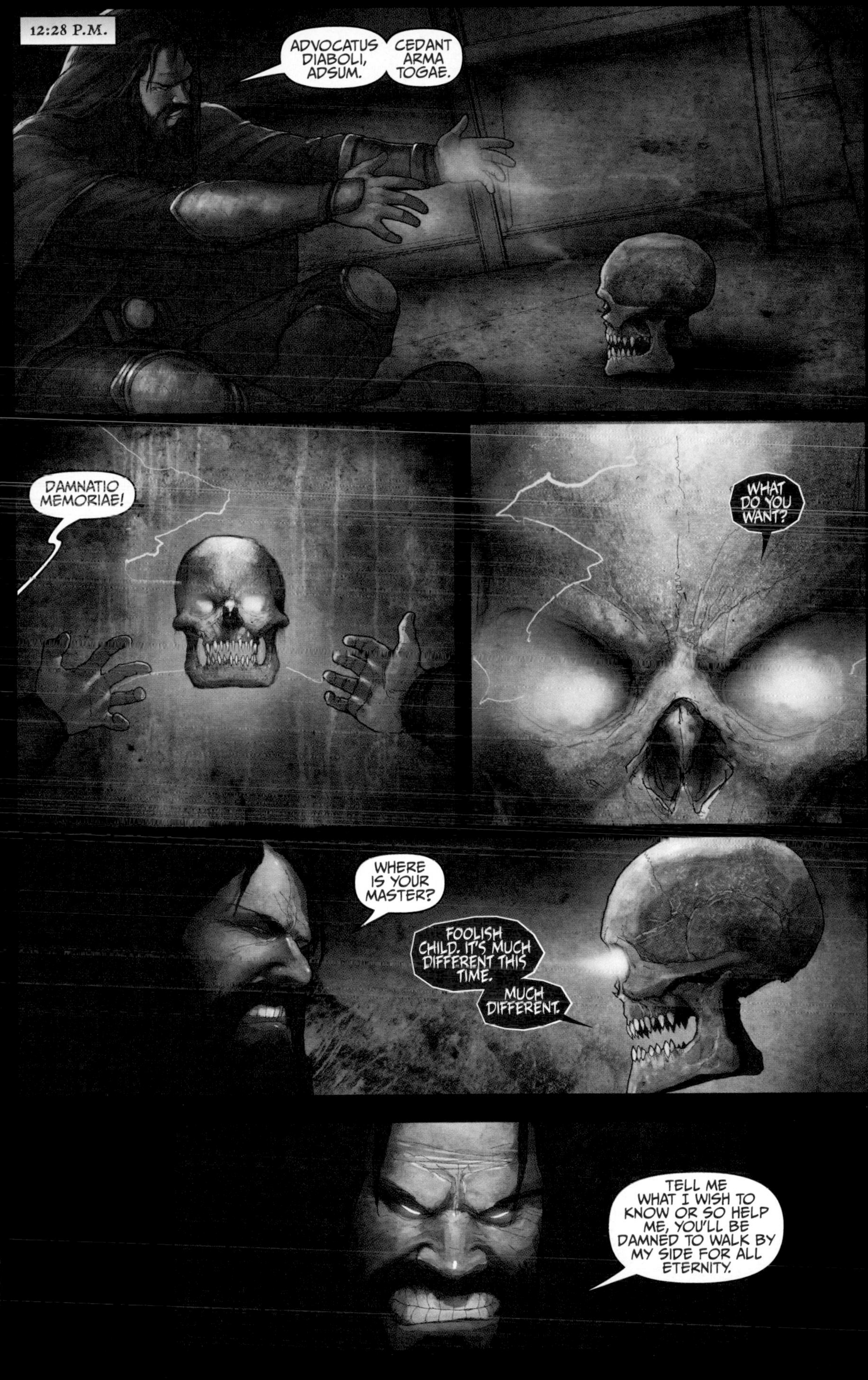
12:28 P.M.
ADVOCATUS DIABOLI, ADSUM.
CEDANT ARMA TOGAE.
DAMNATIO MEMORIAE!
WHAT DO YOU WANT?
WHERE IS YOUR MASTER?
FOOLISH CHILD. IT'S MUCH DIFFERENT THIS TIME.
MUCH DIFFERENT.
TELL ME WHAT I WISH TO KNOW OR SO HELP ME, YOU'LL BE DAMNED TO WALK BY MY SIDE FOR ALL ETERNITY.

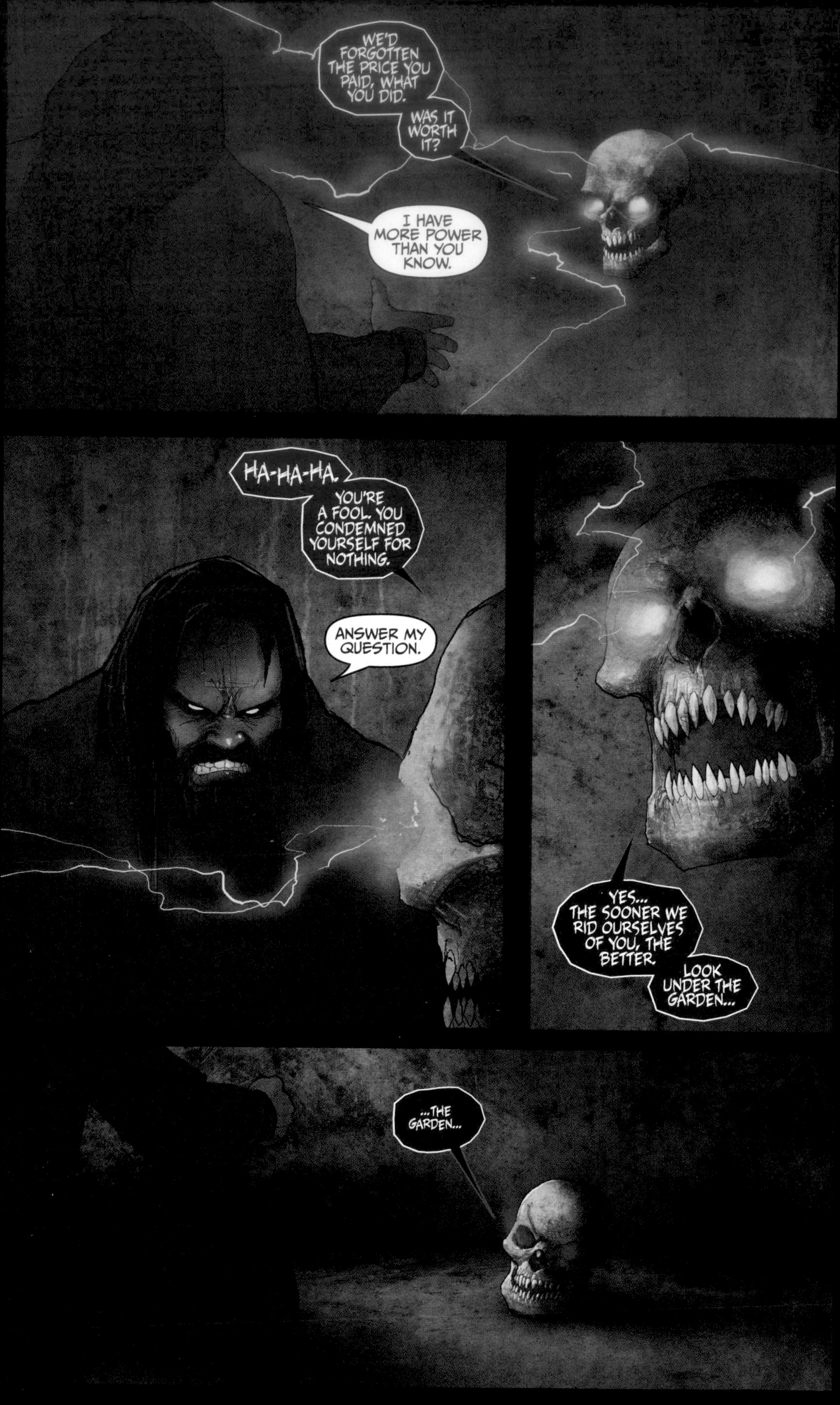

WE'D FORGOTTEN THE PRICE YOU PAID, WHAT YOU DID.
WAS IT WORTH IT?
I HAVE MORE POWER THAN YOU KNOW.
HA-HA-HA.
YOU'RE A FOOL. YOU CONDEMNED YOURSELF FOR NOTHING.
ANSWER MY QUESTION.
YES... THE SOONER WE RID OURSELVES OF YOU, THE BETTER.
LOOK UNDER THE GARDEN...
...THE GARDEN...

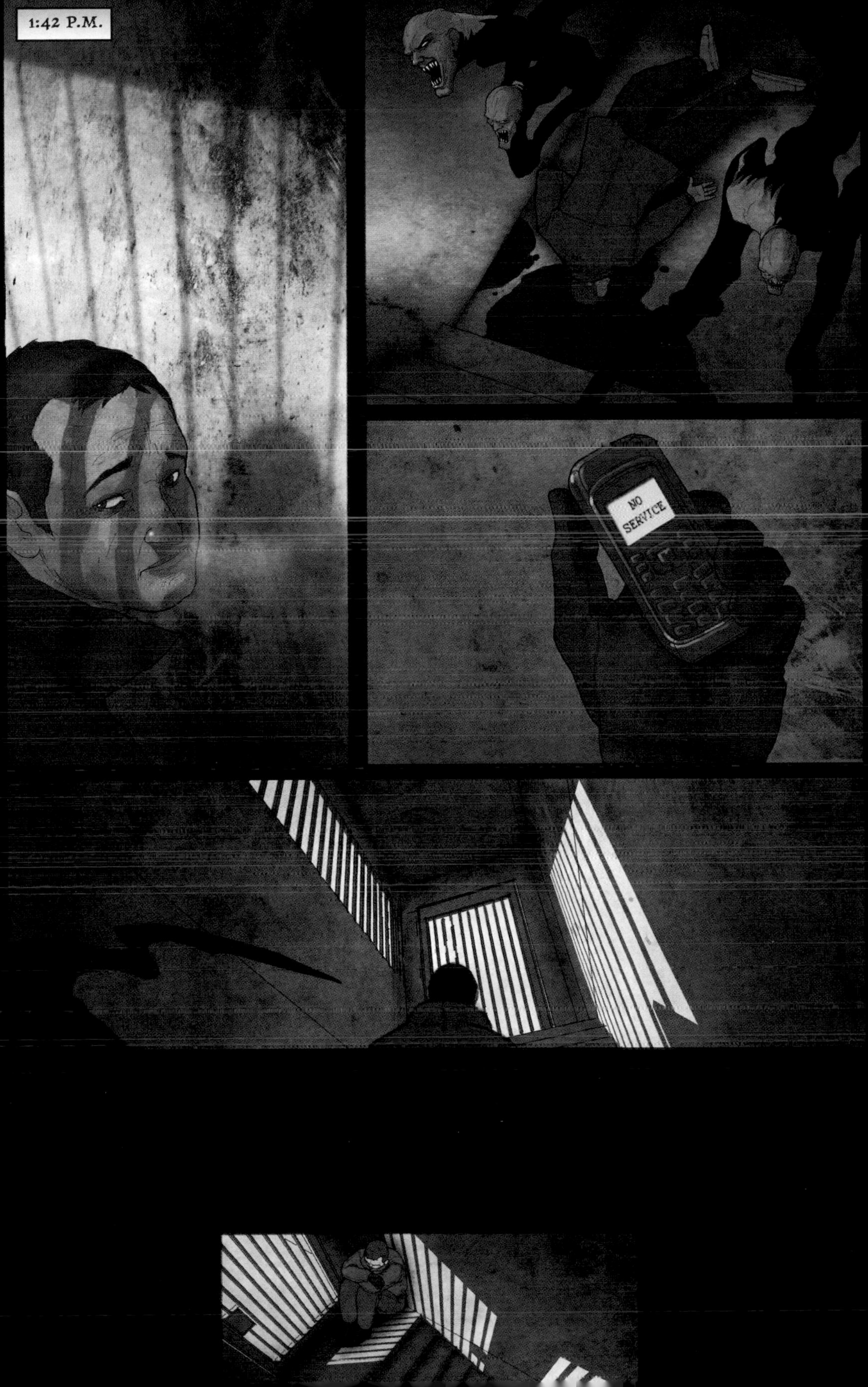
1:42 P.M.
NO SERVICE

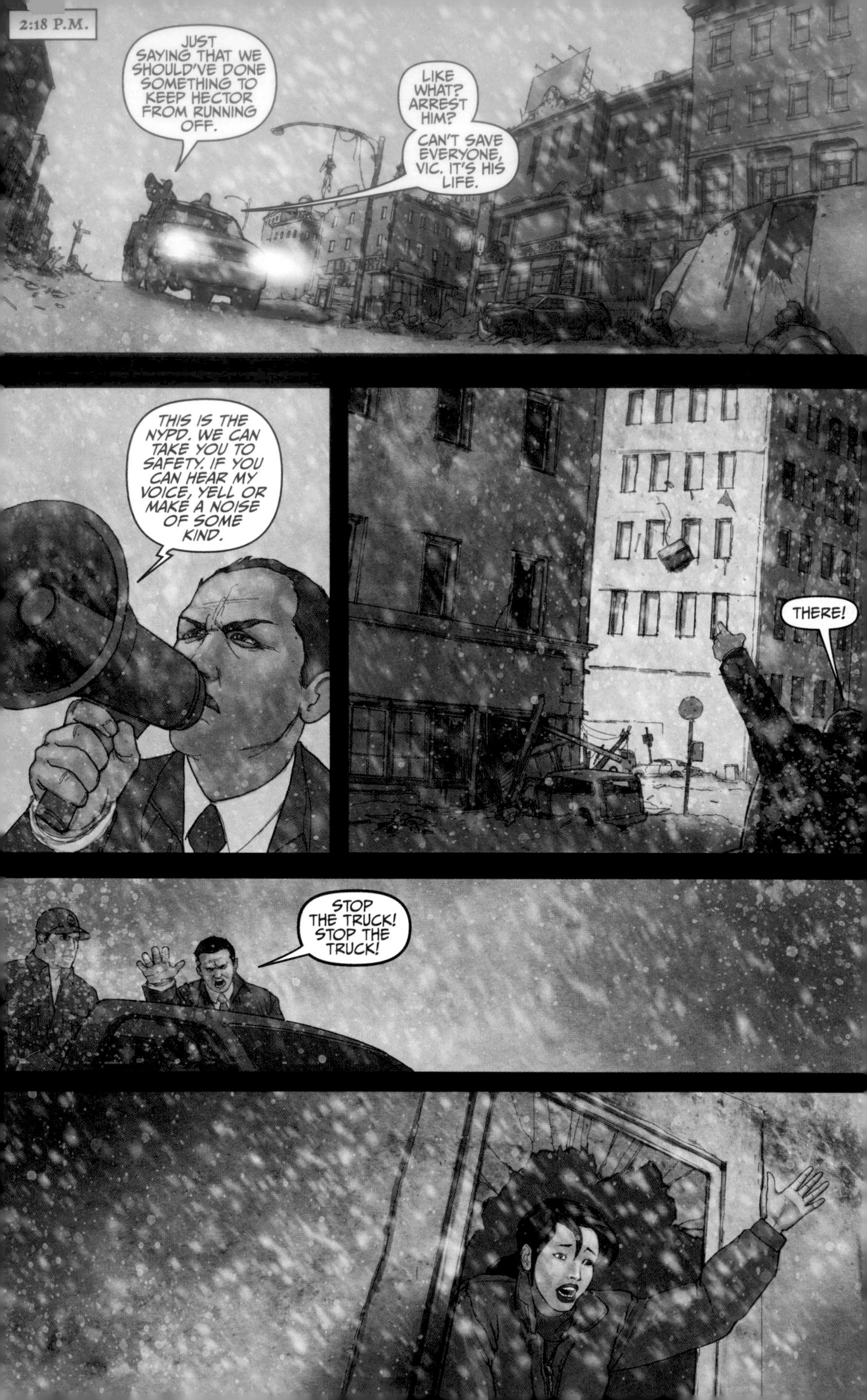
2:18 P.M.
JUST SAYING THAT WE SHOULD'VE DONE SOMETHING TO KEEP HECTOR FROM RUNNING OFF.
LIKE WHAT? ARREST HIM?
CAN'T SAVE EVERYONE, VIC. IT'S HIS LIFE.
THIS IS THE NYPD. WE CAN TAKE YOU TO SAFETY. IF YOU CAN HEAR MY VOICE, YELL OR MAKE A NOISE OF SOME KIND.
THERE!
STOP THE TRUCK! STOP THE TRUCK!

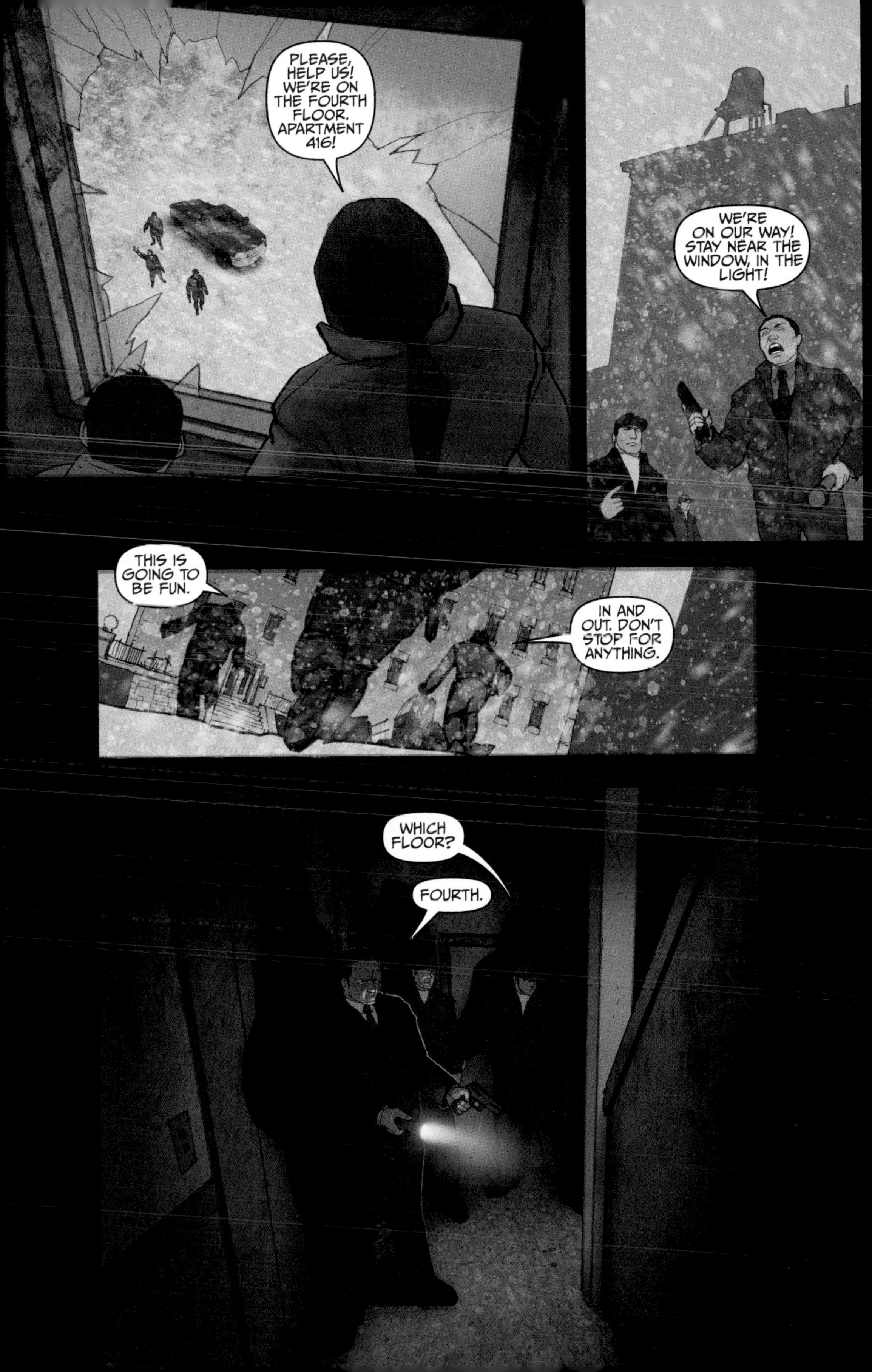
PLEASE, HELP US! WE'RE ON THE FOURTH FLOOR. APARTMENT 416!
WE'RE ON OUR WAY! STAY NEAR THE WINDOW, IN THE LIGHT!
THIS IS GOING TO BE FUN.
IN AND OUT. DON'T STOP FOR ANYTHING.
WHICH FLOOR?
FOURTH.

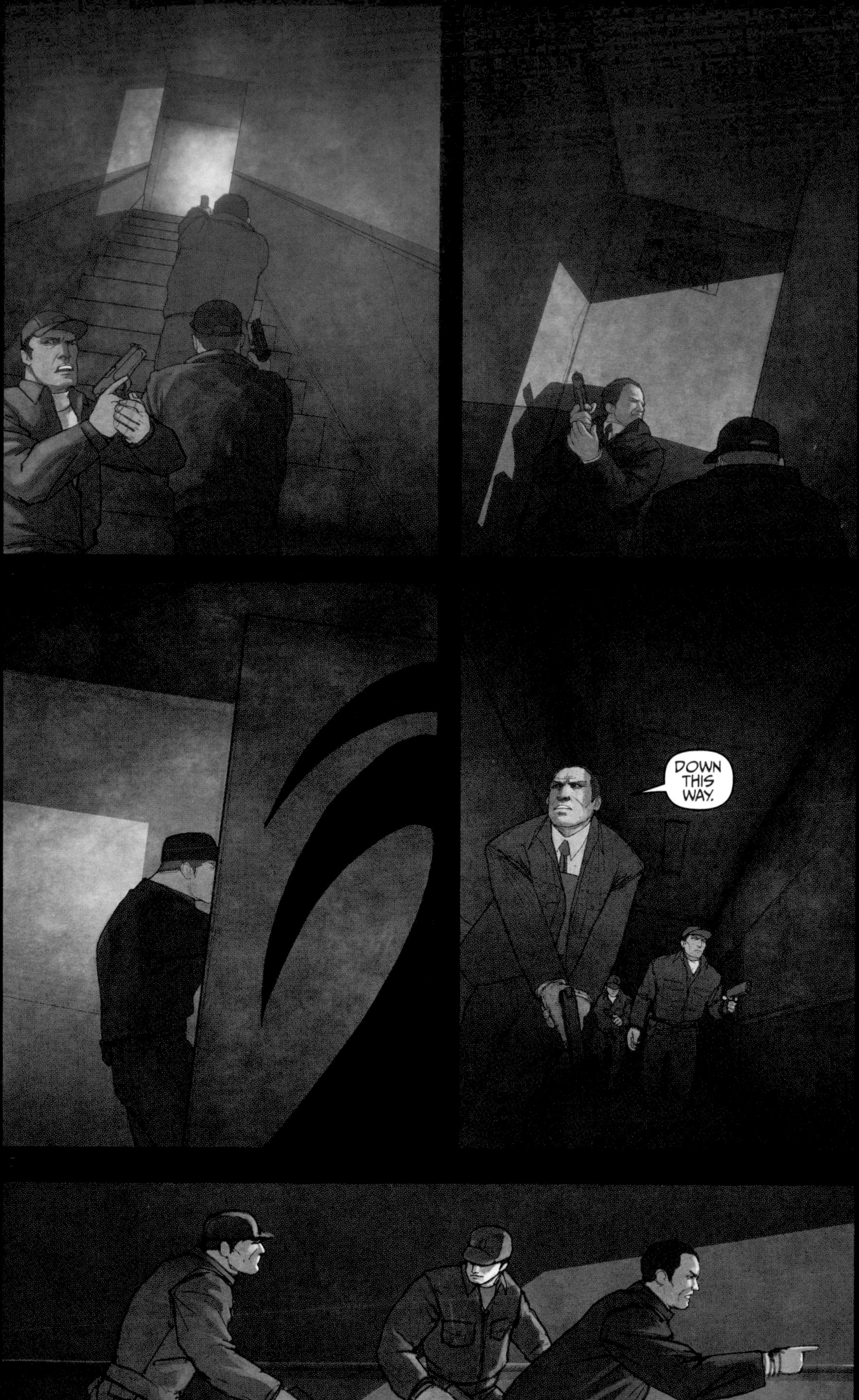
DOWN THIS WAY.

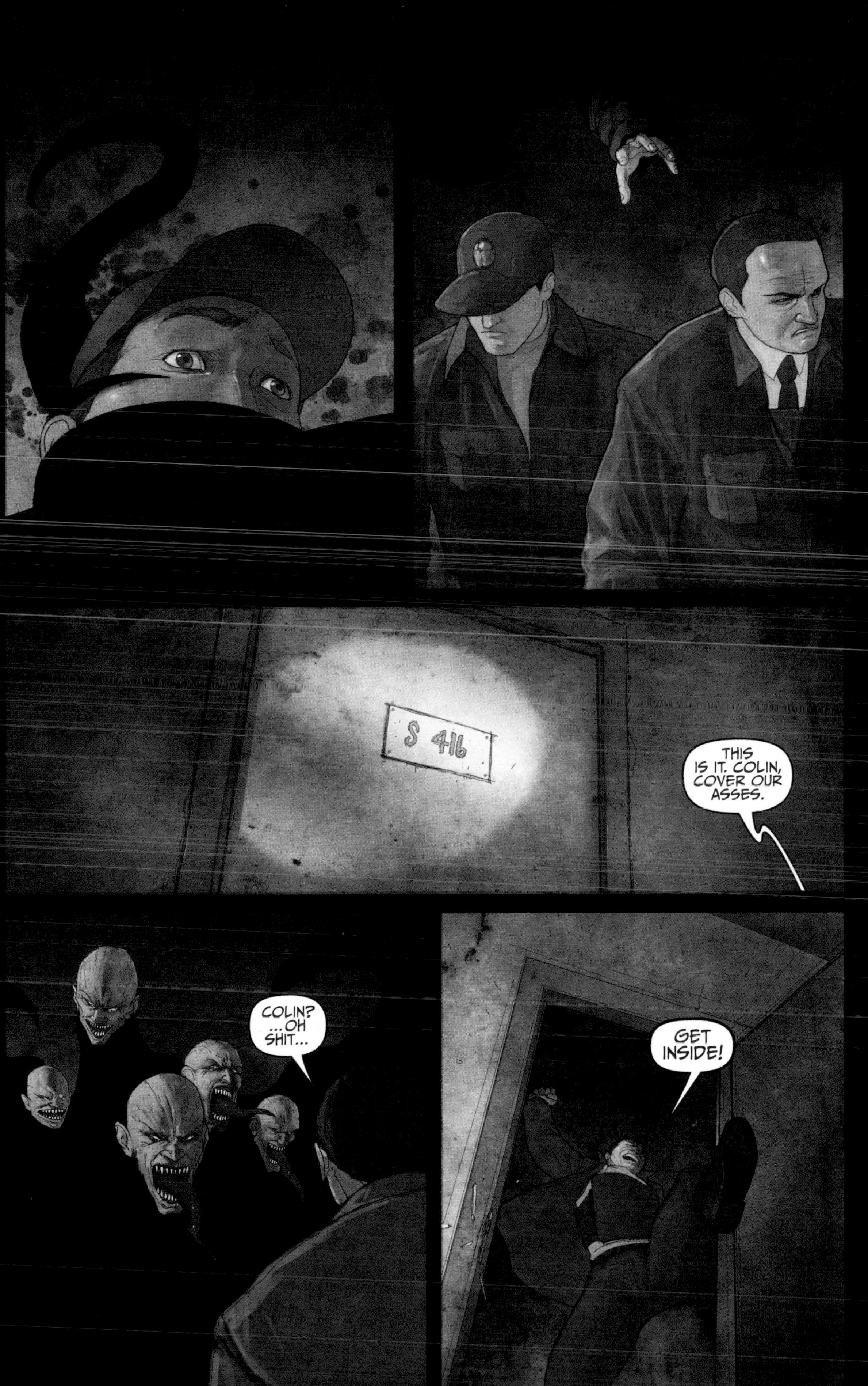
S 416
THIS IS IT. COLIN, COVER OUR ASSES.
COLIN? ...OH SHIT...
GET INSIDE!

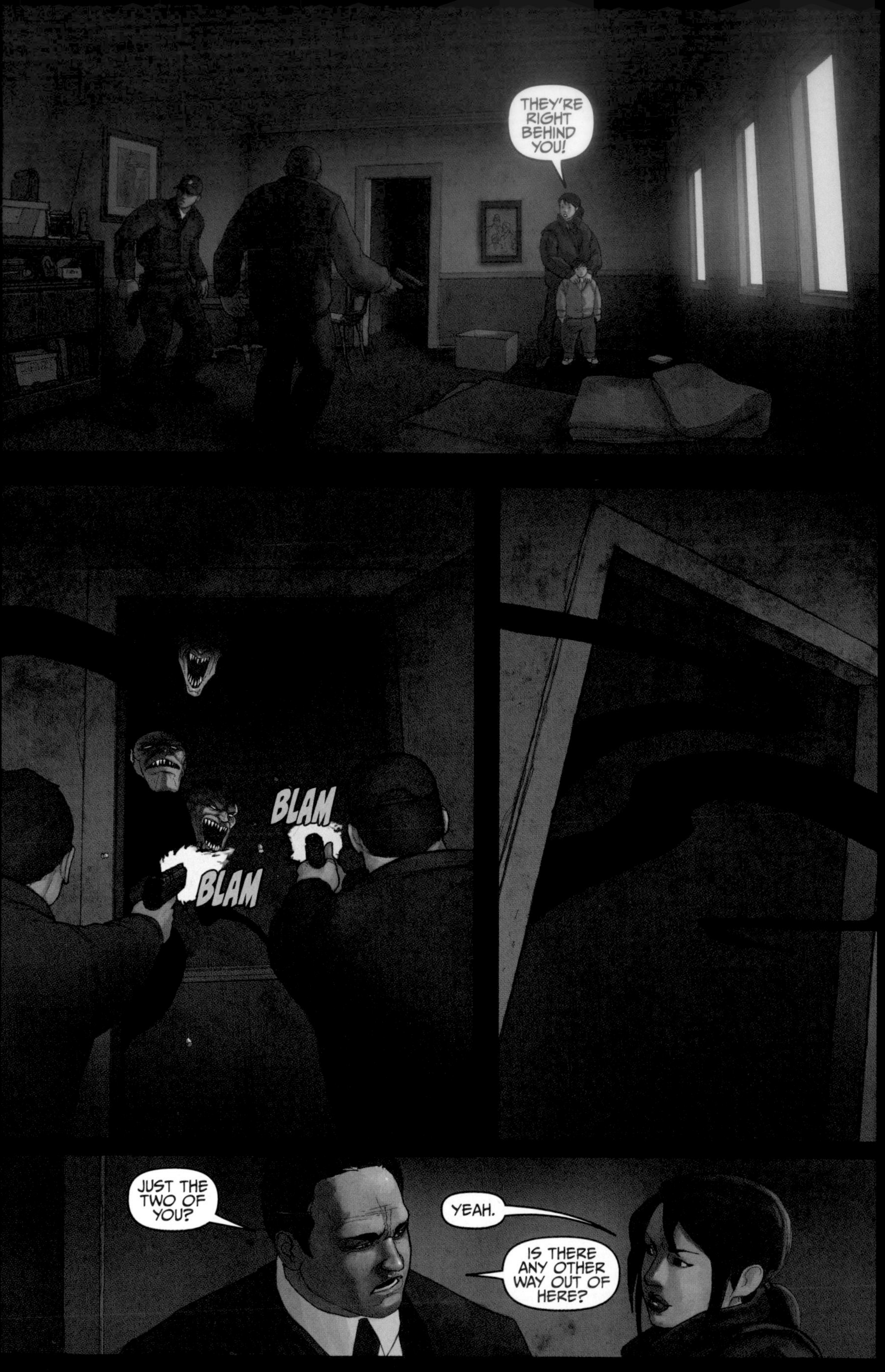
THEY'RE RIGHT BEHIND YOU!
BLAM
BLAM
JUST THE TWO OF YOU?
YEAH.
IS THERE ANY OTHER WAY OUT OF HERE?

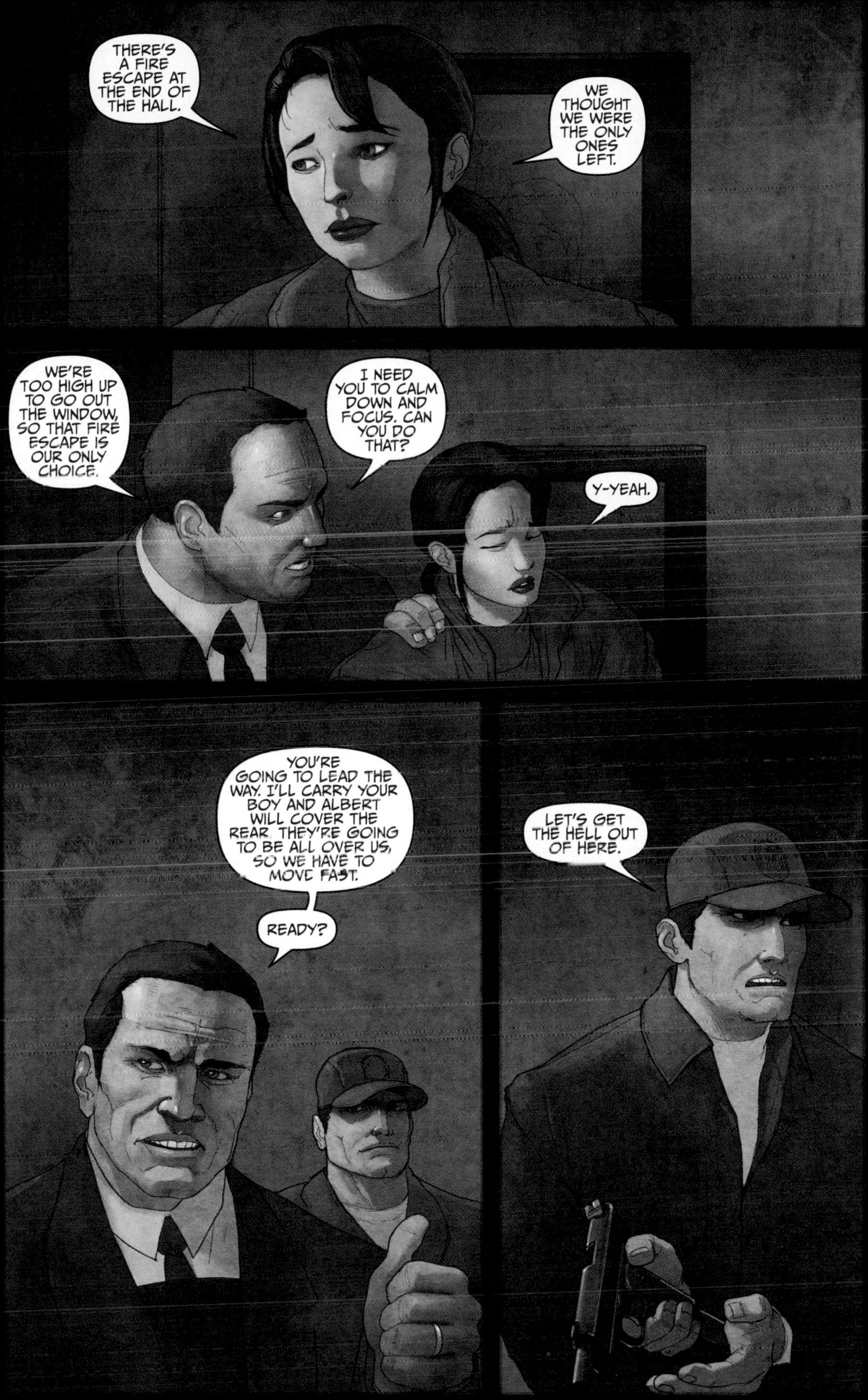
THERE'S A FIRE ESCAPE AT THE END OF THE HALL.
WE THOUGHT WE WERE THE ONLY ONES LEFT.
WE'RE TOO HIGH UP TO GO OUT THE WINDOW, SO THAT FIRE ESCAPE IS OUR ONLY CHOICE.
I NEED YOU TO CALM DOWN AND FOCUS. CAN YOU DO THAT?
Y-YEAH.
YOU'RE GOING TO LEAD THE WAY. I'LL CARRY YOUR BOY AND ALBERT WILL COVER THE REAR. THEY'RE GOING TO BE ALL OVER US, SO WE HAVE TO MOVE FAST.
READY?
LET'S GET THE HELL OUT OF HERE.

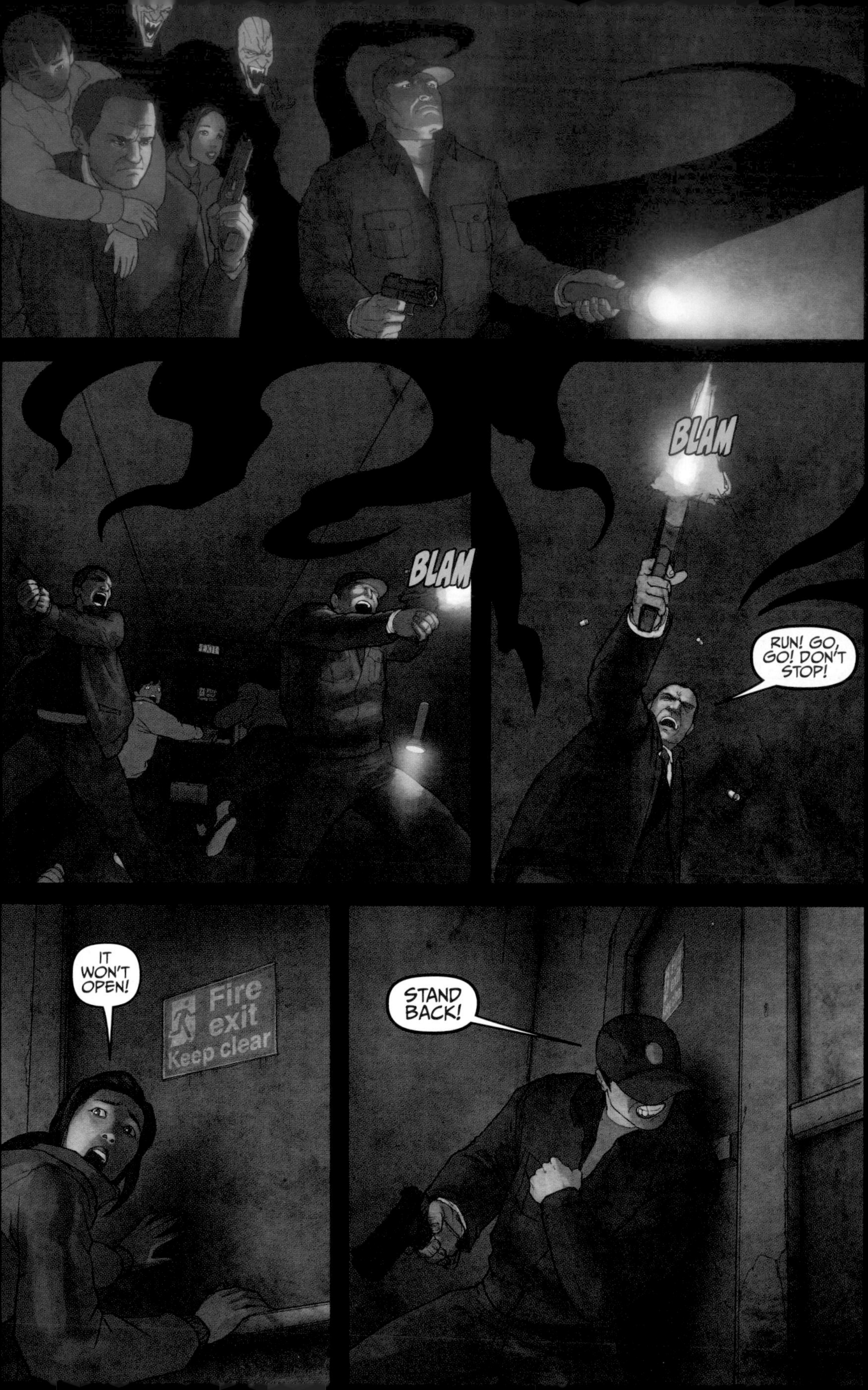
BLAM
BLAM
RUN! GO, GO! DON'T STOP!
IT WON'T OPEN!
Fire exit Keep clear
STAND BACK!

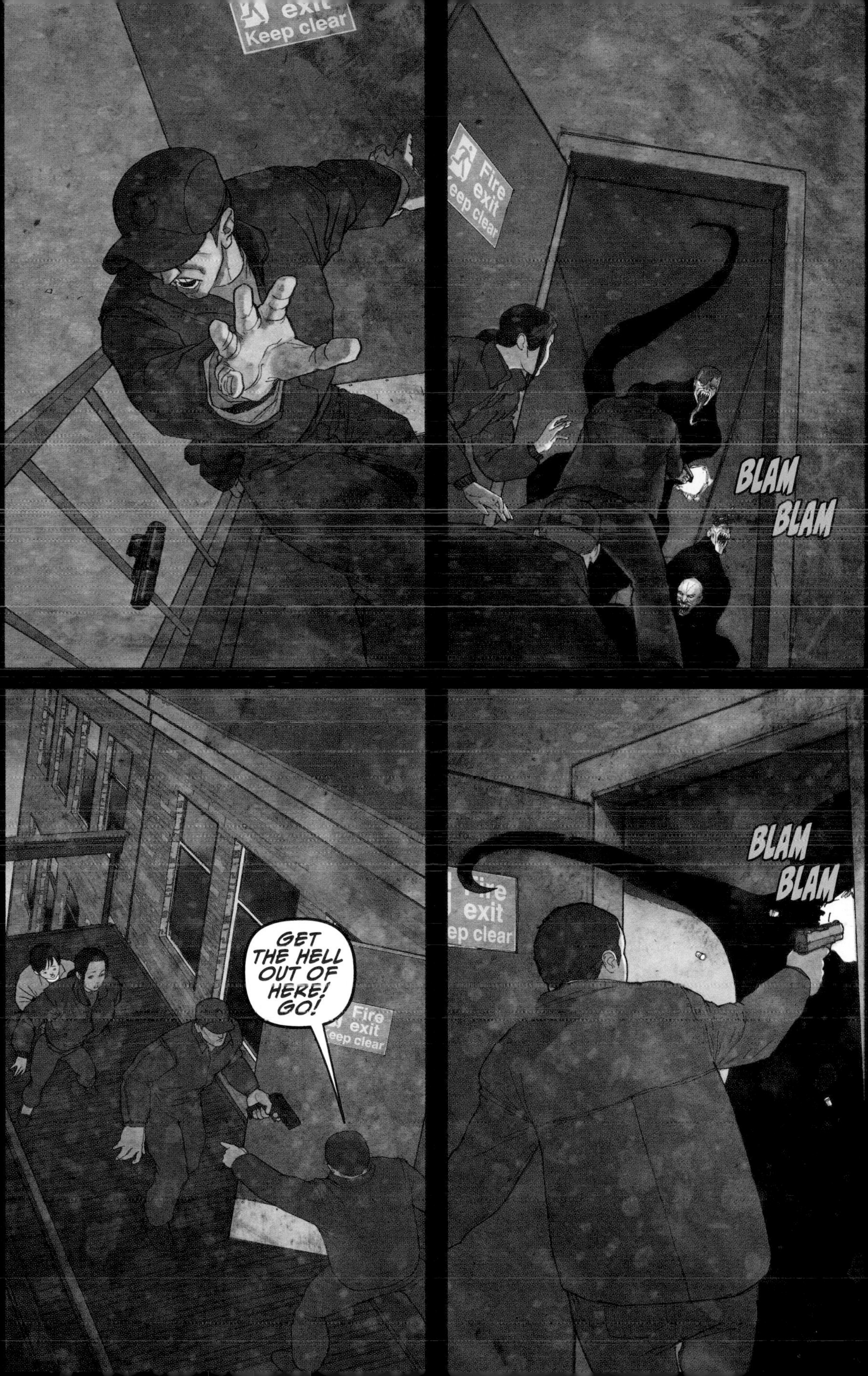
exit
Keep clear
Fire
exit
Keep clear
BLAM
BLAM
GET THE HELL OUT OF HERE! GO!
Fire
exit
Keep clear
Fire
exit
Keep clear
BLAM
BLAM

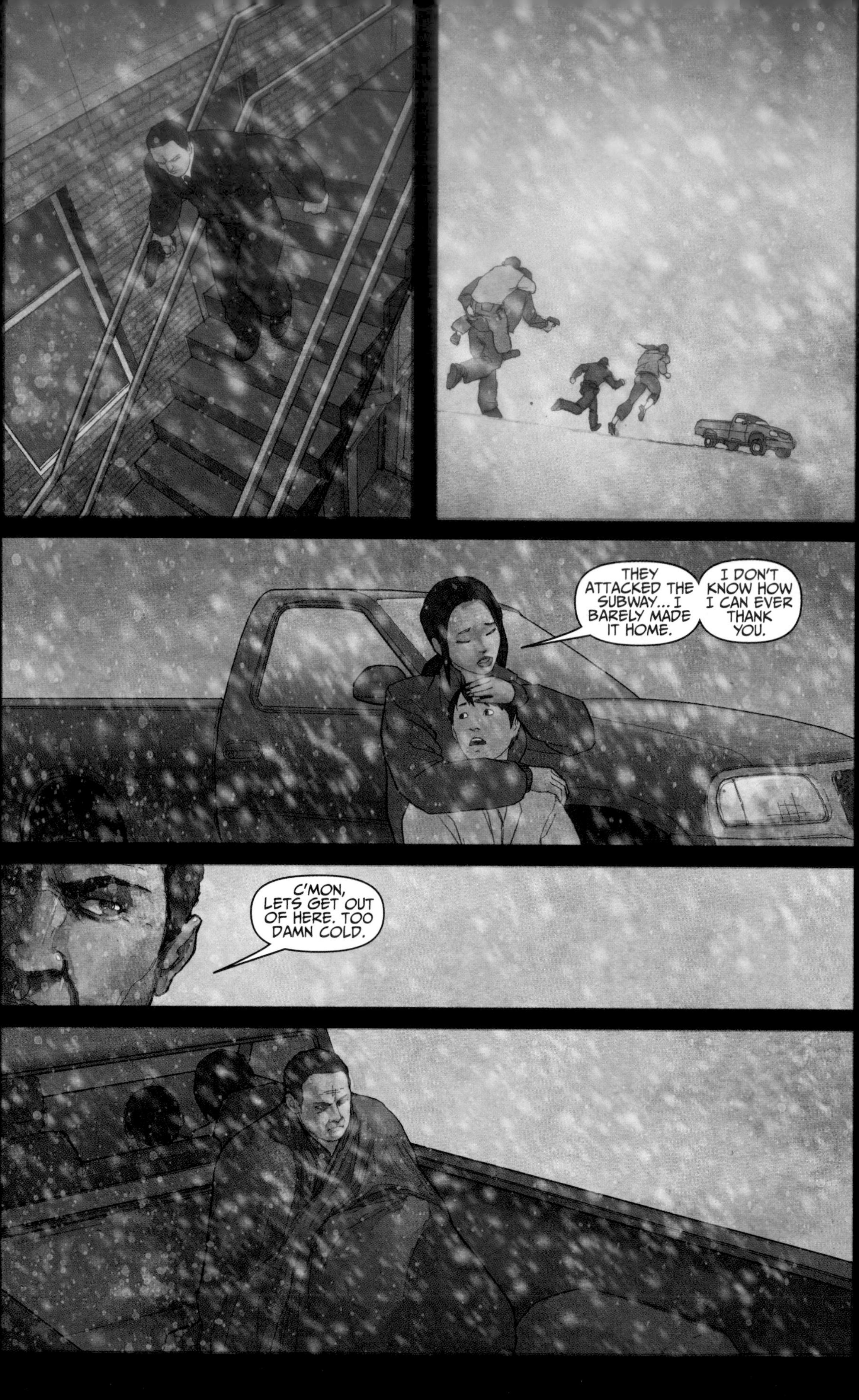
THEY ATTACKED THE SUBWAY... I BARELY MADE IT HOME.
I DON'T KNOW HOW I CAN EVER THANK YOU.
C'MON, LETS GET OUT OF HERE. TOO DAMN COLD.

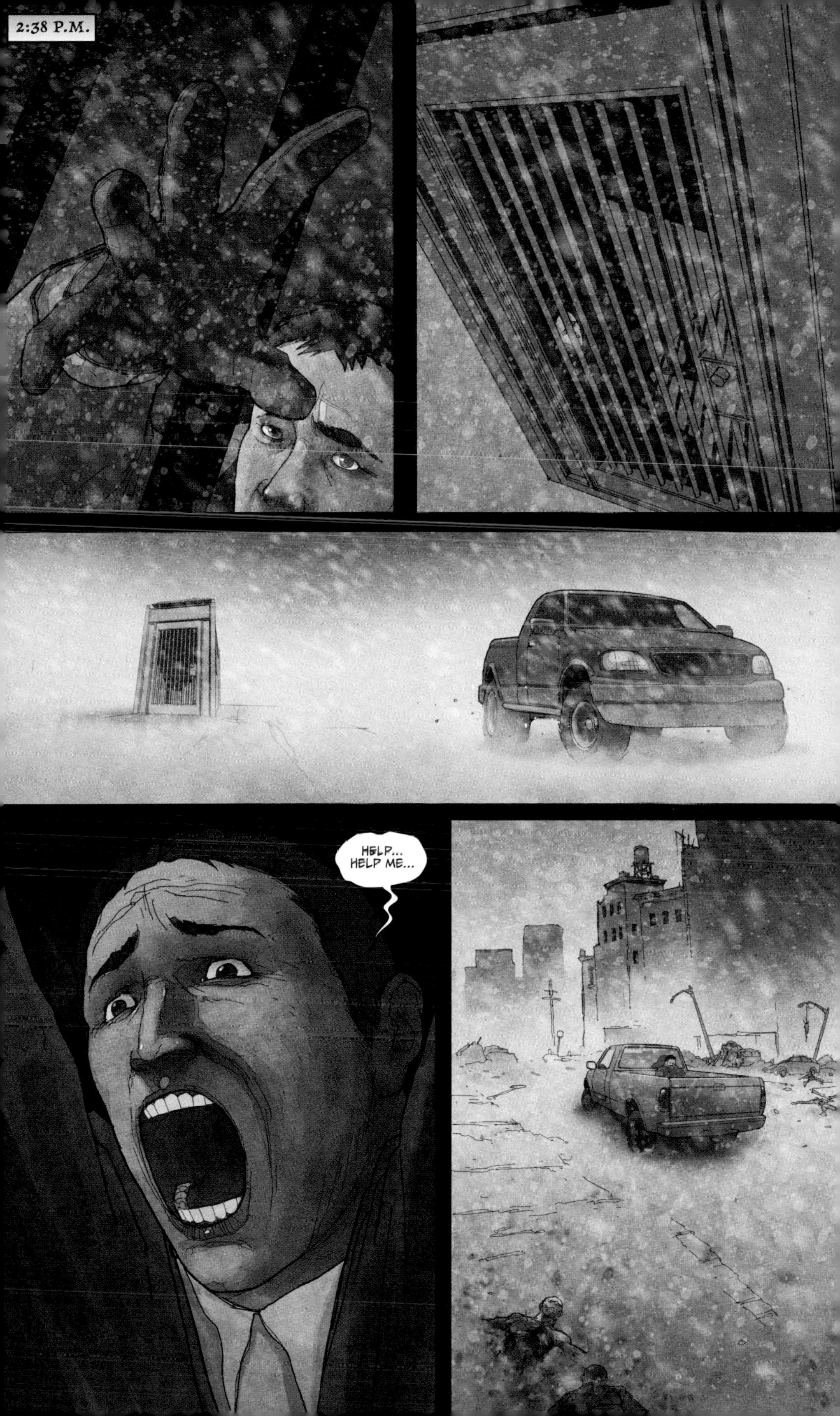
2:38 P.M.
HELP... HELP ME...

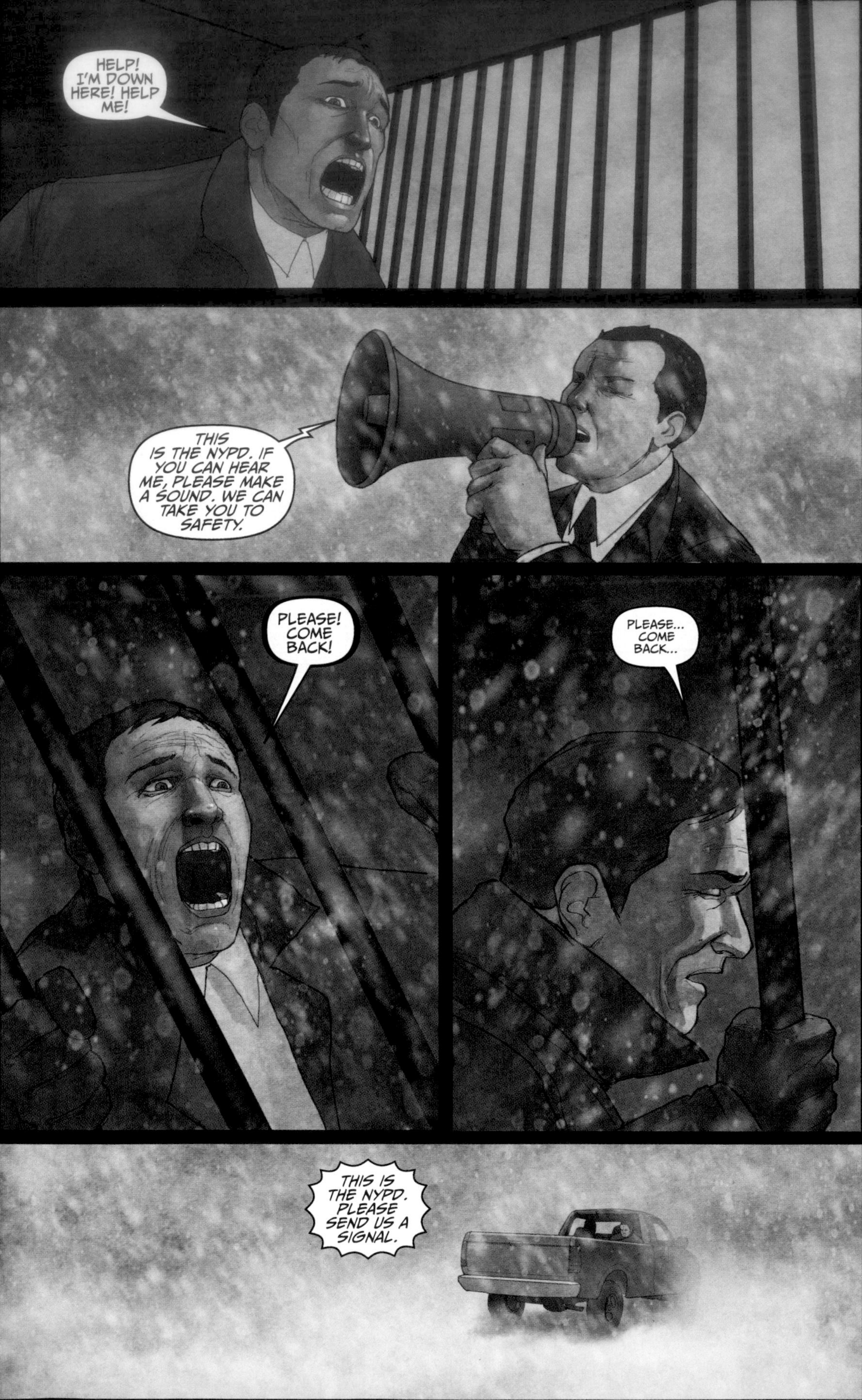
HELP! I'M DOWN HERE! HELP ME!
THIS IS THE NYPD. IF YOU CAN HEAR ME, PLEASE MAKE A SOUND. WE CAN TAKE YOU TO SAFETY.
PLEASE! COME BACK!
PLEASE... COME BACK...
THIS IS THE NYPD. PLEASE SEND US A SIGNAL.

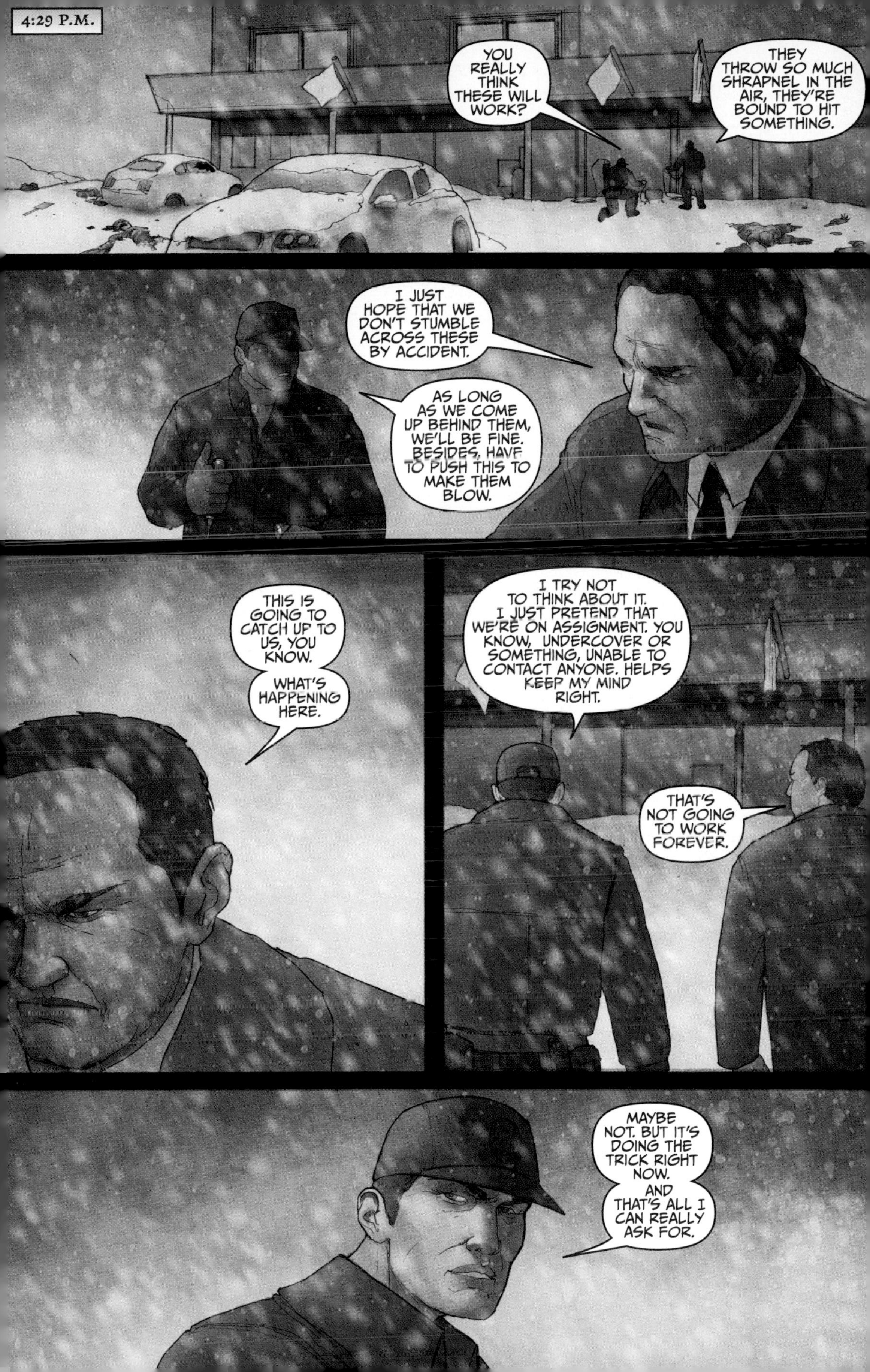
4:29 P.M.
YOU REALLY THINK THESE WILL WORK?
THEY THROW SO MUCH SHRAPNEL IN THE AIR, THEY'RE BOUND TO HIT SOMETHING.
I JUST HOPE THAT WE DON'T STUMBLE ACROSS THESE BY ACCIDENT.
AS LONG AS WE COME UP BEHIND THEM, WE'LL BE FINE. BESIDES, HAVE TO PUSH THIS TO MAKE THEM BLOW.
THIS IS GOING TO CATCH UP TO US, YOU KNOW.
WHAT'S HAPPENING HERE.
I TRY NOT TO THINK ABOUT IT. I JUST PRETEND THAT WE'RE ON ASSIGNMENT. YOU KNOW, UNDERCOVER OR SOMETHING, UNABLE TO CONTACT ANYONE. HELPS KEEP MY MIND RIGHT.
THAT'S NOT GOING TO WORK FOREVER.
MAYBE NOT. BUT IT'S DOING THE TRICK RIGHT NOW.
AND THAT'S ALL I CAN REALLY ASK FOR.

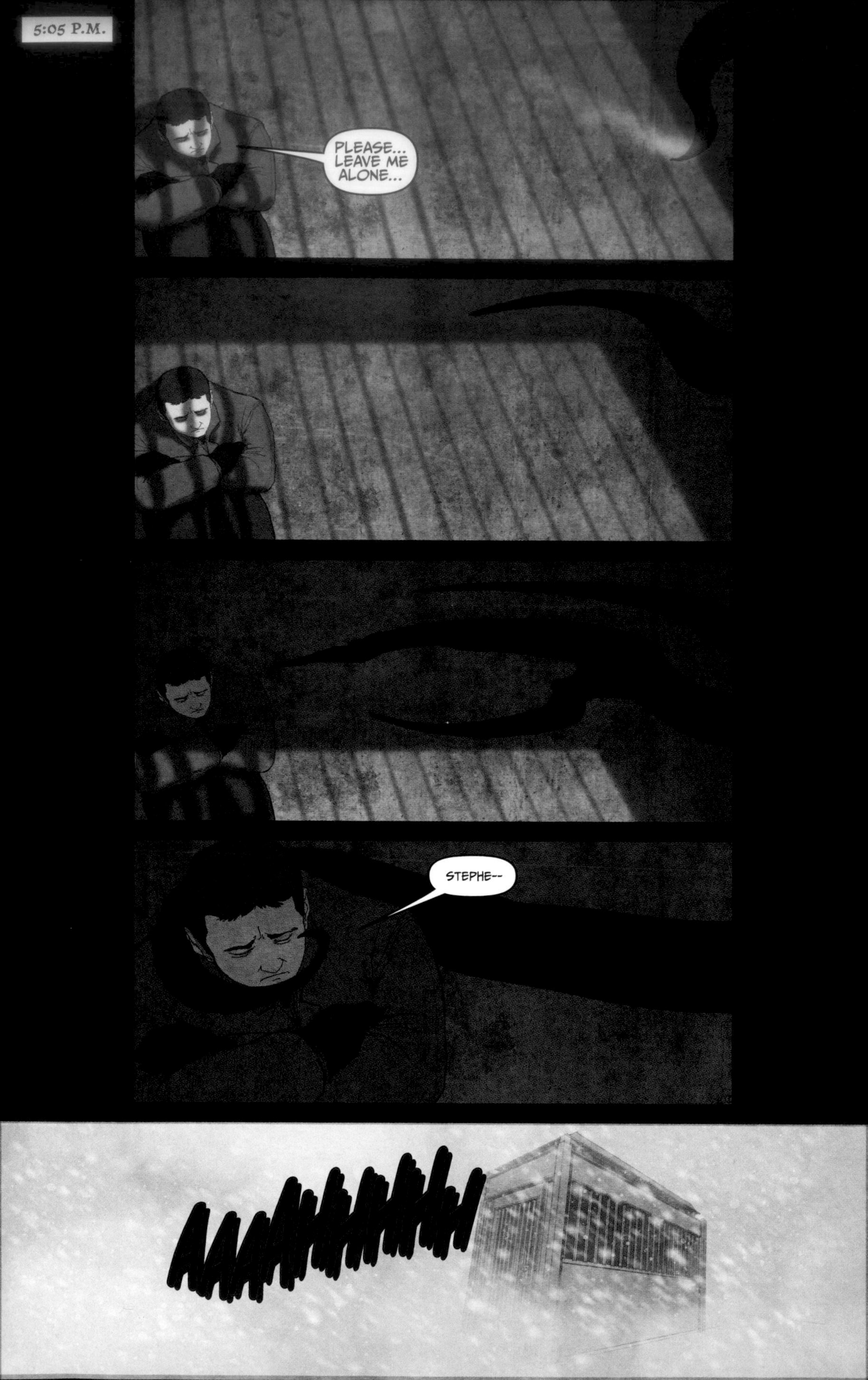
5:05 P.M.
PLEASE... LEAVE ME ALONE...
STEPHE--
AAAAHHHHHHH

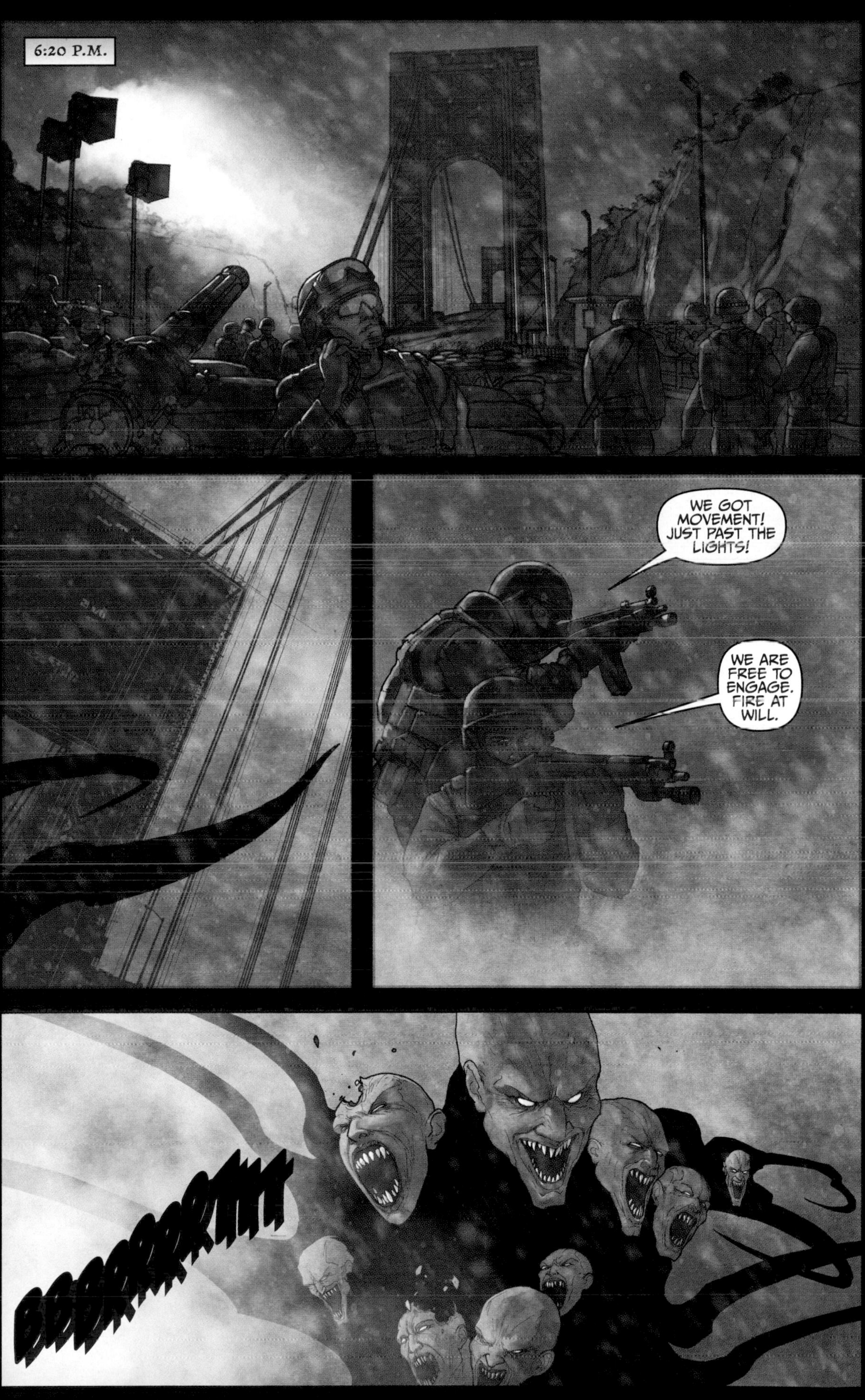
6:20 P.M.
WE GOT MOVEMENT! JUST PAST THE LIGHTS!
WE ARE FREE TO ENGAGE. FIRE AT WILL.
BBBRRRRRTTTT

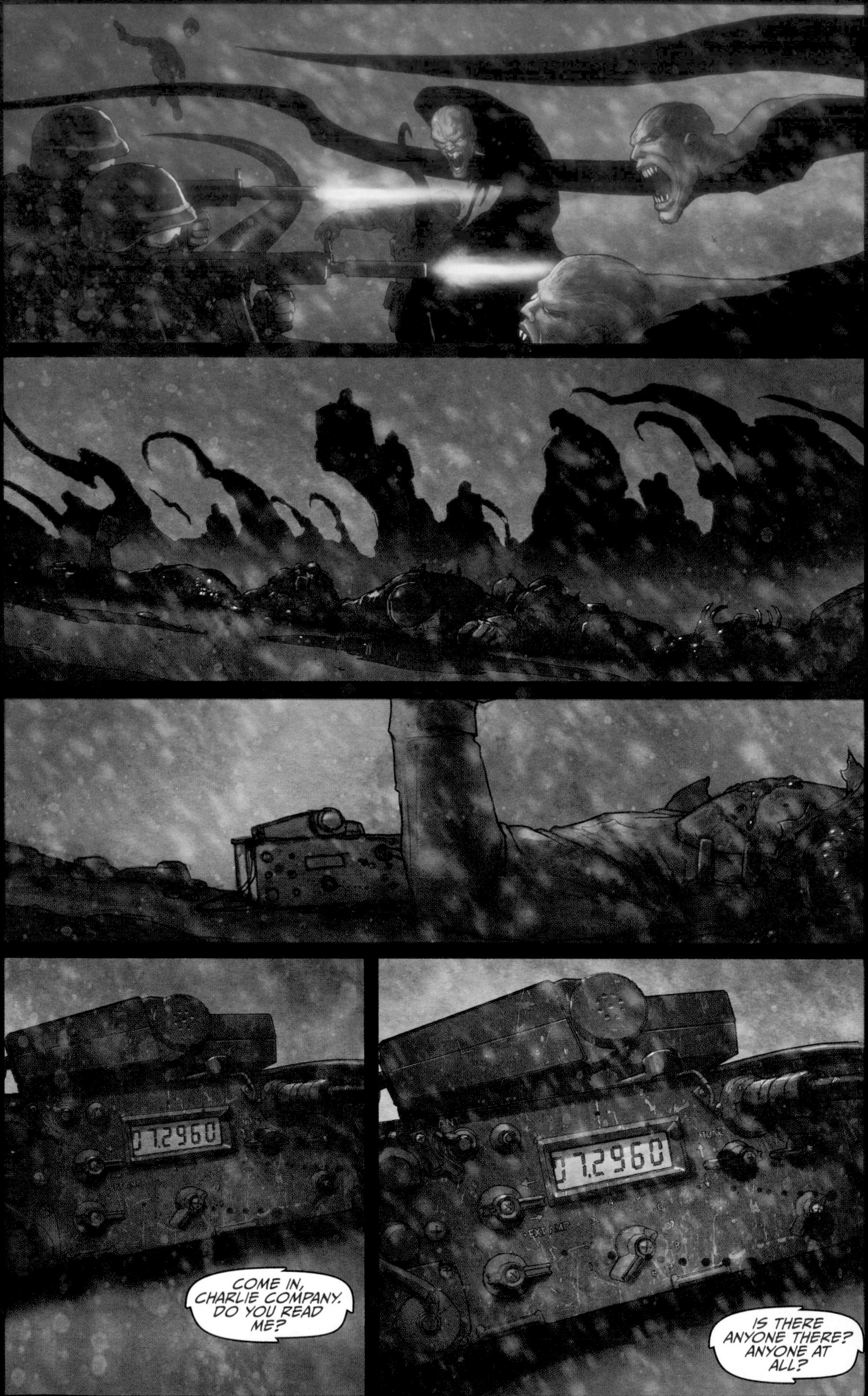
COME IN, CHARLIE COMPANY. DO YOU READ ME?
IS THERE ANYONE THERE? ANYONE AT ALL?

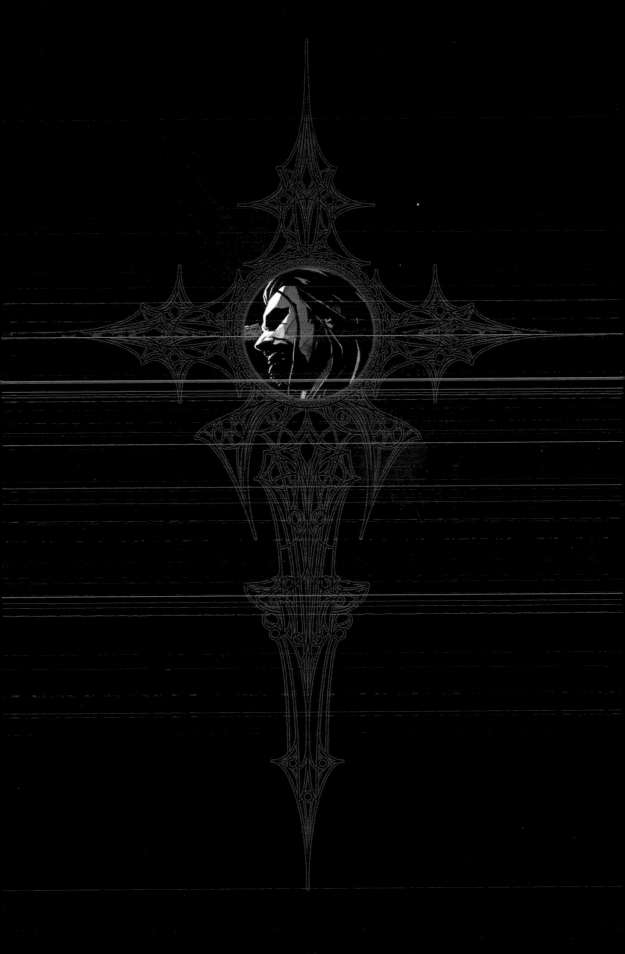

CONFRONTATION
{Issue #6}

WRITTEN BY:
WILLIAM HARMS

PENCILS, INKS & COLORS BY:
FRANCIS TSAI

LETTERING BY:
TROY PETERI

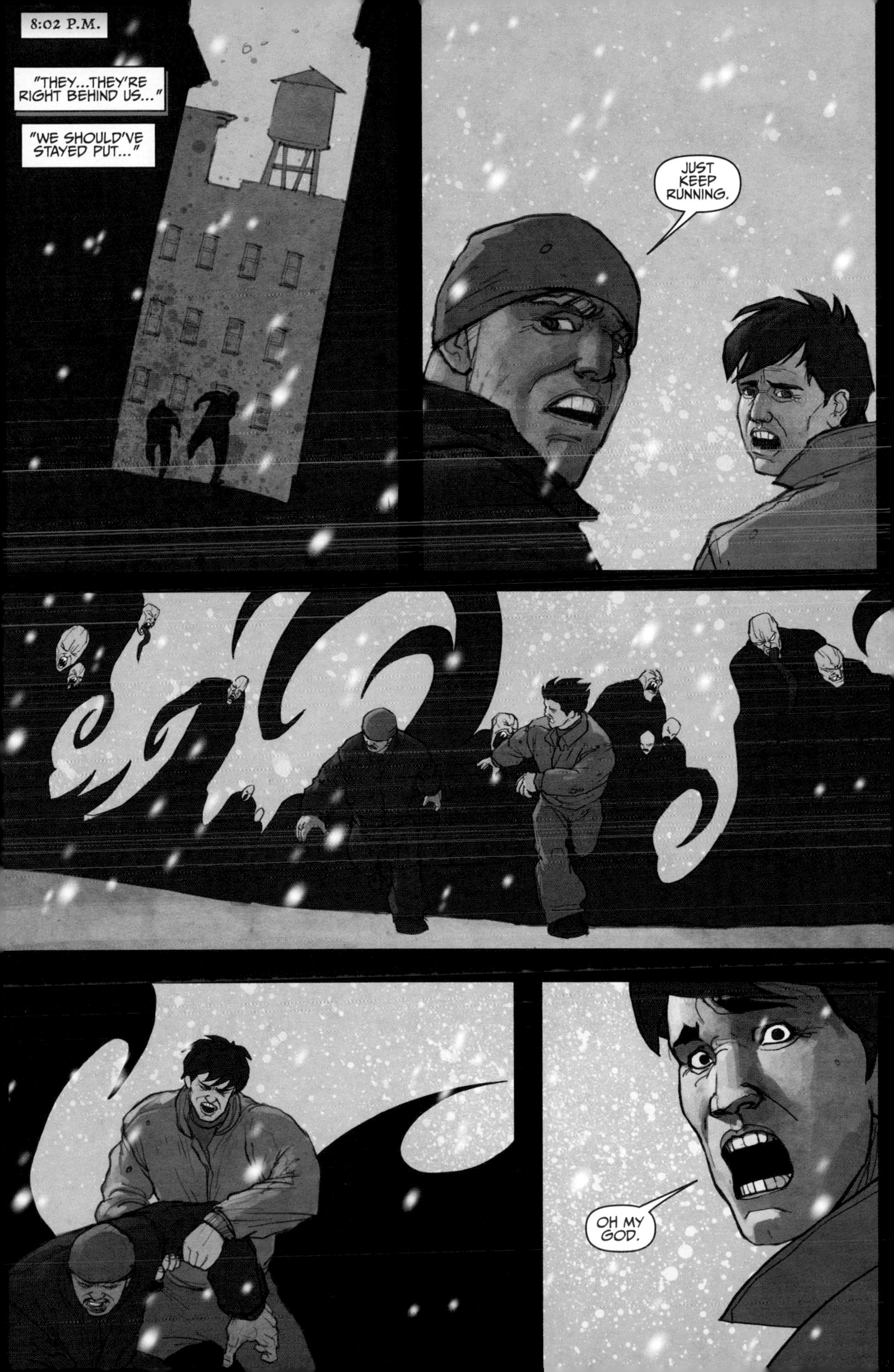
8:02 P.M.
"THEY...THEY'RE RIGHT BEHIND US..."
"WE SHOULD'VE STAYED PUT..."
JUST KEEP RUNNING.
OH MY GOD.

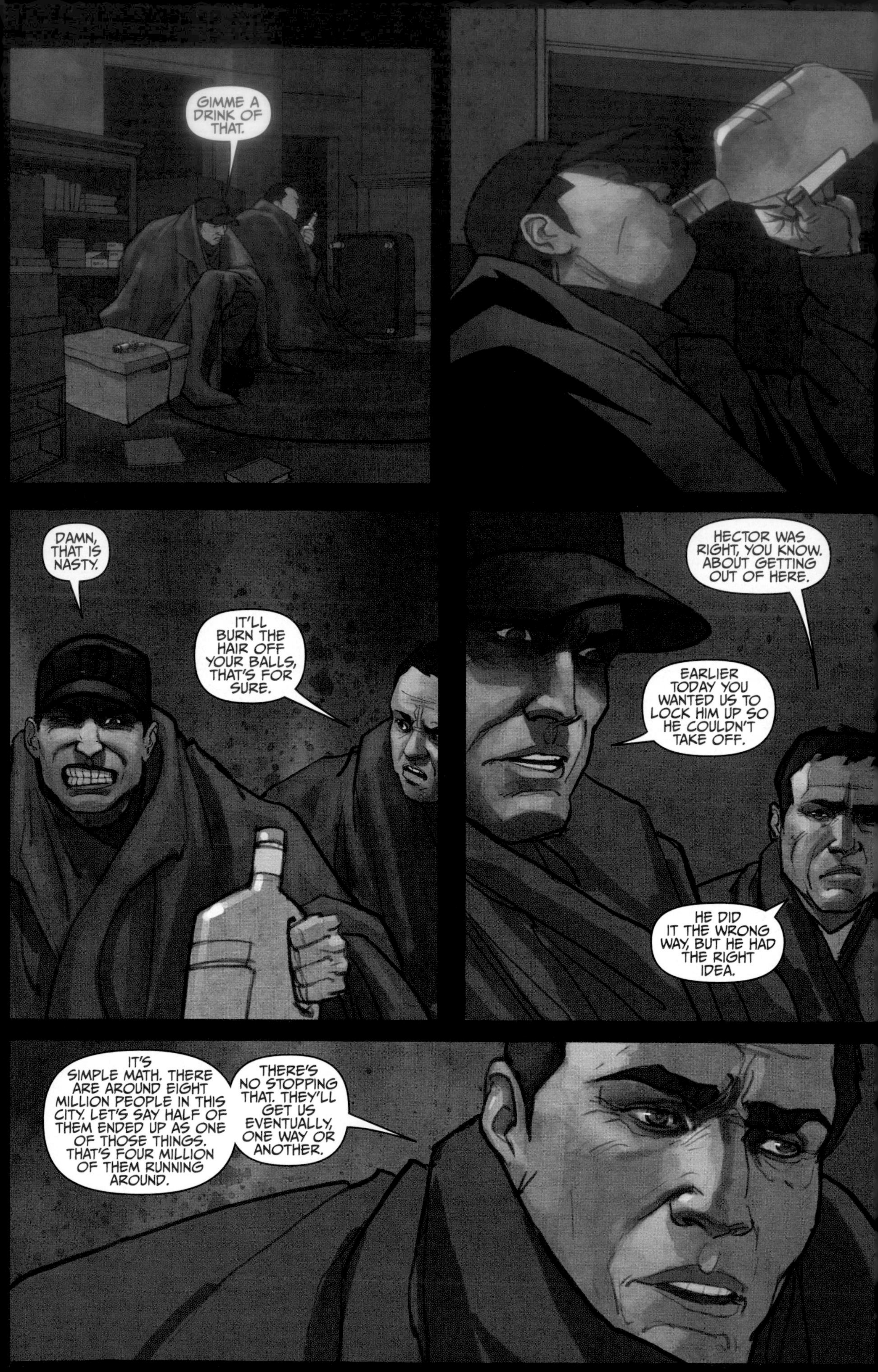
GIMME A DRINK OF THAT.
DAMN, THAT IS NASTY.
IT'LL BURN THE HAIR OFF YOUR BALLS, THAT'S FOR SURE.
HECTOR WAS RIGHT, YOU KNOW. ABOUT GETTING OUT OF HERE.
EARLIER TODAY YOU WANTED US TO LOCK HIM UP SO HE COULDN'T TAKE OFF.
HE DID IT THE WRONG WAY, BUT HE HAD THE RIGHT IDEA.
IT'S SIMPLE MATH. THERE ARE AROUND EIGHT MILLION PEOPLE IN THIS CITY. LET'S SAY HALF OF THEM ENDED UP AS ONE OF THOSE THINGS. THAT'S FOUR MILLION OF THEM RUNNING AROUND.
THERE'S NO STOPPING THAT. THEY'LL GET US EVENTUALLY, ONE WAY OR ANOTHER.

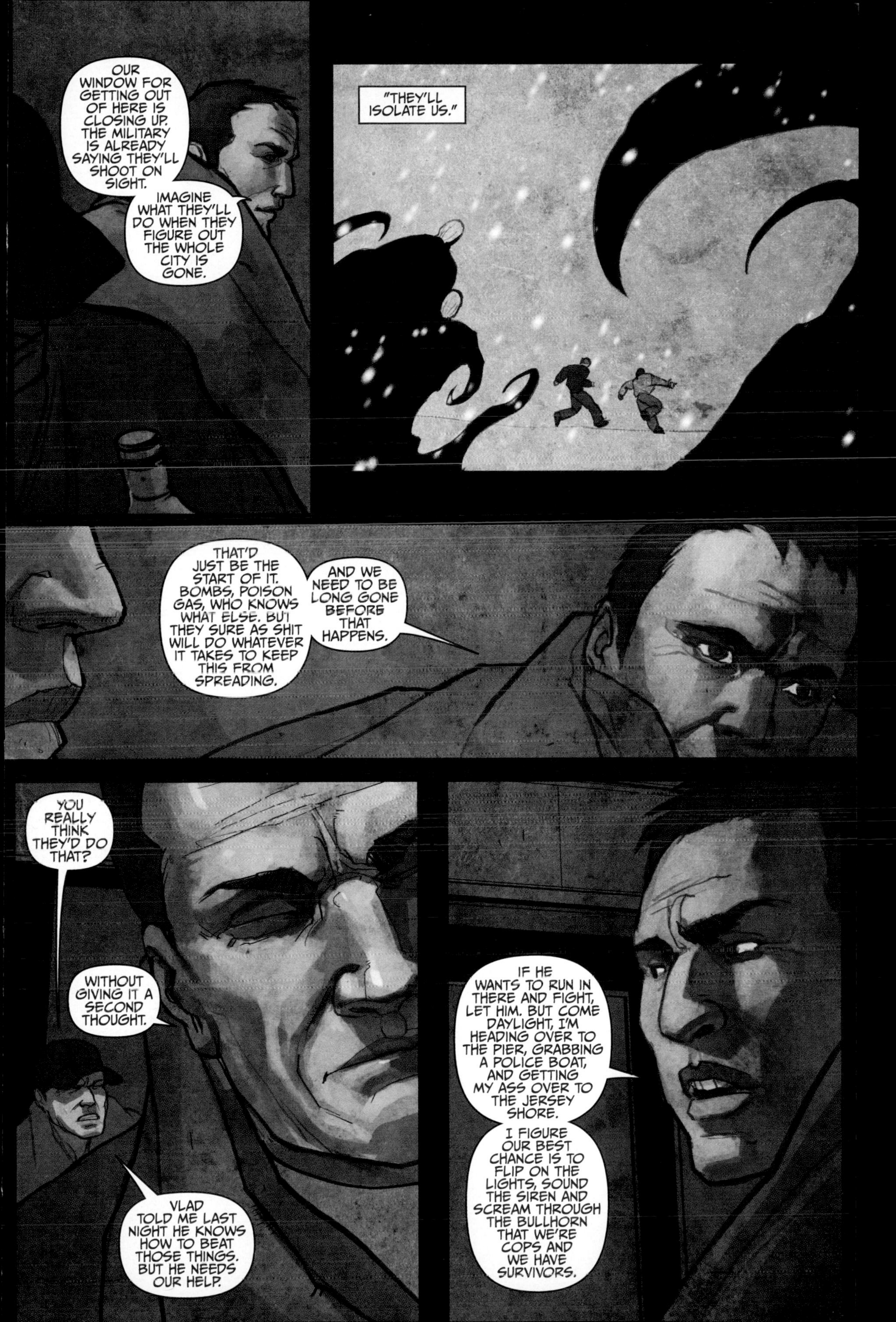
OUR WINDOW FOR GETTING OUT OF HERE IS CLOSING UP. THE MILITARY IS ALREADY SAYING THEY'LL SHOOT ON SIGHT.
IMAGINE WHAT THEY'LL DO WHEN THEY FIGURE OUT THE WHOLE CITY IS GONE.
"THEY'LL ISOLATE US."
THAT'D JUST BE THE START OF IT. BOMBS, POISON GAS, WHO KNOWS WHAT ELSE. BUT THEY SURE AS SHIT WILL DO WHATEVER IT TAKES TO KEEP THIS FROM SPREADING.
AND WE NEED TO BE LONG GONE BEFORE THAT HAPPENS.
YOU REALLY THINK THEY'D DO THAT?
WITHOUT GIVING IT A SECOND THOUGHT.
VLAD TOLD ME LAST NIGHT HE KNOWS HOW TO BEAT THOSE THINGS. BUT HE NEEDS OUR HELP.
IF HE WANTS TO RUN IN THERE AND FIGHT, LET HIM. BUT COME DAYLIGHT, I'M HEADING OVER TO THE PIER, GRABBING A POLICE BOAT, AND GETTING MY ASS OVER TO THE JERSEY SHORE.
I FIGURE OUR BEST CHANCE IS TO FLIP ON THE LIGHTS, SOUND THE SIREN AND SCREAM THROUGH THE BULLHORN THAT WE'RE COPS AND WE HAVE SURVIVORS.

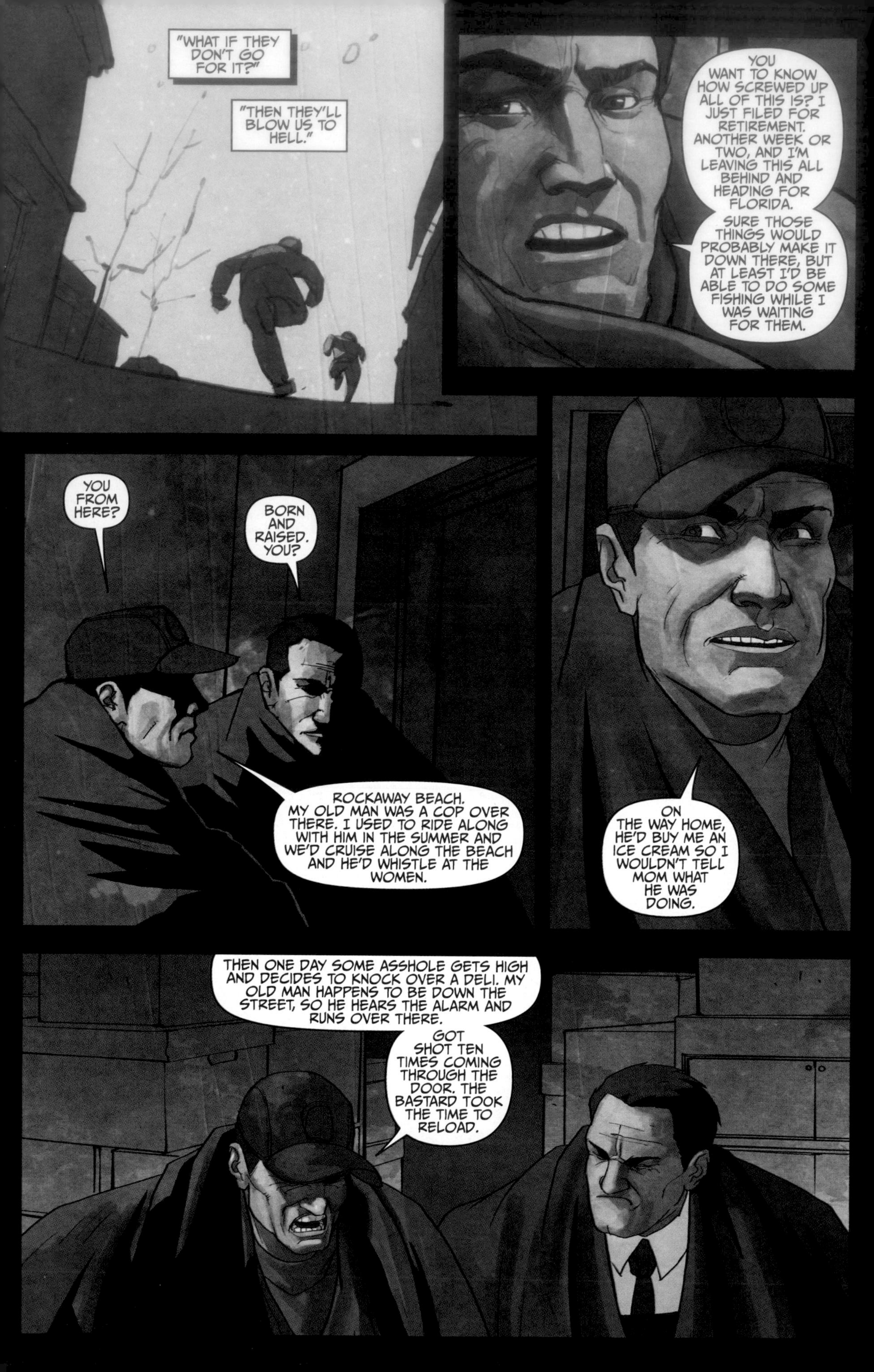
"WHAT IF THEY DON'T GO FOR IT?"
"THEN THEY'LL BLOW US TO HELL."
YOU WANT TO KNOW HOW SCREWED UP ALL OF THIS IS? I JUST FILED FOR RETIREMENT. ANOTHER WEEK OR TWO, AND I'M LEAVING THIS ALL BEHIND AND HEADING FOR FLORIDA.
SURE THOSE THINGS WOULD PROBABLY MAKE IT DOWN THERE, BUT AT LEAST I'D BE ABLE TO DO SOME FISHING WHILE I WAS WAITING FOR THEM.
YOU FROM HERE?
BORN AND RAISED. YOU?
ROCKAWAY BEACH. MY OLD MAN WAS A COP OVER THERE. I USED TO RIDE ALONG WITH HIM IN THE SUMMER AND WE'D CRUISE ALONG THE BEACH AND HE'D WHISTLE AT THE WOMEN.
ON THE WAY HOME, HE'D BUY ME AN ICE CREAM SO I WOULDN'T TELL MOM WHAT HE WAS DOING.
THEN ONE DAY SOME ASSHOLE GETS HIGH AND DECIDES TO KNOCK OVER A DELI. MY OLD MAN HAPPENS TO BE DOWN THE STREET, SO HE HEARS THE ALARM AND RUNS OVER THERE.
GOT SHOT TEN TIMES COMING THROUGH THE DOOR. THE BASTARD TOOK THE TIME TO RELOAD.

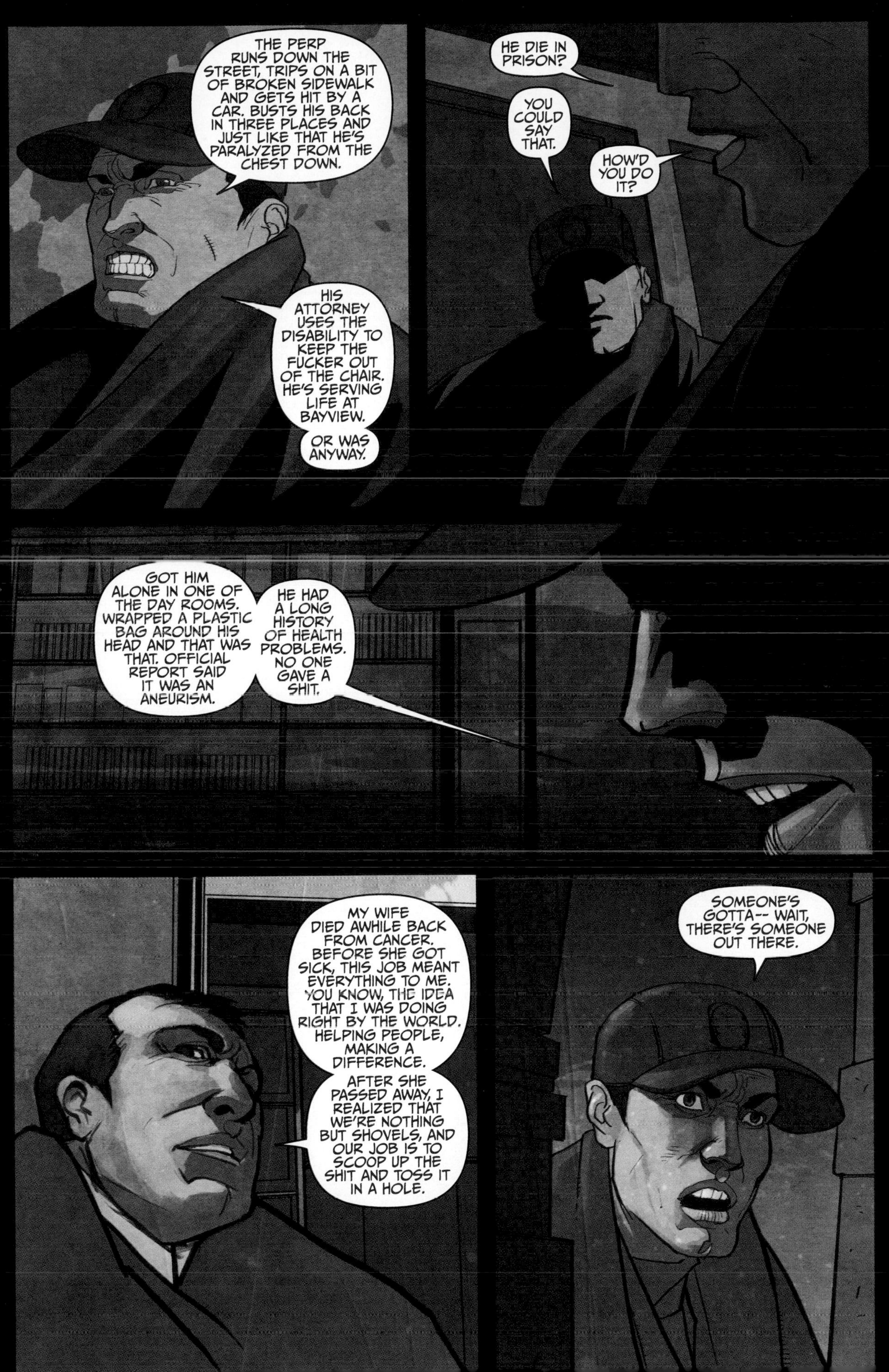
THE PERP RUNS DOWN THE STREET, TRIPS ON A BIT OF BROKEN SIDEWALK AND GETS HIT BY A CAR. BUSTS HIS BACK IN THREE PLACES AND JUST LIKE THAT HE'S PARALYZED FROM THE CHEST DOWN.
HIS ATTORNEY USES THE DISABILITY TO KEEP THE FUCKER OUT OF THE CHAIR. HE'S SERVING LIFE AT BAYVIEW.
OR WAS ANYWAY.
HE DIE IN PRISON?
YOU COULD SAY THAT.
HOW'D YOU DO IT?
GOT HIM ALONE IN ONE OF THE DAY ROOMS. WRAPPED A PLASTIC BAG AROUND HIS HEAD AND THAT WAS THAT. OFFICIAL REPORT SAID IT WAS AN ANEURISM.
HE HAD A LONG HISTORY OF HEALTH PROBLEMS. NO ONE GAVE A SHIT.
MY WIFE DIED AWHILE BACK FROM CANCER. BEFORE SHE GOT SICK, THIS JOB MEANT EVERYTHING TO ME. YOU KNOW, THE IDEA THAT I WAS DOING RIGHT BY THE WORLD. HELPING PEOPLE, MAKING A DIFFERENCE.
AFTER SHE PASSED AWAY, I REALIZED THAT WE'RE NOTHING BUT SHOVELS, AND OUR JOB IS TO SCOOP UP THE SHIT AND TOSS IT IN A HOLE.
SOMEONE'S GOTTA-- WAIT, THERE'S SOMEONE OUT THERE.

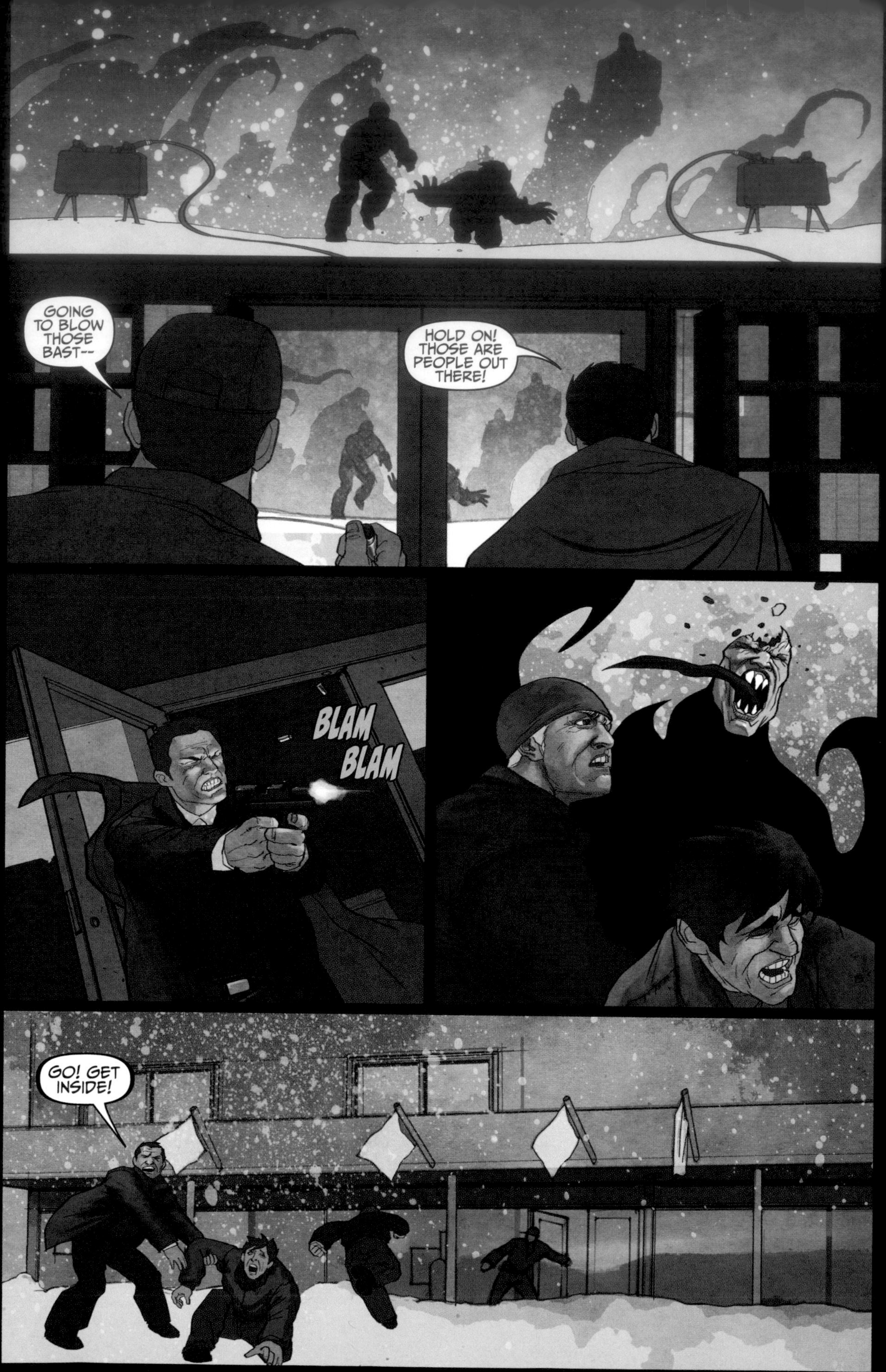
GOING TO BLOW THOSE BAST--
HOLD ON! THOSE ARE PEOPLE OUT THERE!
BLAM BLAM
GO! GET INSIDE!

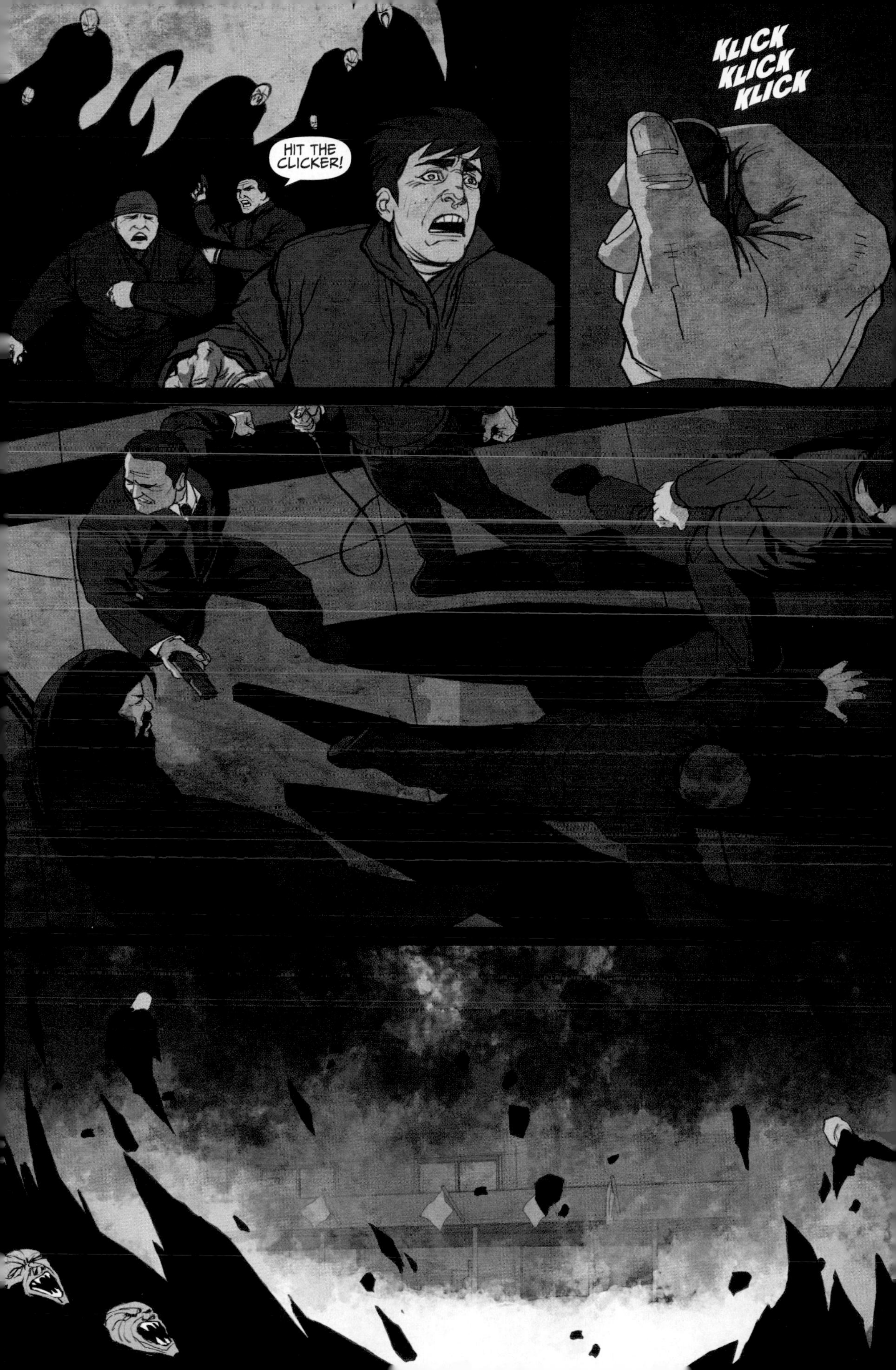
HIT THE CLICKER!
KLICK KLICK KLICK

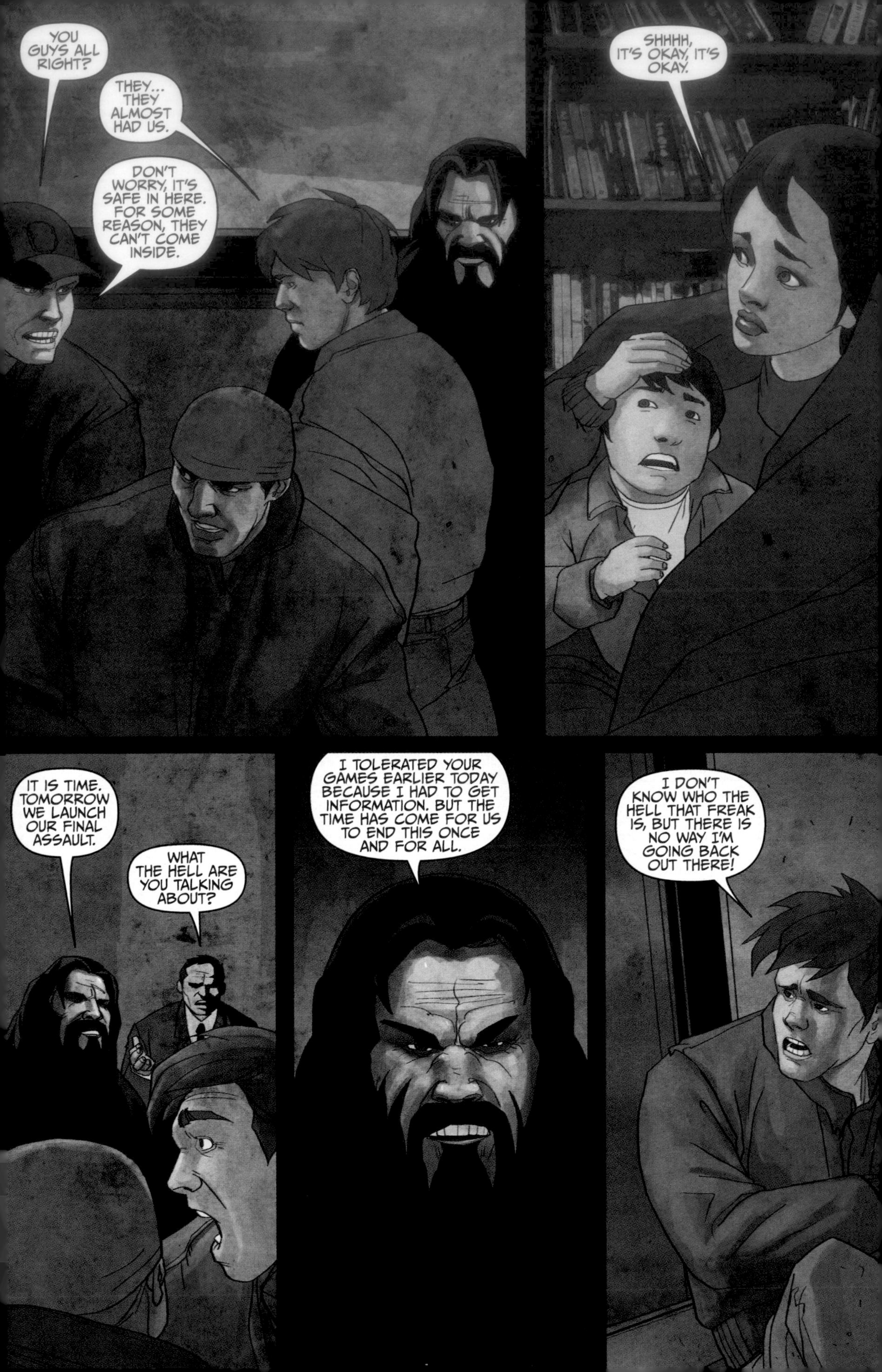
YOU GUYS ALL RIGHT?
THEY... THEY ALMOST HAD US.
DON'T WORRY, IT'S SAFE IN HERE. FOR SOME REASON, THEY CAN'T COME INSIDE.
SHHHH, IT'S OKAY, IT'S OKAY.
IT IS TIME. TOMORROW WE LAUNCH OUR FINAL ASSAULT.
WHAT THE HELL ARE YOU TALKING ABOUT?
I TOLERATED YOUR GAMES EARLIER TODAY BECAUSE I HAD TO GET INFORMATION. BUT THE TIME HAS COME FOR US TO END THIS ONCE AND FOR ALL.
I DON'T KNOW WHO THE HELL THAT FREAK IS, BUT THERE IS NO WAY I'M GOING BACK OUT THERE!

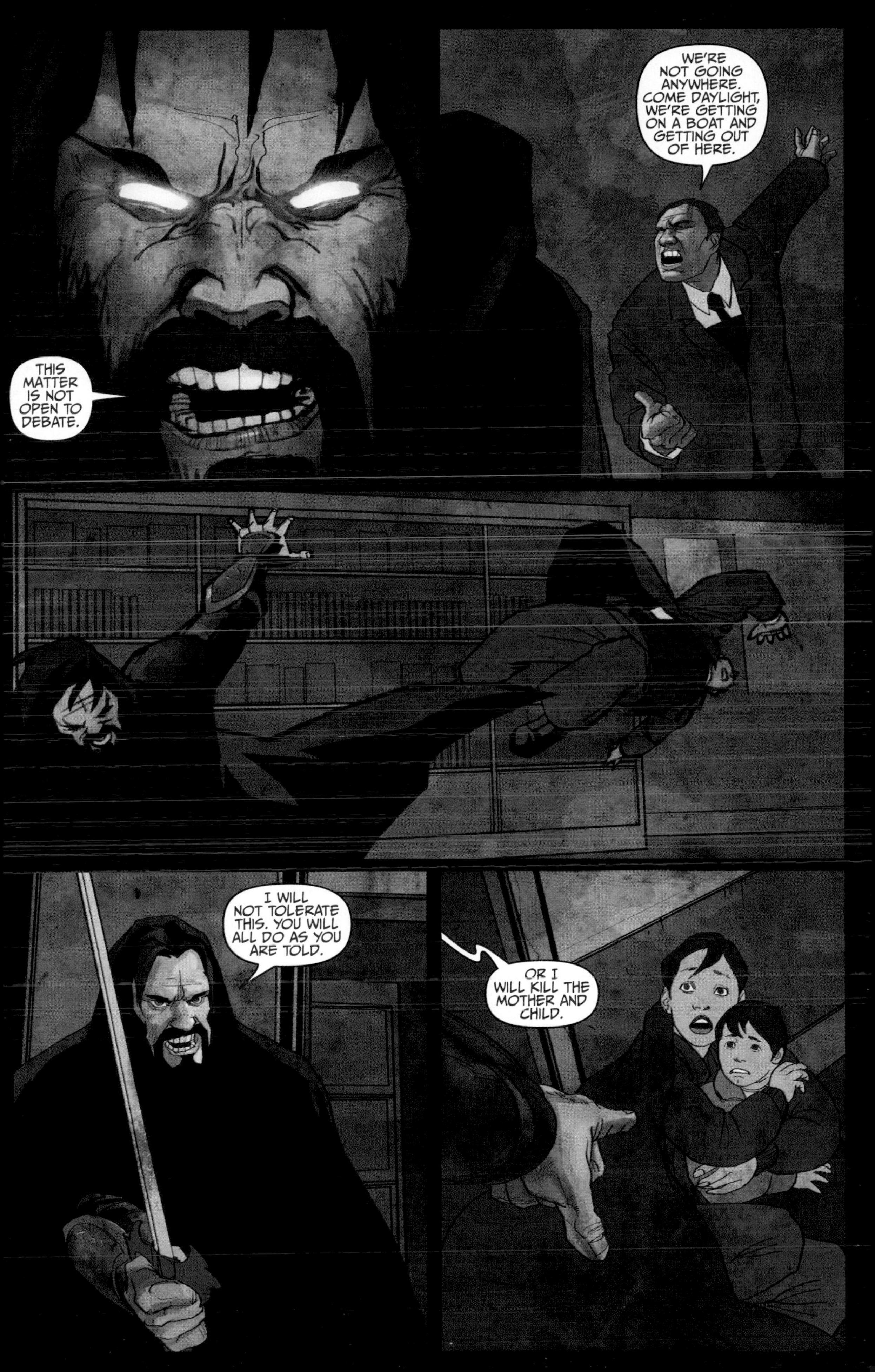
THIS MATTER IS NOT OPEN TO DEBATE.
WE'RE NOT GOING ANYWHERE. COME DAYLIGHT, WE'RE GETTING ON A BOAT AND GETTING OUT OF HERE.
I WILL NOT TOLERATE THIS. YOU WILL ALL DO AS YOU ARE TOLD.
OR I WILL KILL THE MOTHER AND CHILD.

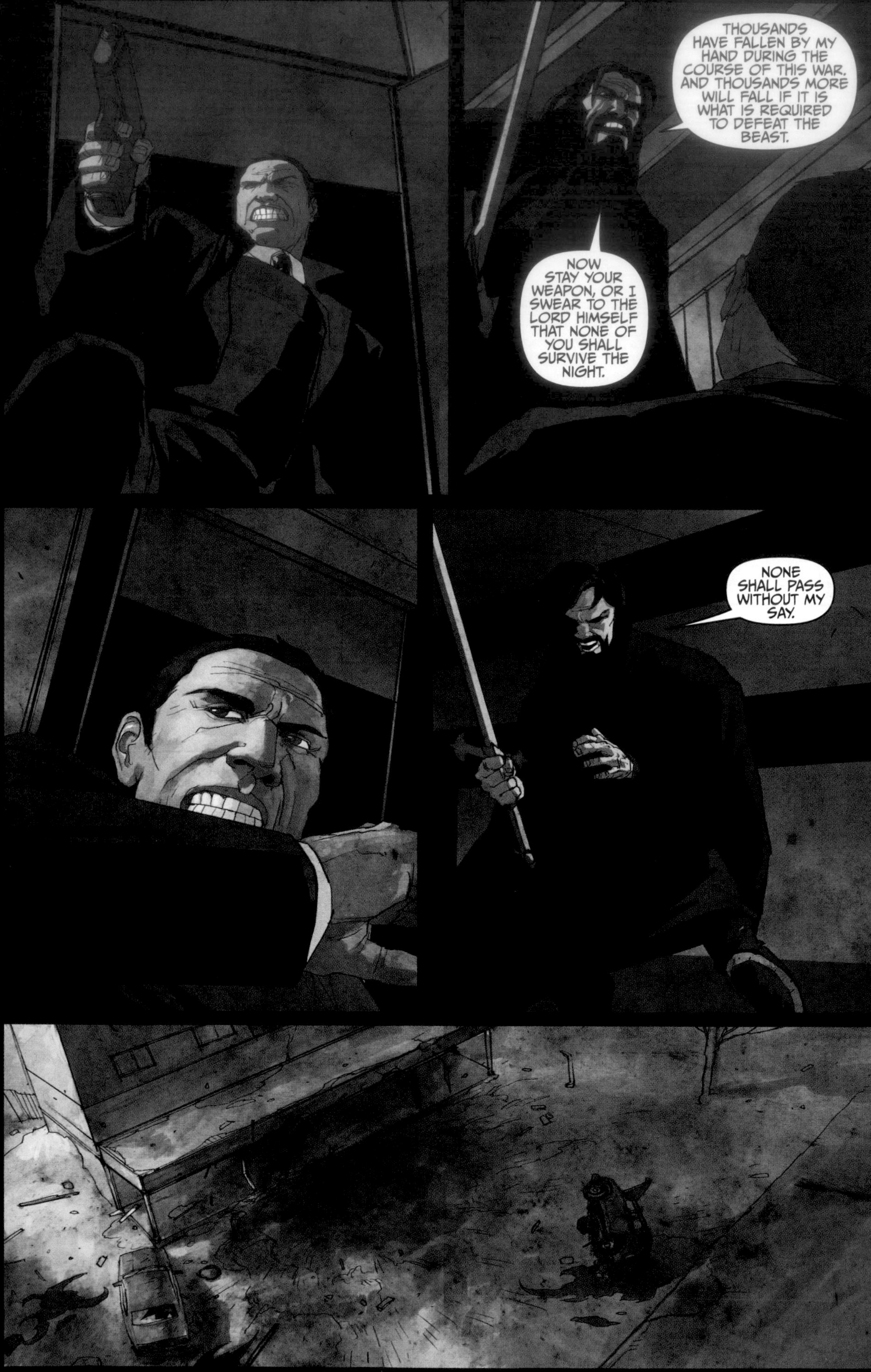
THOUSANDS HAVE FALLEN BY MY HAND DURING THE COURSE OF THIS WAR. AND THOUSANDS MORE WILL FALL IF IT IS WHAT IS REQUIRED TO DEFEAT THE BEAST.
NOW STAY YOUR WEAPON, OR I SWEAR TO THE LORD HIMSELF THAT NONE OF YOU SHALL SURVIVE THE NIGHT.
NONE SHALL PASS WITHOUT MY SAY.

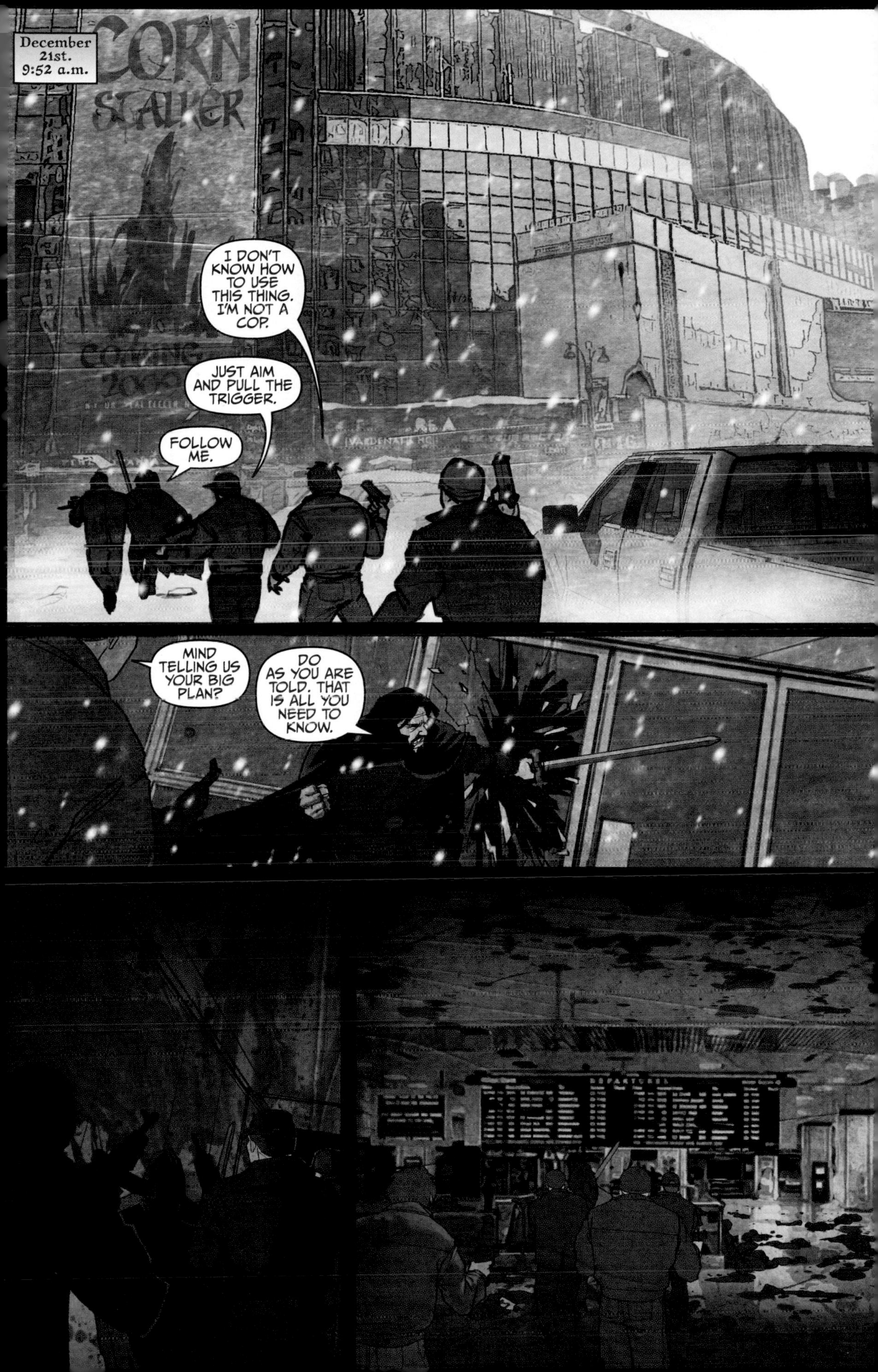
December 21st. 9:52 a.m.
CORN STALKER
COMING 2009
I DON'T KNOW HOW TO USE THIS THING. I'M NOT A COP.
JUST AIM AND PULL THE TRIGGER.
FOLLOW ME.
MIND TELLING US YOUR BIG PLAN?
DO AS YOU ARE TOLD. THAT IS ALL YOU NEED TO KNOW.
DEPARTURES

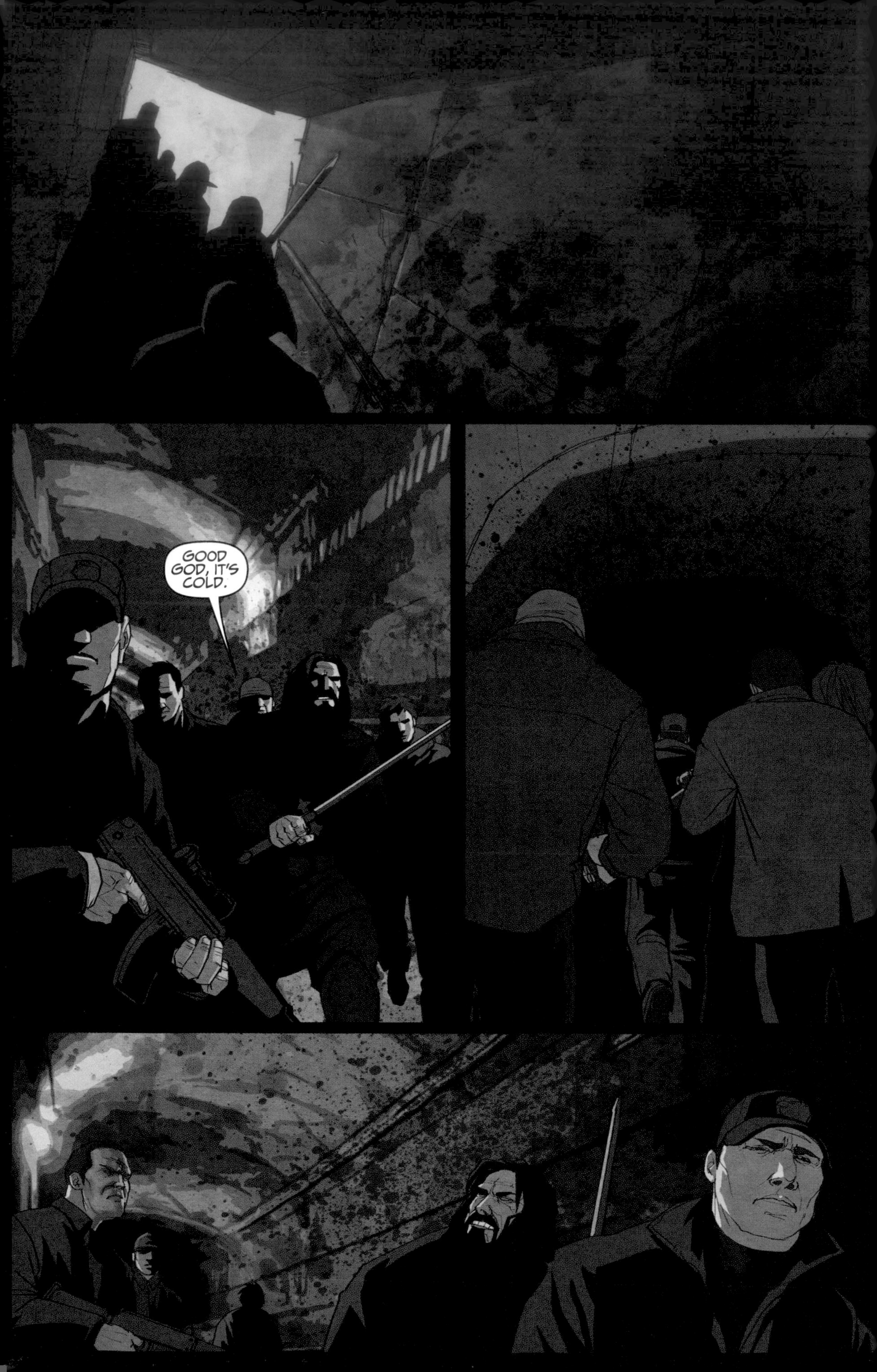
GOOD GOD, IT'S COLD.

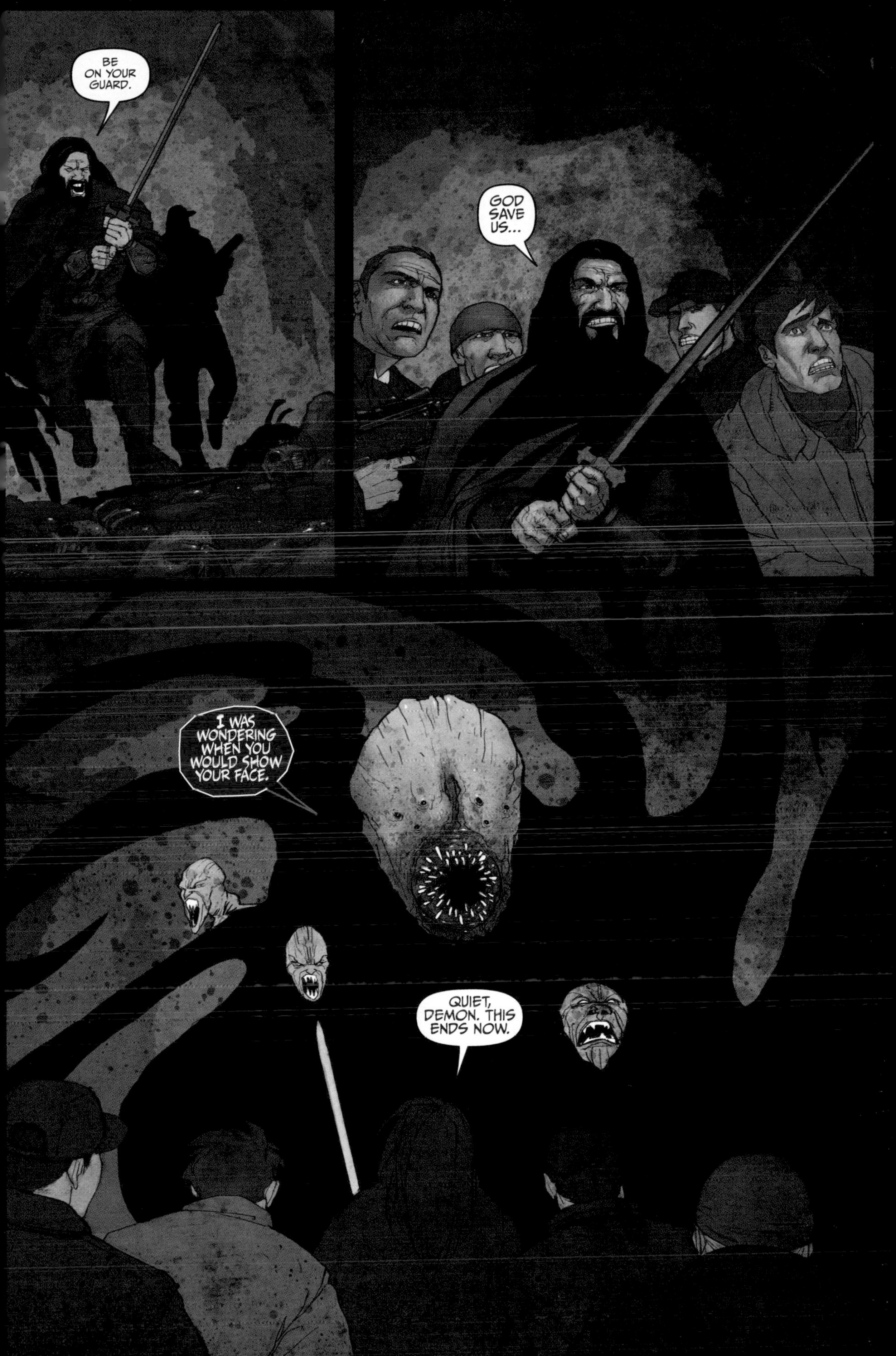
BE ON YOUR GUARD.
GOD SAVE US...
I WAS WONDERING WHEN YOU WOULD SHOW YOUR FACE.
QUIET, DEMON. THIS ENDS NOW.

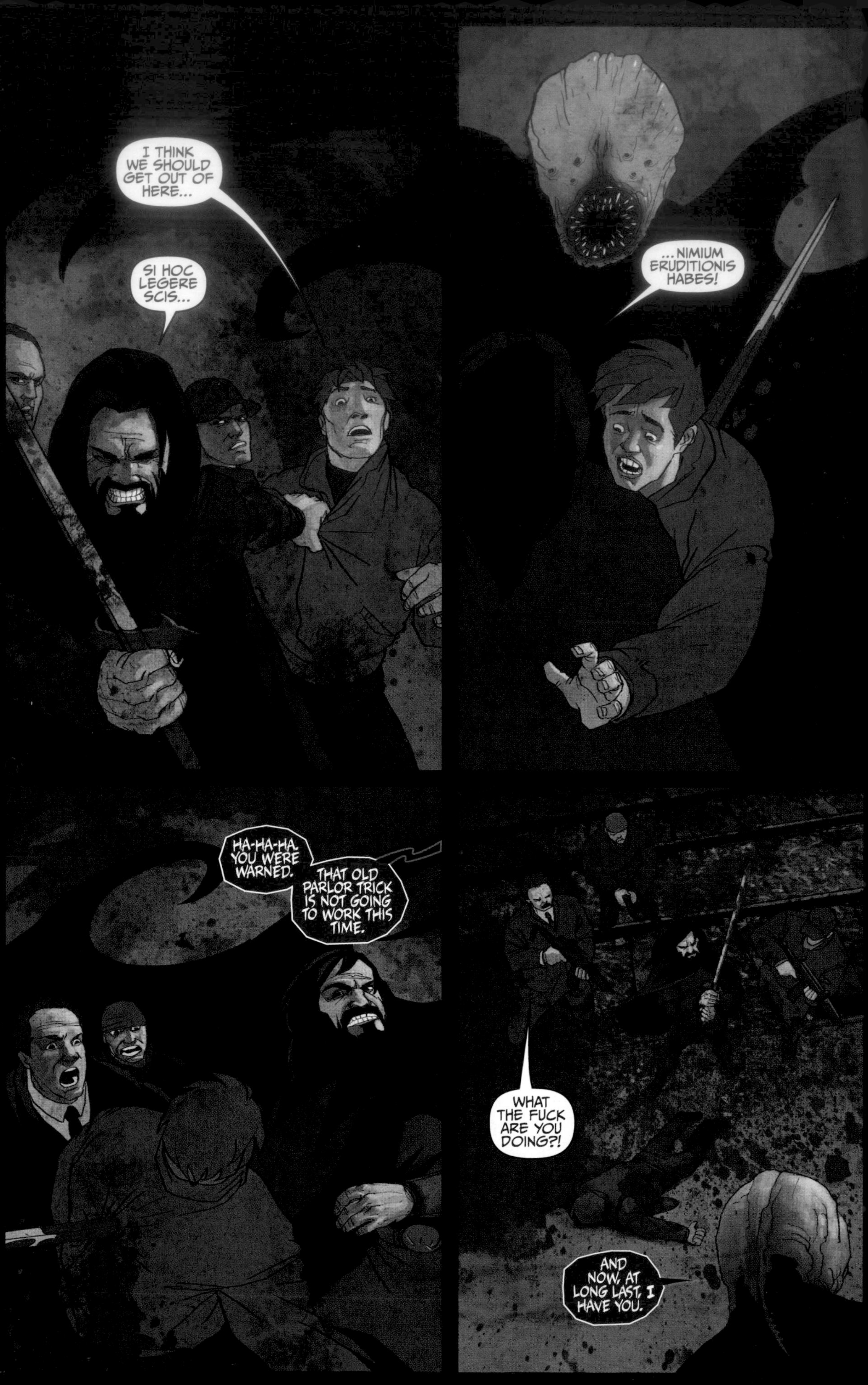
I THINK WE SHOULD GET OUT OF HERE...
SI HOC LEGERE SCIS...
...NIMIUM ERUDITIONIS HABES!
HA-HA-HA. YOU WERE WARNED.
THAT OLD PARLOR TRICK IS NOT GOING TO WORK THIS TIME.
WHAT THE FUCK ARE YOU DOING?!
AND NOW, AT LONG LAST, I HAVE YOU.

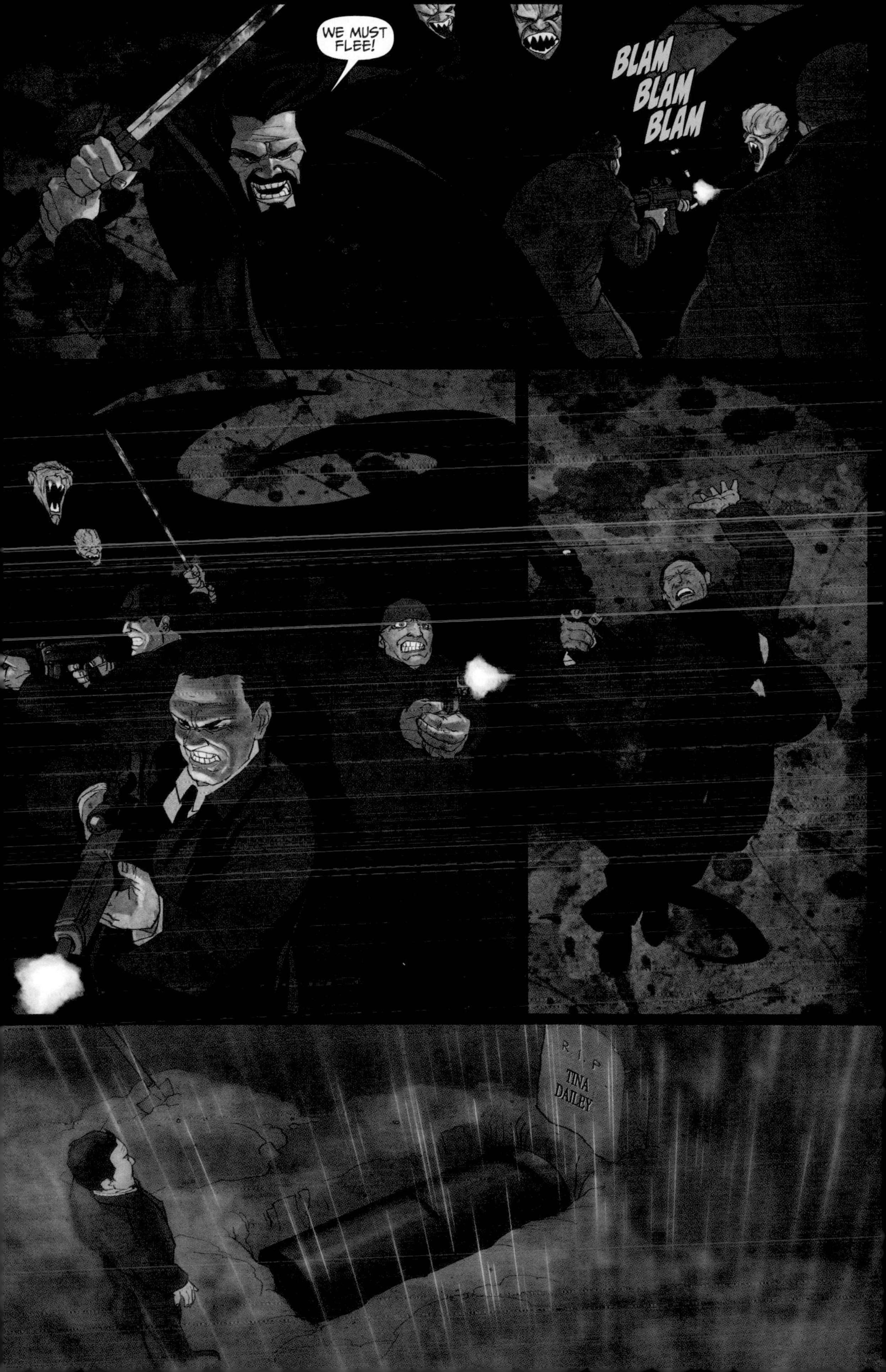
WE MUST FLEE!
BLAM
BLAM
BLAM
R.I.P.
TINA
DAILEY

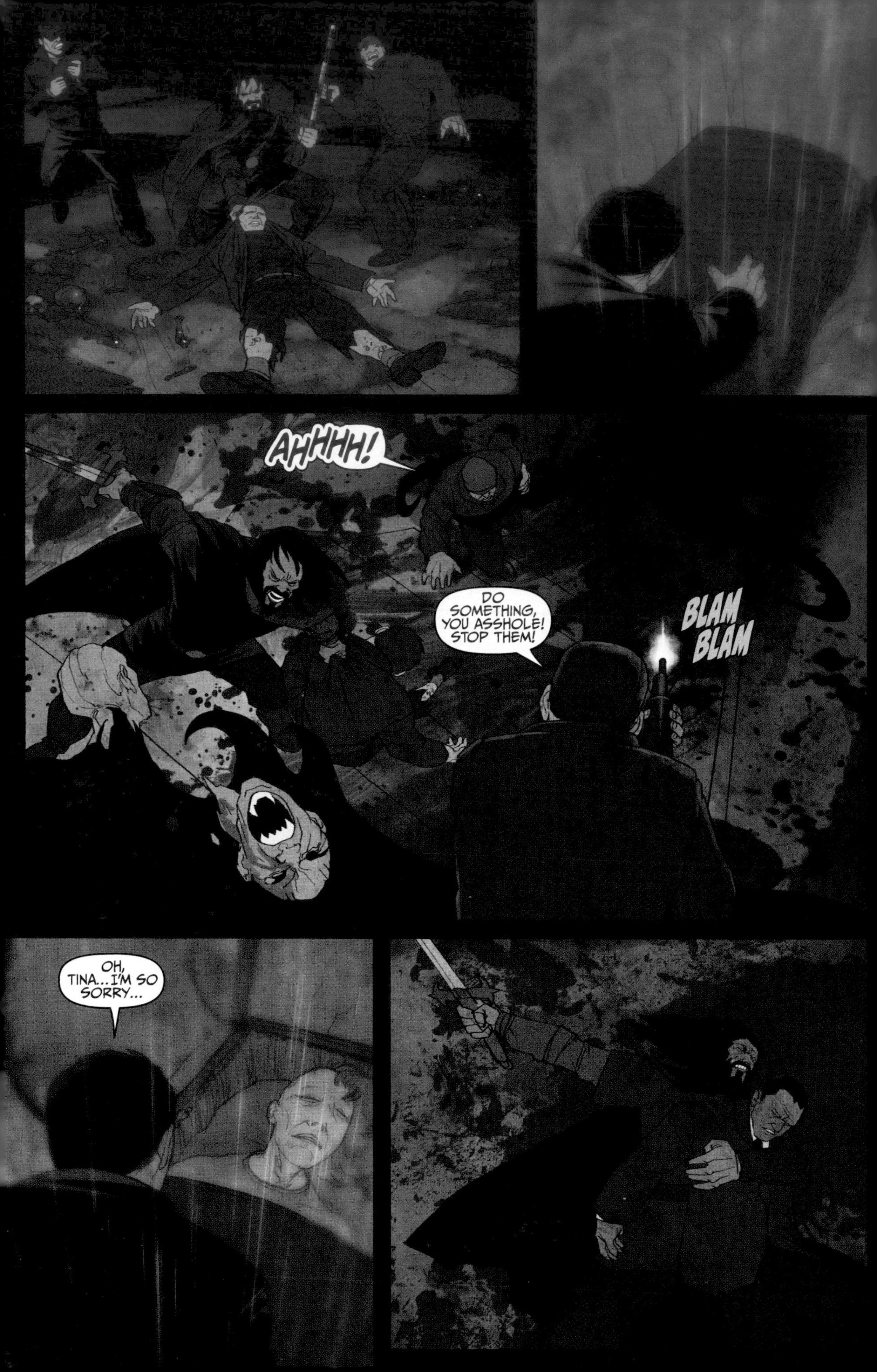
AHHHH!
DO SOMETHING, YOU ASSHOLE! STOP THEM!
BLAM BLAM
OH, TINA... I'M SO SORRY...

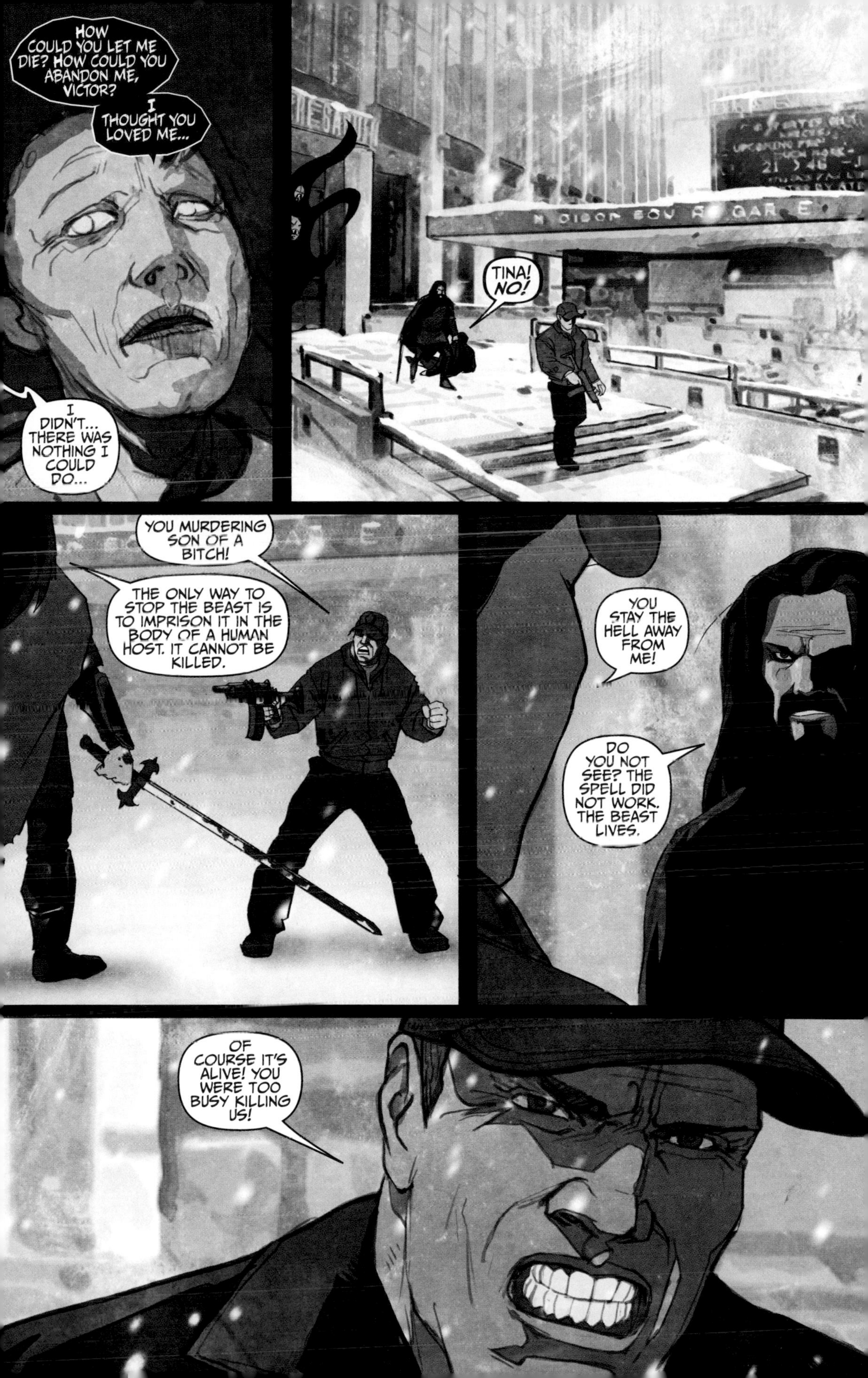
HOW COULD YOU LET ME DIE? HOW COULD YOU ABANDON ME, VICTOR?
I THOUGHT YOU LOVED ME...
I DIDN'T... THERE WAS NOTHING I COULD DO...
TINA! NO!
YOU MURDERING SON OF A BITCH!
THE ONLY WAY TO STOP THE BEAST IS TO IMPRISON IT IN THE BODY OF A HUMAN HOST. IT CANNOT BE KILLED.
YOU STAY THE HELL AWAY FROM ME!
DO YOU NOT SEE? THE SPELL DID NOT WORK. THE BEAST LIVES.
OF COURSE IT'S ALIVE! YOU WERE TOO BUSY KILLING US!

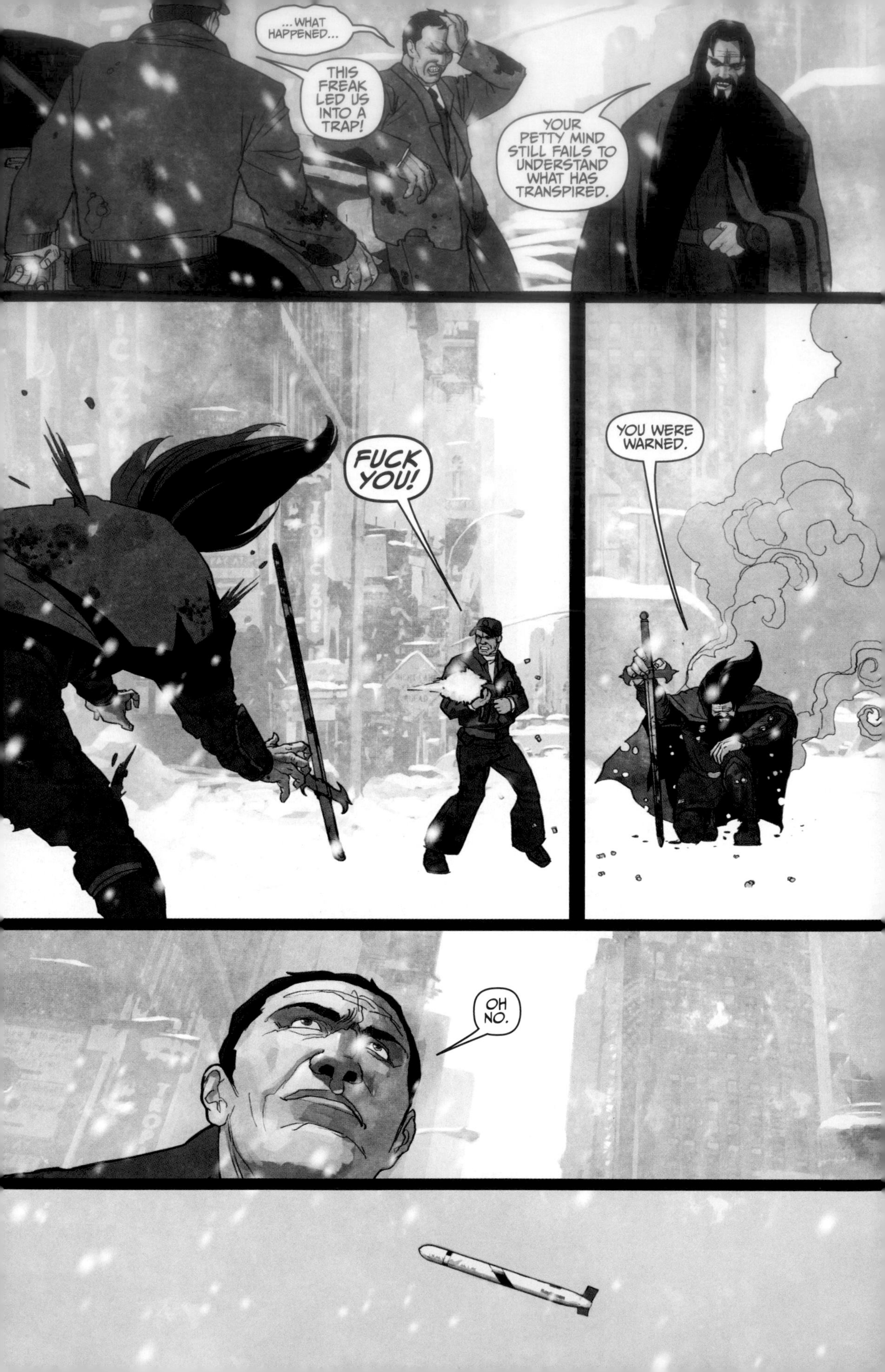
...WHAT HAPPENED...
THIS FREAK LED US INTO A TRAP!
YOUR PETTY MIND STILL FAILS TO UNDERSTAND WHAT HAS TRANSPIRED.
FUCK YOU!
YOU WERE WARNED.
OH NO.

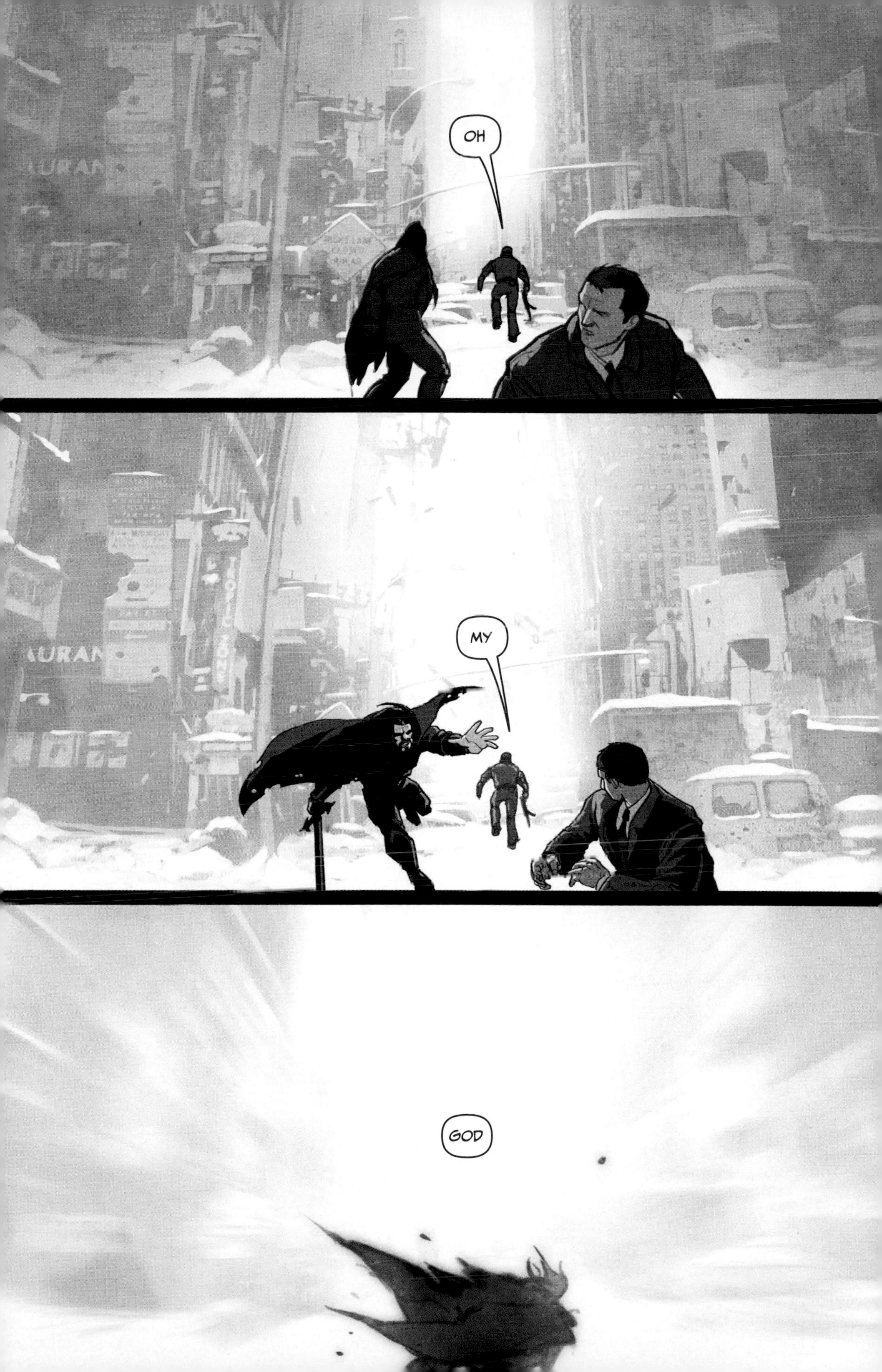
OH
MY
GOD

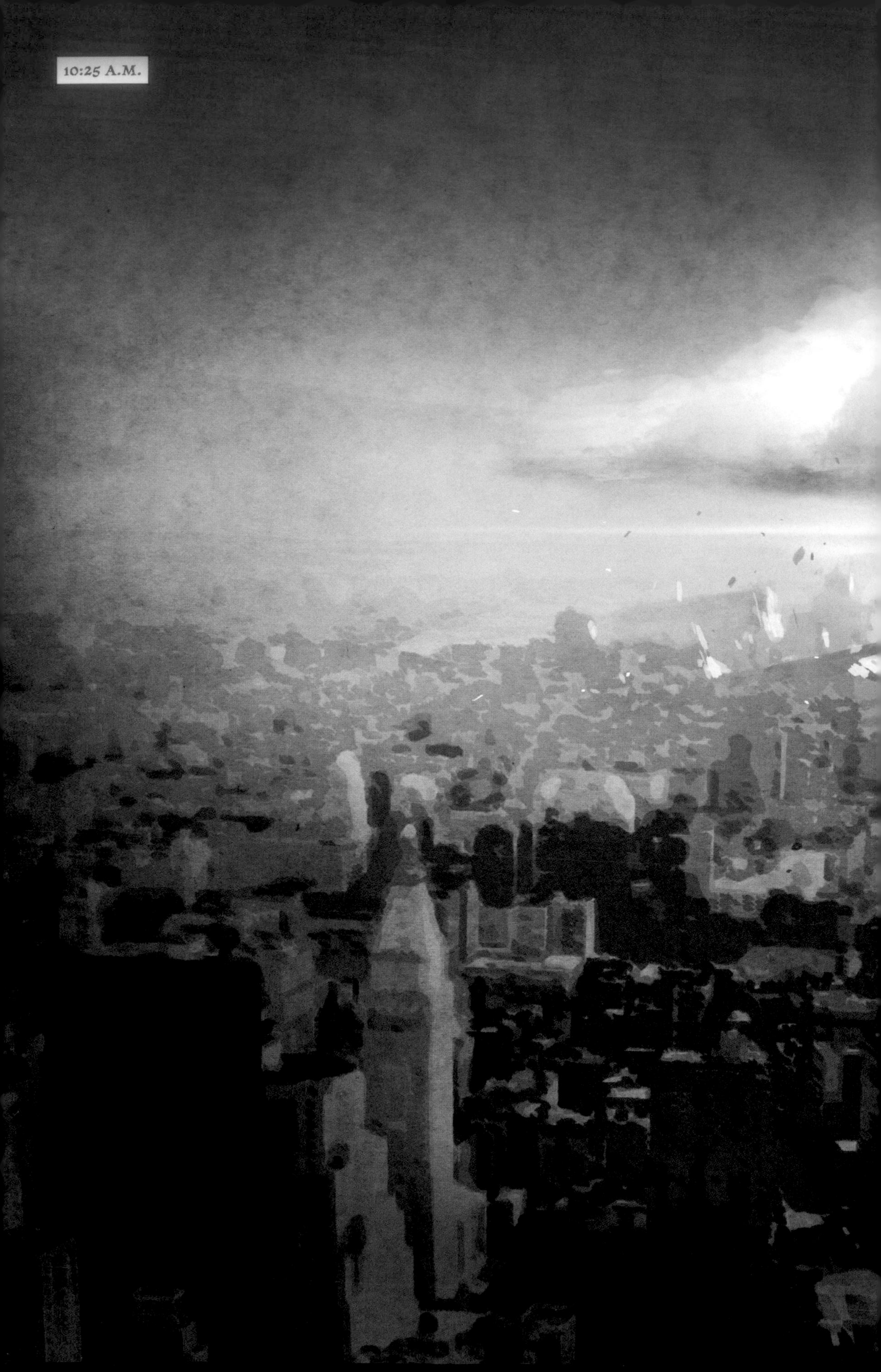
10:25 A.M.

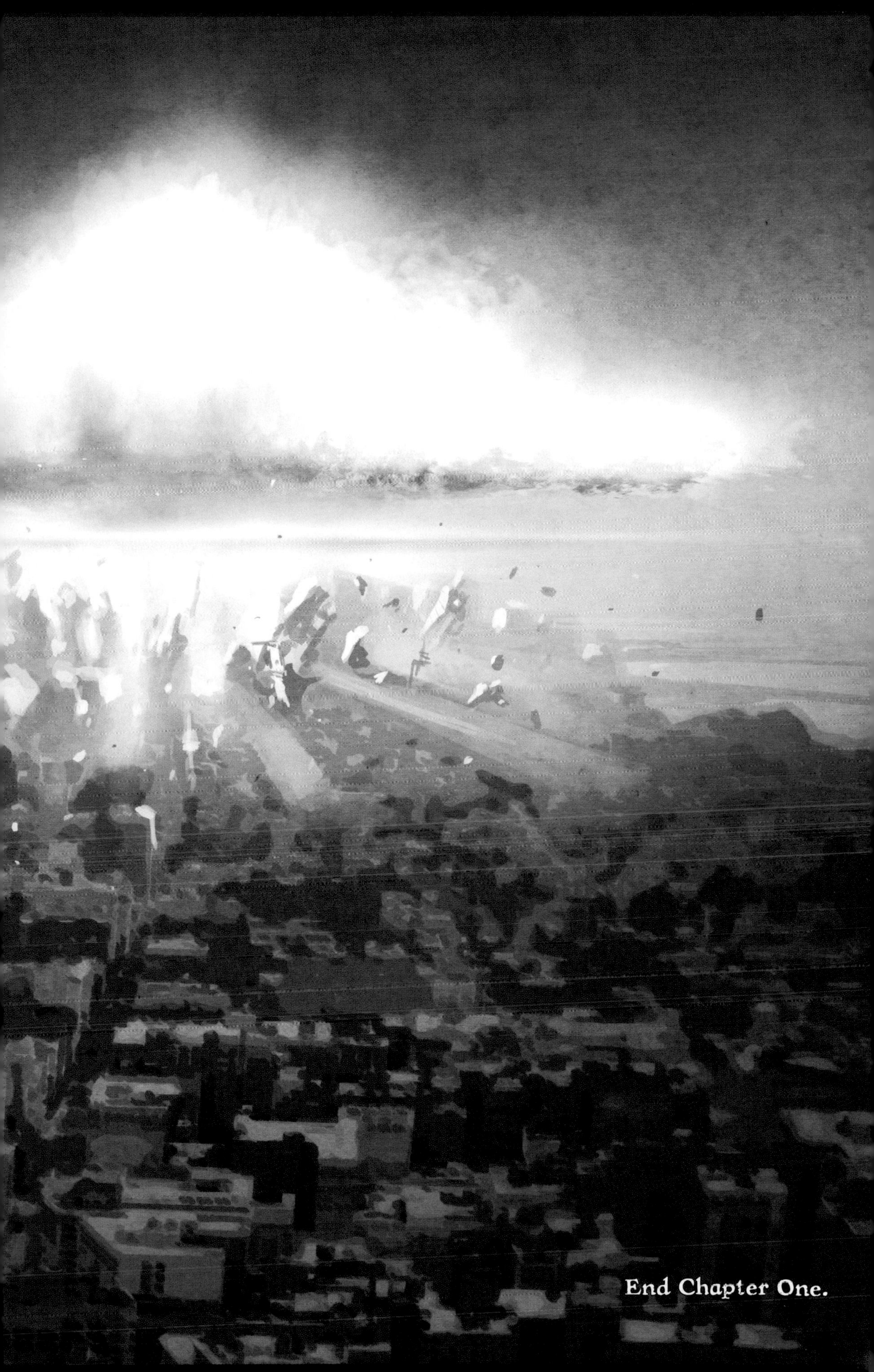
End Chapter One.

AFTERWORD

As a writer, it's always fascinated me where story ideas come from. What's the catalyst that takes your brain from not having a particular idea one moment to spitting out a fully formed idea in the next? And what takes that idea and turns it into a story? Perhaps it takes external forces, things beyond our control, pushing and pulling the idea like a wad of clay.

Case in point: *Impaler*.

For some reason, I remember the exact moment the idea for this comic first appeared to me. My wife Cindy and I were living in Berkeley, California at the time, and I was heading home from work. Or trying to anyway, because the traffic on Highway 24 was about as bad is gets,

For you see, there had been a wreck in the Caldecutt Tunnel, which meant that 24 was a parking lot. Literally. I was tired and wanted to get home and boy was I pissed off. My exit was only about a mile away, but it might as well have been on Mars.

But between the litany of traffic-inspired profanities that were leaving my lips, it hit me: Vlad Tepes, the historical Dracula, inspiration for countless vampire stories, isn't a vampire at all. In fact, he's a vampire hunter. And worse yet, the vampires he faces aren't the normal, run-of-the-mill vampires. Crosses, churches, holy water...none of them matter a whit. You want to take one down, you shoot it in the head. Or impale it with cold iron.

Oh, and the vampires can turn into shadows and morph their bodies into tentacles.

One minute I was wishing that my car would suddenly transform into a snow plow so that I could ram through the cars sitting in front of me, and the next I had an idea for a really cool vampire story floating around in my head.

But an idea doesn't a story make. I've often said that while Vlad may have constituted the genesis of *Impaler*, Victor is its heart. Its moral center. Without Victor, there is no story. There's just a guy with a sword chopping vampires in half.

But Victor didn't show up one day while I was sitting in traffic. He came a little later. And under much worse circumstances.

Shortly after the idea for *Impaler* pushed its way into my head, my wife Cindy was diagnosed with cancer. Cindy's doctor called me at work saying she had the results of the biopsy and that she needed to immediately speak with Cindy. I gave her Cindy's work number and hung up.

I sat there, waiting for the phone to ring, knowing exactly what was happening and trying to get myself ready for it. But nothing can prepare you for your wife calling you to tell you that she has cancer.

So why did I take something very personal and horrible and create its fictional mirror, make it such an important part of this story? I don't know. I think in some ways, it was born out of the fact that for the next two years, our lives were dominated by cancer. Cindy had surgery to have the tumor removed and then began a healing process that took over a year to complete.

From there she went on to become very active in a variety of cancer-related events and causes, including swimming a mile to raise money for the Women's Cancer Resource Center of Oakland, California, and regularly volunteering for the Susan G. Komen Race for the Cure. She took something terrible beyond words and turned it into a positive, not only in her life, but also for the lives of other women struggling with cancer.

Those experiences informed and directed the evolution of *Impaler* and took it from being a story about a guy with a sword fighting vampires to something that really resonates with me on a deeply personal level. It's a story of survival, of fighting against impossible odds to keep ourselves and our loved ones safe from the horrors that lurk in the darkness.

It's about never giving up hope.

~**William Harms**
Redmond, Washington

COVER GALLERY & BONUS MATERIALS

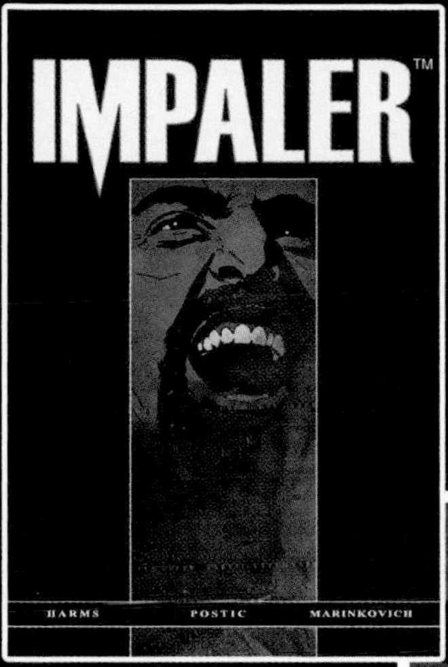
IMPALER™
HARMS
POSTIC
MARINKOVICH

Final Cover Design

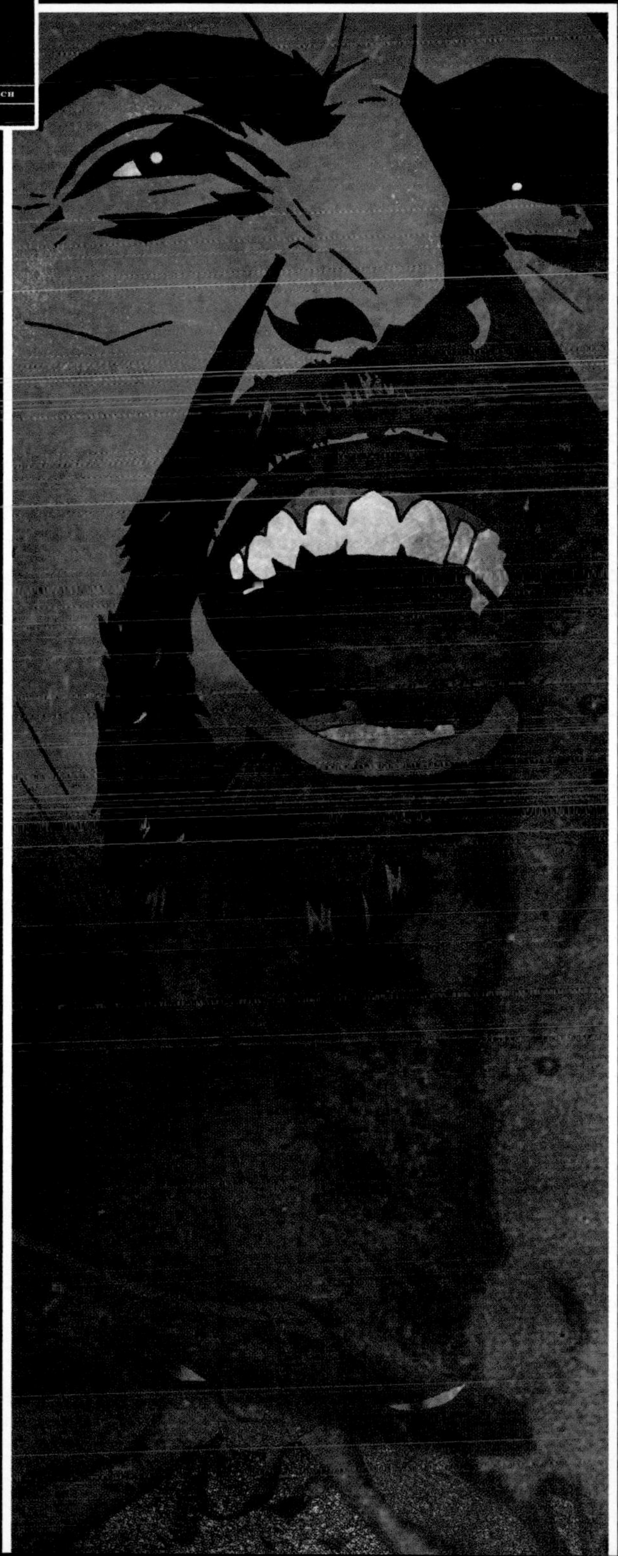

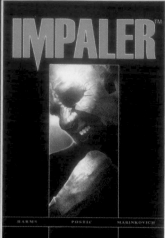

IMPALER ™

HARMS   POSTIC   MARINKOVICH

Final Cover Design

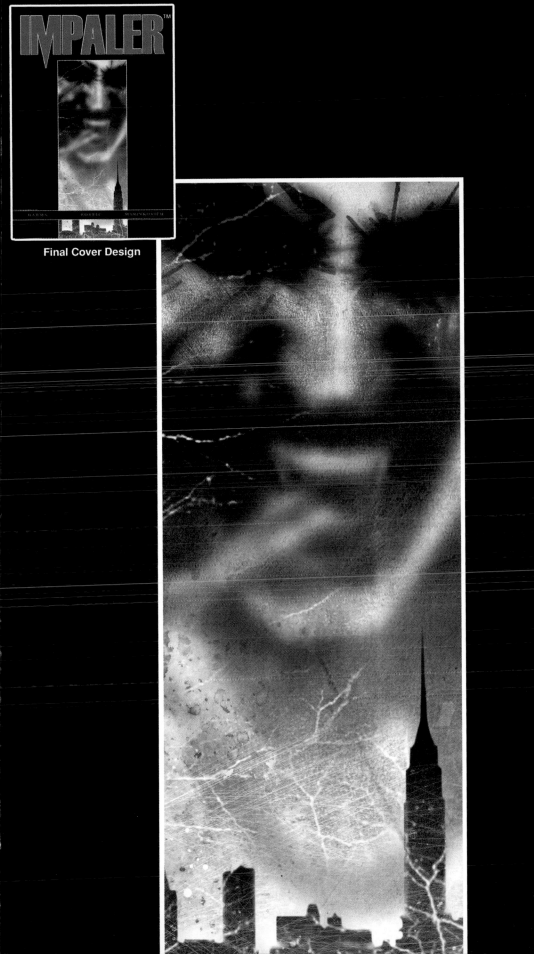

IMPALER™

HAWES   KOSTIC   MARINKOVICH

Final Cover Design

drifting off the coast of Long Island. The ship was returning from an archeological dig in Morocco and the mutilated crew is discovered in the ship's hold. As the investigation into what happened aboard the Demetrius winds down, the remaining police officers are attacked and killed by an ancient vampire, a vampire that was inadvertently released from its prison in Morocco by the Demetrius' crew.

That night, as a blizzard strikes, a wave of horrific killings sweep the city. All told, over 200 people are either dead or missing and the NYPD is placed on high alert, with every officer assigned to solving this horrific epidemic. Every officer except for Dailey, who, because of his retirement, is confined to a desk job, interviewing any witnesses who happen to come in.

The police investigate the killings, and several of them fall victim to the vampire hordes. As darkness falls, an all-out vampire assault strikes Manhattan, the vicious beasts attacking with impunity.

Back at the precinct house, Victor and the other men there come under attack by several vampires. At the same time, Vlad Tepes appears a couple of blocks away, and fights his way to Victor's precinct, killing any vampires that cross his path.

Vlad and the other survivors fight their way to one of the city's holy spots, which is located under a travel bookstore. As the survivors hole up for the night, Vlad explains to them what is happening, how he fought the vampires in the 1400's and has spent the intervening years in Purgatory, waiting for the vampires to return. He imprisoned the Great Vampire in a tomb in Morocco; it cannot be killed, only imprisoned. And now that it's free, it must be stopped before the vampires destroy the world.

During the night, all of New York City falls to the vampires and the city is sealed off by the federal government. No one can go in or out until the authorities determine the proper course of action. The vampires launch an attack against military fortifications around the exterior of Manhattan, easily slaughtering the soldiers and pushing outward from New York. The entire Eastern Seaboard is now exposed.

The next morning, and Vlad wants to immediately launch an attack against the Great Vampire. Victor and the other survivors refuse. They will instead search for survivors. That is their top priority. If the vampires can't harm Vlad, he should go after them himself. Vlad is enraged by this; he is not used to anyone questioning him.

Victor and the others begin to round up survivors, spending the day bringing them back to the bookstore. However, they quickly realize that most of the people in New York City are either dead or have been turned into vampires. In the meantime, Vlad begins to search out where the Great Vampire is located. He learns that it is located under Madison Square Garden.

As night once again sets in, the streets around the bookstore are quiet. The survivors soon find out why—the vampires are now sweeping across the east. There are reports that Washington, D.C. has fallen. Vlad again says that this must end. And Victor finally agrees.

ACT III

At the first sign of daylight, Vlad leads a ragtag team of survivors to Madison Square Garden. As they descend to the tracks below Penn Station, the signs of the Great Vampire are everywhere—bodies strewn about, stacks of bones, etc.

They at last reach the Great Vampire, and Vlad grabs one of the other survivors and rams his sword through him; it is part of a spell meant to defeat the vampire, but it fails. Victor is horrified by what he has seen, and bedlam breaks out as vampires attack from all directions.

Realizing that he has failed, Vlad tells Victor that there is only one thing to be done—Vlad must sacrifice himself. He will attack the Great Vampire and Victor must kill him while he, Vlad, enacts another spell.

Vlad then launches his attack and just as the Great Vampire is on the verge of killing him, Victor runs a sword through Vlad. There is a brilliant flash of light, and not only is the Great Vampire "imprisoned" within Vlad, Victor now has all of Vlad's power. He engages the remaining vampires, but they begin to die on their own. Without the Great Vampire, the other vampires will quickly die off.

Victor now realizes Vlad's ultimate goal—to imprison the vampire and ensure that someone else can pick up his mantle as the timeless vampire hunter. Victor walks back out into the sunlight and looks around the remains of New York City. It will now be his duty to watch over the centuries to ensure that something like this never happens again.

DELETED SCENE

WILLIAM HARMS

After finishing up Chapter Three, I decided that the initial story arc was going to end with New York City getting nuked by the military. I wrestled with when to convey that information to the reader--do I show that it's coming or do I simply let it be a surprise?

I originally opened Chapter Five with the following scene. In the end, though, I decided to cut this out and keep the focus strictly on Victor and the other survivors in New York City. The reader ultimately only knows what they know.

PAGE ONE

PANEL 1: Establishing shot of the White House. It is decorated for Christmas. It's early morning and there is snow on the ground.

CAPTION: Washington, D.C. 6:13 A.M.

CAPTION: "I just got off the phone with the FAA, Mr. President. All flights east of the Mississippi are grounded.

CAPTION: "We also have confirmation that Vice President Cheney is secure, and Speaker Pelosi's plane is scheduled to land at Andrews Air Force base within the next 10 minutes."

PANEL 2: Inside of a ready room in the White House. There is a table with the Presidential seal on it and President Bush, Stephen Hadley, General Peter Pace and a few other generic government types are sitting around the table. All of the men look tired and disheveled. They haven't slept in a day.

There is a large plasma screen on one wall; the screen is displaying a detailed, overhead view of Manhattan.

BUSH: What have you got, Pete?

GENERAL PACE: All UAVs are in position, and we have completed our initial surveillance sweep. A total of 52 unique heat signatures were detected, but we have no way of verifying their origin. Could be anything.

GENERAL PACE: I also have some new footage that you should see.

PANEL 3: Tight on the plasma screen. Grainy, night-vision video that is looking down on Times Square. It is the aftermath of the attack that happened in PAGES 8 & 9 of ISSUE THREE. Hundred of bodies are everywhere, there are burning cars, etc. Some vampires are still visible, feeding.

There is a time stamp at the bottom of the image: 21:34:23. 20-12-08

GENERAL PACE (OP): This was taken a few hours after the primary attack commenced.

GENERAL PACE (OP): Watch what happens.

PANEL 1: Tight on the plasma screen, but now the camera has zoomed in on two dead people. They are lying on the ground, half-buried in the snow, frozen blood pooled around their bodies. It is obvious that they are dead.

Time stamp at the bottom of the image: 21:35:05. 20-12-08

PANEL 2: Same scene, but now the two people are turning into shadows, their bodies dissolving.

Time stamp at the bottom of the image: 21:35:42. 20-12-08

PANEL 3: Same scene. Now both people are vampires, and they're scurrying away.

Time stamp at the bottom of the image: 21:36:59. 20-12-08

PANEL 4: Shot of the men around the table.

GENERAL PACE: Based on our surveillance, we estimate that 42% of the victims undergo this transformation. The remaining 58% are killed outright.

GENERAL PACE: Once they're dead, they stay dead.

PANEL 5: Tight on Bush. He looks tired and worried.

BUSH: That comes to what, three million of those things running around? We've got to find a way to fight this. Get a handle on it.

PAGE THREE

PANEL 1: Tight on General Pace.

GENERAL PACE: We have nine RNEPs that we can deploy within 30 hours. I have identified six primary targets, all of which connect to the subway system.

GENERAL PACE: Our intel suggests that the creatures are using the subway system as their primary method of travel. We hit those, and we'll do some serious damage. Then we'll be in a position to send in ground forces.

PANEL 2: Hadley and Pace are talking.

HADLEY: You're not really suggesting that we use those weapons against an American city, are you?

GENERAL PACE: Because of the reduced yield, collateral and structural damage should remain at a minimum. Each blast radius will impact roughly 20 square blocks and the weather reports for tomorrow indicate favorable wind conditions.

GENERAL PACE: And to be frank, I don't thing we have any other choice.

PANEL 3: Tight on Pace.

GENERAL PACE: Run the numbers, and it's easy to see that unless we do something drastic, we're going to be on the losing side of this one.

GENERAL PACE: All we need is your word, Mr. President.

PANEL 4: Tight on Bush. He looks tired, worn out. A man facing a horrible choice.

BUSH: Do it.

Raw Bits: Pencils

Nick Postic

Artist Nick Postic's style favors clean line work and stark, bold darks and is a perfect fit for the horror comics genre. Below is a closer look at select pages from his four issue run on *Impaler*.

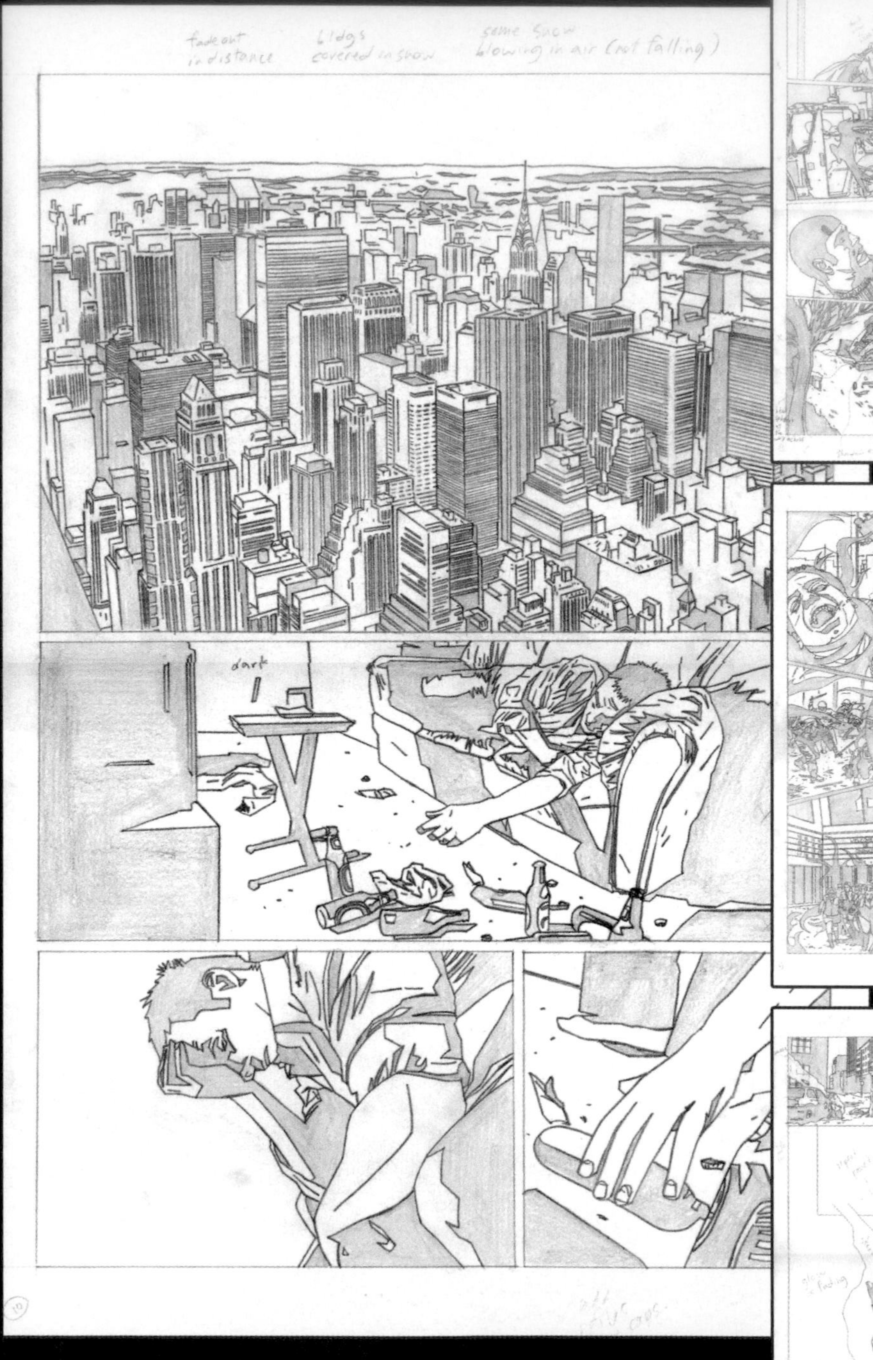

fade out in distance
bldgs covered in snow
same snow blowing in air (not falling)
dark

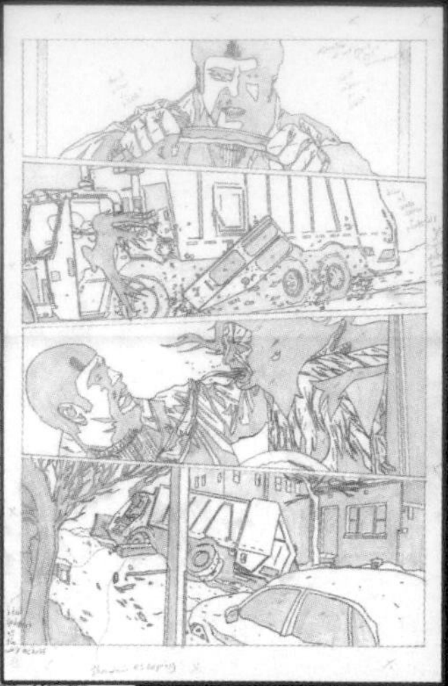

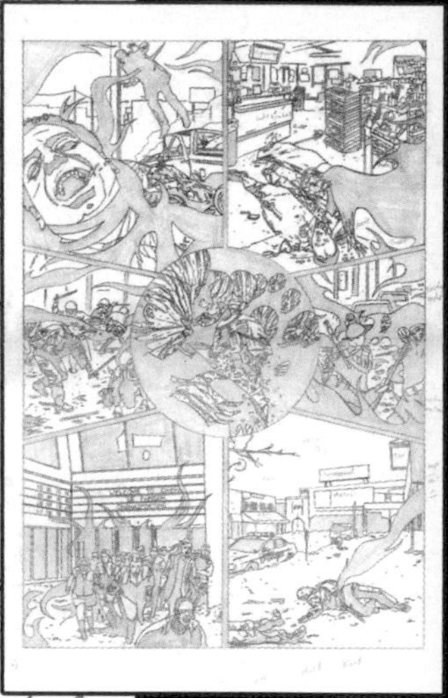

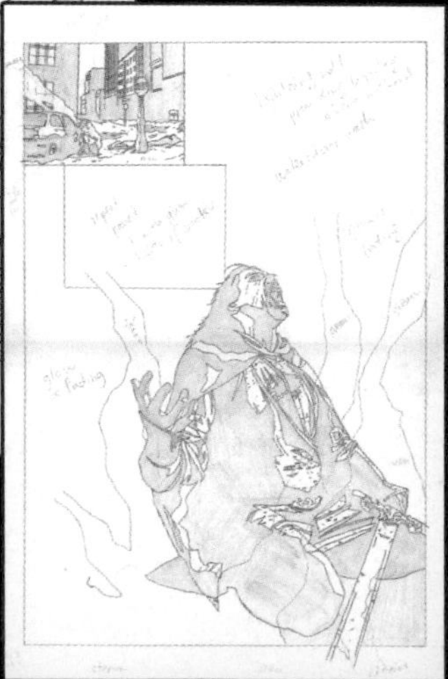

GET IMPALED CONTEST

WILLIAM HARMS

In ***Impaler # 1***, we ran a contest where one lucky winner would be drawn into the book. (And naturally they'd have to die a horrible death.) The winner was **Nick Johnson**, and I'm happy to say that he's the bait that lures Mr. Martinez down into the subway entrance in Chapter 5. Congrats, Nick!

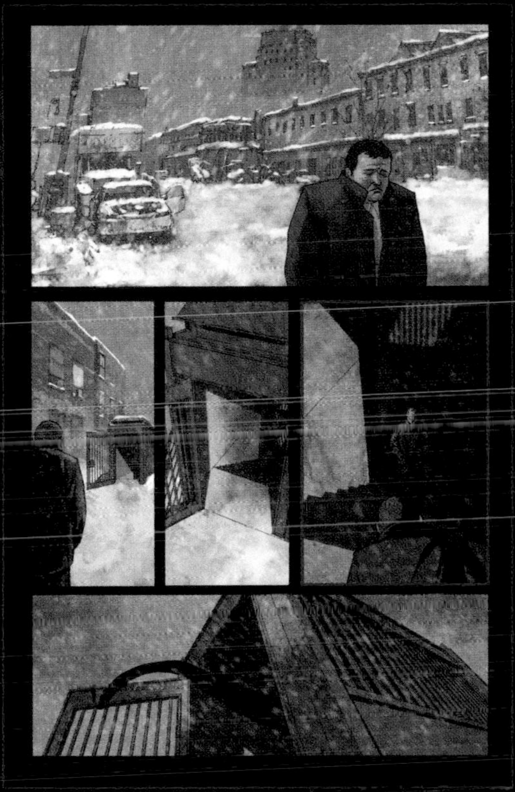

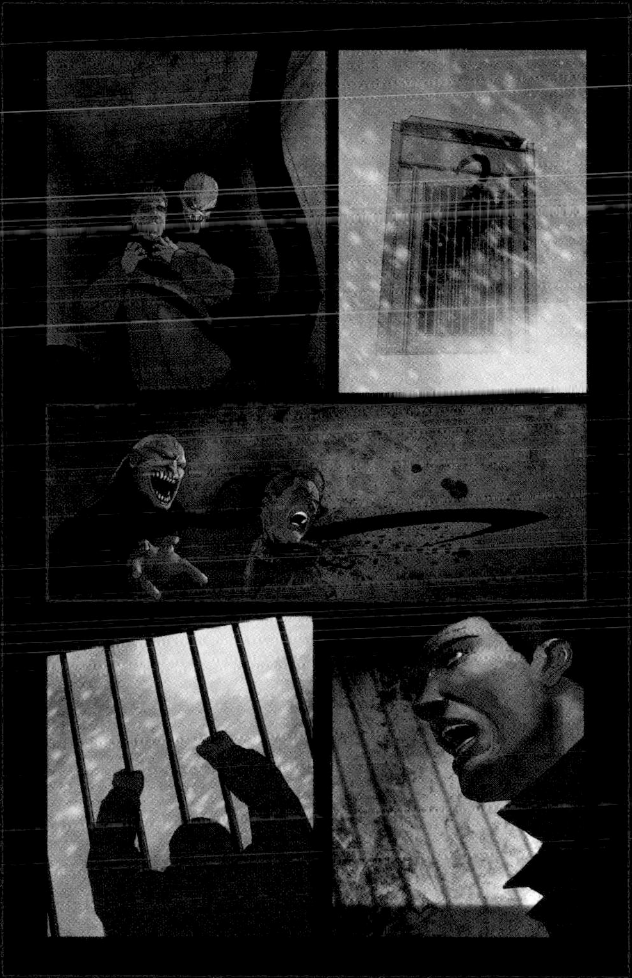

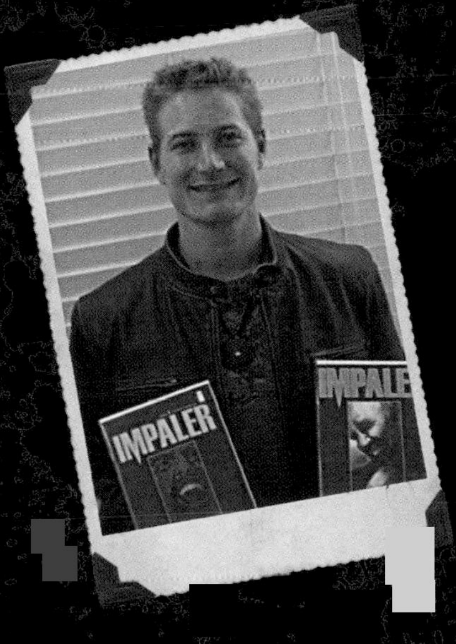
IMPALER
IMPALE

Nick Johnson, luckily, survived his comic book death and is all smiles here, flaunting the very comic book that has now immortalized his likeness.

NEW SERIES PREVIEW

I'm thrilled to present this preview of the new *Impaler* series, which debuts December 2008. The art is by British artist **Matt Timson**, and the pages he's turning in are simply amazing. *Impaler* is my baby, and it was very important to me that we get the right artist, someone who could capture the small character moments, a raised eyebrow, a creased brow. The things that add an extra layer of nuance.

It was equally important that the artist be able to draw large-scale combat, cities being destroyed, tanks being ripped apart. And Matt has delivered on every count. He's the perfect artist for this book and a wonderful collaborator. I hope you enjoy the preview pages as much as I did.

~William

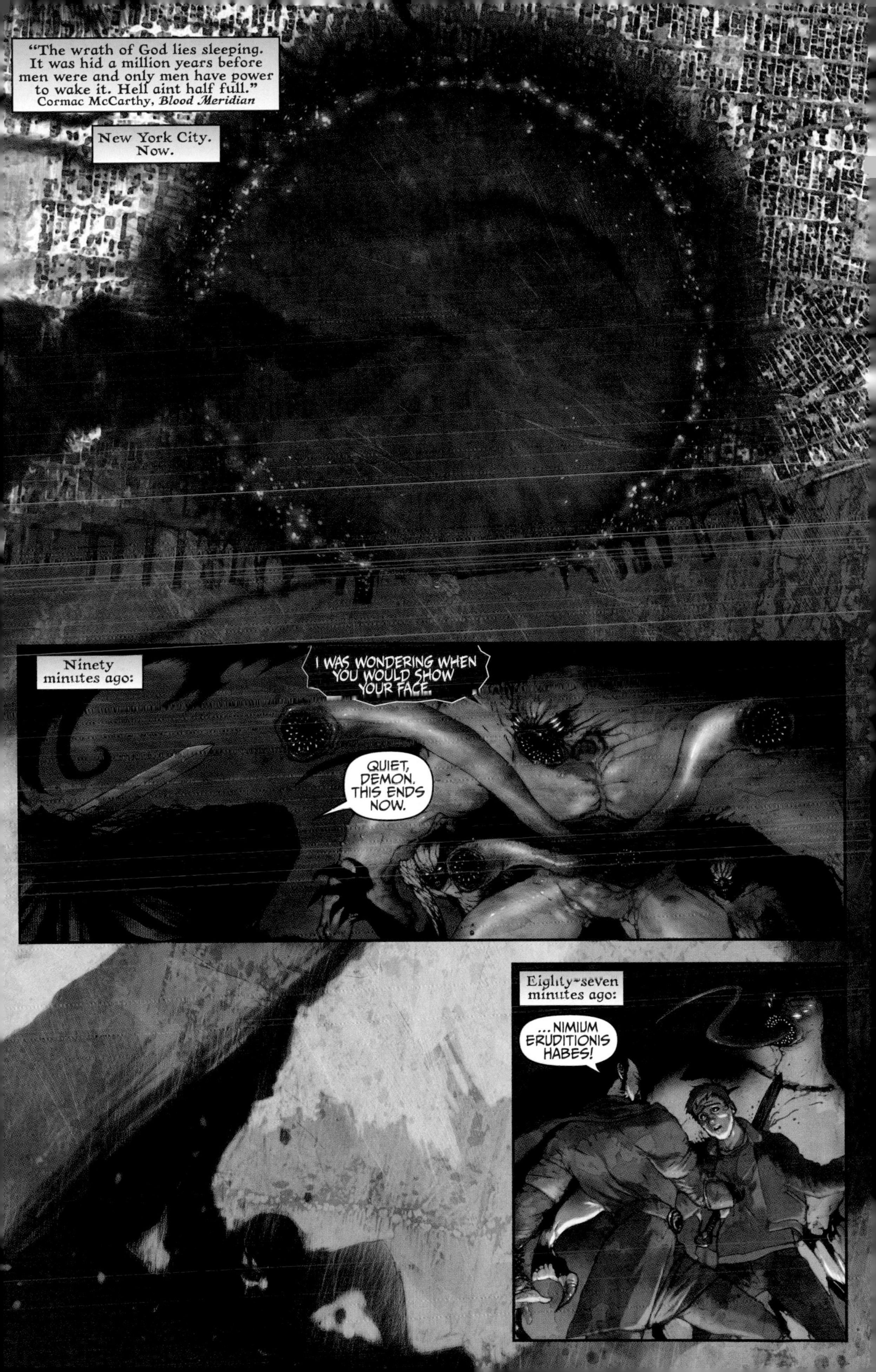
"The wrath of God lies sleeping. It was hid a million years before men were and only men have power to wake it. Hell aint half full."
Cormac McCarthy, *Blood Meridian*
New York City. Now.
Ninety minutes ago:
I WAS WONDERING WHEN YOU WOULD SHOW YOUR FACE.
QUIET, DEMON. THIS ENDS NOW.
Eighty-seven minutes ago:
...NIMIUM ERUDITIONIS HABES!

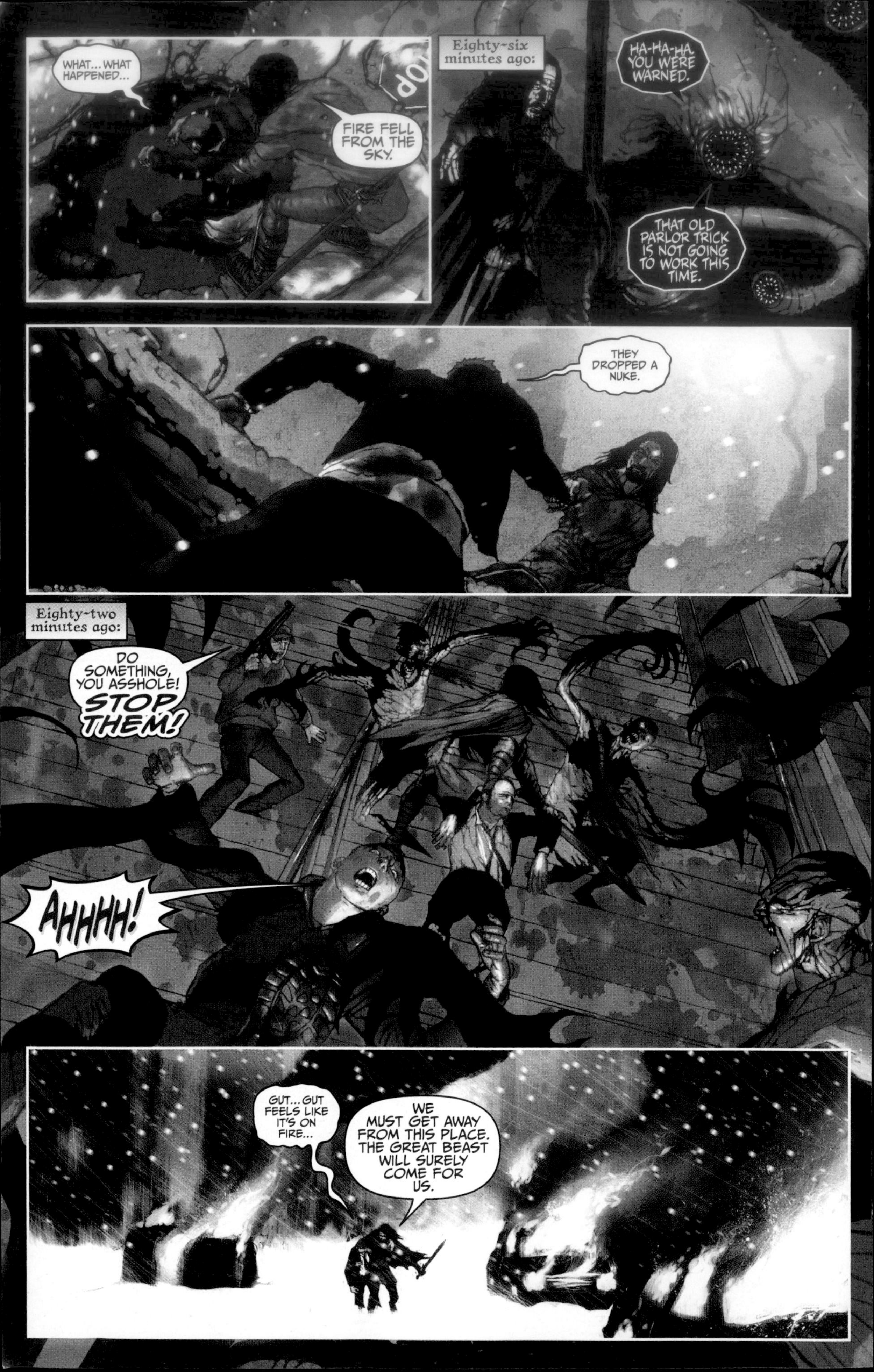

WHAT... WHAT HAPPENED...
FIRE FELL FROM THE SKY.
Eighty-six minutes ago:
HA-HA-HA. YOU WERE WARNED.
THAT OLD PARLOR TRICK IS NOT GOING TO WORK THIS TIME.
THEY DROPPED A NUKE.
Eighty-two minutes ago:
DO SOMETHING, YOU ASSHOLE! STOP THEM!
AHHHH!
GUT... GUT FEELS LIKE IT'S ON FIRE...
WE MUST GET AWAY FROM THIS PLACE. THE GREAT BEAST WILL SURELY COME FOR US.

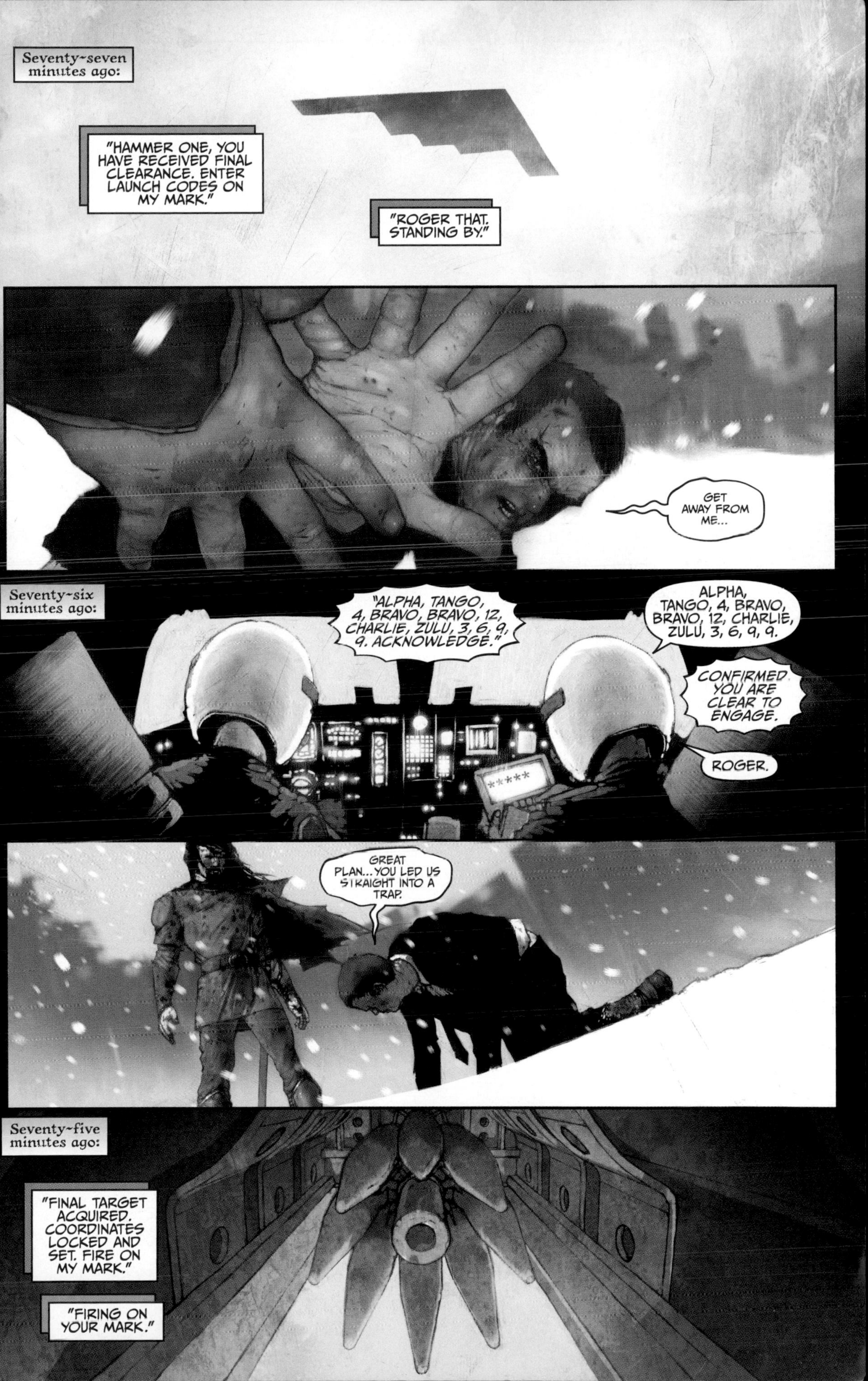
Seventy-seven minutes ago:
"HAMMER ONE, YOU HAVE RECEIVED FINAL CLEARANCE. ENTER LAUNCH CODES ON MY MARK."
"ROGER THAT. STANDING BY."
GET AWAY FROM ME...
Seventy-six minutes ago:
"ALPHA, TANGO, 4, BRAVO, BRAVO, 12, CHARLIE, ZULU, 3, 6, 9, 9. ACKNOWLEDGE."
ALPHA, TANGO, 4, BRAVO, BRAVO, 12, CHARLIE, ZULU, 3, 6, 9, 9.
CONFIRMED YOU ARE CLEAR TO ENGAGE.
ROGER.
*****
GREAT PLAN...YOU LED US STRAIGHT INTO A TRAP.
Seventy-five minutes ago:
"FINAL TARGET ACQUIRED. COORDINATES LOCKED AND SET. FIRE ON MY MARK."
"FIRING ON YOUR MARK."

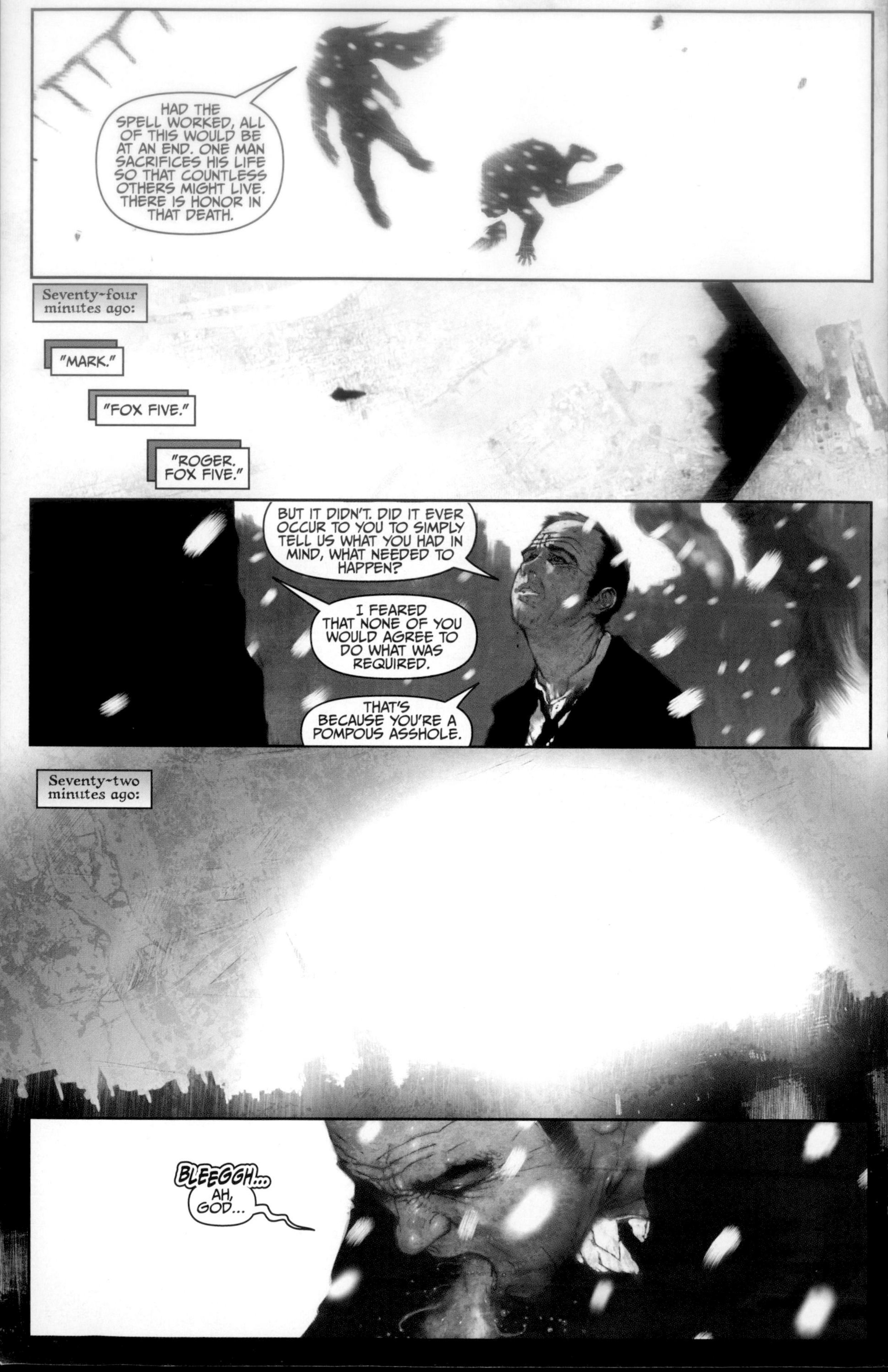
HAD THE SPELL WORKED, ALL OF THIS WOULD BE AT AN END. ONE MAN SACRIFICES HIS LIFE SO THAT COUNTLESS OTHERS MIGHT LIVE. THERE IS HONOR IN THAT DEATH.
Seventy-four minutes ago:
"MARK."
"FOX FIVE."
"ROGER. FOX FIVE."
BUT IT DIDN'T. DID IT EVER OCCUR TO YOU TO SIMPLY TELL US WHAT YOU HAD IN MIND, WHAT NEEDED TO HAPPEN?
I FEARED THAT NONE OF YOU WOULD AGREE TO DO WHAT WAS REQUIRED.
THAT'S BECAUSE YOU'RE A POMPOUS ASSHOLE.
Seventy-two minutes ago:
BLEEGGH...
AH, GOD...

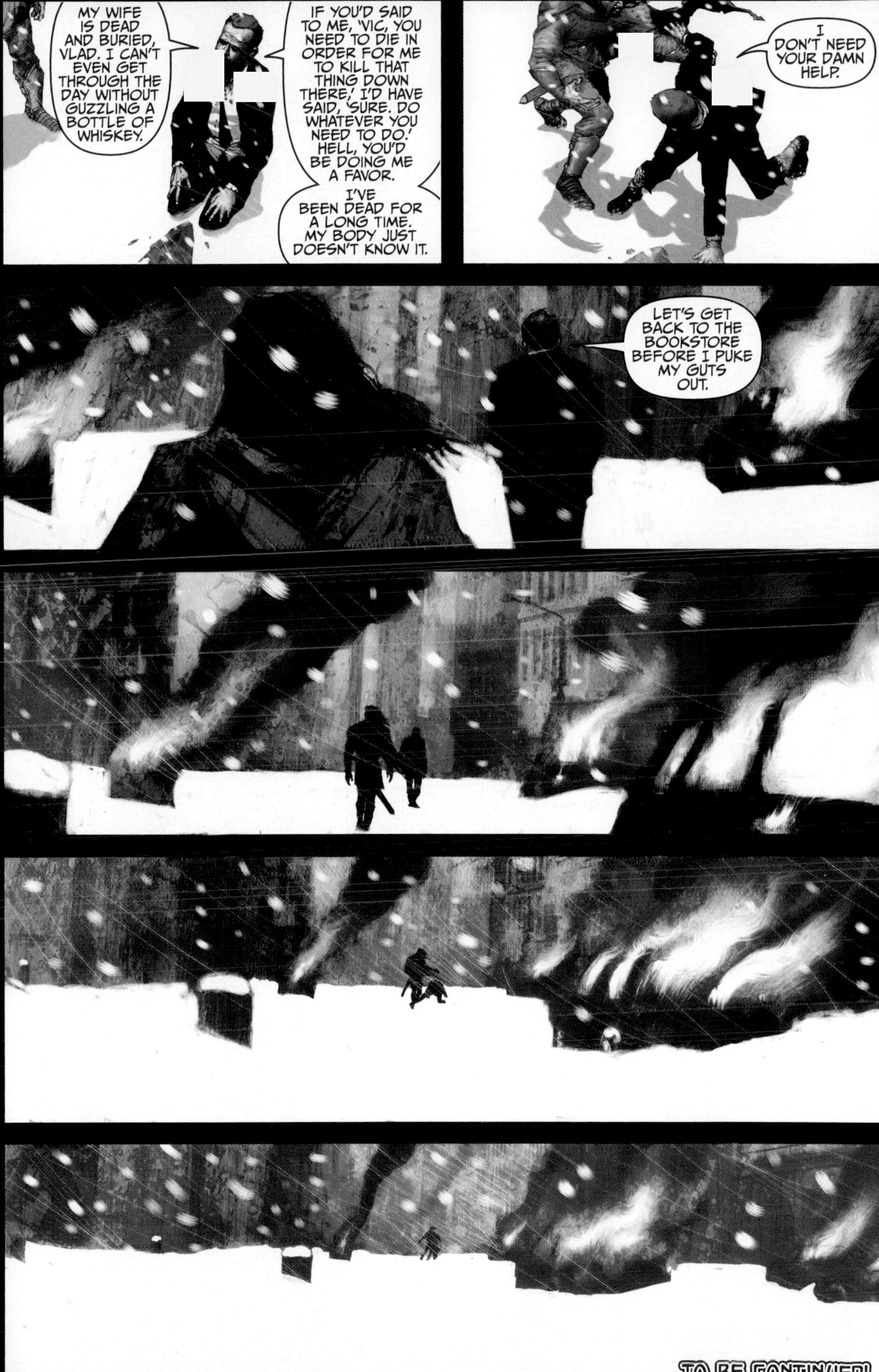
MY WIFE IS DEAD AND BURIED, VLAD. I CAN'T EVEN GET THROUGH THE DAY WITHOUT GUZZLING A BOTTLE OF WHISKEY.
IF YOU'D SAID TO ME, 'VIC, YOU NEED TO DIE IN ORDER FOR ME TO KILL THAT THING DOWN THERE,' I'D HAVE SAID, 'SURE. DO WHATEVER YOU NEED TO DO.' HELL, YOU'D BE DOING ME A FAVOR.
I'VE BEEN DEAD FOR A LONG TIME. MY BODY JUST DOESN'T KNOW IT.
I DON'T NEED YOUR DAMN HELP.
LET'S GET BACK TO THE BOOKSTORE BEFORE I PUKE MY GUTS OUT.

TO BE CONTINUED!

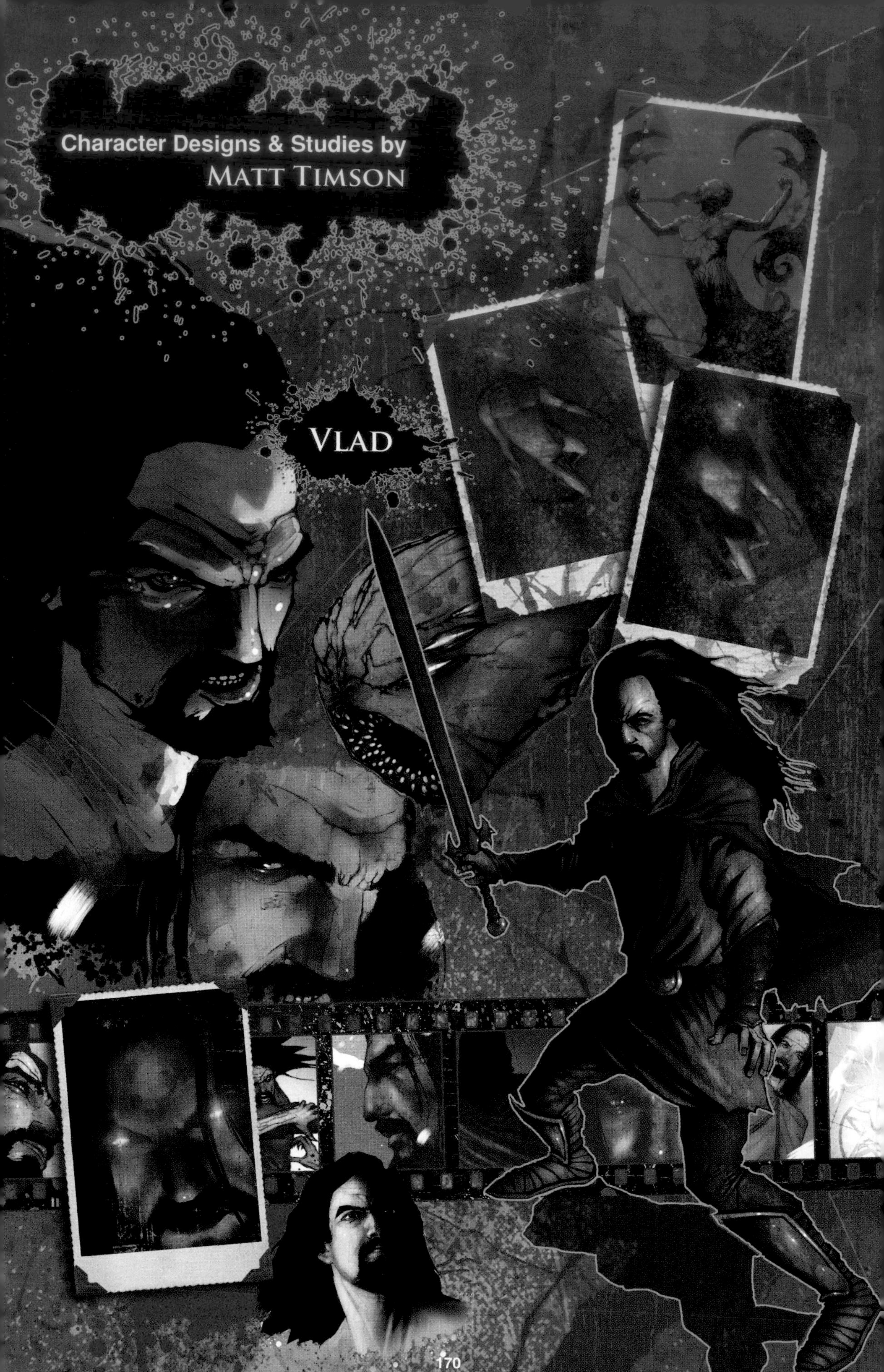
Character Designs & Studies by
MATT TIMSON
VLAD

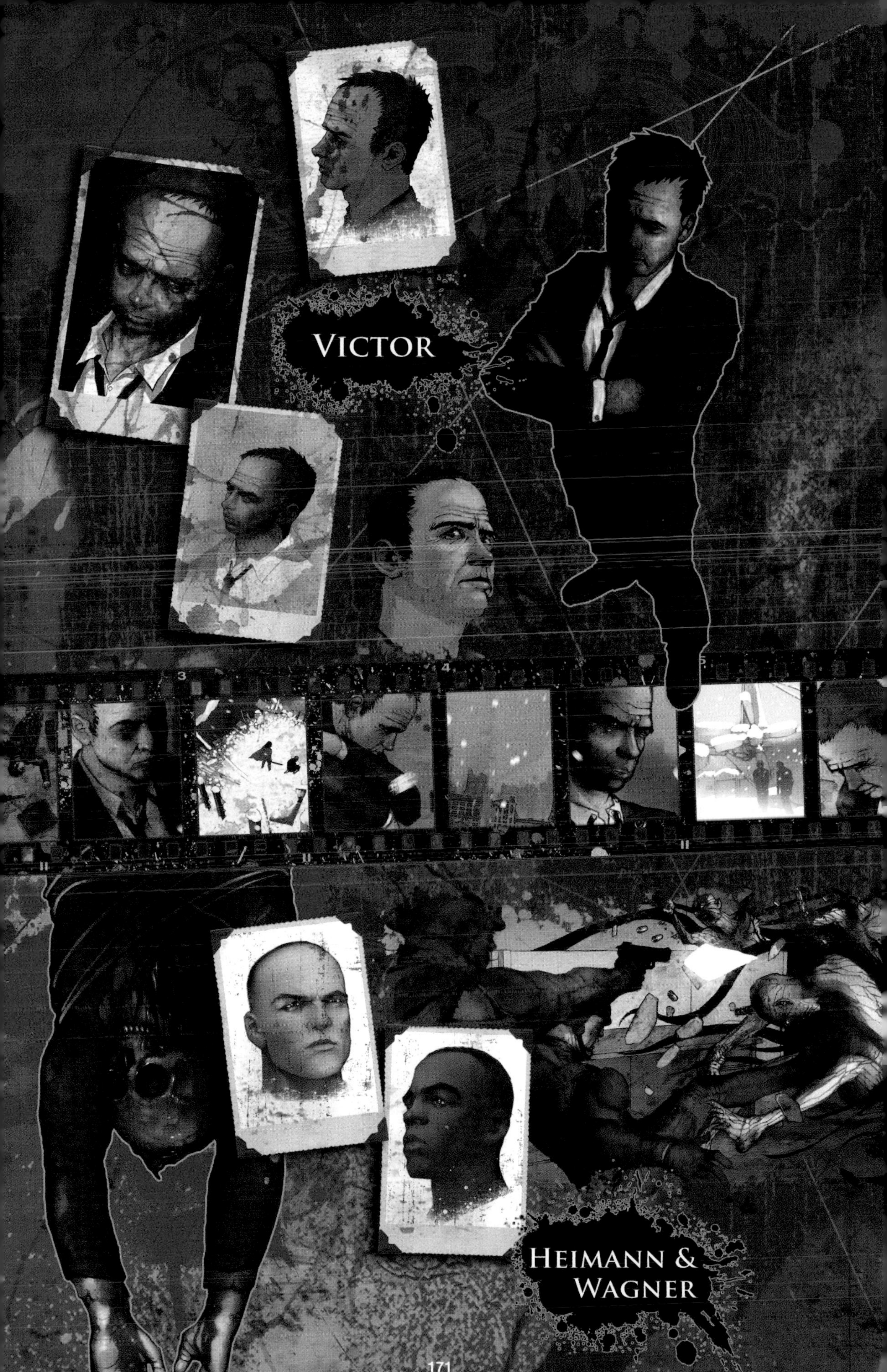
VICTOR
HEIMANN & WAGNER

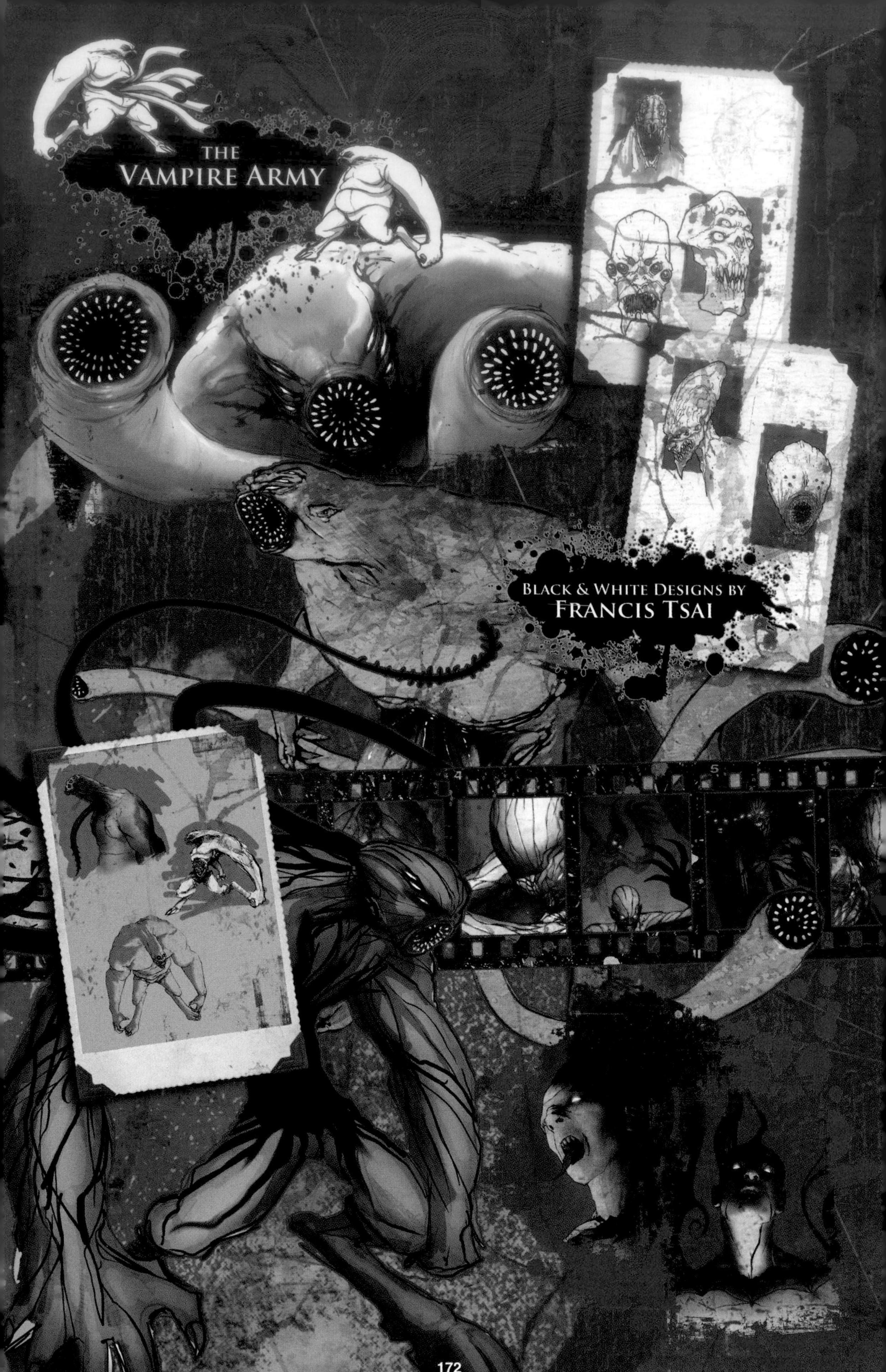
THE
VAMPIRE ARMY
BLACK & WHITE DESIGNS BY
FRANCIS TSAI

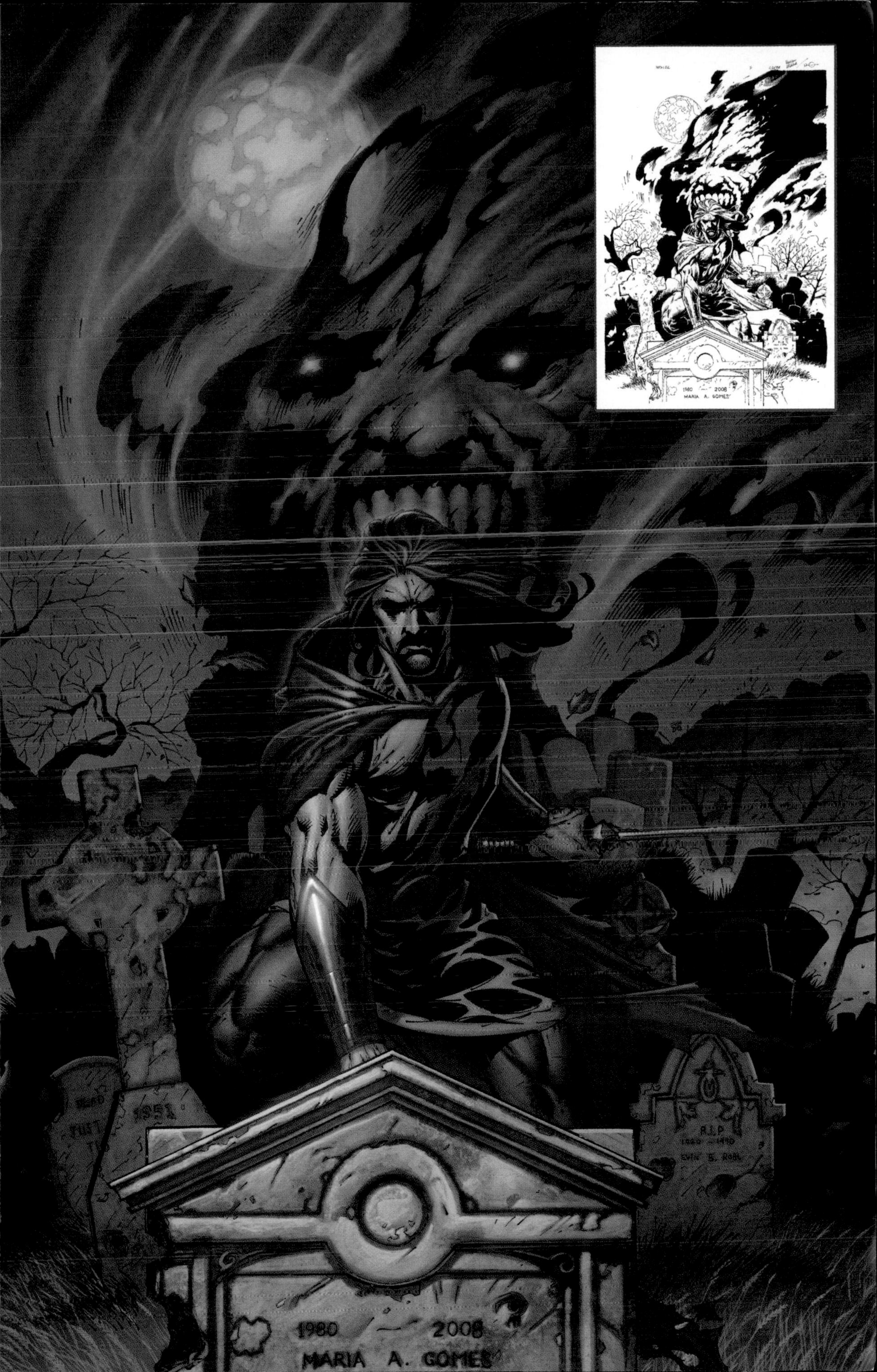
R.I.P
1980 2008
MARIA A. GOMES
1980 2008
MARIA A. GOMES

Check out *Witchblade* in these trade paperback collections.

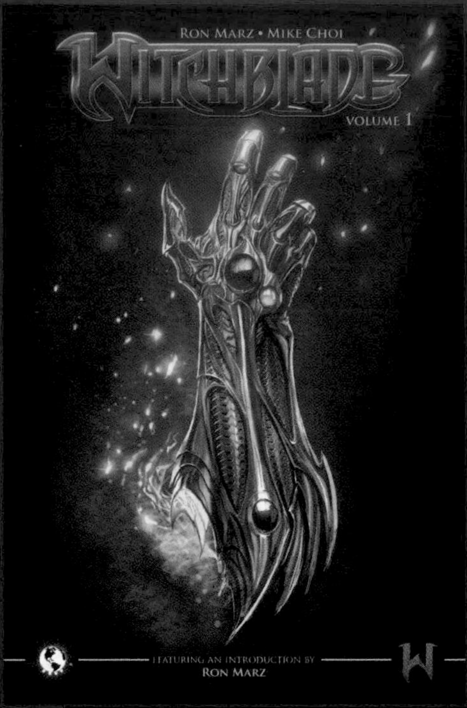
RON MARZ • MIKE CHOI
WITCHBLADE
VOLUME 1
FEATURING AN INTRODUCTION BY
RON MARZ

Witchblade

volume 1 - volume 5

written by:
Ron Marz
pencils by:
Mike Choi, Stephen Sadowski, Keu Cha, Chris Bachalo, Stjepan Sejic and more!

Get in on the ground floor of Top Cow's flagship title with these affordable trade paperback collections from Ron Marz's series re-defining run on Witchblade! Each volume collects a key story arc in the continuing adventures of Sara Pezzini and the Witchblade.

volume 1
collects issues #80-#85
(ISBN: 978-1-58240-906-1) $9.99

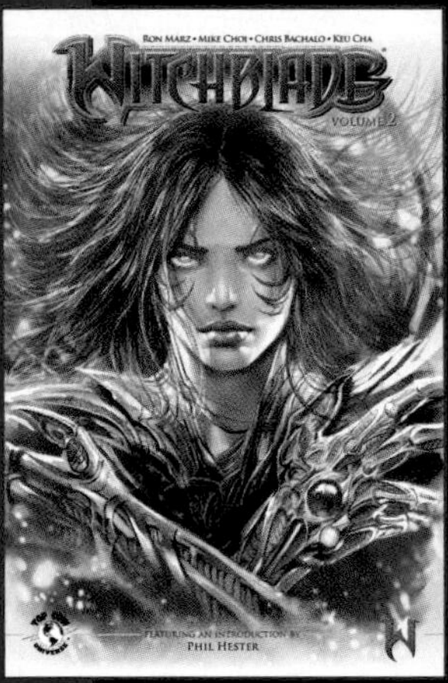
RON MARZ • MIKE CHOI • CHRIS BACHALO • KEU CHA
WITCHBLADE
VOLUME 2
FEATURING AN INTRODUCTION BY
PHIL HESTER

volume 2
collects issues #86-#92
(ISBN: 978-1-58240-[illegible])
U.S.D. $[illegible]

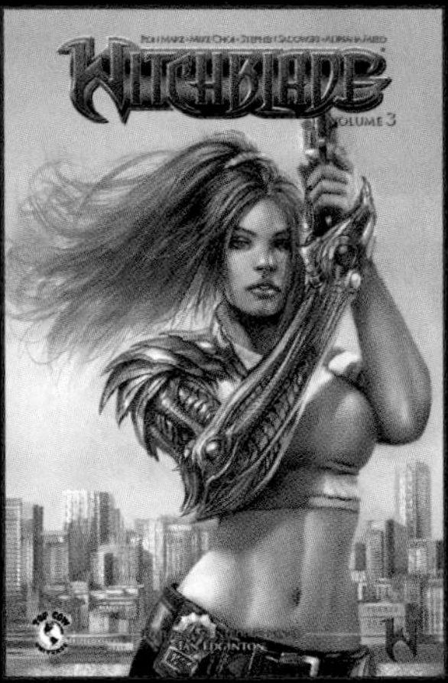
WITCHBLADE
VOLUME 3
IAN EDGINTON

volume 3
collects issues #93-#100
(ISBN: 978-1-58240-[illegible])
U.S.D. $[illegible]

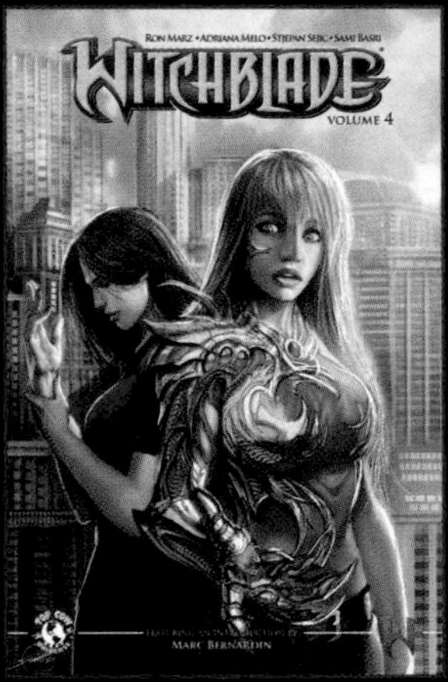
RON MARZ • ADRIANA MELO • STJEPAN SEJIC • SAMI BASRI
WITCHBLADE
VOLUME 4
MARC BERNARDIN

volume 4
collects issues #101-109
(ISBN: 978-1-58240-[illegible])
U.S.D. $[illegible]

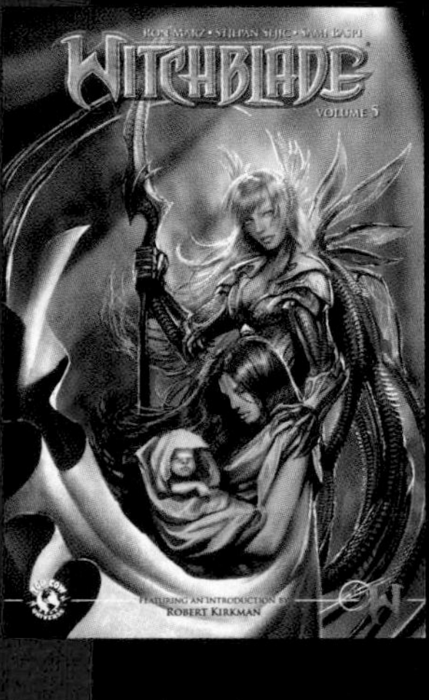
RON MARZ • STJEPAN SEJIC • SAMI BASRI
WITCHBLADE
VOLUME 5
FEATURING AN INTRODUCTION BY
ROBERT KIRKMAN

New York City Police Detective Sara Pezzini is the bearer of the Witchblade, a mysterious artifact that takes the form of a deadly and powerful gauntlet. Now Sara must try to control the Witchblade and learn its secrets, even as she investigates the city's strangest, most supernatural crimes.

volume 5
collects issues #110-[illegible], First Born issues #1-3
(ISBN: 978-1-58240-[illegible])
U.S.D. $[illegible]

Other trade paperbacks and special collections available from Top Cow!

Top Cow Productions, Inc. Presents
The Art of
The Darkness
Featuring an inside look at the conceptual art from The Darkness video game from
2K
union

The Art of The Darkness

Celebrate the 10th Anniversary of The Darkness! Inspired by Art of books for video games and films, this oversized art book features glorious illustrations and commentary from the original creators, all contained in a glossy, thick-papered, beautifully designed book. Covers, splash pages, collectible cards, sketches--the best of the best *The Darkness* art! See it here in its unadulterated form. A decade of work to choose from, this is the definitive Art of book for *The Darkness*! Featuring art by the top names in comics including:

Marc Silvestri
Michael Turner
Dale Keown
Jae Lee
Stjepan Sejic
Dave Finch
Whilce Portacio
and many more!

(ISBN 13: 978-1-58240-649-7)
$14.99

Garth Ennis
Marc Silvestri
Paul Jenkins
Dale Keown
The Darkness
ULTIMATE COLLECTION
The story that inspired the video game by
2K
union

The Darkness

Ultimate Collection
written by:
Garth Ennis and Paul Jenkins
with art by:
Marc Silvestri and Dale Keown

The Darkness: Ultimate Collection trade paperback spotlights the two storylines which inspired the hit video game from 2K Games and made Jackie Estacado and the Darkness an integral part of the Top Cow Universe.

Featuring the complete **Coming of Age** and **Resurrection** storylines, this edition is a must-have for fans of *The Darkness* and the video game.

(ISBN 13: 978-1-58240-780-7) $19.99

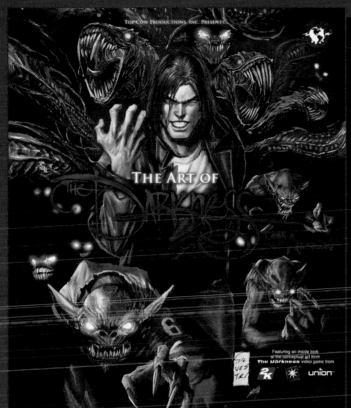

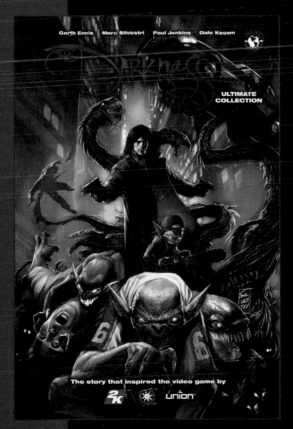

Premium collected editions

ENNIS • WOHL • CONEY • LOBDELL • JENKINS
SILVESTRI • BENITEZ • LANSANG • TAN • FINCH • KEOWN
The Darkness
COMPENDIUM
VOLUME 1
TOP COW UNIVERSE

The Darkness
Compendium vol.1

written by:
Garth Ennis, Paul Jenkins, Scott Lobdell
pencils by:
Marc Silvestri, Joe Benitez and more!

On his 21st birthday, the awesome and terrible powers of the Darkness awaken within Jackie Estacado, a mafia hitman for the Franchetti crime family. There's nothing like going back to the beginning and reading it all over again-- issues #1-40, plus the complete run of the *Tales of the Darkness* series collected into one trade paperback. See how the Darkness first appeared and threw Jackie into the chaotic world of the supernatural. Get the first appearances of The Magdalena and more!

SC (ISBN 13: 978-1-58240-643-5) $59.99
HC (ISBN 13: 978-1-58240-992-7) $99.99

WOHL • JENKINS • TURNER • SILVESTRI • GREEN • CHA
WITCHBLADE
COMPENDIUM
VOLUME 1
TOP COW UNIVERSE

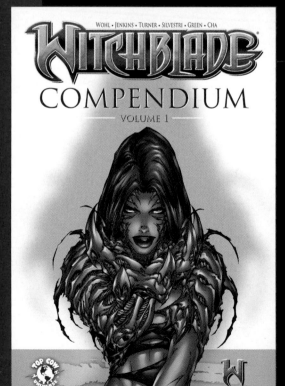

Witchblade
Compendium vol.1

written by:
David Wohl, Christina Z., Paul Jenkins
pencils by:
Michael Turner, Randy Green Keu Cha and more!

From the hit live-action television series to the current Japanese animé, *Witchblade* has been Top Cow's flagship title for over a decade. There's nothing like going back to the beginning and reading it all over again. This massive collection houses issues #1-50 in a single edition for the first time. See how the Witchblade chose Sara and threw her into the chaotic world of the supernatural. Get the first appearances of Sara Pezzini, Ian Nottingham, Kenneth Irons and Jackie Estacado in one handy tome!

SC (ISBN 13: 978-1-58240-634-3) $59.99
HC (ISBN 13: 978-1-58240-798-2) $99.99